A child's history of America

Some ribs and riffs for the sixties
by Charles Newman
The Swallow Press, Inc.
Chicago, Illinois

A CHILD'S HISTORY OF AMERICA

First edition
First printing 1973

Published by
The Swallow Press, Inc.
1139 South Wabash Avenue
Chicago, Illinois 60605

ISBN (cloth) 0–8040–0644–X
ISBN (paper) 0–8040–0645–8
LIBRARY OF CONGRESS CATALOG CARD NUMBER 73–5951

Portions of this work previously
appeared in a somewhat different form
in *The Yale Review, The Antioch Review, TriQuarterly*, and *Prose*

Designed by Lawrence Levy

Against Icarus, that first liberal technocrat, who got
precisely what he deserved—not for flying too high or
even for taking his father's advice—but for trying to
jump the maze when the only way *out* was the way *in:*
I propose Talos, Daedalus' nephew and apprentice,
who, through his invention of both saw and potter's
wheel by the age of twelve, so threatened Big D's
hegemony that he threw the child from the heights of
the Acropolis, this crime necessitating his escape to
Crete and the later more celebrated, if abortive,
"flight." For Talos, then, whose soul flew off in the
form of a partridge, who was murdered not for his dis-
obedience, but his competence, for his second sight,
not his spleen.

And for the children we have denied ourselves

In 1968, that vintage year for delirium, I traveled a good deal because I work best when disassociated in time and place, and kept a journal, since that activity stabilizes me as staying put cannot. I've kept such a journal for some twelve years, but it has evolved from a personal diary and working notebook into a kind of psychic holding action, a strategy to keep autobiography—the propaganda of the missed deed—from obtruding upon my other writing. In effect, this is the record of those experiences which resisted both plausible fiction and straight reportage; and actually, it was only much later that the notes seemed to acquire a shape—an architecture created by no author, but by the recession of events.

There will be a lot of autobiography in the seventies. Such work will undoubtedly pose as omniscient fiction or objective journalism, but it will be autobiography nonetheless—that accounting for all the material of one's life which is otherwise unusable, and testimony to that most contemporary of vices, the desperate equation of one's personal experience with the disparate history of one's time.

Naturally, I would have preferred to offer a systematic analysis, a brutish equilibrium of facts with some fancy sidereal ruminations, rather than merely talk about myself. What follows is too selective to be a confession, too personal to be a manifesto, and inasmuch as I have lived neither a very interesting nor instructive life, I can only offer my thoughts in the lugubrious contexts in which they occurred. The fact that what happens here happens to be true—i.e., actually occurred—does not, in itself, make it worth repeating. Sincerity remains a most oblique tactic.

Nor am I in any position to justify my life or promote this work by describing its odd composition as some new invention of necessity. All I know is that we were not given our minds merely to deal with a reality which is already complete, and one of the pretensions of the sixties was to advertise every small discovery about ourselves as a new genre. Distanced from our history, language and ourselves, literature is all we have; literature and other, lesser, fictions.

Literature always exists in a double sense—as reports on behavior as well as a progress in the evolution of forms. My life in this year was so fortuitously metaphorical that I ceased willing those continuities which make for artifice or argument, and as I did so, the space for inscription seemed to lose its edges. It was not so much a matter of experimentation, but of knowing my own limitations better. After all, language begins to celebrate itself in mere juxtaposition—pre-metaphorical bliss—offering access to both history and the silences which are to come. Writing without genre not only increases the number of voices available to the author, but invites contingencies which do not certify the text as much as they offer access from it. To question one's own means of production is to assist the reader in producing his own text. And it is a marvelous paradox that the recovery of our antecedents requires the reader as collaborator.

Then the day came when I discovered that anything I read anywhere could give me narrative metonymy, that I was filling the margins as a farmer fills his field—not only for profit, but to demark what is not yet *his*—and I realized that my text had entered the world among others, that my efforts, achieved or not, were at an end. My "I" now abided in another body, and it remained for whatever audience it would have to give it further shape, to appropriate the remaining clots of space.

In cranky retrospect, I can only wonder if the idea that the world is our idea is a very good idea. The more we demythologize the world, the more we fail to demystify our selves.

But perhaps that is why, at least in one respect, books are like lives—tunnels with light, nothing save light, such blinding light, at both ends.

CHN

CONTENTS

A short history of the universe and its implications   *11*
Concerning the republican institutions of the United States
and what their chances for duration are   *12*
Son of Henry James visits the psychedelic anthropologist   *31*
Jacobins and anarchists   *36*
The last Yank at Oxford, or, recollections of a light heavyweight   *51*
Contre la regression: fucked up or fucked over?   *73*
Ressentiment   *103*
You're having a very good time, isn't it?   *111*
But that's the way the American people like to do   *119*
Risorgimento   *128*
Letter from the first and everlasting third world   *140*
No one to the left (or right) of us:
Confessions of a white liberal   *192*
Whither Yugoslavia   *221*
A short history of the royal family   *241*
On being ahistorical   *257*
Our buddies, Greece 'n Spain   *270*
Know your Araby   *279*
Envoi   *294*
Soon to be a major motion picture   *301*

February 5, 1968, San Francisco

How to comprehend what those first settlers must have felt—after fighting their way across the breadth of the continent, only to find beyond all those mountains, deserts and cannibalizations— no treasure, no fountain of youth, no noble savage, no spice, no poon- tang . . . just another blue ocean as opaque and terrifying as the first one, accomplishing the one thing they dreaded . . . to come full circle. But they kept it to themselves, somehow, the secret which is now out— that America does not evolve, only expands.

Surviving a journey in which anything could have killed you casually, you arrive at the second shore, no longer an invader exactly, your last enemy disposed of, and as the logical extension of individual rights (have nothing left to escape) take your own life. And, indeed, San Francisco seems largely inhabited by those who, bent upon ridding themselves of conventional successes, are discovering numerous new ways of destroying themselves. This, a utopia of death on demand, where voluntary self-extinction retains a certain willfulness and con- firms the trauma of our pioneers.

"The City," as it refers to itself, much in the same way as if over the lintel of a nifty cathedral door, one were to find the inscription, "House of Worship," *in quotes;* "The City," then, testifies not only to the end of the New World, to that terminality which is our most recent myth, but also to the civilization left behind; homage not to our hard-won uniqueness, but a painful reminder of the unnecessary discontinuity be- tween the old world and ours. However impracticable, one ought to re- turn to Europe from such a place as this; worth a special detour, as the guides say. We suspect the inhabitants of "The City" no longer know the difference between their pride and fear. We suspect that if the Con- ventional Americans they are fleeing can be described as a class with no consciousness of themselves, then this "new breed" might be char- acterized as self-conscious about their unconsciousness. They have, without considering the consequences, put themselves in quotes. And it is here, on the second shore, that those little marks, inverted commas, double apostrophes, words naming words, begin to close in upon us. Why is everything we *say* secured by these dolloped crescents, sixes and nines; are they party ears, exemplary horns, or vestigial antennae?

|11|

A SHORT HISTORY OF THE UNIVERSE
and its implications

Check here the probable reason for your attempted suicide:

☐ Nervous and mental disease

Other diseases:
☐ coronary
☐ vascular
☐ tumor
☐ contagious disease
☐ illness—precise
  aliment unknown
☐ disability (other)

Family conflict:
☐ i.e. with spouse
☐ parent
☐ child
☐ other relative
☐ Family conflict, details unknown

Other reasons:
☐ Blow by fate
☐ Poor school marks
☐ Disciplinary action at school
☐ Unhappiness
☐ Disillusionment over love affair
☐ Financial difficulties
☐ Alcoholism
☐ Commission of a crime
☐ Old age
☐ Abandonment
☐ Shame over pregnancy
☐ Housing problem
☐ Difficulties at place of work
☐ Other
☐ Unknown

❝ *here are yours.* ❞
Wear them proudly

always stay in the Tenderloin because it remains the only conventionally sinful district left in America where you are not, if a reasonably well-built male, in perpetual physical danger. The whores are altogether amiable, the pimps diffident, the bums prouder, the transvestites less arch, the crooks without corporate phlegmatism.

Here, my best friend's abiding off-hours activity is to *seduce* whores; that is to say, to make them *like* him sufficiently to turn tricks for nothing, or in effect, price themselves out of the market, decommercialize their talents. He relies on his 1950s college-boy good looks and an occasional quality Moroccan joint for his appeal, as well as on the worldview that nothing is corrupt if no one profits. It is an engaging thought: making love with parity, without technique, formal procedure, or consequences.

Is this the new man? Or at least the new middleman? The man who moves the goods without regard to supply and demand? The whores love him because he treats them better than do the street people.

"I don't turn no freaks," Ellen said today, "they dirty and they cheap." She despises them even more than their fathers, spillover conventioneers from North Beach trailing their condoms, Right Guard and saddle-scented talc.

"They talk, at least," she muses. "They talk and they pay. The kids got nothin' to say."

Ellen's obsolescent. Between the Haight and North Beach, her profession, her status, is no longer functional. She loves my friend because he prefers her, her competence, her stoicism, her alertness, to the calculated disorientation of the freaks and their fathers, who have now divvied up the world and insist on making their quarrel over it a matter of public debate. She knows that she has been consigned to the periphery of American life, not to the poor and outcast precisely, but to those *other* pensioners—the seamen, the cooks, the artisans, the loggers, the fishermen, longshoremen, dirt farmers—the *handy*men who joke as they shuffle past her cakewalk on their three square trips to the cafeteria. At twenty-four, she is already and forever amongst old men, basted eggs and American fries, between North Beach and the Haight, that putrescent nexus of Organized Crime, Bohemia manqué and *Touris-*

teria, an oligopoly of pretense which will collapse totally the day the last conventioneer sees his first bare tit in public.

Here in the Tenderloin, you can sense the difference only in the cops' lips. They are not yet drawn thin. Here they are still part of a functioning system no matter how you might ultimately judge the lubricant. Crime here remains definable. It is namable. It has its consequences. It is therefore human. I see that only recently, at thirty, I have become afraid of the police. Perhaps that is healthy, part of the demeanor which protects me from street thieves. Nevertheless, in North Beach or the Haight, I give them wide berth, though I was brought up to ask a policeman where to go when I was lost. In some periods of history, perhaps only the police know who they are—and in a very curious way, it is *they* who bring out the violence in *me,* a kind of hyperventilated aggression which I can no longer admire, even in myself. Maybe it's a hatred which will finally prove constructive if I can continue to resist, examine it. For the time being, I steal cops' guns in my dreams. Their faces seem fleshier than when I was twenty.

The cops are keeping our monks out of trouble. Or perhaps they are protecting the monks from bigger trouble. In any case, there are monks all over this town. In the Haight, in North Beach, in the Tenderloin, in front of the Head shop, the Condor, Woolworth's, ubiquitous with thumb cymbals, reed pipes and "the drum," they intone their chant. They also have on their Chuck Taylor Converse All-Star gym shoes, that gym shoe with the mottled pink track I know so well, sweat socks with blue piping, and their heads are shaven against the gym's aridity. Strange to find that the team you played against in the state high school basketball tournament have become Buddhists. It almost makes you ashamed that you won. They still have on their uniforms beneath their saffron robes, those numeraled polyester creations which inflame the nipples, passed on from year to year, stinking of no collectivity, only the naphtha of dry-cleaning hysterical. Old number forty-four with the unstoppable left-handed fadeaway jump, too small for the pros, maybe a starter in junior college, now a vegetarian troubadour. He offers me incense, invites me to the temple for lunch.

Do you have curry?

HARE KRISHNA HARE KRISHNA KRISHNA KRISHNA HARE HARE HARE RAMA HARE RAMA RAMA RAMA HARE HARE

"Hey man," he says, "it's really good food."

What part of Indiana you from, I say.

The crowd has thickened. Upon their foreheads, veins throb beneath the egg-white insignia, the telltale signal for a fast-break or a stall. We petitioners are blocking the door to the Hot Dog Heaven. A small benighted motorcycle cop, a series of intricately folded black vinyl flaps, arrives, and those with incense are asked to lean against the wall in order to create a pedestrian tunnel between the audience and the monks on the curb. The chant reaches a crescendo, then a novice with begging bowl advances on those of us gripping our telltale punk, and it's half-time forever, thirty-five cents for Coach Buddha.

But now we are suddenly joined by an empiricist, a smooth black man with a pint of Thunderbird in a brown bag, who staggers into our pedestrian tunnel. He stares at the drum, observes the audience, and the idea ignites his forehead like a cartoon light bulb. The drum continues. The black man begins to snap his fingers. The head Buddhist, captain lo these many years by virtue of his unselfish floor play and hacking defense, eyes his new initiate warily.

The black man turns to face us, who illuminate the scene. Our odor curls away into the kitchen exhaust of Hot Dog Heaven. Then he begins to shuffle—*his* dance. "Hairy Christmas, Hairy Christmas," he intones. And against the monotone of the cheerleaders, he syncopates, Hai-ry Christ-mas, *vamp!* And between those beats, on the off chord, he spits, whamp! He shuffles, he moans, he rolls his red-webbed eyes, his interpretation against their event, and when his dance is over, the drum is faltering, our tiny daily self-immolations have become merely the flicker of a neon motel sign three hundred feet in the air above us. And then the newest black Buddhist in the world, our Pushkin, turns to those of us with our drooping tapers, and making a bowl of his slender hands, demands *his* offering.

But he is unincorporated, undeductible, this religious fanatic, this bandless music man without a prayer, he is disabused gently enough by the police who know a decent ritual when they see one, and the unde-

Does this mean then that the materialist west is hopelessly decayed and that light shines only from the mystic religious east? No, quite the opposite. It means that the east has definitely taken the western path, that hundreds of millions of people from now on share in the struggle for the ideals which the west has already worked out for itself. What has decayed is the western bourgeoisie, which is already confronted by its grave digger, the proletariat. But in Asia there is still a bourgeoisie capable of championing sincere, militant consistent democracy, a worthy comrade of France's great men of enlightenment and leaders of the close of the 18th Century. |Lenin, The Awakening of Asia|

VACANCY
VACANCY
VACANCY

feated but ineluctably tied team, lately from Rangoon, Indiana, move the franchise up the street through the arbor of their fans.

This morning it occurs to me that my hotel may well be a most historic place. Its permanent residents, almost to a man, are retired enlisted men—naval or merchant marine—who have done a generation's stint and now live off their pensions in this crevice of "The City." Down here, they can see neither the flares of Nob Hill nor the flames of Oakland. They go down in the mornings and lean against the Bank of America, queuing up, waiting. I watch them for a week, but the line does not move a single mote, though there is a definite order: first come, first served. They talk, read the newspaper and wait in that endless static line against the Bank of America. After a week of watching, I have realized why. Over the dilapidated buildings which line Market Street, a blade of sunlight wipes the face of the Bank of America from ten to two. They go to stand in it. The stone flank is warm as meat. Then they go to a cafeteria for a cold lunch where they *never* talk. They talk in the light, never over their food. It is mess psychology. They are still taking their regimental smoke breaks down at the Bank of America.

The transient residents are young soldiers who, having seen *their* war, are here on Rest and Recreation, regrouping for the return to battle. They misconstrue the Tenderloin's old-fashioned seediness for access to the delicacies with which they have been surfeited in the Orient. They want to get laid, zapped, bombed, zonked, but the girls and drugs, as I patiently explain to them, are in North Beach and the Haight. Here, the screwing is expensive and the dope's still scotch. They express a desire, nurtured by the American press no doubt, for a "Hippie Girl" who had "given it all up" who would go down for "anything pointy," not "like those bitches in high school." It is hard to think of them ending up here, and making no connection between themselves and these clean quiet old men. One war at a time. Every generation screwed each in its own way. Each man, putting in his time, each imagining he is as isolated as the twelve clocks showing international time in the Bank of America, each only an hour apart yet at twenty feet indistinguishable from the other.

We are all wakened early by some soundless collective reveille, and together, with Cokes and cream soda, regard the TV in the lounge. A big-titted broad is doing pushups for the housewives, which form our security perimeter, and for which she receives a few appreciative murmurs. She does the weather, then we are gone for the day, a community again only at 6, for the News.

This evening, the President announces that he may need 200,000 more men for the Asian campaign. A young marine, Lance Corporal Fred, is of the opinion that he'll get them.

"You *all* gonna be over there soon," he laughs.

"Not me," grins an elderly Chinese cook with a midwestern accent. It turns out he served the last five of a twenty-five-year hitch tying up the tourist boat on the bridge of the sunken *Arizona* at Pearl Harbor. In the Visitor's Book he says the tourists write "great," "very interesting," "well presented," "the high point of our trip."

"That's why we're at war," he finishes, "but I only got my pension to worry about now."

"You'll see how fast we get this thing over now," Lance Corporal Fred goes on. "With reinforcements, we'll be in Hanoi in a month."

"Those gook bastards are tougher than you think," the USN Reserve Chink cook grins inscrutably.

And Lance Corporal Fred doesn't know quite how to deal with this. But it tops out the surreal edifice nicely. Later, Lance Corporal implores me to take him down to the Haight, "Just to rap, man. I don't need none of that acid pussy."

If there is a collective unconscious, then who collected it? |Sol Yurick|

Never together, rarely in uniform, the Marines on Rest and Recreation make their way to the Haight. Their object is not a pick-up (the hookers downtown are more attractive and less presumptuous) or drugs (they have access to purer stuff) but good old country store dialogue. They've got some things to get off their chests. They want to see their peers for themselves, let them know that *their* trip is worth it.

"I'll listen to anybody," Lance Corporal Fred tells me, "if they got proof for what they say. I can get proof for anything I say in forty-eight hours."

"It's groovy that they come, you know," says Felix the Hippie whom we have searched out, "it just shows how uptight they are."

Lance Corporal Fred and Felix the Hippie are both twenty, both graduated from high school in middle-sized Middle Western towns, and left two years ago to pursue their respective callings. Neither will return because they "can't" after what they've seen "over there." Of his parents, Felix recalls that he "couldn't get it up hard for either one of them." Fred is more circumspect. "Well, they fought for me, didn't they? Now I gotta fight for them."

They look remarkably alike, except for the hair. Felix's is a foot and a half long, affected Afro, settling as if in the first seconds after electrocution; Fred's is so short he has acne on his temples. But both are uniformed, decorated. Fred, stubborn in his dress uniform, theater ribbons, sharpshooter's distinction, yellow diagonals on his arms. Felix in fur trousers, the inverted wishbone of peace on the right, a Hell's Angel 13 over his heart, purple Cossack blouse, and sporting, oddly enough, a dovetailed West Point dress coat with an epaulette missing. Felix has his Christian name painted in phosphorus on his forehead. Fred has his family name laminated over his heart. Both have been awarded something like a black Maltese cross; Fred's pinned, Felix's pendent.

Used military clothes are in great demand here—not peajackets or Eisenhower tunics—rather Franco-Prussian accouterments, World War I leggings, Air Force officer caps with lightning frowning on the bill. One sees girls dancing at the Fillmore in baggy Air Force blues—a child frugging in the shroud of a dead man. These are the hippies at their best, not new at all, but forcing the past down our throats, or at least the past as we ourselves have caricatured it.

Revolution swept the sunny tropical Vietnamese city of Saigon last week, shaking and straining the anti-Communist, anti-French government, while the fires of civil war guttered out in the refugee-crowded streets of Saigon (pop. 2,000,000) . . . Locked in this squalid conflict were precarious hopes of Vietnamese nationalism, the ambitions of French colonials and the committed prestige of the U.S. government. . . . That night in Freedom Palace, Diem's revolutionary committee drew a pistol on Bao Dai's favorite general, Nguyen Van Vy. With a .45 at his stomach, Vy promised that the pro-Bao Dai units in the Vietnamese army would support Diem's government. Some of the excited young rebels wanted Vy shot on the spot, but Diem eventually let him go untroubled into the night. . . . At this point, the outcome depended upon the attitude of the army. Who did the articulate young army officers want to run their country, colonial puppets or the nationalists. . . ? The situation is encouraging . . . but bad blood also owed between the two big overseeing powers, France and the U.S. Encouraged by Diem's performance, the U.S. (which is pumping $400 million a year into South Viet Nam) coldly urged the French to reverse their position and support the legal government. . . |*Time*, May 9, 1955|

If Fred could only remember the comics and movies he grew up with, he would recognize the friendly faces of his childhood in the Haight— Mandrake the Magician, Harpo Marx, and, for that matter, Little Orphan Annies without eyeballs. It is not a long step from Captain Marvel to the *Oracle,* the psychedelic newssheet; from blowing the monster up to just blowing the monster.

There is a newspaper strike on, and the hippies are making good money selling the *New York Times.* Which is fine until you open your paper and discover it's at least twenty-five years old. A befuddled conventioneer protests in front of the Hilton: "Uh, look, I know where I been, I wanta know where I'm going."

"But get this, man," the vendor replies with unfailing politeness, "ROOSEVELT DECLARES WAR!!! I got one on Hitler visits Poland too."

At scalpers' prices, they sell us back the images of our life, putting our tails in our mouths. But Fred, "one of the leaders of the future," to use his Commanding General's words, sees it as simple inflation, a temporary imbalance in the free market. "They don't know what a revolution is," he confides to me, comparing it to his Asian experience. What he means is they don't know what it's like to be on the winning side of a revolution.

Both kids use the phrase "zapped out" to express their highest emotions, though for Fred this conjures up the use of an anti-tank rocket against a man on a bicycle, while Felix expresses it in terms of an Oriental mandala, all consciousness collapsed to a single liquid center. To zap, or be zapped, these are the only questions. One wonders how that Cong on the bike would describe it.

But their lifestyles are too complementary to let mere language intervene. They need each other. And each has a fund of statistics to support his experience.

"We got one thousand communes in San Francisco alone," Felix says, "leaderless communities based on love."

"I seen more love in Vietnam than what you got here," Fred counters, "those people *really* love each other . . . an' we're getting one thousand defectors a week."

"Ky's a Fascist."

This was a most accursed, wicked, barbarous, cruel, unnatural, unjust and diabolical war. It was conceived in injustice, it was nurtured and brought forth in folly, its footsteps were marked with blood, slaughter, persecution and devastation; in truth,

"You got Commies in this government right now."

"Hitler, Stalin, they're all like little dolls now. It's *you* that have taken us to the moral abyss."

"Aw, if they let us do what we wanted, we could clean that place up in a month."

"Well, I hope they get you before you get them, you prick."

"Hey, that really pisses me off!"

"I don't mean to put you down, man. But look, why don't you shoot your officers?"

Fred thinks this over for some time.

"Wal," he says finally, "Why should I do that? I mean if I was to shoot a 'capitalist warmonger,' I'd shoot the President now, wouldn't I?"

A white band of flesh above Felix's eyebrows as he grins.

"Okay man," he says, "be free."

They break off, conserving their energy.

My friend Felix is a meth head. If we are to believe our doctors, he has about a two-in-five chance of living to twenty-five. Fred is also voluntarily extending his tour. If we are to believe our doctors, he has—under fire, with his specialty—roughly the same chance of making it.

Perhaps the psychedelic anthropologists are right. Substitute LSD for saltpeter in the Army's bill of fare, pay off the Mafia to push syringes of Beefeater in the Haight. War is too important to be left to the military, protest too important to be left to *its* pros.

Assuming Fred and Felix survive their statistics, it should be instructive to be present at their generation's reunion.

everything which went to constitute moral depravity and human turpitude were to be found in it. It was pregnant with mischief of every kind, while it meditated destruction to the miserable people who were the devoted objects of the black resentments which produced it. The mischief, however, recoiled on the unhappy people of our country . . . the nation was drained of its best blood and of its vital resources of men and money . . . the expense of it was enormous, much beyond any former experience, and yet, what had the British nation received in return? Nothing but a series of ineffective victories or severe defeats; victories only celebrated with temporary triumph over our brethren, whom we would trample down or defeat, which filled the land with mourning for the loss of dear and valuable relations, slain in the impious cause of enforcing unconditional submission, or narratives of the glorious exertions of men struggling in the holy cause of liberty. |William Pitt, On the American Revolution|

Went to hear Janet Baker's Debussy, walking the mile to the Opera House. How I love walking in February without practically dying from cold. How I love walking in an American city without being killed. Along Mason Street, some guy in front of me walks into a parking meter, drops his cane and falls heavily into the gutter. I bet it's a trick. When I bend over to pick him up he'll roll over with a revolver and demand my Travelers Cheques. But I know how to handle his kind. I either stomp him right in the face before he can make a move or, if he gets the drop, I ask him to take the money and give me back the wallet for sentimental reasons. He rolls as I hover over him, his eyes open and pupil-less. I see he's blind.

Going to the opera? I ask, helping him up.

"Trying."

You know, of course, it's *Pelléas et Mélisande.*

"Yes, let's hurry. Don't worry about me."

May I take your arm?

"Please."

You go often?

"Depends on the weather. It's hard with these hills, you know. I usually make it two out of three times. Sometimes I just give up and go home if I get lost. Many times, someone will take me, like you."

Why don't you take a cab?

His pupils come into view like a crescent moon on the heels of a red-streaked sunset.

"They seem to ignore me when I wave," he grins and taps.

How blind are you, actually?

"Just enough to improve my hearing."

I get him into the lobby of the Opera all right. The head usher recognizes him and escorts him to his seat. The guy doesn't thank me but the usher winks. Janet Baker saves Debussy from himself once again.

Went out to Berkeley to fill in for a friend's Creative Writing class. It's a nice class as such things go. A retired Hell's Angel in a Pierre Cardin suit and with an aluminum plate in his forehead. A strawberry blonde with no bra but two afghans. Other extremely earnest people. They want to know why there aren't any great writers in America today. I mumble something about there are probably more good writers in America now than at any other time in history.

"So why haven't we heard of them?"

"Maybe it's because," one kid says, "they don't act like writers."

That's quite brilliant. What these kids want is to *live* like writers. Sleep late, punch no clock, be respected, put your neuroses to good use, market your *Angst,* work at what you want, fuck the system and live off it too. Only *art* as a way of life provides such a strategy. And real democracy is possible only when every man is an artist.

The discussion then centers about the necessity for drug experiences to get you out of the "word bag," as they say. After hearing several confessions from people who probably haven't written down more than ten thousand words in their entire lives, hearing how their "blocks" were cured by various drugs, I can only mumble that the basis of all good writing is sufficient motor control to actually hold the pencil firmly to the pad. This struck them as a novel idea. The act of writing as an *event.* More confessions. It's not very interesting how everyone now feels compelled to trade on personal experience with narcotics to prove they know what they're talking about. At length, I have to detail my own drug experiences in order to have the right to argue against their cruel cause and effect. The pathetic fallacy, a student notes. Right on. At length, a barefoot guy with very impressive hair stood up and said that in high school he was in the top ten in the country in math aptitude, and it was only through drugs that he discovered how essentially meaningless that was. In fact, he was now out of math for good. I said that was certainly something literary people could appreciate, but the only thing I could say was that there are hundreds of thousands of opium heads in the world and only one *Kubla Khan,* and mathematically that was an instructive ratio. They were not charmed by this, but they wanted to trust me. So we walked the Strip together, I marveling at the obvious wealth of the students, and also at the potential of the university, as much as I detested the institution. Here was perhaps a beginning for a true medieval university, and in places like the Strip, there seemed to be the possibility of a buffer zone, a necessary hiatus in American life for us all to survive for a better time, something like the College of Paris offered to marginal citizens of the fifteenth century. Still, in a time so marred by the simplicity of survival strategies, how could I continue to believe in a kind of education which could really only be justified if it processed geniuses—that one man, one architect, one engineer, one artist, one politician, who could imprint our time with his own uniqueness? And if I doubted myself in that way, what

I studied politics and war that my sons will study mathematics and philosophy, so that their children will study art. |John Quincy Adams|

Art, which certainly never began as "art for art's sake," at first found itself working for tendencies which are now, for the most part, extinct. |Sigmund Freud|

The comic comes into being just when society and the individual, freed from the worry of self-preservation, begin to regard themselves as works of art. |Henri Bergson|

There is no revolutionary art as yet. |Leon Trotsky|

rhetoric could I use to warn them of the rage they will feel when they discover they have been lied to, that being praised for both their gentleness and their violence, they will find themselves lost in their mid-twenties, unskilled in the largest sense. Unable to protect themselves, victims of their weakness and/or their most ruthless peers who will inherit the positions of their fathers, having no past save the strangulated fury of their adolescence. How to tell them how very hard it is to discipline oneself in important matters when one has not accomplished the petty measurable, and how the shit will hit the fan when they end up selling cars like everyone else, how instead of the revolution we will have a movie of the future which has already passed us by. And for all my hopes for a democracy created (or at least preserved for a time) in this most elitist of institutions, I did not see that man coming out of this training. Those few solitaries of every age who, for better or worse, can *use* or abolish institutions, can drain them, divert them by the mere contingency of their own minds.

I articulated this badly. The students were patient, and in the end advised me to consult a psychedelic anthropologist who lived up the hill, and I said I would.

The evening was given over to other literature. It began in a bar with a notable poet monologuing a visiting Yugoslav poet/critic about how during the Second World War our anarchist/pacifists used to meet at a certain delicatessen in New York and argue out the Trotskyite split. The Yugoslav shrugged politely throughout this and then mentioned how, in Novi Sad, the Hungarian cadre securing the Nazi front had marched several hundred Serbs out on the ice of the Danube, ignited gasoline on the ice and, from ranks, had observed the Serbs slip into the January water. His father was among them. He shrugged again. "I am very sorry, but I cannot understand your pacifism or your anarchism, any more than your Vietnam now. You do not know what it is to be invaded."

Scarcely anyone, in the more educated classes, seems to have any opinions, or place any real faith in those which he professes to have . . . it requires in these times much more intellect to marshall so much greater a stock of ideas and observations. This has not yet been done or has been done only by the very few: and hence, the multitude of thoughts only breeds an increase of uncertainty. Those who should be the guides of the rest, see so many sides to every question. They hear so much said, about everything, and they feel no assurance of the truth in anything. |Matthew Arnold|

Then a late-nite tour. The place where Lawrence Ferlinghetti wrote poems before the sandwiches got thinner! The back room where, we were told, a most relevant folksongstress, to celebrate her thirtieth birthday, went down that night for each of her years, something on the order of waiting in the line which never moves for the twelve clocks at the Bank of America, and finally to the bar where Jack Spicer, that first and last beatnik, toppled over for the last time. The Yugoslav replied disdainfully that whoever Spicer was, he wasn't the first writer to prove you could drink yourself to death. I tried to interject that Spicer actually was a pretty remarkable poet, but the damage was done. Several veterans of his time, their brains viscous with something more than scotch and water, began to surround us. There is nothing more powerful than an idea whose time never came.

The Yugoslav asked me if I thought there was any difference between American prose and poetry.

I said I guessed not except that the poets all knew each other and the novelists didn't, which was what I should have said to the students when they wanted to know why there were no more great writers.

"Of course," he said, "literature has become theatre. The literature of the twenty minutes. An oral tradition for the moment. But nothing is passed on. No more lyric poems. Poems now exist only when they are connected with the person of the poet. Novelists exist only when their novels become movies or they serve on panels. We live in an age of secondary rights. Our work becomes real only when it is meat for another methodology. Like love, you Americans believe in poetry only through the science which explains it or the demonstrable freedom it gains the practitioner. The writer functions now only to the extent that he can explicate and paraphrase his own work, or when he becomes a celebrity. You are a country of two classes: celebrities and eremites. That is why you are all teachers. . . ."

The Yugoslav ends by berating the poets for their self-confessional streaks when they should be polymaths.

"Why are we so unhappy in these goddamn universities?" a poet interrupts. "Because we are captives even more than the students?"

"Not at all," says the Yugoslav, "I tell you it is because you are valued only insofar as you can make your art discursive. You are being paid for creating an atmosphere, the last gasp of bourgeois humanism. You are paid to do everything *except* produce your own work. To read, to teach, to analyze. Talk about alienation! You are allowed to have the products of your minds and your minds themselves *as long* as you are able to reduce them to a common jargon. We, of course, understand this well. It is a very subtle kind of revisionism going on all the time." One drunk poet slams his glass down. "No, it is we who are the *church*. *They* are the hangers-on."

"Acolyte? Sexton? Bell ringer perhaps. No, those are all wrong too. Did you ever see an Eastern Orthodox Mass?"

Much shaking of heads at the Yugo.

"There's a lay fellow in a simple robe who holds a rope separating the people from the priests. He potentially controls the scene, as it were. And he could get more attention than he does. But he'd rather just hold the rope. Oh, the outrageous things he could do. But he'd rather just hold it. There you are."

He asked how many poets we thought were in this country now. I said around fifty thousand probably. The bartender interrupted, "And an awful lot are in California, I bet."

The poets were now angry with all of us. The poets are pressing closer. One of them asks me what my sign is. When I tell him Gemini he nods knowingly but becomes extremely irritated when I don't know what my rising sign is. After some calculation he announces that his Gemini is across mine, and that we can have nothing else to say. . . .

In my next life, I resolve to have nothing to do with writers, myself included.

Went to an old college friend's home for dinner, one of those wonderful frame jobs with octagonal bays to catch the light. Now it's a kind of authoritarian commune. His wife split a year before; now two very funny-looking girls live here, I guess about sixteen, and a thirteen-year-old boy. They bring six enormous loaves of bread to us for dinner. "What's in it, Ray? It's really good."

Very soon we shall see the reappearance of universal apathy, of beliefs in the end of the world, of Messianic claims. But lacking a theological foundation, where can this unconscious fervour find a basis? Some will seek it in the flesh, others in the old religions, and, yet others in Art, and like the Children of Israel in the desert, humanity will adore all sorts of idols . . . I believe, on the other hand, that rules of all kinds are breaking down, that barriers are tumbling and the earth falling to a dead level. This vast disorder may perhaps bring liberty. At least Art, which is always in the vanguard, has followed this road. What is the prevalent poetic form nowadays? Broad construction itself is becoming more and more impossible, with our limited and precise vocabulary and our vague, confused and fugitive ideas. All that we can do then is, out of sheer virtuosity, to tighten the strings of the overstrummed guitar and become primarily virtuosi, seeing that simplicity in our age is an illusion. At this point the picturesque has almost completely died out . . . Perhaps beauty will become a useless quality to humanity, and Art will be something halfway between algebra and music. |Gustave Flaubert, 1852, to Louise Colet|

"Sperm and speed, Charlie; Larry here makes it."
The thirteen-year-old nods indifferently. His eyes are rather like those of the connoisseur of the opera. The manna becomes a bullet on my palate. Two children are brought forward. Ray refers to them as his "former children" since his wife left. He says one of them is on speed. Violence rises in me again. There was a time when I thought I would never be angry like that again. Women who are no longer women, men who try too hard to be men; that's acceptable. But kids who are no longer children . . . what am I going to do, turn Ray over to the cops?
I decide to come at him in a different way, turn my reproach against myself, so I tell him about the students I have just talked with, since this man had been ticketed as one of the most promising young scholars of his time. It is not much fun to teach literature in an egalitarian atmosphere, I said, because writing is not something you want to be *fair* to; and if you are constantly programmatically impartial, you will wind up being merely amiably indifferent, and that is the beginning of self-hatred.
"Well, I was wondering how long it would take you to get it together," he said; "you stayed on longer than most."
He speaks so slowly now. Maybe it's *my* reaction to *his* drugs. Maybe I'm the one who, through a relatively untampered and censorious metabolism, is actually speeding up, out of phase.
"I left school," Ray said, "so I could *stop* writing. Writing is shit. I wasn't afraid of selling out, you know how good a student I was. I didn't drop out because I couldn't make it."
I acceded. He was, in fact, of the top ten in our class. If many more drop out, I think, I'm going to end up in the top ten by default. I look around, wondering if this isn't better than a middle-class family. Not quite a captive audience and the parasitism at least out in the open. Can you live off just your hate? Maybe so. Maybe that's how you find out what you're good for. And then I wonder at myself for making such a comparison at all.
The girls had swabbed off the paper plates, put them up to dry, and disappeared. I mean to get around him.
Well, one thing I don't understand, Ray, why do you fuck ugly girls? I

|25|

Man lives in the sagalike country of utopia where the thing-in-itself tapdances with the categorical imperative. |Jean Arp|

know that sounds simple-minded, but they're really pretty awful.

"Ah," he said, "I like it because they don't care."

You mean no guilt?

"They don't care if they're ugly," he said. "And if they don't care, then why should I?"

There is a lot that wasn't ugly in that.

Well, okay. But the children, are they, actually, you know, *yours?*

"They are not mine, not ours; they are *the* children."

I feigned, passed.

"You see, you've got to understand, the community as we tried to set it up is gone. We didn't have the discipline to sustain it. It's not just that the Mafia is into drugs, or that the cops are on our asses. We've been co-opted. Our resistance has been packaged and sold back to us in bite-sized morsels. It isn't ours any more. It's not that we're being exploited exactly, it's just that we've become another commodity. It's incredible how fast they picked up on us. Now we're going to end up as the *petit bourgeois* of psychedelia."

I had nothing more to say. A spaced-out kid was sitting motionless in my lap. Ray had fended me off perfectly. Taken the argument at face value and proved that, sure man, I can still be lucid. Lucidity conquers all our objections eventually. Just as language outrides all our actions in the end for better or worse. I'd have a hard time explaining that to his kid, his system already full of scientific terminology he will never be able to name.

"I'll tell you one thing that really got me," Ray went on. "You're one of the few guys I could talk this way to anymore, because you knew me before—even if we're now in two different worlds. . . . I got out of the army—you know, my shrink got me out—on the homosexual dread bit. And then I got into the Movement. I was old for the Movement you might think, but in fact I was the youngest guy involved in our particular group, so it ended up with me counseling students how not to go, and how to get out, and then there were the guys that were going to go to jail—in spite of everything we could do to get them out legally, they were *determined* to go to jail. Well, that wasn't for me. I wasn't going to be another of those great gurus who tell 'em not to go, and I realized

We are cannibals, cowboys, Indians, witches, warlocks. Weird-looking freaks that crawl out of the cracks in America's nightmare. Very visible and, as everyone knows, straight from the white middle-class suburban life. |Abbie Hoffman|

that I was powerless to tell them anything because I wasn't afraid any more of what might happen to me. *I* could do anything—I could tell them to do anything—and nothing would happen to me because I no longer cared about myself. It was they who would pay. Well, then I thought about going to jail—but who would give a shit if old Ray blows his cool and goes to jail? I got very hung up on this and wondered how I could become a celebrity on short notice just to be able to use it, see, just like we used to talk about making a million bucks before we were thirty so we could 'do what we wanted to.' I was taking a lot of acid then, and baby, if I hadn't, if I *had* been in control and actually faced my unconscious, if I had been able to 'act out my normal aggressions,' as the shrink used to say, I'm positive I would've shot Reagan or some-body. So, the next time you put down drugs, just think of it this way—the streets are full of omnicompetent middle-class assassins who have voluntarily sterilized their violence. Heroic narcosis. And then I saw a very strange thing, that a lot of the guys in the Movement were getting their kicks out of the war. Now maybe that's puritanical or something, but I knew they didn't really want it to *end*—that they looked on these stupid kids, right out of high school, as some kind of *proletariat*—they looked on them in exactly the same way that recruiting sergeants love those younguns 'cause if you get 'em early and gung ho they'll do any-thing you tell 'em to. No wonder we're losing the war. It's their four-teen-year-olds against our nineteen-year-olds. So what happened to me is so obvious, you're polite not to mention it. It's not just the drugs. My strategy was simple. I became an *un*-celebrity, a totally anonymous per-son, and in that way I'm testimony to a man who's willing, not to give up his leverage, but himself—as little as it may be. Not dehumanized but just dysfunctional.

The notion of the void has lost its critical edge and is thoroughly reactionary . . . |Harold Rosenberg|

"Somehow, by giving up one's *place,* one acquires *weight.* I don't know how else to explain it. I'm no masochist strictly speaking; I just gave up the only thing I had. I can't refuse the Nobel prize. I can't re-fuse a battle order. This is the only kind of mourning I know. Do I sound presumptuous or melancholy?—I'm not at all that unhappy about it. I just *know* now I don't fit in. I blew my chance for status. I don't regret it. I couldn't have handled it. People like us don't know how to use whatever is fortunate in their lives. My business now is to find the holes I don't fit in and then by sitting there, staring at those unfilled holes while I die, maybe somebody else, somebody stronger than me, will see me looking at those holes, and be moved beyond pity and do something about it. You could walk right by now and not notice those holes if it weren't for people like me just sitting there and staring at them. And this I must warn you about, friend. One day, a man is going to come along who understands this psychology, a leader, see, we're all gonna get up and follow him and you had better pray he's a good man, because if he isn't, it's going to be the end of everything."

I looked hard at Ray then. And it struck me how easily a little success at the right time in his life would have bought him off. A rave in the Sunday *New York Times*—something as simple as that. Without it, he was crazy. A considerable intelligence turned upon itself, and which could now only crave, not revenge, but only release from itself. Polonius' advice is not a platitude. It is the establishment insuring its hegemony by insuring paralysis and self-hatred among those energies that threaten it. "To thine own self be true, Ray. Otherwise, you could be dangerous. . . ."

I would confirm this suspicion by drinking myself beyond them. Ray went on, but began to repeat himself. How much I loved him then, even admired him. And he was right, particularly on one count—that our society was not sick because it could be blamed for making him what he was, but rather because it could not make use of what he had made of himself.

I awoke at dawn on the floor, my liver like a creel at my side. Ray, all five of my hosts were asleep entangled upon an enormous water bed. It was a kind of family, but I would not yet lie with them. A family has to be more than "interesting," as it once had to become something more than an economic unit. And I have had enough of survival tactics for this month.

I can truly say that I am not in the world and this is not a mere mental attitude . . . Moreover, it matters little, I prefer to show myself as I am, in my inexistence and uprootedness . . . [but] the reader must believe that it is a matter of an *actual* sickness and not a phenomenon of the age, of a sickness which is related to the essence of the human being and his central possibility of expression . . . |Antonin Artaud to Jacques Riviere|

To put it more precisely, this is how I see the matter: the mind is fragile in that it needs obstacles—adventitious obstacles. If it is alone, it loses its way, it destroys itself. It seems to me that the mental erosion, the inner larcenies, the destruction of thought and the substance which afflicts your mind, have no other cause than the too great freedom you allow it. It is the absolute that throws it out of gear. In order to grow taut, the mind needs a landmark, it needs to encounter the kindly opacity of experience. The only remedy for madness is the innocence of facts . . . There is no absolute peril except for him who abandons himself; there is no complete death except for him who acquires a taste for dying . . . . |Riviere to Artaud|

Went to a demonstration in front of the Fairmont Hotel. Paint all over the façade signifying blood. Humphrey et al. inside. Broken glass. Girls up front and screaming. But it still sounded like a high school basketball game. A cop pushed me over a fire hydrant. They clubbed a lot. It is easy to make too much of this. The point is, not one of us, whatever our persuasion, wanted to be there. It was a witless demonstration, banal repression. We are beating on each other because we are helpless for each other. We are a nation looking for a policeman to tell us how far we can go, so we can find out where in hell we've been.

In this legendary marble palace on the crest of Nob Hill, there is scarcely any occasion when a patron need step outside to satisfy his needs . . . whether you stay at the hotel or not, a trip to the tower top is a San Francisco must . . . if you do stay, you'll appreciate such lavish extras as twice daily maid service, sprigged percale blanket covers, a maid to "turn down" your sheet at night, TVs, shower baths, Muzak, electric shoe polishers, and a large walk-in closet in every room. But such elegance does not come cheaply. . . . |Brochure found on pavement in front of Fairmont Hotel|

Ray gives me his car for the weekend. He is going into the hospital for a complete 48-hour rectal-respiratory investigation. He must drink a quart of barium to illuminate his digestive tract. That's the hardest part, he says, harder even than the proctoscope, that anal telescope the size of his car's radio antenna with a little light on the end. Oh, it unwinds, uncoils, you betchum. Despite our different heads, our different foods, Ray and I share the same weak stomach. That's what gives one hope. The tummy, like the brain, is vulnerable, finally, only to itself.

It's a great big car, too big for the coast road in the fog. Too big to drive, too thick to see, too cold to swim. A semi goes off the road ahead of me, its brakes steaming blue in a grove of redwoods. I stop at an inn. The few visitors are not panicky, though they have had to abandon their cars along the coast road like cordwood. A lovely, soft, abstracted blonde, a friendly fetus apparent behind her jeans, serves us curry. Behind the bar, she secretly tastes each portion with a goodly finger before she serves. *Wow,* she says each time.

An elderly couple ask her what's her name?

"Waitress," she beams guilelessly.

"That's nice. Where you from, dear?"

"Here."

"My wife means where did you come *from,* miss."

"Here. This is where I'm from."

"But there's no town here. This is just a restaurant."

KIMOSABE TOURS BIG SUR

|29|

Later: "Maybe she was born here, Frank. Maybe her father owns the place."

"She's knocked up, that's all."

"Frank!"

In the morning, the fog lifts just enough to reveal the road. Before she goes back up to the lodge to get breakfast, she says I should come back when there's sun; but I prefer her mist to any tan.

We wander out to retrieve our sullen autos; the sea might as well not be there, only the first twenty feet of the deciduous sienna redwoods are visible. Notice how calm people are in the fog; when they're abstracted from their own perception. It is something very close to tears—the response to incalculable beauty is the same as that before inexplicable destruction. It occurs to me we are slowly able, not through courage as much as a kind of desperate curiosity, to learn to let our consciousness roam apart from our will, a strategic retreat from the codified despair which has become so professionalized, so respectable—this metaphysic of being down on ourselves. It's not Freudian, in the sense of confronting repressed desires, but an exteriorization, an extension of the senses, learning to accept ourselves apart from the psychopathology of survival. For a people who have no politics, whose pride once lay in an illimitable future—which is now only a disdain for the past which is to come—it is perhaps inevitable that self-acceptance should take on an erotic, a tactile form, at least in the beginning. In this fog we are neither free nor fearful, and among the redwoods planted to amaze us, we know that our fate does not have either the certitude nor the inevitability of tragedy, that we are neither free in a vacuum nor pawns in a premeditated game. What we do know is that we have sources of life hitherto unexplored . . . that we are engaged, even against our will, and do not comprehend either the sources or uses of our considerable power. We have already described ourselves dying, and if we are capable of watching ourselves *lose* our consciousness, then we can resurrect it, not through psychotherapy or history, but by the very ability to be *separate from our own minds*; that which began as cosmic theology and ended up a housewives' complaint.

America's dirty little secret. That self-liberation has ultimately little to do with self-realization. Oompah.

|30|

I like to think (and
the sooner the better)
of a cybernetic meadow
where mammals and computers
live together in mutually
programming harmony
like pure water
touching clear sky.

I like to think
*   (right now, please!)*
of a cybernetic forest
filled with pines and electronics
where deer stroll peacefully
past computers
as if they were flowers
with spinning blossoms.

I like to think
*   (it has to be!)*
of a cybernetic ecology
where we are free of our labors
and joined back to nature,
returned to our mammal
brothers and sisters,
and all watched over
by machines of loving grace.
|Richard Brautigan|

Our waitress knows the sea is there though she couldn't prove it, just as she knows that it's breakfast time though there's no chimes. Imagine, we've been handed down an entire philosophy, predicated on what is theoretically verifiable. You can make a statement about the moon because theoretically you can go there and test it empirically. So now we go to the moon and our words are as opaque as ever. The moon cannot verify our words about it.

The waitress too, coming down the mountain to work, a lunar beauty, slightly out of phase, as lubric as if she just rose from the sea. No child of nature she. No metaphor, you sweet. Just a pregnant waitress who lives on the place, where we can test her empirically, take her invention from her by night. Verifiable as she may be, can she verify our words about her? If I ever have a daughter, I will call her Verifiable or, perhaps, Honey.

His ward opened the front door a crack, the chain clinking straight as a pike. A gentle boy who is finally persuaded I am neither fuzz nor media, and a lovely large-breasted young woman, his wife, who says she's a Pisces as she serves us rose-hip tea. The psychedelic Anthropologist is rotund, and has no secondary characteristics.

"Ultimate religious and ultimate sexual experiences are identical with psychedelic drugs," the large, soft and not stupid man begins, "and drugs are a necessary antidote to Christian culture which has always, from the beginning, separated the two."

The young man and young wife and I all nod affirmatively. He presents his plan for the "Alternative University": To study *cosmic* history, by a leap through space-time, to o'erleap anthropology which is the "science of death."

He is known as a man who engages in polemics, attacks faculty wives at receptions. He spent the first part of his life drawing excruciatingly

SON OF HENRY JAMES VISITS THE PSYCHEDELIC ANTHROPOLOGIST

boring but meticulous kinship patterns. It's quite conceivable he also was in the top ten in math aptitude in the country when he was 20. "Our Hualapai Indian informants know that one has to eat in order to conceive, and one has to be conceived in order to eat. They believe that they can eat anything they conceive of and conceive anything they can eat. And as we know from an occasional tale brought back from travelers to remote areas, heaven is up, and, therefore, earth is down. Now earth is matter, and matter is *mater*, and mater is mother, and mother is nature. If nature is down, then culture must be up. Therefore, we conclude that *emic* is culture, and *etic* is nature, and that the latter is to be put down."

It's all so odd, this lovely house in the Berkeley hills, this quiet triple, this man-child who began by mastering algebraic transposition, and now through chemicals would put down History itself with a New Hegelianism.

He asks me how many doses of LSD I've taken. I lie about the number. What was it like? he says, what did you feel? A lot of lights, I said, like I was in a . . . cartoon. My mind was outside my own body, that is to say I had no peripheral vision, and everything receded from my grasp.

"What was the dosage?"

I have no idea.

"Then the dosage wasn't strong enough," he says, "or it probably wasn't good stuff. I've taken over 280 trips myself. Paul here has taken nearly 200." Paul nods.

"If you take pure stuff in the right dosages, the total symbolic net which is our language and culture begins to collapse by folding in towards itself. As the two extremes begin to approach one another, they approach identity, and eventually they will reach the point of zero difference. One has a firm grip on one's own tail. . . . When the collective unconscious is reduced to a single point, the individual has, at that moment, a snapshot of the entire content of the collective unconscious. And at that point, he knows all there is to know. But since the collective unconscious is language, the veil of Maia, he believes that Maia is a reality. At that moment, he believes that he knows and encompasses all of reality and therefore concludes that he is God. But he is suspended in the ulti-

The history of the human race, viewed as a whole, may be regarded as the realization of the hidden plan of nature to bring about a constitution, internally and externally perfect, as the only state in which all the capacities implanted by her in mankind can be fully developed. |Immanuel Kant, Eternal Peace|

Originally, the ego includes everything, later it detaches from itself the external world. The ego-feeling we are aware of now is thus only a shrunken vestige of a far more extensive *feeling—a feeling which embraced the universe and expressed an inseparable connection of the ego with the external world. If we may suppose that this primary ego-feeling has been preserved in the minds of many people . . . it would co-exist like a sort of counterpart with*

mate of all symbols, the single word which is the timeless, motionless, unchanging and absolute void. In other words, while he feels that he continues to exist, everything else has come to a halt. He is frozen in the ultimate symbol. It is no wonder that he may experience isolation and loneliness on a cosmic scale, and he then has two recourses, either to return to the differentiated levels of the collective unconscious or to proceed downward. Down is Nirvana, orgasm, entropy, individuation and magical science. Only *there* do we escape cultural relativism, for only in culture can we have such a thing as relativism."

The man not only wants to have the *last word*, I think, he wants to *be* the *word*, in the beginning. He wants to be *my* symbolic net. And as a matter of fact, if you gear back the rhetoric about 20 percent, he is only describing quite commonplace feelings.

"Today," he continues, "we take our children from their play when they are four and put them to work. We do not call it work but education. We take children who are full of life and love, and force them to sit quietly in schools while teachers, who have been selected for their inability to love, force them through an apprenticeship which will ultimately make them valuable commodities in the market. It is the most horrible and systematic exploitation of children that has occurred in all history, and the human being differs from the animals in only one way. The animals may love their children, but may not eat them. Humans may not love their children, but may eat them. The forbidden fruit which Eve ate and then gave to Adam to eat was her own children. And original sin was not sex, but the directing of sexual energy to pervert the hunger drive."

Do you have any children, I ask him earnestly.

"No," he says, "We cannot afford them."

"I don't want any," his wife interjects quickly. "We have all our family now."

What about genetic damage? Aren't you afraid at all?

"Not until women are free to love their own children will the way to paradise be reopened. The exit from the maze is through the entrance."

I'll take you more seriously when you produce that child.

The rose-hip tea has taken its toll. I am excused to take a leak. The

the narrower and more sharply outlined ego-feeling of maturity, and the ideational content belonging to it would be precisely the notion of limitless extension and oneness with the universe . . . 'oceanic' . . . I can imagine that the oceanic feeling could become connected with religion later on . . . |Freud, Civilization and Its Discontents|

Freud . . . has not given a scientific explanation of the ancient myth. What he has done is propounded a new myth. The attractiveness of the suggestion, for instance, that all anxiety is a repetition of the anxiety of the birth trauma, is just the attractiveness of a mythology. 'It is the outcome of something that happened long ago.' Almost like referring to a totem . . . it may be an immense relief if it can be shown that one's life has the pattern rather of a tragedy—the tragic working out and repetition of a pattern which was determined by the primal scene. There is of course the difficulty of determining what scene is the primal scene—whether it is the scene which the patient recognizes as such, or whether it is the one whose recollection effects the cure. In practice, these criteria are mingled together. |Ludwig Wittgenstein, Conversations on Freud|

|33|

bathroom wall is papered with Paul's poems. Lord God, are they awful. Is this the cost of a new consciousness? No language at all? Or just lousy language? Does a more human living room, a frankly political foyer, mean bad poems in the john? (By keeping ourselves from dying, we are keeping ourselves from living, he says.)

Well, he is not dying, not yet. Nor am I. And my guess is that Ray is right, that what he has garbled so ceremoniously in cultural analysis, in the aesthetics of drugs, is essentially a political wish, the desire to blow everything up, and since he's repressed that, he implodes his own mind. Well, live or die, fella. Take your symbolic net, your Maia, and stuff it up your ass. Leave me a few contingent if impure words. Have your mind any way you like it, and call every word repression if you like—divide life into those who speak and those who feel, but get those shitty poems out of your bathroom. . . . Whoever supposed that books and bodies should be weighed on the same scale? So it's Culture versus Nature, is it? Well, I have a little Zen paradox for you, my friend. Life is language, but language is not life. Poems are not worth lives nor vice versa. We ought to be able to do better than that in an "alternative university." Divvying up the world in this way, no matter how you reconstitute it, is our oldest sickness. You treat your body as if it were a book, as if it could hold time; I treat books as if they were bodies. And that is no source, my friend, for a quarrel. It's a phony dialectic. And we meet from either side of your Damoclean mimeographed sheet, where I have an irony for every monopolemic you can muster. OK, language is a circle. For you it's vicious, for me it's magical. And that's a matter of rhetoric, which is to say, free choice. And we are brothers because we have been denied the same things. But I'd give myself over to you, to Paul even, before I'd give it over to an impersonal chemical. And yes, I know I drink too much. . . .

He takes me down the hill to catch the bus back to the city.

Does your wife take acid too? I asked innocently.

"No, she had a very bad trip once."

If you don't make it at the Alternative U, what are you going to do?

"Oh," he says, "My wife's getting her Ph.D. in sociology here. We'll be okay."

|34|

I have rejected these poems for the same reason that made Arnold withdraw his "Empedocles on Etna" from circulation; passive suffering is not a theme for poetry. |W. B. Yeats|

It is not urged against cuticles that they are not hearts, yet some philosophers seem to be angry with images for not being things, and with words for not being feelings. |George Santayana|

We embrace briefly at the bus station. I look back at the campus on the hill. How I despise those who do not have the patience to take him on, this strange good man assaulting an entire historiography from his mimeograph machine, writing off writing with writing, who wants to have his Time and eat it too, who wears such marvelous contradictions so innocently, discovering in the laboratory of his body what the greatest prophets and poets discovered through their texts, that moment when the imaginative realization of dying becomes the determining climactic experience of living. But how would he call forth the light in his body without the words of the prophets?

On the bus, I am chilled by the thought that we could be brought together only by an extraordinary *political* act.

And there, sir, lies the entire problem, to have within oneself the inseparable reality and the material clarity of feeling, to have it in such a degree that the feeling cannot but express itself, to have a wealth of words and of formal constructions which can join in the dance, serve one's purpose—and at the very moment when the soul is about to organize its wealth, its discoveries, this revelation, at the unconscious moment when the thing is about to emanate, a higher and evil will attacks the soul like vitriol, attacks the word and image mass, attacks the mass of feeling and leaves me panting at the very door of life . . . |Artaud|

The imagination will not down . . . If it is not a dance, a song, it becomes an outcry, a protest. If it is not flamboyance it becomes deformity; if it is not art, it becomes crime. Men and women cannot be content any more than children, with the mere facts of a humdrum life—the imagination must adorn and exaggerate life, must give it splendor and grotesqueness, beauty and infinite depth. |W. C. Williams|

I made my plane reservation for Europe, then decided to go down to the Haight for a last look. It had turned around the previous fall, lost its momentum, and now one sees an occasional kid, no older than ten, spread out on the steps of some high-vaulted rooming house, The New Malnutrition in his cheeks—"Look at me, Ma, I'm a commodity too. . . ." Then is what rises in me only a residual puritanism? Any serious attack upon the bourgeois order must take these kids into account. Love without fear, they say. How can one possibly love without fear when such children exist, even potentially, lost in the fallopians of society? Oh, they're not eating the right things, but then they never have. I am beginning to believe that the Church is right—we have no more right to destroy ourselves than others. Camus said that the only philosophical question left was that of suicide. To that one might add, the only metaphysical question left is that of conceiving children.

When you take your pill it's like a mine disaster. I think of all the people lost inside of you.
|Richard Brautigan|

have this special banker's suit: three piece, blue, Brooks Brothers, which was given me on the occasion of my graduation from high school, and which I still use now and then for fund-raising, weddings, as well as wakes and riots. In those early nostalgic days of the Civil Rights Movement when the police still respected the niceties of class, that suit kept me from getting shoved around during many demonstrations, and on occasion it even protected others. Once in Atlanta, when The King was riding high, a cop rushed at a group of us sitting in; as he got to me, he raised his club high, then at the last moment passed on to belabor a comrade in a more ill-fitting herringbone. Only a Nigerian in a dashiki and I were spared that day, and in the paddy wagon it became clear that we were thought to be "foreign reporters." That was not far off the mark, and the lesson was not lost upon either of

JACOBINS AND ANARCHISTS

or how, when conditions are equal and skepticism is rife, it is important to direct human actions to distant objects.

us. Superman's workaday disguise is, after all, the safest one he could choose. Had I known then what kind of aesthetics would eventually be offered as surrogate politics, I would have capitalized more on aloof insinuation. I was still young enough to act out the moral pieties and redundant strategies which did in that particular form of high-toned liberalism. In retrospect, I should have been more the ruthless dandy than the ingenuous amateur. Perhaps I would have then anticipated to what extent our resistance was doomed by its very style; the presumption that we could be politically effective by "being ourselves" in public— Lord, what a lousy strategy. It allows your enemies to predict you, and I see now that I could have protected more people by posing as a faggoty cultural attaché from The Netherlands than a respectable kid gone mad or moral. In any case, "the suit," although it looks as good as the day the whining tailor let the crotch out two inches and hustled me off for my first certificate, is worn now only in airplanes, about the only institution left which I feel disposed to get dressed up for. I'm always amazed, for example, when I see a woman in slacks on an airplane. Not appropriately funebrous, I suppose. When one is packaged so fragilely, one should dress accordingly.

Today, my Pan American formality comes in handy. The sidewalks are solid with residents taking the Sunday air, the boutiques doing a brisk, supererogate business; in a loft, somebody's playing an electric organ with his elbows. Haight Street itself is jammed with cars which are in turn jammed with tourists, faces pressed against the windows, leaving dots of fog and mucus upon the glass, ogling the hippies, precisely like those peasants against the panes of the ballroom doors in *Madame Bovary*. And it's quite right to look upon these kids as *our* aristocracy. Our rich lack the requisite *chutzpah* to create an elite, the right has only managed the demeanor of a provincial court, and our liberals have always lacked the requisite fatuity to create class out of a political dynasty—so, given American life, we have manufactured as best we can an aristocracy of the young, an ersatz bohemia, a fun ghetto, a buffer zone of privileged minors. Alienated just sufficiently to be charmingly inarticulate, but sufficiently paranoid to strike at the insult rather than at the cause of the insult. Their hatred remains only representational.

|37|

An American should never be led to speak of Europe, for he will then probably display much presumption and very foolish pride. He will take up with those crude and vague notions which are so useful to the ignorant all over the world. But if you question him respectfully, respecting his own country, the cloud that dims his intelligence will immediately disperse; his language will become as clear and precise as his thoughts. He will inform you what his rights are and by what means he exercises them; he will be able to point out the customs which obtain in the political world. You will find that he is well acquainted with the rules of the administration and that he is familiar with the mechanism of the laws. The citizen of the United States does not acquire his practical science and his positive notions from a book; the instruction he has acquired may have prepared him for receiving those ideas, but it did not furnish them. The American learns to know the law by participating in the act of legislation; and he takes the lesson in the forms of government from governing. The great work of society is ever going on before his eyes and, as it were, under his hand . . .
|de Tocqueville|

They know no essences. It is an anger which stinks of theory. For its full expression, it requires their other half, their double, the suburban nuclear family come to see it like it is; and for these sociologists sealed in their obdurate autos, the hippies oblige their audience with, if not precisely impromptu, at least amateur, routines. How curious that their sole endeavor seems to be to prove the clichés about each other. The commonplace and banal are demonstrated with such perfervid execution, such requisite discipline. Our appetite for stasis is awesome. The bourgeois stereotype being well documented, one ought to catalog the clichés about the other half. They are intelligent but not literate, critical but not analytic, self-conscious but not intuitive, confuse the aesthetic with the political and vice versa, and so are neither. Having no sense of the self, they project, exteriorize their consciousness. They practice that traditional American expropriation—creating a form in the world for their minds. This is seen by the envious bourgeoisie as an acceptance of their bodies, but it is not that, rather acquiescence to the penultimate split between mind and body. In other words, the body exists only when it is aware of itself, when it is outside itself. And the mind only when it is acknowledged materially, has a *place*, a reversal of the usual Western notion. The body becomes subjective, the mind takes on the quality of a paralyzed physical gesture. And as the body becomes spiritualized, etherealized, the mind becomes an organ, at worst a loathsome one; the body a mystery, at worst a mystery story. . . .

In the Haight, the cars are lined up end to end, radiators beginning to steam, air conditioners flush upon the asphalt, electrical systems short out involuntarily in a parody of honks. Across the gutter, they eye each other obliquely. Only the shatterproof tinted glass of the car windows separates them. The organ has ceased and the Aristocrats have turned as one, as if to take down their pants, their doublets, lifting their gowns and codpieces to press their busky arses against the pane. Gotcha, peasants, gotcha!

The peasants recoil from the ballroom windows in horror. The world is changing roles. The cop at the intersection is deluged. His walkie-talkie hangs upon him like a goiter. They have stuffed mums in his pistol belt. The tourists are honking themselves deaf. In my formal attire, some still make way for me. You can see it in their faces, the readout. Too expensive a suit for a detective or a reporter, not a tourist either, exactly. Why so natty, man?

I'm a crab, fresh-cut bait, and I have ears only for the barracuda.

I am able to see exactly how it started. The traffic breaks for an instant, both cars and a clot of pedestrians leap for the open space, a leashed mutt is nearly struck by a car. Brakes slam, a family of four's heads strike leatherette abutments. The Pontiac's bumper guards waver an inch from the mutt. His master, a study in static berserk, lives up to his costume. Hair thrashing furiously, he removes his belt and begins to lash the snout of the Pontiac, causing our nuclear family to turn mauve. Head of nuclear family's eyes narrow, then widen. Driver feels himself helplessly across the chest. Cop's mouth is open. Dog is urinating convulsively on the tire which had nearly crushed him a moment before. The residents gather protectively about their pet, a girl picks him up and a stream of urine inscribes the air, spattering on the hood where it beads upon the Simonize. Cop yells to get dog out of street, the honking crescendos, and the crowd leaves the sidewalk, breaks the proscenium, pours into the intersection and engulfs the cop. Now he's on the walkie-talkie. Kids run up and down the stalled line of autos spitting through a few open windows, slapping the autos like penned cattle until the Haight rings with pain. The cars are so close, enraged husbands cannot open their respective doors to get out and fight like men.

Cop yells that the pedestrians are blocking traffic.

"The traffic is blocking itself! We gotta cross the street sometime."

The horns are now unbearable.

It is intermission.

Sirens are heard. Reinforcements. A phalanx of motorcycle cops, at least a dozen on two-wheelers, appear at the crest of the hill, then break formation and careen up the sidewalks, heel and toe, barely able to keep the heavy Harleys upright in close quarters at low speed. A few of the boutiques begin to close, but most of the crowd has now been driven off the sidewalk to the parked cars upon which they lounge until their coils and shocks sigh as the wind. The organ has been wheeled to a second story window and reactivated. In the cramped space, the kids join hands and begin to snake-dance between the cars, taunting the cops.

"You got five minutes to clear the street." And then the first bottle arrives. A gallon jug of mountain Chablis, I believe, exploding in the midst of bullhorns and boots.

I dodge a cycle and turn the corner, encountering a crowd of troglodytes and witches running full upon me, bare feet splatting on the pavement, medals and beads ajangle, screaming, not with fear precisely, but like a lady who's been goosed in the subway. They flow around me, pursued by dismounted cops on foot with nightsticks at the ready, occasionally cracking them on legs or asses. Implausibly, I stand my ground as I note them run through me. I have not forgotten the Fairmont. I'm so tired of getting the *symbolic* shit beat out of me. The cops are upon me; a blow to the calf shuts my eyes. Then they surge by. I'm untouched, left spinning in their wake like some cartoon character who's been bopped on the head, blown up, ravished a thousand ways, but after a singed whiskered grimace, reconstitutes himself in the next frame, for the next scenario. I turn around, Buster Keaton-like, only to find the same crowd now come full circle, round the block, although screaming more naturally this trip. Not pressing my luck, I step into a doorway as the phantom coppery passes at a clatter.

Now as it darkens, bottles are bursting in the street, windows lose their reflections, and somehow the visitors' cars have rapidly dispersed. There'll be some stories around the old barbecue tonight. And within an hour, the street is deserted save for two hundred police. Above them, on the rooftops, more romantic shadowy figures, hurling the containers of their lives; they crouch like Indian scouts taking dumb aim behind a single tree upon a literal forest of bear. The hail of glass and garbage is constant. A cop is hit with a Clorox bottle, leaps back expecting blood and then goes sheepish as he realizes it's plastic and empty. Another, however, with his helmet visor raised, has a lip torn away. At my feet is a milk carton on the backside of which is a public service message.

HELP OUR P O W' S
WRITE HANOI

The restaurant advertises "soul food." A lovely large Ghanaian woman hands over some Beef Stroganoff. It tasted OK at first, but then my eyes began to water. Then my nostrils began to burn unfamiliarly, not with curry, nor exotic spice, but the tear gas I first tasted in the South. A squad car goes by telling us to stay indoors; the Ghanaian woman is *truly* crying, moaning how much the neighborhood has deteriorated. I go back outside.

The street now reoccupied, the battle lines less fixed, a lot of unpremeditated crying. A young man is yelling knowingly, "Don't rub your eyes, it's Mace, it's Mace. The crystals will blind you." He takes a girl into a doorway. She has a water-soaked handkerchief with which he douses her eyes.

"It'll just make it worse," I tell him, "don't put water on it."

"I've been maced," she says flatly, proudly.

A couple of the more daring kids throw the tear gas canisters back at the cops. Nobody can throw very well, but there is this one kid, obviously with minor league experience, who hurls the canisters fifty yards down the street with great accuracy. I stop to pick up one spinning at my feet and heave it back; not a bad shot at all, a cop has to jitterbug to avoid it. My bursitis is killing me.

A couple of the younger cops are rapping with some barefoot chicks. "Let's get off the street," they're saying, "and get on home."

"It's *our* street!"

The cops shake their heads. "Nope. It's your sidewalks. It's our street." Plainclothesmen with more scoped rifles arrive, but no one has fired yet.

A freak yells at one of the sergeants, "Hey man, why don't you get out? If you get out, it'll stop."

The cop turns unconvinced. "It ain't finished yet, brother," then flashing a peace sign, "you started it."

Finally, the street is barricaded with a pride of squad cars. The dusk is lowering, the revolutionaries are running out of empties. Will they now resort to their larders? Ah no; it's dinner, dinnertime.

What's important to note here is the scarcity of dialogue, the lack of material with which to reconstruct the world. So we should not com-

Write:
PRESIDENT HO CHI MINH
DEMOCRATIC REPUBLIC
OF VIETNAM
HANOI, NORTH VIETNAM
POSTAGE 25¢

YOUR EXCELLENCY:

I am disturbed about the condition of American prisoners of war held in your country. I ask you in the name of humanity to return these men to their families. They are of no military value— and to link their fate with war aims is a flagrant contradiction of the spirit of the Geneva Convention , which you signed in 1957.

Sincerely,

Signature _____

plain that art cannot sufficiently render life in such instances, but the fact is simply the reverse; this afternoon, we have all become refugees from a bad novel. The only possible aesthetic response in such a situation is to orchestrate these voices—for they have been given one of the worst librettos ever—and, through a single consciousness, establish an essence where there are now only representations. No doubt, the fact that I will be in Europe again in eight hours enhances this possibility. For to be in Europe is to be *back* in the audience and to be judgmental. To hear these old dialogues rehearsed so badly, uplifted not even by tentativeness, one is thrown back upon the writer's natural paranoic voyeurism, or perhaps that disdain which is the last vestige of liberalism, that peculiar scorn which the bourgeois intellectual once reserved for the idle rich, and now applies to the new aristocracy—with all your advantages, why aren't you more effective? The liberal, that lost liberal, does not hate the random violence which has taken his leaders from him, not even the self-indulgence and pathetic self-congratulation of these children. What he cannot stomach in the end is their incompetence, their lack of a methodology for reality. So to be absolutely honest, what we really despise is the lack of *effective* violence. If you're so pretty, why ain't you won?

In such disdain, nevertheless, there exists the possibility of common ground, for here the liberal makes precisely the same error as these kids have done today. That is, by superimposing the grand paradigm of European social change upon a long and undistinguished street of a mid-century American city, they are not even acting out old movies; they are miming old gravures. We blame them for not exposing themselves in their exposure of the system, and write off their petty insurrection as one which will not determine the character and purpose of whatever revolution is to come. But it is not helpful to define these kids as *a*historical. They are utterly historical. They just don't know it. It is not fear of the future as much as the lack of any usable past which fuels their aggression. And if they model their activity after such figures as Che, Mao, et al., then we cannot have it both ways by calling such figures inappropriate to American experience, and implying that we won't take the kids seriously until they display the courage or *class* of such

A lived event is finite, concluded on the level of experience. But a remembered event is infinite, a possible key to everything that preceded it and to everything that will follow. . . .
|*Walter Benjamin on Proust*|

We could go somewhere else as we had always had the right to go somewhere else and as we had always gone . . . |*Hemingway,* A Moveable Feast|

. . . in spite of the elastic freshness and vigor of her youth, she is far from being a model for the earth to copy. |*Dickens,* American Notes|

figures. If the cops are not those of Batista or the Kuomintang, and we are not Trotsky or even Engels, then the kids are not Mazzinians or Fenians or Red terrorists, and therefore we should not discount their efforts because they didn't arrive on a sealed train and read the situation correctly.

It would be simple as well as comforting to see sexual determinism here. But in this case at least, Marxism remains a better principle of analysis if only because it identifies the particular point of mystification which the sexual metaphor cannot. First of all, the most obvious thing about this confrontation is that these kids do not seem to want to admit that they are resisting laws which their upper-class parents made, and which must be, in the end, enforced by lower-class people. This is neither to excuse the brutality of the reaction nor question the legitimacy of the grievances, but it does suggest that the true revolutionary must know who his actual enemy is, and acknowledge the source of his enmity. In our society, it is easier to tell a policeman off than one's own father, and further, to attribute to the policeman one's father's mixed motives. This cops-and-robbers mentality has poisoned more than our politics, and from a strategic viewpoint it has had two particularly debilitating effects: first, it avoids yet another opportunity to understand who "they" are. The policeman represents an unenlisted mentality without which no revolution can succeed; the police as exemplary proletariat.

Secondly, it is to forget the somewhat ancient truth that to truly destroy one's enemy, one must first sympathize with him, identify with him in order to be able to predict him, and what happens when all experience becomes politicized is that political consciousness has nothing against which to test itself, no principle of self-criticism. It is consciousness neither raised nor repressed; only diverted. All that has happened so far is that politics have become *sensualized,* a quest for a kind of public virility which overrides all ideological objections. That was the secret of the Kennedy style, after all, and when virility cannot be established with grace and shape, it must assume a more grotesque and radical momentum. Having no specific object of desire, it must flaunt, feign, float free, fuck and run. Eroticism, the only private guarantee of one's iden-

Artistic alienation is sublimation. It creates the images of conditions which are irreconcilable with the established Reality Principle but which, as cultural images, become tolerable, even edifying and useful. Now this imagery is invalidated. Its incorporation into the kitchen, the office, the shop; its commercial release for business and fun is, in a sense, desublimation—replacing mediated [sic] by immediate gratification . . . True, the Romantic pre-technical world was permeated with misery,

|43|

tity, becomes the basic weapon against the oppression which has yet no name.

Liberalism fails in this context because it does not sufficiently capitalize upon its own American uniqueness; i.e., it constantly reconstitutes itself only in terms of *parliamentary* strategy. It is the old story of Social Democrats who invariably must drive out their own anarchist elements in order to attain a working majority with the center and right. And even our anarchists have confused themselves too much with their European counterparts. After all, President McKinley was not a Hapsburg prince, Henry Clay Frick no King Umberto of Italy. What is overlooked is that random violence cannot bring down an elected government, and in fact simply opens the breach for the right to reassert itself. How lucky we are that Kennedy was killed by such an inarticulate leftist, and that he was not allowed to testify. Had he been as lucid an ideologue as those wild-haired men who accosted bourgeois juries after their assassination attempts in the nineteenth century, we could be in much more repressive times than we are. What is most discouraging about our liberalism is that while, for a time, it effectively isolated the right, the price was to purge itself of its anarchist impulses (its virility), and what is most discouraging about the present anarchism is that it does not see how intelligible a tradition it has to draw upon. Kropotkin says, "All laws have a double origin, one relating to the principles of morality of a particular society, but at the same time, the law crystallizes generally approved customs to introduce, in disguise and under their sanction, some new institution that is entirely to the advantage of the governing minorities." Thus, when anarchism is effective, the "second origin" of the law is tested by using the morality of society itself to expose mere custom and strip sanction from these "new" institutions. It is easy to see why what's left of the old left has little sympathy with what's left of the new, and why we, the middle generation, reject the latter's cult of action out of hand, as we once rejected the former's concern with ideology. (A pragmatist these days is one seemingly able to discount both theory and practice.) In any case, it should be no surprise to the veterans of the Trotskyite or McCarthyite wars, that these kids mistrust state authority quite as much as private,

toil, and filth and these in turn were the background of all pleasure and joy. Still, there was a "landscape," a medium of libidinal experience which no longer exists . . . . With its disappearance, a whole dimension of human activity and passivity have been de-eroticized. The environment from which the individual could obtain pleasure has been rigidly reduced. The effect is a localization and contraction of libido, the reduction of erotic to sexual experience and satisfaction. . . . Thus diminishing erotic and intensifying sexual energy, the technological reality limits the scope of sublimation. It also reduces the need for sublimation. |Herbert Marcuse|

and that they *necessarily* have *nothing to put in its place,* as they say. Their strategy, sloppy as it is, is with mutual aid and protection, and the ideal which informs their actions is simply the removal of authority, not the strategy of how to replace it with another Utopia. It's quite as simple as that; social contract in its legalistic form is rejected. We must recall that the old left was just as determined by the Depression as by the bourgeois whom it attacked, and that the liberalism of the fifties differed only insofar as it posited affluence as a fact which would presumably make a radical redistribution of wealth unnecessary. What informs these kids' barrage is the internalization of the idea that *there is enough for everybody.* This may not in fact be true. But they do believe in their bones that as long as there's enough to go around, why not share the wealth? This is quite a different thing, quite a different attitude, than that of the leftist ideologue who grew up in a non-affluent age, and for whom the question of redistribution of wealth implies much more complex motives of revenge, not to mention the taking of power by his own class.

The bullhorn again demands the streets be completely cleared. The sidewalks are rivulets of ground glass. Vast clouds of tear gas boggle the street lights. The police, for no reason at all that I can see, charge an abandoned theater occupied by kids. At the door, a girl is hit. A trail of lymphy blood stains her blonde pressed hair and she goes blue. I use my suit and gall to get through. Her friends pick her up and take her away. Don't move her, I tell them, she's in shock.

For not even those thunderstorms, nor fiercest lightnings of the war, have purified the atmosphere;
—Let the theory of America still be management, caste, comparison! (Say! what other theory would you?)
Let them that distrust birth and death still lead the rest! (Say! why shall they not lead you?)
Let the crust of hell be neared and trod on! let the days be darker than the nights! let slumber bring less slumber than waking time brings!
Let the world never appear to him or her for whom it was all made!
Let the heart of the young man still exile itself from the heart of the old man! and let the heart of the old man be exiled from that of the young man!
Let the sun and moon go! let scenery take the applause of the audience! let there be apathy under the stars!
Let freedom prove no man's inalienable right! every one who can tyrannize, let him tyrannize to his satisfaction!
Let none but infidels be countenanced!
Let the eminence of meanness, treachery, sarcasm, hate, greed, indecency, impotence, lust, be taken for granted above all! let writers, judges, governments, households, religions, philosophies, take such for granted above all!
Let the worst men beget children out of the worst women!
Let the priest still play at immorality!
Let death be inaugurated!

The cop says please move along sir.

Get an ambulance. This girl's been hit.

He gives me a dirty look. "Could have been worse," he screams. He's not more than 22 himself. "The next time you reporters talk about the city police, remember what *could've* happened!" A boy, almost naked, is sobbing over the girl. "They gotta stop throwing that shit," he waves at the roof. "They're gonna bust everybody."

Who's up there, I ask him.

"Weirdos, assholes, I don't know."

What do you mean you don't know?

"What good would it do to know who they are?" he wails. A group of young blacks on bicycles in the alley back of the theater get out of the way when an ambulance arrives. "We oughter get some guns," they say.

"Jesus," the naked boy screams, "why can't they just leave us alone?"

"The pigs, man, those fuckin pigs are out of their minds. Hit her while she was lying down."

"What the fuck we gonna do now?"

"We oughter get some guns."

Let nothing remain but the ashes of teachers, artists, moralists, lawyers, and learn'd and polite persons!
Let him who is without my poems be assassinated!
Let the cow, the horse, the camel, the garden-bee—let the mud-fish, the lobster, the mussel, eel, the sting-ray, the grunting pig-fish—let these, and the like of these, be put on a perfect equality with man and woman!
Let churches accommodate serpents, vermin, and the corpses of those who have died of the most filthy of diseases!
Let marriage slip down among fools, and be for none but fools!
Let men among themselves talk and think forever obscenely of women! and let women among themselves talk and think obscenely of men!
Let us all, without missing one, be exposed in public, naked, monthly, at the peril of our lives! let our bodies be freely handled and examined by whoever chooses!
Let nothing but copies at second hand be permitted to exist upon the earth!
Let the earth desert God, nor let there ever henceforth be mentioned the name of God!
Let there be no God!
Let there be money, business, imports, exports, custom, authority, precedents, pallor, dyspepsia, smut, ignorance, unbelief!
Let judges and criminals be transposed! let the prison-keepers be put in prison! let those that were prisoners take the keys! (Say! why might they not just as well be transposed?)
Let the slaves be masters! let the masters become slaves!
Let the reformers descend from the stands where they are forever bawling! let an idiot or insane person appear on each of the stands!
Let the Asiatic, the African, the European, the American and the Australian, go armed against the murderous stealthiness of each other!
Let them sleep armed! let none believe in good will!
Let there be no unfashionable wisdom! let such be scorn'd and derided off from the earth!
Let a floating cloud in the sky—let a wave of the sea—let growing mint, spinach, onions, tomatoes—let these be exhibited as shows, at a great price for admission!
Let all the men of These States stand aside for a few smouchers! let the few seize on what they choose! let the rest gawk, giggle, starve, obey!
Let shadows be furnish'd with genitals! let substances be deprived of their genitals!
Let there be wealthy and immense cities—but still through any of them, not a single poet, savior, knower, lover!
Let the infidels of These States laugh all faith away!
If one man be found who has faith, let the rest set upon him!
Let them affright faith! let them destroy the power of breeding faith!
Let the she-harlots and the he-harlots be prudent!
    let them dance on, while seeming lasts!
    (O seeming! seeming! seeming!)
Let the preachers recite creeds! let them still teach only what they have been taught!
Let insanity still have charge of sanity!
Let books take the place of trees, animals, rivers, clouds!
Let the daub'd portraits of heroes supersede heroes!
Let the manhood of man never take steps after itself!

|Walt Whitman, from "Respondez!" excluded from *Leaves of Grass*|

The old feeling of helplessness, the redundance of demonstrations re-turns. This will be the last one for me, in any capacity, in any country. The old homicide is resurfacing again. Yet the recurrent instances give me no clue to its sources or uses. When bending over that young girl, for example, I suddenly had a flash, remembering when I worked in Washington in '62. It was on that little train which connects the Capi-tol Building with the Senate Chamber. I used to ride this with the florid-faced, boutonniered Senators and invariably, seated next to these personages, my attaché case filled with arguments some liberal would need in his speech that' day, I found myself sucking back a hatred and violence the dimensions of which I was totally unprepared to admit. I wrote it off at the time to competitiveness, or perhaps simply to that despair which always accompanies the sight of powerful men at private leisure. Never try to be chummy with a man you admire for his prin-ciples; he will always disappoint you—and you will always betray him. However gratuitous, this accumulated bile could not be denied. I could no longer see myself as the victim of an idiosyncratic nervous system, but of a culturally transmitted disease—and there was nothing in my culture with which to isolate it.

It is clear, now, why I spent the best, if not the largest, part of the last decade in Europe—to defuse that particular rage, prevent it from turn-ing on myself—for Europe after the war was not resuscitated by the re-covery of its own sense of self, but because it was still *not* America. These days, that fact alone can provide a nation with a *raison d'être*. And twentieth century Americans, like those nineteenth century Eu-ropean travelers to the New World, had the luxury of not only expe-riencing the turmoil of their own estate at one remove, but of testing their own undeveloped political fantasies against another landscape— which is precisely what those gentlemen did to us. It was their mythol-ogies about us which gave them not only perspective, but actuality, hor-rified as it was. And it is we who are escaped, to tell the tale.
As I took the bus out to the airport, it occurred to me that when we look back from whatever new authoritarianism we choose, while we will not be quite able to forgive these children's foolishness, we will

I shall never again be as free as I have been in England and Italy . . . while the United States are fit for many excellent purposes, they are simply not fit to live in. |Nathaniel Hawthorne, to his publisher, 1858|

homage their fragility. They are testimony to what has been denied all of us in our nation's ascension to power. I also realized that there is an extremely heavy price in keeping oneself free at all costs, and further, that if this is in fact a revolution, I have a good chance of ending up in jail, no matter which side wins.

Do we really ever seek happiness? No, rather the free activity of whatever is newest in us. |Gide, Journal, *1905*|

This plane has for some reason begun to jettison fuel over the ocean. The drink carts are very busy and the two-ounce limit has been waived. Our fuel flies out behind us like piss. Sabotage, or is the airplane just not feeling well? We return to New York somewhat later, switch planes and are on our way again. There, Benjamin Spock is leading an anti-war parade in Manhattan. Several prominent literary critics were arrested before dinner.

Englishwoman, next to me, is just returning from these United States. She has come from pleading the Biafran cause on the late night TV talk shows. For some reason she has a copy of the alumni magazine of my university and a manuscript of Nigerian translations which she offers me to pass the time.

She talks to me, with that peculiar British straightforwardness, of the starvation she has seen, which, at thirty-five thousand feet, after several drinks, a glut of hors d'oeuvres and a forced landing, I find more than appalling.

I ask her why she came to the United States. I mean, Biafra's really a British problem, right?

"Oh," she says, "of course, but we can't do anything. You know that. We are helpless in such matters. Only the States can help in this case. If not the government, then the people."

Oh lady, I groan.

"You must admit you are certainly both the most generous and the most powerful country on earth, even the most compassionate?"

Oh lady.

I begin with the necrology in my alumni magazine (for the first time, the number of deaths of men in their twenties and thirties approaches

First time Biafra
Was here, we're told, it was a fine
Figure massively hewn in hard wood
Voracious white ants
Set upon it and ate
Through its large emplaced feet
To the great heart abandoning
A furrowed, emptied scarecrow.

And sun-stricken waves came and beat
*   crazily*
About its feet eaten hollow
Till crashing face down in a million
*   fragments*
It was gleefully floated away
To cold shores—cartographers alone
Marking the coastline
Of that forgotten massive stance.

In our time it came again
In pain and acrid smell
Of powder. And furious wreckers
Emboldened by half a millennium
Of conquest, battening
On new oil dividends, are now
At its black throat squeezing
Blood and lymph down
Its hands and feet
Bloated by kwashiorkòr

Must Africa have
To come a third time?

|Chinua Achebe|

those of the classes of 1897–1910), and read back through the Class News.

"Your young people are embarking on an entirely new life style. A true adventure. You want to have a world with values!"

There's something to that, all right.

"I had a lot of coverage on TV. Don't you think it will help?"

Oh lady, please.

"There's just one thing I can't understand. This Vietnam business."

Lady, I am not the Pentagon, you are not the Ministry of Defense. Let's forget it, OK?

"Why are you going to England, dear?"

To see why I hated it so much when I lived there before.

We get off together at the funky airport. The customs man holds me up despite my suit. Maybe the hair and beard get him.

"How long will you be in England?"

I haven't the faintest idea.

"Do you have a work permit?"

I won't be working. (What to say? That I've come again to gain . . . perspective?)

"What is the purpose of your visit?"

Nothing in particular. I'm a writer.

"Truly, now let me have this again, please. You have no purpose to your visit, you will not be working and you do not know what you will be doing here. . . . Pardon me . . . How much money do you have?"

It's all right.

I take a roll of Travelers Cheques out of my pocket and throw it on his table.

"Where will you be going after you leave here?"

Well, I don't really know.

"I suppose to the Continent?"

It's certainly close, isn't it.

"To France?"

Yes, to France in all probability.

"What will you do in France?"

Nothing. Really nothing there.

Frank Beane of the Pittsburgh National Bank reports that his second son, Christopher, was born last September. Dorrance Belin has graduated from the University of Pittsburgh Law School and is working in Washington, D. C. From nearby Rochester comes word that Dr. Roger Bernard is an instructor and research fellow in surgery at the University of Rochester and Strong Memorial Hospital. After graduating from Yale in 1965 with an M. A. in industrial administration, Clint Brown joined Smith, Kline & French Labs in Philadelphia. He is in their research and developments section which is composed of a small team of globetrotters who locate and negotiate for potential new products. Since fall of 1966, Dale Collinson has been an assistant professor of law at Stanford, specializing in private international law (international business transaction, law and institutions of the European Common Market, and admiralty). Bill Corrigan is finishing his fourth year as a financial marketing representative in IBM's data processing division in St. Louis. A daughter, Tracy, is abroad with a second child due this month. Skip Koff will marry non-engineer Wilki Dyer of Drexel Institute of Technology this month. No children to speak of yet. John Latona, San Francisco Mayor's deputy for social programs, writes that his wife Kay graduated from the University of California (Berkeley) Phi Beta Kappa. Their new baby, Jane Elizabeth, was born July 26, 1967. After completing a one-year tour of duty in Vietnam last November, Captain Doug Guiler has been assigned to Fort Benning, Ga. in advanced branch schooling. Jeff Lammy has forsaken the rat race of the East and Midwest and become the manager of the Moscow Chamber of Commerce. Moscow is the "Dry Pea Capital of the World" and home of the University of Idaho. Jeff would like to hear from fellow Yale Alums in the Pacific N. W. Bill Levitt, formerly in the U. S. Foreign Service and recent graduate of Harvard Law School, is with Davis, Polk, Wardwell, Sunderland & Kiendl in New York. Jim Lusk, who was recently married to Janet Armstrong of Riverside, Conn., is an assistant treas-

"You have no purpose in this visit?"
None whatsoever.
"If you get a job," he says with a deep sigh, not knowing whether to be smug or envious, disbelieving that this man of his own age might arrive having no more idea why he was there than the man in the moon, a dollop of American Express in his pocket . . . "If you should seek . . . employment," he sighs again, "you will have to inform the Ministry."
Behind me, an endless line of Americans, the final solution to the Biafran problem, begin to shuffle impatiently, and the official lets me through.

urer in the municipal bond division of Bankers Trust Co. in New York. Dan McFadden married Barbara Miki Briggs in Honolulu on June 21, 1967, and is presently coaching football and basketball and teaching U. S. History at the Harvard School in Hollywood, Cal. Ed McGonagle is still in Washington D. C. with the Navy Dept. while finishing up his M.A. in history from Georgetown University. Dick MacKinnon has relocated to White Plains from the Boston area to work in IBM's data processing division headquarters, industrial development/finance department. Dick, who has an MBA from Harvard, was married to Skidmore graduate Patricia Goorhead in 1965. Dick's brother Bill MacKinnon is living in Rye, N. Y., and is working in the treasurer's office of General Motors. After two years as curate at St. John's Episcopal Church in Georgetown, Ron and Mary Miller have returned to New York where Ron is a graduate student at General Theological Seminary. Don Crabtree is presently doing market research programs for Benton & Bowles, one of Donavan Data Systems' accounts. Don is very optimistic about the future of this small company. Vern Loucks has been appointed administrative vice-president for Baxter organization in 1966 as assistant to the president. He is director of the John L. and Helen Kellogg Foundation, a trustee of the Chicago Latin School, and an associate of Presbyterian St. Luke's Hospital and resides with his wife and two sons in Chicago. Jim Crooks, assistant professor of history at Hollins College, Va., has been named chairman of the department of history for the 1968–69 year. Jim received his M.A. and Ph.D. from Johns Hopkins University. Randy Fleming recently completed demolition training, diving school, and parachute school, qualifying as a member of the Navy's UDT. He will depart on May 27. "My wife keeps me busy refinishing fine solid pieces of furniture and plotting trips to see historical and natural wonders; the latter seems to introduce us to hosts of people with whom we exchange Christmas mail once a year."

raduating from high school to Elgar, I was grim. My parents asked me why. "Boy," I said, "are you ever going to miss us." I knew very well that the deepest reality for most of America was behind me, and had congratulated myself on finally escaping it. What I didn't know was that I had made no actual progress beyond the culture; the culture had simply shriveled, and was receding from one who had been fixed, in every sense.

Four years later, in 1960, when I again marched to Elgar, I knew it was time to truly flee, and so I timorously entered the lists for a fellowship to England. Rather than stay home and become a great hater, I preferred to become a great Anglophile. A gentler way of being lonely. If my strategies were contemptible, my reasons were not. I cared not a whit for the *entrée* Oxford credentials promised, nor even for the contemplative leisure which it presumably afforded—I simply felt that the *mesure* of that country would help me to deal with considerable hatred I had developed for my own, and that I would learn somehow to either confront or ignore the injustices that I had come to feel as profoundly as possible when one is not a victim of the first order. I would have settled for either the amusing aloofness of a Waugh or the moral passion of an Orwell, and took the politics of each style as a consequence. At the least, I might develop a taste for expatriation, for English eccentricity. Standing lost in thought with one's hounds in a herb garden seemed preferable to forever screaming in the fastness of the bright, slightly collodial American forest.

However clear it was, as Nick Carraway's father reminds him, that the "fundamental decencies are parceled out unequally at birth," the appearances of competition had to be preserved. Therefore, we were rehearsed for our *real* interviews by old Yalies, as they say, to "hone our edge"; a preparation not only for the competition, but also to educate our potential "winners," prevent their embarrassing our mellifluous young colleagues-to-be, so well versed in the pure language and the only civilized Socialism ever. After my first mock interview, I was told I looked presentable enough, that my record showed that I had done a number of things reasonably well (emphasis on the adverb) but that I had to remember one small thing:

THE LAST YANK AT OXFORD

or, recollections of a light heavyweight

We turn with pleasure to the contemplation of that small but glorious band, the fourth class of the Friends of Freedom *whom we may truly distinguish by the name of thinking and disinterested Patriots. These are the men who have encouraged the sympathetic passions till they have become irresistible habits, and made their duty a necessary part of their self-interest, by the long continued cultivation of that moral taste which derives our most exquisite pleasures from the contemplation of possible perfection, and proportionate pain from the perception of existing deprivation . . . Convinced that vice originates not in the man, but in the surrounding circumstances; not in the heart, but in the understanding; he is hopeless concerning no one—to correct a vice or generate a virtuous conduct he pollutes not his hands with the scourge of coercion; but by endeavoring to alter the circumstances would remove, or by strengthening the intellect disarms, the temptation. The unhappy children of vice and folly, whose tempers are adverse to their own happiness as well as to the happiness of others, will at times awaken a natural pang; . . . |Coleridge, Conciones ad Populum|*

"Don't say 'yeah,' say *yes*."

OK, I said.

"And don't say 'OK,' say *yes sir*."

Sure . . .

"And please, don't say *that* either."

Having come to be effete, to learn what our vague elitism was good for, prepared to be bored at the slightest provocation, to turn a natural competitiveness into a witty dandyism, it was disappointing when Oxford served only to heighten our latent and most powerful egalitarian instincts. I arrived punctually under an outrageous pink sky which then puckered and drooled for 57 straight days—not hard enough to do any damage, like those midwestern storms which sterilize everything in the name of fecundity—just enough to spoil things. On the residence list I found my name between Norway, Crown Prince Harold of, and the Nawab of Pataudi.

And upon first seeing the spacious green lawns of the college—known, a good scout informed me, as the "College of Prime Ministers"—I was truly awed, particularly at the sign which stated only the "Fellows" could walk on the grass. My first reaction was that if I were a non-Oxbridge Englishman, I should like nothing better than to tear the entire establishment down, brick by brick. And so England was to provide the very thing both of us least expected of her, contact for the first time with a visible working class, or rather with people who *looked* and acted differently from people who were not "workers." Most of us had been active on the fringes of Democratic party politics long enough to realize that our unions were simply accomplices of their employers, and while we voiced the populist rhetoric at their meetings, our lack of interest in them as political and/or human beings was rather complete. Our eyes were for the war chest, to be used against their employers, against our own class. We looked (rightly, I believe) upon Management and Organized Labor as some vague conspiracy to trivialize civilization. In England, I thought each day, "If only *our* working classes respected us as much, what political leverage we could exert."

So while the English pressed us to see Tintern Abbey, Mount Snowden

As you will not try to make the best people the most powerful people, persuade yourselves that the most powerful people are the best people. It is part of the universal principle on which Englishmen have acted in recent years. It is a place for humanizing those who might otherwise be tyrants or even experts . . . if these universities were destroyed, they would not be destroyed as universities. If they are preserved, they will not be preserved as universities. They will be preserved strictly and literally as playgrounds. The lads at Oxford and Cambridge . . . are only larking because England in the depths of its solemn soul really wishes them to lark . . . Oh, what a happy place England would be to live in if only one did not love it! |G. K. Chesterton, Oxford from Without|

you cannot create a culture for a class behind that class's back. |L. Trotsky, 1924|

and Stonehenge, we were falling down before every Victorian railroad station and public house, before the BMC factory outside of Oxford and the tenements in which most of us boarded, amazed at the artifacts of the Industrial Revolution, the barbaric relics of that time, the cost to the landscape and inhabitants. I could smell the dung heaps, hear the screams of child labor, and sense the historical trauma which had been so submerged in America by the *enbourgeoisement* of the lower classes. This was enforced daily by the visitations of our "scouts," come to make our tea and beds. England was not to be the paradise which one American expatriate don saw as "all the advantages of living in an underdeveloped country with none of the guilt."

At first, we chose to view the English class structure as an oddity, a brief entertainment concocted primarily for our discomfort, but finally and for the first time, I think, we saw the possibility of working unpaternalistically with uneducated people, and to make use of that abstract hatred for those who did so visibly live off the work of others. And we paid the subsidized dues of the liberal by directing a good portion of that hatred toward ourselves.

We were learning, all right. Occasionally, this took humorous effect. It was discovered that there was a young college scout of about 30 who had four children, and when someone casually asked him how much he earned, it turned out his salary was $25 a week. This naturally resulted in massive tipping by Americans at the end of term and subsequently severe rebukes from our Anglo fellows. American spoilage again. This led to the taking of yet another collection, and the next month our good scout emigrated with his family to Australia, courtesy of Americans at Oxford. The Warden was not pleased.

The "boys" as opposed to the "old boys" at Oxford were not all that overwhelming. Rather than being pleased to discover our cream of the crop was as heavy as theirs, we were appalled to find that these arch lads had a more guaranteed *entrée* to the *governing* life of their country than we. To see a little fart on the floor of the Union speaking with the assurance of one who would, in a few years after graduation, so obviously occupy a seat in the Parliament of his nation, or at least the civil service, threw us into spasms of rage, and brought out that very hard-

nosed practical skepticism of our businessman fathers which we had
come to discredit. Though we came from every stratum and region of
American life, and while we knew what gangsterism and sheer good
luck had gotten us here, our Humanism had only prepared us for the
professions and to make money, while what we were interested in was
either total freedom and/or power, whatever leverage it took to either
change or transcend the social relations of our culture. *Change or transcend:* this ambivalence is crucial to understanding the paralysis of
American liberalism. But indeed, the more one took that education seriously, the more it seemed to disqualify one by temperament, interest
and ability to enter public life, particularly in any elective capacity.
And that is why Kennedy was so popular, for he held out the hope that
private personalities (being private, alas, has nothing to do with having
integrity) could be effectively integrated into public life; that personal
elitism could be maintained within political service. As a friend would
write me several years thereafter, "Well, it *is* amazing that almost all of
us did go into 'public service,' the only effect of which," he went on,
"was that we didn't make as much money as we could've." So it was
difficult, then, to abide those whose credentials would entitle them to
automatic credibility in public life, while for us, equal papers guaranteed only security in a university or other corporation, or perhaps a leg
up in making an inordinate amount of money. Here we were, surrounded by acned adolescents who couldn't have made the Red Shirt
squad in our local high schools, already assured of their place of leadership in their society, absolutely devoid of paranoia, and oblivious, we
felt, to the fact that their country was obviously heading towards disaster—here they were, the little buggers, their entire culture crumbling
about them, running after beagles in the woods, attending their heraldry club meetings, debating pacifism and moral rearmament, while
we, rather than being groomed for *our* rightful role, were only putting
off a return to some grueling profession, and hoping that one day, before we were senile, a dullard in the political ranks would weaken, and
having done the requisite shitwork for the duration, we could blow into
the breach with our shrewd and up to then secret program of reform.
Talk about the system breaking down!

How the English put up with us, our cliquishness, the garrulity which we believed to be a new sensitivity, our scorn for their harmless rituals, our combativeness (once after forearming a rugby opponent in the face, he wiped the blood from his mouth and muttered, *"Chacun à son goût"*), chasing their women with horrifying enthusiasm, mimicking their intellectuals, cursing their pigeons, cuisine and curriculum, our heads banging off their rafters and arches, nasal accents yippeeing amongst the desultory citizenry, I shall never know.

While our politics were uniformly leftist, uniform in the derogatory sense, we nevertheless retained a stronger nationalism than we supposed or preferred. This took its penultimate form in demonstrating to a bewildered native population how it was possible to throw a rugby ball farther than most of them could kick it. (There was a brief effort to convert rugby strategy to the forward pass, but bullet after bullet pass, clothesline peg on the run, they invariably dropped the ball. "How the fuck could you drop that one, Algernon? It was right in your bloody gut!" It was a lovely game, despite its viciousness. One was rarely hurt, largely because the turf was so soft.

My first morning, I woke up to face my large roommate who asked, "Why did you start the Korean war?" I mumbled something about containment strategy, suckering the yellow hordes down to the tip of the peninsula so we could surround them, Indian-style.

His father had been a brilliant Communist MP, the kind of magnanimous ideologue which only the British aristocracy can produce, and his son could indulge his own version of the British Museum Marx while becoming a pediatrician. Although we were perfectly prepared to adapt our manners to the Edwardian, we knew well enough that our petty violences would betray us in the end. Communists we might well become; Aristocratic Marxism would take much more training.

He then went on to explain how the Marshall Plan was employed merely to preserve American markets.

I allowed as how that might very well be the consequence, but you

POLITICS, OR (SIC, SIC, SIC)

couldn't understand America's failures in foreign policy unless you understood that, however venal and war-warped we were, we were not cunning in that sense. One can only understand Vietnam, after all, not as an attempt at some Machiavellian coup, cornering the bauxite, some logistical aberration, but the response of men who actually believed it was their moral and legal duty—which is of course why our folly remains doubly heinous. You will never be aware of the real dangers of America, I said, unless you are prepared to understand that these were *righteous visions. . . .*

We went on wonderfully happy marches then, demonstrations at the Aldermaston US Air Base to oppose the "American presence," accompanied by priests, philosophers, housewives with babies in prams. It had all the joy and effect of a hayride. Upon our arrival, the Commander invariably sent out thermoses of hot tea as we camped around his base perimeter. Air Police joked with the crowd. One had put on his helmet so tightly that he couldn't loosen the chin strap; one of the wives helped him. At first, I loved the sweet reasonableness of these constitutional exercises, though they would be poor preparation for Georgia and Mississippi. Gradually, however, I became aware of my impotence in such demonstrations, and this gave way to fantasies of violence. I dreamed of cornering one of our gum-chewing pockmarked surly southerners who'd been recruited with the promise of rocketry and was now a military policeman, mashing him with his own carbine.

Then the Bay of (capitalist) Pigs.

It was somehow indicative that none of us had sufficient facts to really argue until *Time* magazine came out. It was the first inkling that our "rest period" was up; in any case, forced marches with parlor Communists would no longer be therapeutic.

"See, this *proves* you started Korea," my Commie roomy said.

No, it doesn't, I said morosely, it just proves that we expected too much from Kennedy, that he's more scared than we thought.

Several meetings of Agonized Americans Abroad were held; the same ones who had roared at the televised Kennedy-Nixon debates giggled at that clod who in every high school becomes treasurer of the prom, as-

Above all, I sincerely believe that the public institutions and charities of this capital of Massachusetts are as nearly perfect, as the most considerate wisdom, benevolence, and humanity can make them . . . |Dickens, American Notes, Etc. 1850|

suming, because he lost the debate, he would never have the gall to re-surface. We had purposefully held both our disgust and potential radi-calism in abeyance and had been betrayed. . . . For what? For a style, for a seriousness which couldn't turn back upon itself. We believed that any substantive shift in priorities had to be accompanied by a change in manner, and Kennedy caught us up not because of his glamor or his pseudo-intellectualism, as conservatives would have it, but precisely be-cause of his relative toughness, the edge of cunning and irony which underlay that nouveau patrician demeanor. It was the cutting edge that we identified with; we knew what calm and taste were worth. It hinted at the possibility of a new public virility—without the he-man postur-ing—the possibility of being tough without being vulgar, the promise that we could cure ourselves of congenital American violence and still hold the line against the Philistines. (This is veering into nostalgia, so let me give an example quickly: I once heard Kennedy at a reception in 1962, talking to a group of pacifist students, addressing their complaint that too many poor people were being drafted. He looked very pained, almost jaundiced at the time, and, after agreeing, added wearily that the war was unfair, and life was unfair, some people were sent to Paris NATO and some people were sent out to be killed, some were elected President and others were thrown in jail. And, he went on, unless he could do something about it, he knew he would pay for it, "and I don't mean politically," he said more than mysteriously. That may seem a rather inconsequential or even a callow remark now; at the time, how-ever, it seemed refreshing in its candor, echoing that paradox that runs through the *Declaration* and *Federalist Papers,* particularly Madison, which recognizes that precisely because people are *un*equal in ability, every effort must be made to make them equal before the law. It is a liberal response based upon a conservative diagnosis of society, and as close to a synthesis, perhaps, as our politics has ever achieved.)
But it was now clear that the entire American left had been com-promised to the extent that they identified with Kennedy. In retrospect, there were two more important consequences. It was demonstrated, for all our nasty in-fighting, how much we shared in common, and this

promised a unity of purpose *beyond* competition, a virginal experience
for many of us. Such minority solidarity, however, would increasingly
manifest itself as paranoia, until that would become the predominant
political style. On the other hand, the very commonality of our cause
demonstrated how narrow the range of our alternatives for protest was,
how feeble a texture of opposition we had developed. Some cried out
for a new theoretical understanding of American imperialism (as if we
needed another dialectical category). Others saw Cuba as merely a random adventure with politically disastrous consequences for the Democratic Coalition (as if it were still intact).

One Harvard man related a story he had just heard by transatlantic
telephone—it seems that a group of Harvard faculty and students had,
upon hearing the alert, started to drive to Washington with petitions to
present to their friends and colleagues so lately conscripted into the
highest echelons of public service, and who suddenly could not be
reached by telephone. About halfway down, news of the debacle came
over the radio—they threw the petitions of gentlemanly concern out of
the car and went home. (Rumor has it that SDS was formed on that
abortive trip.)

Political scientists among us quickly diagramed the argument into justifiable historical strategies on the blackboard. It went something like
this:

U. S. MILITARY INVOLVEMENT

OK	Dubious	Stupid and/or Evil
Revolution (?)	French/Indian	Mexican
World War I (except for Russian Expedition)	1812	Indian
World War II (except for Hiroshima, Dresden, etc.)	Civil	Spanish
	Korea	Cuban
		Asian

"Christ!" someone stood up in the back of the room, "Is that what
we're being educated for?"

Another shouted, "So you've got your goddamn categories! *Now what?*
What about the *politics* . . . ? How do we *stop* the fuckers!"

What came out of this finagling was the usual protest petition, delivered to our Embassy where an enormous bronze bald eagle hung like a de-monic shitbird over the Georgian facade of Grosvenor Square. This pa-triotism only gained for us a contingent of CIA men on the Oxford beat, who occupied themselves by following a boy who was dating the daughter of a famous Labor minister, and a severe warning from the military attaché to those who held ROTC commissions.

A record number of Americans left Oxford after that year. There were, of course, many other reasons—the crummy girls, the lousy curriculum, the slightly jarring discovery that we could no longer accept our lei-sure—whether we were frightened of it or manfully rejecting it, it is still too early to tell. Most of us went directly to work for Kennedy or Civil Rights. The hardest thing for an ambitious American in the early sixties was to create a calculated hiatus for himself. The most recent young have shown us how to do it, and also why we were wrong to want it.

The insidiousness of the entire business was lost on me until later in the year when I struck up a friendship with a retired American foreign service type in London, an aging model of those small-town boys who yearn for a life of travel and intrigue. He lived an ascetic and cranky life, eating nothing but omelets, still trying to escape his Christian Sci-ence background by taking abrasive young Americans to the theater. One night, he asked me if I knew there were CIA agents at Oxford; I replied sure, everybody knew about them. He warned me that if I ex-pected any more government fellowships I should watch what I said at public meetings. He added I should feel no need for censorship in what I wrote, but somehow what one said in public always became part of one's dossier. It reflected the mentality and energy of the agent more than any concise policy, but I should stand forewarned.

I was, of course, elated by this. "What do they think we're doing?" Maybe we were a real *threat,* after all, considered dangerous, of *con-sequence.*

"Don't flatter yourself," he said, "they're simply doing their job. It's a wage game with them."

I asked him how he knew. It happened that he'd been a CIA agent, had entered the service a week after Masaryk had been pushed out of the window in '47 and had served, apparently, with distinction.

Well, why'd you quit then?

"I couldn't take the monthlies," he said sadly. "Every month they cross-examined me about my personal life."

Well, Christ, you were a spy, right? Isn't *that* part of the game?

He looked at the ceiling, crossed his hands, cracked his knuckles. "They did it with sodium pentathol," he said.

Well hell, I thought, maybe we did start Korea?

I had supposed I would "read English," that being a fit topic to pursue in England, but when it was pointed out that no books written after 1800 would be studied, my enthusiasm dampened, and I turned to the most unlikely thing I could, economics. A strange experience, for surely this is the most mystical of all formal disciplines. Far more arcane than literary criticism, laced with those lively illustrative graphs and opaque formulae, it was magical precisely because it was the most literary, secretly value-laden, and subjective of all "sciences." And it had all the appurtenances of power as well.

We had never faced the fact that we were Socialists in all but name, but all's in a name. We couldn't call ourselves that—for we could not argue the issues in ideological terms in our own country, if for no other reason than we did not wish to be identified with losers. The right was right to color us pink, though the fact that they could only namecall and invoke the rhetoric of free enterprise deprived us of the only enemy against which we could have defined ourselves. The American left has always been in trouble because the right has always been so inarticulate. That's why we openly envied the English—for even though we thought them wrongheaded and parochial in much of their centralization, they could *talk* about a wider range of problems without using code words, without worrying about translating everything into the rhetoric of frontier individualism. They were not more honest, and in a way were trading on a legacy of humanitarian socialism which they had no right to regurgitate. But the frame of their analysis was wider; there

The reader is forewarned that a rather abstract if necessary discussion of ideas here ensues.

was more room for a variety of exchange between left and right, and even if finally masturbatory, as in the Union, the amplitude of their debate remained an impressive civilizing fact. We should know our parts so well.

Galbraith's economics were naturally quite in vogue in England (though the dons were unaware his thesis derives directly from David Potter as do his statistics from Bator and others) and he was quintessential for our liberalism as well. It was soon clear, however, that the English did not take to him so much because he made sense, but because he possessed a cynical disdain for bureaucracy by the middle classes, and an ironic literary style which recalled Keynes, who also delighted in making his own class uncomfortable. Galbraith's elitist elan intrigued us as well, but it was the reassurance of his thesis which was so compelling—that our *priorities,* not our structure, were wrong, and that it was a matter of reallocating our investment without any fundamental change in the political process or social system. A little of that Defense Department budget pushed over into HEW, put the telephone wires underground, penalize the people who buy big cars; there is enough to go around if only we have the guile and taste to bring it off. (All we need is four more liberals in the Senate, and wait for Kennedy's second term; we've got the votes, baby, and the pricks will be out for good.) Who knows? To use that lively economist's hedge—*ceteris paribus*—all other things being equal—maybe he was right?

It is, of course, the Affluence Thesis, and I mean the thesis not the fact, which most influenced American politics of this decade, both left and right. Galbraith's popularity rests upon a curious inversion of Keynesian theory, for Keynes' economics are morally neutral, can be applied in the service of any statism, and his celebrated argument that socially wasteful investments might be economically useful becomes, through Galbraith's lens, the idea that economically wasteful activity (from a strict capitalist viewpoint) might be socially useful.

Our acceptance of this elegant cynicism, whatever its relative merits, had severely deleterious effects on our politics, for it opens up these sorts of questions.

1. If there's so much affluence, one may ask, then why can't the poor

Enemies of the American way of life have attempted to put capitalism in a bad light by picturing our people as being ground under the heels of a handful of men who hold nearly all the nation's wealth in their hands and control our economic system for their own greedy ends. . . . One thing the opponents of capitalism . . . disregard is the fact that the American economic system consists mainly of small farms, small shops and small industries, and that nearly all the big industrial corporations are owned and controlled not by a few big financiers, but by the millions of ordinary stockholders, bank depositors and insurance policyholders. For instance, one of our largest corporations is owned by more than 1,000,000 individual stockholders, not one of whom owns even a tenth of one percent of the total stock. |Boy Scouts of America, Citizenship Merit Badge Series|

make it up the ladder on their own? (A reinforcement of the conservative free market economics, and opposition to such alternatives as guaranteed annual income.)

2. If there's so much affluence, then society can be perfected by a gradualistic redistribution of wealth by selfless, civilized administrators (i.e., *us*).

3. If there's so much affluence, then the entire notion of *who* owns the means of production, and one's relationship to commodities as well as one's own work, becomes obscured by the replacement of outright competition with allocation by the state, and ideology goes out the window.

4. Most importantly, if the idea that there's more than enough to go around is absorbed by the bourgeoisie, then in our sort of society, it only intensifies the clamor for a "fair" share of the pie. That is to say, it breaks into more sharply defined minorities what was once a loosely held consensus; and each group sees it to their advantage to fragment the power base of opposition in order to claim their share of the goodies. It further atomizes an already ghettoized society, utterly obscures the question of how we should treat each other and how decisions are made; it is the ultimate trade-unionizing of politics.

Finally, such an analysis overlooks the consumption habits, the way of life, as they say, of most people in the country who are not "affluent" (*pockets* of poverty, indeed) and pretty much blithely waves away the question of *which* commodities ought to be given priority, and *who* decides this. It is a fundamental reassertion of marketplace theory, an *estatiste's* critique of private oligopoly, implying that if only the consumers had the requisite information, then the system could function justly as well as efficiently. As in the endless argument as to whether advertising meets or creates demand, it is never spelled out *who* should have fewer choices, whether there should be simply fewer products (choices) in general, more competition between widely differing products, or what?

Galbraith is of course an honorable man, and it is not his fault that his liberalism, to use his own words, evolved a "conventional wisdom" struck down by events. It was not so much that his reformism was too

What is at stake in our economic decisions today is not some grand warfare of rival ideologies which will sweep the country with passion, but the practical management of a modern economy. What we need are not labels and clichés but more basic discussion of the sophisticated and technical questions involved in keeping a great economic machinery moving ahead. . . .
I am suggesting that the problems of the fiscal and monetary policies in the Sixties . . . demand subtle challenges for which technical answers—not political answers—must be provided. |John F. Kennedy, Yale Commencement Address, 1962|

gradualistic, but that both his thesis and tone gave the impression that all American economics needed was some Europeanization (more centralized, domestic public spending) and, further, that what American political life needed was some cosmopolitanism. To the extent that the Kennedy style confirmed this, it masked the underlying cold warrior. "Did they teach you to hate suffering at Yale?" an English Socialist once asked me.

Nope, I said, but they teach you to hate the people who don't hate it.

With my economics tutor—reputedly a member of the shadow cabinet, which he exemplified in his demeanor—I was prepared to be the devil's advocate, defending Capitalism, then Communism against State Capitalism in its various forms, but found myself defending, for the first time, instead of *rights*, those *needs* of the English worker as I saw them darkly.

He opined that I had been drinking too much with my friends at the BMC factory and avoided the college altogether too much.

I suggested to him that if *I* were a worker, I think I would rather have a car and a washing machine and a telly than centrally planned shopping malls or even complete health care. But that not being a worker, I would argue for shopping malls and complete health care against cars, telly, etc., even if he could have both of them, which didn't seem to be the case. What's the implication of that split, I asked him.

He replied that the aim of Socialism was to create a new man who would not value such things, who would work with dignity and joy without such things.

You mean, I hope, the Tolstoyan thing that if a single commodity takes a single life then we should do without that commodity but we cannot do without that life? (I always used novels to justify my econometrics.)

"An exemplary way to put it."

But in the *interim*, I persisted, nearly hoarse, what does he do on weekends? What does he do with his *life?*

"We do not," he murmured, "share your obsession with mobility. . . ."

I am now going to state three facts, which will startle a large class of readers on this side of the Atlantic, very much. Firstly, there is a joint stock piano in a great many of the boarding houses. Secondly, nearly all these young ladies who work in the factory subscribe to circulating libraries. Thirdly, they have got up among themselves a periodical called The Lowell Offering, "a repository of original articles, written exclusively by females actively employed in the mill," . . . of the merits as a literary production, I will only observe, putting entirely out of sight the fact that the articles having been written by these girls after the arduous labors of the day, that it will compare advantageously with a great many English annuals. It is pleasant to find that many of its tales are of the mills and

Fair enough, I said, but is it only the Garden and the Pub? If you gave him the choice between a car and free eyeglasses, which would he take? "It doesn't matter which he would *take*. It's what is made available that counts, actually."

I quoted Wilde to him hoping to touch a more local chord. "To sweep a slushy crossing for eight hours a day when the east wind is blowing is a disgusting occupation . . . to sweep it with joy would be appalling. . . ."

You know, I said, at last, nearly choking, you, you are keeping them alive in the name of an *idea* . . .

He interrupted with a yawn.

"Did it ever strike you that Russians and Americans have a great deal in common?"

I was speechless.

"Oh dear," he continued, "I mean we in the West are *all* Americans now, like it or not. . . ."

I'm not an American yet, I snapped. I'm not even English.

There was another, happier intellectual legacy to that exile, nevertheless, the synthesizer in this case being an enormous Jaguar sedan—property of a titled young Scot of noble heritage, hyphenated last name, and spectacular wit, who insisted on driving to Paris at least once a week. We never had much to do with each other at either end of the trip (he affected kilts, monocle and a sword) but for some reason he would seldom go without me. I knew nothing of the damp, erratic ignitions of Jaguars; indeed he never once let me drive, though I longed for that burled chestnut steering wheel. Looking back, he must have thought me some kind of good luck charm; when you travel fast, leave home, take an American along. Whatever, to pass the time, which wasn't long since he always had his car flown across the Channel, we would pretend we were Positivists until we reached Eastbourne, and from Calais on, *Existentialistes*. Sometimes we would play Wittgenstein monologuing an Indian graduate student on the nobility of silence, or reconjure Jaspers and Heidegger arguing in Sid Caesar German in a *Gasthaus* about all-enveloping transcendence.

of those who work in them; they in-culcate habits of self-denial and con-tentment, and teach good doctrines of enlarged benevolence.
|*Dickens*, American Notes|

However flip such routines might sound, they did much to preserve my sanity, for it was a matter of some terror to me that two such formidable systems could exist separated by a few miles of brackish water, while never acknowledging the other's existence. While communication was presumably the major concern of both philosophies, there was seemingly no communication between them. Their different polemical strategies seemed so strongly and so unconsciously to dictate their respective lifestyles and cultural roles, and their thinking seemed so nationalistically circumscribed, it profoundly depressed me—what metatheory were *we* locked into, or were we circumscribed by *lack* of a theory? To sit in Oxford on Wednesday and hear all sentences begun with *actually*, implying that every statement was made in contradistinction to a previously unexamined truth, as well as a modestly verifiable *fact*, and then in Paris on Thursday to be machine-gunned by the inevitable *alors*, implying that each sentence was an organic outgrowth of every sentence uttered previously in all history, was to be immersed in *lucidité* like a potato in hot fat. I submit that if one day you listen to a lecture on the "seven moral proscriptions of the word 'ought,'" the next to a talk on the "something-universal-which-is-hidden," on one day to speak of "unavoidability and indeterminism," the next of "authenticity and inauthenticity," to establish one day the impossibility of "empirically grounded praise and blame," the next to evaluate "things seen and things used," to talk one day of "unnecessary bifurcation of the spirit," the next of "existence preceding essence," to have one's prose criticized one day as "rather too vivid" and on the next to be warned to "shoulder one's anguish" and be open to "the ecstasy of time," to eliminate all "pseudo-problems" and then celebrate Sisyphus pushing his bloody stone up that slope, to one day hear A. J. Ayer mumble something like, "If I am constrained I do not act freely, but in what circumstances can I legitimately be said to be constrained?" and the next to confront Kierkegaard quoted lovingly in French: "One might say that I am the moment of individuality. But I refuse to be a paragraph in a system"—it can really screw you up—and to forget doubly, if in two quite different ways, what it means to be alive. For an American, this was further complicated by the fact that

Incidentally, I *know* this sounds rather synoptic, and it is strange to see experiences so quickly converted into cultural and ideological formulae—but that is, in fact, how I lived at the time—for the one thing of which I was certain was that you could change the world only by reconceptualizing it, and you could know yourself only by understanding the ideas that others had about you. I am no longer able to think in such a way, and perhaps it is impossible for a writer in our time to do so; but I like myself now for having once been able to.

the quarrel no longer seemed between Freudian and Marxist determinism, and the ''action'' seemed to be between two little cultures carrying out an isolated night guerrilla action against each other, but who would never admit to an enemy.

Obviously, the man who could resolve this would be able to penetrate to the heart of the 20th century and just as obviously, no one was about to come forward and do it. The implication was that no one could ever know enough, anymore, to make the necessary connections, to possess the sheer will, much less intellect, to proceed through either one of the systems while remaining open to the other. This confirmed, not so much by their methodologies, but in their isolated existences, the utter subjectivity of history.

On the other hand, it was encouraging to see the smartest men in the world giving their careers to discover what any American plugger can learn by just looking out the window—that there is no such thing as ontology—of defining how we are in the world—and that the only suitable subject for philosophy in our time can be epistemology—how the world *is* in *us*.

There is, of course, a further irony—that insofar as existentialism owed its tone and concerns from being forged in the Resistance—that total breakdown of politics—by the time it had been filtered through to the next generation, it offered an *egress* from political consciousness, insofar as the rhetoric of absurdity and *Angst* made most disciplined action utterly self-conscious. The concept of *engagement* is indubitably aesthetic in nature, particularly in a Cold War context. If existence precedes essence, then epistemology precedes metaphysics, aesthetics precedes ethics and ontology goes out the window entirely. The effect of internalizing the relativism of a Sartre, a Camus, was to diminish the very moral involvement which they urged, and it is my feeling that the aesthetics of the early sixties prefigured and to a large extent spawned the ''revolutionary'' politics of the late sixties, and further, that this accounts for the failure of those politics.

Similarly, the effect of Positivists' isolating concepts like ''freedom'' and ''liberty'' from their semantic ambiguity and richness, both their poetic and historical contexts, encouraged not so much a healthy ana-

This sentence contains no information whatsoever.
This sentence contains more information than the preceding sentence.
Because this sentence says, ''This sentence contains less information than the preceding sentence,'' it contains more information than the preceding sentence.
This sentence contains the same information as the preceding sentence.
This sentence contains no more information than the following sentence.
This sentence contains no less information than the preceding sentence.
|Jack Anderson|

For already we hear the swelling chorus of objections from the self-styled bearers of a new culture: 'but we do not want a tried and tested knowledge to rule us, to decide over our actions; our aim is not to think and to know but to live and to do'. . . the next addition to the collection of intellectually fashionable words will doubtless be 'existential.' I can see it springing up on all sides. Before long it will have landed with the public at large. When, in order to convince one's audience of profundity, one has said 'dynamic' long enough, it will be 'existential.' |Huizinga, 1936!|

lytic skepticism but an oblique and specious neutrality, an ahistorical neutrality already certified for most of us by New Criticism, and for all their talk of statements not being verifiable unless they were couched in "scientific *or* ordinary" language, it was clear to me for the first time that language could be *owned* by a certain class and could be used as a means of cultural mystification. We knew who did the "verifying," just as we knew who determined which consumer needs were "artificial." All this business about the non-signification of words, the reduction of language to an involuted game for isolated specialists, did not depress me; on the contrary, it only served to confirm that language was, in Heidegger's phrase, "the house of being." After all, despite the Existentialist's insistence that all the world was discourse, that literature, criticism and everyday speech were simply branches of the same metalinguistic activity, and despite the Positivist's insistence that language had to be cleaned up, reduced in amplitude in order to clarify the world—both invariably ended up justifying their notions of freedom of the will by what they called "creative activity," by which more often than not they meant literature, an activity to which most of them could not hope to aspire. If the hydraulics of the urinary tract remain the only bodily function of which science cannot reproduce a model, then literature remained a single mental domain which could not be reduced to a discursive model. Through the default of philosophy, literature became transcendent. Accepting this philosophy was, in a large sense, to free oneself from the necessity of a philosophy. As Jean Wahl has said somewhere, "Perhaps it is necessary to choose between existentialism and existence?"

It now seems clear that Structuralism represents as much of a synthesis as we shall ever have of these seemingly opposed systems—for with its emphasis on "presentness," and upon an epistemology of radical doubt, it operates with a distinctly existential notion of fate (including the fact that it has no principle of self-criticism), and while it luxuriates in the ambiguity of language as the Positivists could not, it carries on the latters' linguistic empiricism by distinguishing problems, levels and elements in various philosophies of existence.

But what is interesting about Structuralism is that it incorporates much

Modern philosophy, after all, encountered these problems long before modern literature, painting or music [but] . . . however hard Philosophy, under the influence of Idealism, tries to liberate concepts of space and time from Temporal and spatial particularity, literature continues to assume their unity. |Georg Lukács, 1956|

of the Positivist obsession with predictability, and throws onto language all those determinisms which Marx and Freud sought to locate in history or the psyche—language being a symbolic net which cuts us off from our origins, a series of analogies with no instrumental relation to the world. Language is what veils the truth, and our only hope is that it veils it *systematically*. In this sense, Structuralism betrays not only an incurable nostalgia for some kind of prelinguistic paradise as well as an apocalyptic view of the future but, more to the point, it returns to the essential ambivalence of existentialism—for if we really come out of a *nothingness* which cannot be named—then *why* should we make an act of faith, a decision to *be*, why should we push that bloody stone up the hill only to see it run down again—and more than that, why is this *nothingness*, so schematic, so transcendental in its force, always described in terms of forlornness, nausea, alienation, etc.? Why does dwelling upon death and neurosis reveal more of "existence" than concentrating upon life? There is a peculiar brand of American "nothingness," after all, which has always been profoundly, if just as a-priorily, optimistic. So just as ethical action cannot be deduced from any situation without some value beyond reason, then if we do live in a world of signifiers, why describe it as vicious rather than magical, in the terminology of circumscription rather than access? Indeed, the more ambitious and sophisticated the critical method, the more it appropriated the world, the more it seemed to confirm the essential mystery of literature.

I had been first taught that language was a mental function; then that the most ambiguous language was the most poetic, the hardest poem best; then that the most reductive language was the purest, then that the best literature was hallucinatory; and finally, I was told language was what made me man, and miserable.

Between those Englishmen who used language as a methodology and those Frenchmen who used it as a phenomenology, I wished to live nowhere but precisely within those symbolic nets which they alternately fondled and slashed. I cared to dwell no more on my origins than on my death. And I knew that I could become fully alive only if I could somehow learn to write not well nor even easily, but simply write books that no one else could write; for the difference between everyday

The trial of art has been opened definitively and is continued today with the embarrassed complicity of artists and intellectuals dedicated to calumniating both their art and their intelligence. We notice, in fact, that in the contest between Shakespeare and the shoemaker, it is not the shoemaker who maligns Shakespeare or beauty but, on the contrary, the man who continues to read Shakespeare and who does not choose to make shoes— which he could never make, if it comes to that. The artists of our time resemble the repentant noblemen of nineteenth-century Russia; their bad conscience is their excuse. But the last emotion that an artist can experience, confronted with his art, is repentance. It is going far beyond simple and necessary humility to pretend to dismiss beauty, too, until the end of time, and meanwhile, to deprive all the world, including the shoemaker, of this additional bread of which one has taken advantage oneself. |Camus, The Rebel|

speech and literature is that the former is the established record of our interpersonal reverberations, and this established language at any one time threatens to silence us as much as it frees us. But literature is the continuous assault upon the established language of the moment. The way in is the way out.

Every American I knew at Oxford, and I do not exaggerate, kept a novel going in the lower drawer of his desk, waiting, one presumes, not for a publisher but for his mother to die. I am told this has been the rule for the French for some time, that the English gave it up when D. H. Lawrence laid down his pen and died, and I have also been told that we are the last generation in our country to do so. I cannot say that I care much either way on the matter. Literature, after all, is the art which is exclusively both produced *and* consumed in privacy, isolation, in the silences which are to come. And if that sort of communication becomes irrelevant, then it simply means that man will have become another species. We can only wish it well.

I remember one fellow, much justifiably esteemed, with a brilliant undergraduate record of publishing reviews which destroyed the books of his professoriat. He worked on *his* novel before a leaded window in one of the courtyards I passed each day, and naturally I would glance in to see how he was going. I was not ashamed that my heart leaped up when for weeks at a time I could see that he had not progressed beyond his topic sentence. Every click of his typewriter platen buried all of us further in our non-produce. Power we would give up to the strongest, women to the most indefatigable, but literature to no man. This should have told us something very important about ourselves, something which we desperately needed, but I suppose it was written off as just another instance of our lugubrious competition.

One evening, while a good many Americans were gathered in a pub complaining about the size of the hamburgers, someone inadvertently

Or, to put it another way

produced a handbook detailing the "achievements" of Rhodes, Fulbright and other scholars, and began to read aloud in a high nasal voice against the shrieks and groans of the cream of the crop. Apart from a few establishment diplomats, one or two minor scribblers and some lawyers turned Senator through their inheritances, the past elites were all too recognizable:

"Chairman of the chemistry department at Montclair State Teachers' College," the roll call rang, "District Sales Manager, Vita Corporation . . . Associate Actuary for Aetna Life . . . Cultural Attaché to Dahomey . . . Junior partner in Scoville, Whitman and Wood . . . 'I have three daughters, and Felicia remains active in the League of Women Voters!' "

The drinking increased as the gold star victims mounted, and then a pall fell over that group which I will never forget. It was as if their brief and dubious honors had already circumscribed them, that they had expended their strength, and for all their good will and stubbornness, the chances of their breaking the "success" circuitry looked bad. We had come as elitists and found ourselves more egalitarian than we thought possible—as pragmatists, more moral than we thought practicable. We believed that our society required only technical correction, but we knew nothing of technical matters. In that sense, we were literary humanists and poor accountants though our daily experience confirmed the opposite. The politicians among us desired style and brilliance; the artists, power and community. As exiles, we could return home with no reserve of bitterness or desperation, but knowing precisely what banal catalog of petty successes, what droll escalator, awaited us. If freedom was simply being unpredictable, or merely the absence of constraint, then it would no longer do. Arriving respectful of the English language and despising the class system, we left scoffing their moribund literature, and with a grudging respect for a social system which, whatever its inequities, was at least capable of diffusing rage. Looking for charm and self-indulgence, we rediscovered our puritanism and aggressiveness. Having come out of admiration for their socialism which was yet to be, we left despising their capitalism which was no more. Was it true that by escaping the devil of Imperialism they had also driven out all

If Liberals had been defeated, something much worse seemed about to befall Liberalism. Its faith in itself was waxing cold . . . "We know all about you," these parties seemed to say to Liberalism; "we have been right through you and come out the other side. Respectable platitudes, you go maundering on about Cobden and Gladstone, and the liberty of the individual, and the rights of nationality, and government by the people. What you say is not precisely untrue, but it is unreal and uninteresting." . . . "It is not up to date," finished the Imperialist. "It is not bread and butter," finished the Social democrat. Opposed in everything else, these two parties agreed in one thing. They were to divide the future between them. Unfortunately, however, for their agreement, the division was soon seen to be no equal one. Whatever might be the ultimate recuperative power of Social Democracy, for the time being, in the paralysis of Liberalism, the Imperial reaction had things all to itself. The governing classes of England were to assert themselves. They were to consolidate the Empire, incidentally passing the steam roller over two obstructive republics. . . . Their government, as conceived by the best exponents of the new doctrine, was by no

angels of innovation? Looking for leisure, decadence, we found only unfocused, involuted energy. Looking for a new aesthetic, a stance, we had to settle for a neophyte politics, a constructive weariness. Willing to be protean, polymaths, crazy, compromised, cut off, it seemed we were to be only relevant; more or less.

I left then, leaving my barbell and rugby shoes to the boys' club. Each year since, I have received a handwritten note from the Chaplain thanking me for my gift. That same week, a brace of peacocks which had disturbed the college with their mating calls were disemboweled and served with the ubiquitous brussels sprout at High Table. I went to say goodbye to the Warden. In his gloomy office we were surrounded by volumes of constitutional law. He chided me about my creased clothes. How to tell him I was permapressed?
"Leaving us then?"
Yeah.
"You forfeit the degree . . .?"
OK.
"Hopefully, you have benefited . . ."
Sure.

*means to be indifferent to the humanitarian claims of the social conscience. They were to deal out factory acts, and establish wages boards. They were to make an efficient and a disciplined people. In the idea of discipline the military element rapidly assumed a greater prominence. . . . The rest of the world was peopled by dying nations whose manifest destiny was to be "administered" by the coming races, and exploited by their commercial syndicates. This mood of optimism did not survive the South African War. . . . The Tariff Reform movement was largely inspired by a sense of insecurity in our commercial position. . . . All the powers of society were bent on lavish naval expenditure, and of imposing the idea of compulsory service on a reluctant people. The disciplined nation was needed no longer to dominate the world, but to maintain its own territory.
|L. T. Hobhouse, 1911|*

My last evening, a friend and I walked down the playing fields laced by the Thames. I could be *safe* here was all I thought. In a tearoom along the road a sign in the window announced FOOD. In America, a similar establishment would have said EAT.
Ahead of us on the winding road, before the tennis courts, we saw a woman lying face down, beating the cobbles with her fists and screaming. An ugly man stood over her wringing his hands. We ran up to offer our assistance. The woman immediately drew herself up, dusted her knees and announced that she was perfectly fine, thank you, and that

this was none of our business. As we withdrew, she threw herself down and began to scream again and scratch the cobbles.

On the way to the Channel, I could not decide whether I loathed England more for conceiving the idea of Empire in the first place, or for giving up on it—leaving it to those of us who understood neither the sources nor uses of our power.

But as the ferry drew away for Calais, that horrible insistent voice which I had gone to such lengths to escape resounded in my chest, and to the beat of Elgar, my tinny American advice, my plea for England, echoed off the soft receding cliffs . . . *produce; produce or die.*

I tried to found a heresy of my own, but when I put the last touches to it, I found it was an orthodoxy.
|Chesterton the Younger|

April 4, 1968. This morning, I am wretched again with loathing for their insularity, practiced inefficiency, the fifteen-year-old apprentices already at work in the shops, the filth, and drab homogeneity. Then I pick up the morning paper and, like a character in a melodrama, flee to France.

MARTIN LUTHER KING SHOT DEAD

|72|

April 7, 1968, Paris

Ionesco has been invited to the States by a big magazine to cover the conventions. Genet has already agreed to go. Ionesco's wife tells him he cannot. His analyst tells him he will propose him for the *Académie Française*. A fellow Rumanian exile tells him he must not go. "You will die in America, Ionesco. You are not strong enough. You will end up just like Dylan Thomas."

Christ, if Ionesco can't take it, who can?

There are riots in my Chicago. Big Lemon has issued shoot-to-kill orders. Genet says that Chicago reminds him of a beast trying to mount itself. If that is so, Paris is a beast which has *made it* in perpetual, measured lubric congress with itself. Its elaborately disguised grunts only heighten our pleasures, this unceasing effort of its citizenry to outdistance the obscenity of the norm. Everyone here is either an intellectual or a *fonctionnaire,* preferably both. Everyone has a novel in his desk like a Bordeaux from an iffy year that could well be *merveilleuse par chance.* It is a civilization held together by taste. Taste is the cement, the consensus, *la béchamel* of the Fifth Republic.

And to govern by taste is neither as repressive as students would have it, nor as truly authoritative as Malraux must believe. It is simply the coercion of voracious greed by pride. And pride, above all things, insures the status quo. It is unpleasant to realize that when life becomes so defined by the redundant exercise of taste, taste itself becomes unabidable, and government must take refuge in the one-upmanship of splendid aloofness. New York is rough because every step in the streets is the beginning of a small fall. In Paris, the shoving and the rudeness are calculated, deft, even efficacious. One pushes briefly, strikes out, in order to keep everyone else upright, and if everyone pushes, one becomes a connoisseur of the shove, and society is held together by centripetal rebounds. Unable to master that stoicism of the northern provinces, the Parisian falls back upon his phlegmatism which he believes to be ironic but is only, in the end, self-parody. Unfortunately for him, even his abuse has no cutting edge; his attitude towards himself is at once ascetic and decadent. When depravity is no longer gorgeous but democratically competitive, the exercise of taste becomes simply a mat-

CONTRE LA REGRESSION:
Fucked up or fucked over?

ter of preferring anything beyond oneself to oneself. Today a former resistance fighter, now a Gaullist deputy, told me, "You must not think
that we support him through some memory of the war. It is what he has
done in prosperity that truly matters. In the war, we kept ourselves
alive, each in our own way. In the last decade, he has kept us alive
when there seemed no point in living."

And so Paris, like a declawed spayed cat, cleans herself in endless ritual. Malraux has sandblasted the façades from the grays of Utrillo and
DuBuffet back to the "original" patinas of limestone and shades of
rose. What would be the point in similarly restoring American cities?
To reveal the patina of . . . what? For Malraux it is obviously the gesture of recapturing the texture of history, the chimera without the
nightmare. If one has the worst opera in the world, what does one do?
Voilà, we put in a new ceiling by Chagall!

We were never so free as during the occupation. |Sartre|

Marginal to God, marginal to the world, and to ourselves—always in the margin! |E. M. Cioran|

In my hotel which overlooks the Sorbonne, the people who run it complain to me of the extraordinary number of Americans who are cancel-
ing their reservations. The owner shows me the file of letters; he is beyond even a shrug. A retired Air Force colonel from Indianapolis has
canceled his annual tour with his wife and two children because of the
hostility of de Gaulle.

"I fought three years in France and some of my best buddies were
killed. And that's one reason I always come back every year. But as
long as you seem to hate us so much, I am sorry, but I don't think we
should help you any more with our tourist dollars. So we will be going
to Lake Michigan this summer. . . ."

The owner's wife asks me if I will translate a reply for them.
There is both hurt and anger in her face. She will never know the difference. Neither will our Colonel.

Mon Cher Colonel:

You must please understand, I beg of you, that no one in this hotel in any way determines the foreign policy of *la France.* We remind you fervently that the great majority of the French people retain their ad-miration and affection for the American people: We look forward to your visit when you feel it more appropriate. With all sincerity.

When I first came to France at nineteen, I naturally thought I was
Christopher Newman in James' *The American.* My paternal grand-

parents fancied themselves Huguenot Parisians—their ancestors had come to the U.S. in the nineteenth or so century via the Antilles and New Orleans. My grandfather had studied at the Sorbonne and Vienna and returned to St. Louis as a surgeon. After his death, his wife founded the Huguenot Society in St. Louis to preserve French culture there. It must have been quite a job. My grandfather's mother had taken to bed at age forty, surrounded by French literature, the leathery editions of Balzac, Hugo interspersed with red editions of the Complete Mark Twain. The books were piled to the very ceiling. Dr. Newman had lunch with her every day until the day he died.

To be really French! Now that would be something. I practiced incessantly to get the language out of my throat and into my septum, a midwestern nasal gone profound. I would search out my relatives in Paris, tell them of the New World and in return be introduced to Parisian society where I would be abducted for their most lascivious uses. I would be pliable, but proud. There were some things I was sure I would not do. Alas, unknown to me, my Parisian relatives had not acknowledged the *émigré* branch of the family since the turn of the century. For all practical purposes, we were considered dead, lost in the wilderness, and they refused to answer any of the letters of introduction my relatives sent. I had their address, nevertheless, a large gray house in an outlying *quartier* with four holes where a plaque had been bolted above the faded courtyard entrance. With my James literally under my arm, just like Newman before the house of the Carmelites demanding Madame de Cintre, I plagiarized: "Give her back to me in the same state in which you took her from me." I demanded my culture, my roots, my perspective, my history. I wanted that bloody culture back, so I could finally dispense with it.

But no one answered my ring, then or on subsequent visits. Were they "lost beyond recall," as the dapper Jamesian gentlemen said, did they espy me from a boarded window, or were they merely *en vacances?* No matter, let them go, I thought, let them go. I only wished that I could maintain an empty gilded apartment in Paris like Christopher of the novel, for he knew before I did that if one could not have history itself, the next best thing was to have a luxurious vacuum—a bomb shelter

within history—my charlady's wages to be drawn monthly by a
Rothschild representative and deposited in a great pink Sèvres vase in
the foyer, while I . . . traveled? To Hell with them. "Never mention the
name of these people again. Their secret is not worth having."

A decade later, of course, I wouldn't have entertained my relatives if
they languished for me in hotel lobbies around the world. My curiosity
has outdistanced them. I have accepted (without much grace, it is true)
my pastlessness. And I bring no tidings from the New World; our message is clear enough, and its intent I, for one, refuse to bear. I now see
that I was a threat, far more of a threat than was old Christopher. A bar-
barian standing on the rim of the civilization he is about to appropriate,
only to be civilized in spite of himself, a redundant eremite. We want
our Europa back in her *original,* her *imperial* form, so that through our
differences we can come to know ourselves. To the extent she is like us,
we are not interested. Yet in our search for her secret, we make her
like us. And we love in her what we most despise in ourselves: her imperial remnants.

(He imagines he is getting older. He imagines he will settle for less. He
is before the house of Death once again and he is indifferent to it. They
are correct in their suspicions. . . .)

As Mrs. Tristram says to Christopher, "You are not so good a man as I
thought . . . you are more, more ungiving . . . you look wicked—you
look dangerous."

"I may be dangerous," Newman can only reply, "but I am not wicked.
No, I am not wicked."

Ah, there it is again. The familiar whiff of *boeuf stroganoff?* No, tear
gas. I throw open my French windows and watch what has been denied
for days, even among my closest friends—the occupation of the Sorbonne. The gendarmes in their capes loom like Yucatecan buzzards in
the haze. Only the chestnut trees and the statue of Victor Hugo are indifferent.

. . . *Society is not a recreation for him,
but a serious toil: he weighs your
least actions, interrogates your looks,
and scrutinizes all you say lest there
should be some hidden allusion to af-
front him, I doubt whether there was
ever a provincial man of quality so
punctilious in breeding as he is; he
endeavors to attend to the slightest
rules of etiquette and does not allow
one of them to be waived towards
himself; he is full of scruples and at
the same time pretention; he wishes to
do enough, but fears to do too much,
and as he does not very well know the
limits of one or of the other, he keeps
up a haughty and embarrassed air of
reserve.—|de Tocqueville|*

The open air Theatre of Cruelty which had a promising first run in San Francisco is now playing to packed audiences in Europe. As is often the case, however, the facilities here are more suitable to the production; above all, Paris is a city made for riots. Violence itself may be as "American as apple pie," but for all the recent talk of conspiracies, our national criminality has been traditionally expressed through the works of isolatos. So, though we have recently surpassed our forebears in both collective and unofficial barbarism, Europe remains more congenial to the mob.

The historical turning point, scientifically speaking, in this form of popular expression was undoubtedly the invention of the cobblestone. This object, of an officially determined volume and density, is easily detachable from any Parisian street, and can be used to erect barricades or be thrown, and yet—in this lies the genius of its construction—only half the distance to an intended object, no matter how close the object may be. And it is replaceable as easily as it is detached.

Are all the people who can really throw, reactionary?

European technology has also kept pace not only with the balconied boulevards which provide a safe and unobstructed view for the audience, but also with cunningly designed cars, light enough for even the most effete student to place where he will, yet just heavy enough to trip up even the burliest policeman. With our sleek synthetic streets, our immense and obdurate autos, our unbreakable non-flammable products, where shall we find materials with which to reconstruct the world? With neither set nor audience, no wonder we resort to guns and solitary ambuscade.

We lack a chorus of workers as well. No one to provide the lyrics of the old marching songs, as we can only barely hum them. It cannot be simply because our workers know who's paying for the education of these new haters. Can they suspect that the high-consumption leisure society no longer needs responsible workers? Or perhaps they are willing to subsidize and tolerate the costumes and theatricality of the young because they know they're going to end up selling used cars like everyone else. Who knows? The young are our only proletariat, as they are the only aristocracy. Theirs is the only articulated class-consciousness, though the European has the advantage of being able to defect to the proletariat at certain strategic ceremonial moments, while there is nothing left for the American but to make a *career* of youth.

Cause and effect again? The American knows it better than his European counterpart, though he lacks the richer means to express it. At base it has nothing to do with learning or politics or art or even sexuality—hence the scorn of the older generation of radicals and ideologues—indeed, if these children were really interested in *either* education or reform, they would truly and utterly destroy this university. No, it is fact that the entrance to middle-class security is no longer a matter of will or money or manners or luck, but one of *certificate*. And the university as dispenser of certification is the most visible manifestation of a society which has hierarchized itself out of existence, unable for even a brief moment to stop and *take stock*. As long as growing up is reduced to awaiting certification, the only possible official reaction to dissent is that of accelerating the process of certification. If one must make a career of youth, then it should start early, and there should be no distinction between it and maturity. If education has nothing to do with learning, and learning nothing to do with privilege, and privilege nothing to do with life, then clearly, there should be no discrimination between educations. So this Communist party slogan now adorns the façade of the Sorbonne, and it is apt in every respect. But the party as official opposition is as blind to the dirty little secret as the government: that the most efficient way to kill bourgeois life is to insure that everyone lives like a bourgeois.

At the Sorbonne of the XVeme century, studies were long . . . the Doctorate of Medicine required eight years study, four theses, and practical examinations in other subjects. However, the remedies taught were limited to three: purges, enemas and bleedings. Charles Bouvard, for example, physician to Louis VIII, gave him in one year 47 bleedings, 212 enemas and 215 purges. As a result he was made a noble . . . |Guide Michelin|

TUE LA VIE BOURGEOISE!

Well, what started it? The right would prefer to believe, it would seem, that, Hitler being as dim a memory as Attila the Hun, these children were simply condemned to repeat history's errors. The left takes the credit that, through its patient tutelage, the young have finally been able to read history straight. All the initial rhetoric polarizes about these assumptions. My own guess is it's somewhat simpler, a revolt of the middle classes against themselves with the usual attendant masochism, and insofar as it is ideological, it is revolt *within* the left, a truly internecine, involuted struggle. The old cliché about the communists wanting to be Catholics and the Catholics communists seems to be borne out.

The first real sign anything was wrong was when the *petit bourgeois* began to tape their shop windows. They sensed what was coming even before the police. They have the nose for it. They remove their cheeses and wines and croissants to the rear.

Query: If America is the most bourgeois of nations, whatever happened to our *petite bourgeoisie?* Where's *our* croissants? *Our* pâté?

It would be pleasing to see these splendid outbursts in some context—if not as a plot, then at least as a concealed pattern come to the surface. But what if the contradictions reduce themselves to only this—that French higher education is the most moribund in the West, that the lecture halls of the Sorbonne stink like the locker rooms of a grade school football team with thirty-four consecutive losses, that the abjectness and crowding of these universities is unconscionable, that the system of advancement for both students and professors is manifestly unfair and encourages the basest copy work and toadying, that curriculums are absurdly long and irrelevant, that the administration is hopelessly bureaucratic, and that this produces in the higher faculty an arrogance, bitterness and rigidity unequaled even in Germany in the late nineteenth century; in the young faculty, a humiliating protégé relationship; and in the student a resignation which only the most career-oriented can turn to his advantage? Imagine—a man as distinguished as Michel Butor cannot get a job teaching in a French university. He smiles wanly when he tells me this, but this is what the Ministry of Culture should be attending to, rather than scraping the pigeon shit off their façades. No wonder the French *professeur* comes off as a fool in most French literature. Molière farce is strict realism. When I was hanging around the Sorbonne a decade ago, I first thought that the lectures were staged for summering Americans as an extension of that banal arrogance and petty meanness which awaits all who try to divine French culture. Imagine my surprise to find that young Frenchmen and Frenchwomen were treated precisely in the same manner.

It's instructive to recall that even this system could have worked as long as it remained elitist, but with the new influx of students, it had to break down utterly. For this is no revolt, but an insurrection against *self*-repression, for that is precisely what the system encouraged. Elitism works, not because it culls an aristocracy of talent—though it may occasionally do that as well—but because it offers a *quantity* of places commensurate with the ambition of those who aspire to these places. It is a full-employment, closed economy. And the very availability of places defines the nature of the ambition. Elitism breaks down when it creates a new proletariat. As it defines the slots, it dies by the slots.

This new proletariat consists of two different classes, without the welding of which there can be no revolution. There is the passive class that wants the *certificat d'entrée* into the bourgeoisie as rapidly as possible, announcing, quite properly, its constitutional right to a guaranteed life style. The other class is the activists who think of power as something beyond consumership, or even free choice on a profounder level. Their assumption is that no one has the *right* to be a bourgeois, and they question the fact that their education seems irrelevant to much beyond the conditions of entry to that estate.

Revolutions expire in two ways—from excess and from success. Marx could not anticipate the excess of totalitarian reaction; his was still a world of limited revolt. Indeed, for him the process of revolution seemed to generate its own bounds.

This is discomforting if it is true, far more affecting to us than any conspiratorial theory of history, for Marx suggests more about ourselves, our democratic gradualism. He understood our revolution better than that of his disciples.

When the French bourgeois overthrew the rule of the aristocracy, it thereby made it possible for many proletarians to raise themselves above the proletariat, but only insofar as they became bourgeois . . . |Marx, German Ideology|

The facts of injustice and the sovereign antidote of minority rights have been with us for a long time. But a corollary to these rights has intrigued us for almost as long, from the French Revolution at least: i.e., this idea that no one has the *right* to be a *bourgeois*. That may be the outcome of one's rights; but they are not gauged to that end. Marx insisted that man cannot be viewed biologically, as an abstract, isolate entity, under God, but rather sociologically, in the totality of his social relations, amongst Laws. He was not alone in challenging the narrow outlook of the bourgeois *right*. "These changes," says John Stuart Mill of his effected reforms, "had been attended with much less benefit to human well-being than I should formerly have anticipated, because they had produced very little improvement in that which all real amelioration in the lot of mankind depends on, their intellectual and moral state; and it might even be questioned . . . if deterioration . . . had been at work . . ." (!)

Mill's doubts are less threatening than Marx's certainties, but his skepticism is a benchmark for leftist ennui.

Those alienated, as Mill was, might be defined as those who do not wish to be *bourgeois* for a variety of motives, and *these* are the chickens who've come home to roost.

As my friend the Structuralist says, "The socialists want all of the advantages of modern social conditions without the struggles and dangers resulting from them. They desire the existing state of society minus *both* its revolutionary and unjust elements. They want a bourgeois/proletariat graft. And now they've got it both ways. They've created an ersatz proletariat in the students, and the university provides a theater to act out revolution in the grand Alexandrian tradition. Everyone was of course surprised at the sympathy with which the students' initial demands were greeted. But being essentially actors, they could not genuinely believe in their audience. Once the theatrical demands were met, they had to concoct new demands for the audience, assault them with new alienation effects, without realizing that once the audience discovers this might lead to more than vicarious, symbolic revolution, they will leave. Shortly before the Commune, Marx said, 'Insurrection

It was this mixture of greedy desires and false theories that engendered the insurrection and made it so formidable. These poor people had been assured that the goods of the wealthy were in some way the result of a theft committed against themselves. They had been assured that the inequalities of fortune were as much opposed to morality and the interests of society as to nature. This obscure and mistaken conception of right, combined with brute force, imparted to it an energy, tenacity and strength it would never have had on its own. |de Tocqueville, Recollections of the 1848 Revolution|

now would be an act of a desperate fellow.' The audience likes its theater right up there on the stage, thank you very much. But if you break the proscenium, you're in trouble.''

In the first violent confrontation, the students seem so frail, and all the more so considering the viciousness of the police, particularly the CRS [para-military] in their gray fatigue uniforms. It's almost as if after ten years of frustration, having no Algerians to torture, they are released, this Foreign Legion *manqué,* upon the imaginary Araby of their own populace.

''They should have fought so well against the Germans,'' my concierge mutters.

There is something truly schizoid about the police. The American cop invariably tries to stand as tall as he can, throw out his chest, expose his bulky forearms, project, in other words, his *policeness,* and when the blows come there is a long baseball-like upswing, rather like a man felling a tree. This was the technique in front of the Fairmont; it was the technique in the South. I have managed to get out of the way many times—as American police are always trying for the home run, bless'em, one can usually escape them. Theirs are like the blows of a gorilla, exaggerating the natural force of the swing, loving the process of weaponry more than the execution itself.

Here, the CRS lounge in their vans, sticks between their legs. Even when *en cordon,* they still slouch, trying to be invisible. Once they are challenged, however, they form into a charging, helmeted phalanx, and that's when they think they are musketeers, attacking rapidly, using their truncheons like rapiers, hands barely raised above their heads, feet dancing like dervishes. Such poking is much more difficult to avoid than the American cut-down-a-chestnut-tree style, and much more painful when they make contact. I have seen them on the Ile de la Cité come up to a *clochard* sleeping beneath a bridge, and crack him expertly, exactly on the balls of the feet, and they are similarly on target when attacking a crowd. The rumor is that there are convicts among the CRS. They scurry about like mandrills.

The professional *gendarmerie,* of course, are another matter. Listlessly brutal, they stand erect, in the knowledge that they can slice off your head with a mere flick of their cape. To return to the hotel to sleep, I must always breach their line. I explain where I live, show the receipt, and Inspecteur Jean Gabin corrects my grammar. It seems that I have used the past conditional with regard to where I live. Inspecteur Maigret frowns behind him. "Allow the tourist through."

Christ, it's Atlanta and the blue suit all over again, and the cordon releases merrily. "Are you a student?" asks one of the gendarmes.

Non, professeur, I giggle.

"Where?" he laughs, "Berkeley, Columbo?" Much laughing and jostling.

"I will give you some advice, my dear friend," the Inspecteur Maigret breaks in, "if you go to the Right Bank tonight, go early and come back late."

He's right. Later, the police block the bridges across the Seine so that the Left will not infect the Right. If the revolutionaries were truly strategic, they could merely take the subway, bus or taxi and reemerge behind the lines. But this would not meet the demands of the aesthetic. They must go *en masse*—without the jostling they are lost.

*Epater la nostalgie
de la boué bourgeoisie.*

I feel something must be wrong with me to have such equal disdain for both the left and right. And I also wonder what people do at night who aren't writing or rioting.

But tonight, in the rue Gay-Lussac, it isn't funny any longer; no banker's suit, no tourist visa will suffice. By midnight, a dozen cars are burning, the barricades no longer symbolic. The fighting is truly awful, and I spend most of the evening hunched in doorways brandishing an umbrella if anybody gets near me. The medical school has set up a heroic manual ambulance service, and these sober, glassy-eyed students drag the wounded through sheets of flame. The *flics* are repulsed, and some of the students are actually brave. It is extraordinarily moving. At one point, I trip a CRS with my umbrella. I don't regret it, even though it's chicken shit. A student tells me that the "underworld"—can this possibly be the word he means?—has now enlisted itself against the police, and it is obvious that the few muscular young men wielding chains are not studying literature at the Sorbonne. One is pointed out to me as a well-known syndicate hoodlum from Tours. Imagine that. Our criminals versus their convicts; that's worth the price of the show.

Am going crazy with the claustrophobia; no place to work up a sweat. No wonder they're revolting! There isn't a gymnasium in all of Paris. If you want to play tennis with Irving Wallace in a skylit dome, I suppose that's one thing. Yesterday I ran through the Tuileries in my hooded sweat suit and was stopped and frisked—running being the only possible thing one could be arrested for in the Tuileries. Today, I stumbled into an elegant underground steam bath near the Place des Vosges, and for one steam bath and sauna, I must now give up a week's lunches. In the steam room, a *fonctionnaire* lectures me on copper and its property faults. I ask him where I can go to work out as I can't afford this. "Ah," he says, "there's a soccer field for law students about thirty miles north. On the other hand, there are Turkish baths near the Vendôme." In the paper I find two gymnasiums advertised. The first is naturally some kind of Franco-American club with a swimming pool the size of a bedroom filled with tepid saffron water. Some mad Frenchwoman about fifty does the flying breast stroke for the twenty feet. There are algae in that there pool. She hauls herself over the edge. She is a nun.
The second gym is an octagonal room—the front parlor of a mansion with venetian blinds drawn. I peek through into the darkened fetid air. Twenty young French boys with no calves or chests in immaculate white linen are shrugging a medicine ball about the room. Compulsory calisthenics for the Commune! *Purgation du Phlégmatisme!*

Chien lit is coined! *Mon Général est retourné de Roumanie, en retard,* and Frenchmen everywhere scramble for the *Larousse.* The elitist's dream, the perfect word in the wrong context. *Sensibilité* over prudence. A last gasp of taste. He won't be around much longer. "He's not using the tube like he could," an American tourist pronounces in a bar.

. . . je souhaite que mon sang puisse cimenter le bonheur des Français . . . |*Louis XVI*|

The literary leftist must realize that freedom of inquiry and speech, in an oligopolistic democracy, has no bearing upon the change of the economic or social structure. Free speech has a place only where it is censored. De Gaulle plays this masterfully by giving intellectuals free rein, as it were, but controlling TV; i.e., you are free to say what you will, except in those media which reach large numbers of people and cost a lot of money. And so we are subject to a kind of subtle cultural jamming—not by static, but by trivia, blandness, commodities, which constitute the true resuscitation of the status quo. No wonder the indifference of the average man for civil liberties. The French Communists remain frightened of free speech, because of the nineteenth century Russian experience. The Czar made the mistake of letting those poor exiles live and write out there in the country. He could have had Marx shot down in front of the Elgin Marbles. No, theirs was a literary revolution, which accounts perhaps for its reactionary quality. Is it that the closer politics get to the text, the more totalitarian these politics will be? This evening, over the radio, Alexander Dubcek, beginning *his* revolt from above, quotes Heraclitus: " 'There must be more than one path to the heart of the universe.' We must insure dissent." Man, we could sure use each other.

I am caught up with my student friends in the parade tonight, my hands crossed between two pert Jeanne d'Arcs, hair cropped short, and I'm embarrassed since I know I'm not supposed to think of them as sexual subjects but as comrades in arms, as it were. We march singing, the banners fluttering above. One nice thing about the left is that it gets more ass. I'd rather be *engagé* than engaged.
We sweep into the Boulevard St. Michel and I fear my French is sud-

denly going, as I can't understand the words of the "Internationale." Or maybe it's just my ears. And then I realize that no one in this crowd (we are in the midst of a Communist trade union) knows the words of the "Internationale" after the first two or three lines. The vocal phalanx wavers; we hum and fake it.

The general strike goes on. Much marching in the streets, and sporadic violence. The students are beating the shit out of more cars. The police are getting tired, irritable. They don't throw any better than the students, regularly heaving their tear gas canisters through the windows of restaurants and shops. Then they frown, rub their shoulders, and slouch off.

The mass meetings in the Sorbonne are interminable, boring, noisy, out of control. Tonight, Sartre appeared in the grand amphitheater, walleyed, nervous, strangely humble; he tries to make a distinction between socialism and liberty. "The dictatorship *of* the proletariat turns out often to be *on* the proletariat." He ends by mentioning that the students are not impressing the workers. The workers are not politicized yet, they have only stopped working.

A voice screams from the back, "Sartre! Good art, bad politics!"

Poor Sartre. I should have thought it was the other way around. Here he is, impervious to official criticism; he has become a commodity, a cultural treasure of the state, co-opted by his success, isolated by his very distinction. He can put on a cap and hand out the banned Maoist literature, expose himself in public, incite people to riot, and the state will never touch him, not wishing to create a symbol, a precedent, a martyr. He knows that awful secret of Western intellectuals: that they will be allowed to do things denied the ordinary people they are attempting to mobilize. He knows that his own revolutionary rhetoric will be co-opted both by the state *and* the left, he knows that he must act in a way to show those less privileged that he knows how they *should* act, while knowing that if they follow his example they will be subject to a much greater penalty than he. He is closer to my friend

Ray than either would imagine. It is a noble spectacle, and it is largely lost on this crowd. One senses tonight that he will live out his life in increasingly bitter and vitriolic attacks upon the state, and this action on his part will always be undercut, stained by the sloppy language and uncritical thought of those whom he is addressing. Yet, in the same breath he rails against the authoritarianism of language and culture, he will be making cultural distinctions and cleaning up the language for those less impervious to repression than he, and this is a marvelous paradox to which even his dialectical genius could not do justice.

Cohn-Bendit is impressive as well, a perfectly remarkable and likable fellow—time and time again in crowd situations he refuses to exercise the ego-gratifying charisma he obviously possesses. His rhetoric *alone* is assimilable, for the style of the revolution (and its language is pure style) is clearly opaque. "We believe," he says tonight, "in spontaneous resistance to all forms of domination. . . ." Once one is an *ideological spontanist,* however, it seems that action is more infected by thought than ever. It divorces itself from goals and becomes only redundant self-acknowledgment, a language which is a desperate attempt to circumvent its own symbolic functions. The new official opposition, as it reflects itself through the average student, is, apart from the lovely aphoristic graffiti, neither literary nor strictly political. Insofar as it reflects the resentment of the passive consumer, it guarantees that one's intellectual consumption also remains in desuetude. It is the language and syntax of the social sciences, sociology *manqué* for the middle class—Humanism puréed by the Academy, possibly the most stilted language ever. A structure in which the code words of colloquial insult are burnished by superannuated abstraction. It is a language which neither a serious intellectual nor a worker could possibly understand, and that is why this revolution, despite the fact that its passion has enlisted both the Mentone observatory and Folies-Bergère, will fail. Its passion, analysis, and form of expression are finally at odds with one another.

During the recent struggle, many student militants became hero worshippers of the working class, forgetting that every group has its own part to play in defending its own interest, and that, during the period of total confrontation, these interests converge . . . we do not pretend that we can be leaders in the struggle, but it is a fact that small revolutionary groups can, at the right time and place, rupture the system decisively and irreversibly.|Daniel Cohn-Bendit|

Onomatopoetically, it is the opposite of the church's ritual which can be mastered phonetically then run over the tongue without a thought. Every sentence of the new litany is like a ditch. You must either crawl through it or jump over it. Needless to say, it is extraordinarily boring. Beneath all this swirls a desire:

Not to bring the world into the university, or to make the university more worldly, but to make the world more like the university. If the language is bankrupt, the revulsion is nevertheless pure, and the program for decentralization genuinely moving. Part of the problem is that *lucidité* (and literacy itself) is now so closely associated with the Establishment that it must be viscerally discredited. And listening to the government attempt to right itself, particularly through the subtle intonations of cool Couve de Murville, one senses just how much official *lingua* might be considered culturally oppressive. Yet, is not this new behaviorist jargon even more totalitarian? Is it any more of a reorientive enterprise?

What has died is neither revolutionary passion nor the objective possibility of revolution, nor objective language, nor even literature—what is dead is the literary revolutionary. Perhaps a good thing. Nevertheless, while I can strike at the imposture of the past as well as the current intellectual masturbation, I confess I still secretly prefer that my epitaph might read: "He made the revolution literate." Or if not, then: "He made the revolution at least interesting."

What's instructive about the kids' strategy?

1. They have used their bodies, their best feature, all that they have, to their best advantage. They have broken through bourgeois sex-hoarding patterns, not by attacking them openly, as their bohemian predecessors, but by ignoring them precisely as they deserve to be.

2. They have a greater *money* sense than even their parents, for they

The real poverty of the student's everyday life finds its immediate, fantastic compensation in the opium of cultural commodities. In the cultural spectacle he is allotted his habitual role of the dutiful disciple. Although he is close to the production-point, access to the sanctuary of thought is forbidden, and he is obliged to discover "modern culture" as an admiring spectator. Art is dead, but the student is necrophiliac. He pecks at the corpses in cine-clubs and theatres, buys its flesh-fingers from the cultural supermarket, consuming unreservedly. He is in his element: he is the living proof of all the platitudes of American Market Research: a conspicuous consumer, complete with induced preference for Brand X (Camus, for example) and irrational prejudice against Brand Y (Sartre, perhaps). Impervious to real passion, he seeks titillation in the battles between anaemic gods, the stars of a vacuous heaven: Althusser—Garaudy—Barthes—Picard—LeFèvre—Lévi-Strauss, Halliday—de Chardin—Brassens. . . . And between their rival theologies, designed like all theologies to mask the real problems by creating false ones: humanism—existentialism—scientism—structuralism—cyberneticism—new criticism—dialectics-of-naturalism—metaphilosophism . . . |De la Misère en Milieu Etudiant|

The poetry of the revolution-to-come has remained in the hands of a well-intentioned young bourgeoisie who derived their inspiration from their psychological inspiration, from the antinomy of their ideal and their class, from the ambiguities of the old bourgeois idiom. We must acknowledge that it is the present circumstances of the class struggle which keep the worker from expressing himself poetically. Oppressed by technology, the worker wants to become a technologist because he knows that

know, at the same time they are complaining about commodity fetish, just how much a complex consumer society depends upon their technical expertise and cooperation. They are threatening to cut intake. It is their greatest leverage, and they know it even if they can't express it. By defining themselves as their parents' most valuable commodities, they are able to prolong the rebellion. . . .

To be charged against them is that they still don't see how much their own bourgeois elitism counteracts their democratic tendencies, how it prevents them from constructing a broader alliance, and what they are *really* asking for is to be treated like the elite they will become, only sooner, less judgmentally—this is all hopelessly disguised by a populist, even Luddite rhetoric. Having placed too much emphasis upon the closed constituency of youth, they have based their claims on the one prerogative they must necessarily lose—their age. At their worst, they are anarchists who want their institutions destroyed so that *they* might take them over, Jacobins who want status without the institutions which confer such. It is in one sense a brilliant synthesis or strategy, in that it is equally tentative about both the past and the future. But this in itself constitutes no commitment to the present. The demand for relevance is, in effect, asking for the right to *study* revolution—to have it as a matter of curriculum along with the bread and butter—revolution as the subject of vocational education.

In the arcade of the Sorbonne courtyard, across the nineteenth century oil panels by Weerts, have been scrawled the words, "Destroy these terrible paintings." This gives me a twinge, for while it is true they are terrible and while there is a definite connection between this sort of decadent institutional art and decadent institutions, I believe they would have done the same to Chagall had he borne this commission. The courtyard is a circus of literature booths, Maoists, UJCM, Trotskyites, JCR, Anarchists, and I can't help thinking again how much more focused the ideology would be if there were a genuine censorship. The avant garde in literature and politics coincides here in that

technology will be the instrument of his liberation; if he is ever to affect management, he knows he will do so only by scientific, economic and professional knowledge. |Sartre, Black Orpheus|

What makes them representatives of the petite bourgeoisie, is the fact that in their minds they do not go beyond the limits which the latter do not go beyond in life, that they are consequently driven theoretically to the same tasks and solutions to which material interest and social position practically drive the latter. This is in general the relationship of the political and literary representatives *to the class that they represent.* |Marx, The Eighteenth Brumaire of Louis Bonaparte|

it cannot exist without an establishment coherent enough to attack or censor it. Their rage is entirely too assimilable.

A friend, terribly excited by the revolution, tells me mournfully, "Ah, we Frenchmen have no secrets. We speak, we speak, we are so *non mystérieux*. We need a little *refoulement* (repression) to tell us who we are."

In the streets, burned out shells of cars are left for the crowd's astonishment. Strangely beautiful, these gutted Citroëns, like the skeleton of a trout broiled over charcoal; they should be put in the Louvre. In the courtyard, red and black flags protrude from the dome of the church of the Sorbonne. Inside lies Richelieu reclining on his bier, upheld by a figure of "Religion"; at his feet, the figure of "Science" in tears. A daffodil has been placed in his nostril. The crypt is reserved for university professors who have "died for their country."

HUMANITY WILL ONLY BE HAPPY
WHEN THE LAST BUREAUCRAT
HAS BEEN HANGED BY THE GUTS OF
THE LAST CAPITALIST.

DEFENSE D'INTERDIR
(FORBIDDING PROHIBITED)

PROFESSORS – YOU ARE DEAD

FREUD IS A GUIZOT

GIVE UP COMFORT AND SECURITY.
IMAGINATION NOT *RAISON*.

THE MORE I MAKE REVOLUTION,
THE MORE I WANT TO MAKE LOVE.
THE MORE I MAKE LOVE,
THE MORE I WANT TO MAKE REVOLUTION.

I HAVE NOTHING TO SAY,
BUT I WANT TO SAY IT.

ART IS DEAD.
MAKE YOUR LIFE THE QUOTIDIAN.

|ON THE WALL OF THE SORBONNE|

I am prepared to be bored by the man who murders me. |John Barth|

But I keep thinking about those defiled paintings. How does Culture come to us? Am I being merely respectful? I recall when I first came to France, after losing the relatives with which to people a past, I had to settle for Culture. I wandered about the Louvre, but the great paintings were badly positioned, too numerous to absorb. Their glare was too much for me. With those I could directly confront, I could never rid them of my shadow, my ghostly face in their protective glass. As soon as I moved they became opaque; as I left the gallery it became a corridor of mirrors. I was a medallion pendant in the sun, random, inchoate and timeless, the still point. I wrote this off to a conspiracy of curators until I discovered that those artifacts took their shape from the way *I* lived, and I could never salve myself with any determinism—erotic, economic or existential—from that time on.

I had secured a room in an old town house, which, as the plaque above the door announced, had been built by a consort of Châteaubriand, and from which Paris appeared as a green boulder-strewn field after a storm. My landlady, a wisp of a woman with cheekbones so sharp they would surely burst the flesh if she ever had occasion to laugh, wore pearl-gray gloves and confessed that she wrote poetry in her spare hours. The room *"plus haut mais sans bruit"* opened upon a cylindrical inner court at the bottom of which hovered a cut-glass skylight. The once intricately carved panes were now milky with age, and the design had been long obscured with refuse. Only a small turret of stained glass remained free of debris, blossoming bands of rose, amber and violet as the sun forced its way into the shaft each morning.

Madame C'est-à-Dire (she took her name as most people should be given theirs—by the words she used most often) arrived promptly at eight each morning, muttering in execrable French as she placed croissants and coffee on a table by the window. *"Enlevez, Monsieur l'Américan, vous avez faire aujourd'hui les choses magnifiques!"* Upon opening the shutters she immediately turned her back on the light and teetered from the room—as if out of respect for the life framed in the other rooms which opened on the cylinder. I was less respectful. Seated before the window, I involved myself in the imaged life of my neighbors and the spiraling bands of light which interwined them. I even began to keep a journal, unselective but printed meticulously as if in the hope that the observations would evolve their own principle of order through faithful reproduction. I opened it today for the first time in eleven years.

"Stallion-man charges wife to bed. Usually after breakfast when the children have gone to school."

"Inevitable artist paints before window which looks out upon nothing but gray stucco wall, never once turning his easel so that we might judge his work."

"Young girl with acne on back. Exposes it to sun in the morning. No shame."

"Open love. Hidden language. Bare necessity."

"If I wanted to take the man's wife, medicate the girl's back, or see the artist's work, I must go downstairs and then upstairs and come in on the side of their lives that is prepared. They allow each other to see the other side because they would have to forfeit light and air if they did not. But there is an accepted and common blindness here, and it is one which I cannot share. I prefer my position to knocking on their doors. I have waved to them but they ignore me, and if I tried to touch them I would fall silently and be killed in a splintering of glass. Yet this is the same blindness which passes between me and the solemn doe-eyed personages of Velázquez's royalty in the Louvre. They are practiced; they wait to time their blink with mine, their indifference as feigned as that of my neighbors. It is they who are judging me; their interest in me is purer than mine in them."

Then one day the sun struck my windows in the same way that it struck through the skylights of the Louvre, and all that was before me was my face, and the gauzy refracted interior of my poor room. And I understood the principle of acculturation within us—that for every desire in the museum to invest those characters with life, to penetrate the frame, there is a concomitant urge to freeze real life, subject one's neighbors to the proscenium, and that this urge, no matter what cheap psychology may say, is basic to staying alive. It is the delicate membrane which connects the twin solstices of one's perception and reflection.

Once in the Métro, as the crowd engulfed me, I found myself pressed against a young girl. She wore a loose white armless dress and smelled of violets. The shoving passengers forced us together and we both tried to avoid eye contact, as a strutting bird flinches when he discovers another in a window glass. But gradually the mass enveloped us, our hands raised to the straps above as in a Roman salute, and we were forced into a locked stare. I could feel the warmth of her breasts against my chest, my head full of her sweetness. We were crushed together. Involuntarily we relaxed as the oldest of lovers, dependent only on each other's gentleness. Without some absurd craning of the neck, all we could do was smile. It seemed as though my entire life with all its omissions and petty triumphs came down to what I would do with this girl. But as I was about to shout my name to her face, the train broke from a

tunnel into a sun-bleached white canyon tufted somehow with blue
wildflowers, and as the door opened, the shuddering crowd released us.
I started to follow her, to call, to *initiate,* but then I realized I wanted
the moment more than the girl. I wanted her across the cylinder, in her
frame. Had I gone mad? To see analogies in everything?

In the Métro, life as art. While in the Louvre, I reversed it. In a dark
unvisited alcove of her basement, I once encountered an obsidian
sphinx, three times as long as myself, her eyes on a level with my chest.
The only real god, eyeless feline wisdom crouched perpetually in the
wastes. I reached across the velvet restraining rope, coated white with
dust, to touch her paw. It was not cold but barely cool, like a live
hound's nose, a wine glass, caviar, a woman just come in from running
through the rain, vellum, an empty rifle, a sacramental wafer, a silent
lathe, a canoe just beached, a leaf of rhododendron, all those things
which remind you simultaneously that you are alive and about to die,
refueling the impulse to make something that will outlast you, that impulse which unites you with the human family. Then I was between her
ribbed paws, my face against her stylized jowl, with the words of the
Hasidim in my heart—"Whosoever would have truth itself must drive
hence the spirit of victory. . . ."

The guards had led me politely but firmly, one for each arm, to the office of *Le Directeur.*

"What if *everyone* touched it?" he whined. "It would be mutilated. You
are an American, a student of history, you must understand."

So what? So it lasts half as long? All art that lasts is spoiled art, everyone should *touch* it, embrace it . . . let *it* be pawed. . . .

I was released on recognizance. And so I know what those students
feel, even those who carve their initials in the art which they could
never achieve themselves, bad as it may be. And that is why I would
also have them arrested. Otherwise the gesture would be meaningless
as the brush strokes of old Weerts himself, who lived to be eventually
touched, even in such a way.

There is that famous anecdote attributed to Giacometti—that if there
were a fire in his studio, which would he save, his cat or a Rembrandt?
He opted for the cat.

But it is a phony question. What must be asked is: Which would he save? The cat or the work of Giacometti?

Happily, we will never resolve this.

The entire Sorbonne is cordoned off now. The police have retaken it, complaining bitterly about the garbage. The proclamations on the walls are torn down in the night. Many of the students have left, and we are now occupied by international hippiedom, succubi on the bones of a past enthusiasm, like those little long-legged birds one sees feeding off the backs of rhinoceroses in the Transvaal.

I meet a poet, famous for his past radicalism and a few poems, in the Cluny. He chides me for going back to my room to work when there is a revolution going on.

It's an insurrection, not a revolution, and anyway, it's over, I say. Can't you see? The jackals are out.

He wants me to introduce him to my friends in the Movement.

They are confused enough already, I plead. Leave them alone, for God's sake.

He waxes pale. "When I was your age," he says, "I did the same thing. I was wandering through Europe, traveling around in '38, writing poems. Lord, did I write poems, none of which I suppose were very good. If I'd only kept notes on what was going on, reports, even a journal, think of the historical value that would have had! Lord, what a self-absorbed fool I was!"

It wouldn't have helped your poems, I think.

He takes me along to the house of a certain countess, where he is to meet with some of the activist faculty of the Sorbonne to get the lowdown. They are now said to be in negotiation with the student leaders. The countess's apartments are the only place in Paris I have been which is totally quiet; a lovely walled garden full of carefully ruptured

urns, a philodendron at least a century old. In the drawing room, six
Klees I have never seen reproduced anywhere hover above my elbow
on the couch. I get goose pimples from touching the frames. In another
room, amongst *chinoiserie,* a Yugoslav butler serves tea.

The poet asks a professor of sociology which texts have primarily influenced the *enragés:* Marx, Lenin?

"*Mais non,* they despise them."

"Lévi-Strauss, Adorno, perhaps?"

"Oh, *mais non,* they are considered reactionaries, much too Hegelian."

The poet asks the countess what she thinks of Lévi-Strauss's position.

"I have not read that man," she says, "but I shall quickly disembarrass
myself of that peculiarity."

The poet counters, "He's kind of Zen Judaism."

No one laughs.

"Well, how about Marcuse?" the poet begins again.

"*Mais non,* ah but well, at least they know his face."

Countess: "Is he a handsome man?"

Professor: "No, I mean they do not *read* . . . at all . . . you see. They
have no antecedents."

Poet: "But all revolutionary movements in the past have had, you
know, some sort of concrete ideology."

"Oh," interrupted the countess, "but certainly the people who partici-
pated in them didn't know that. It must have been very much as it is
now."

"Except, countess," the poet interceded, "that the regime has, if anything, been strengthened."

"And your little 'angels,' " another professor broke in, "have necessi-
tated a counter-revolution. Already our only honest journalists are
being fired. Soon people will be leaving the country, just as in England.
How do you say, brain-drain?"

The countess: "Not to the United States?"

"To the United States, assuredly."

"Well, certainly not to the colonies," the professor intercedes.

"I must say," the countess continues, "I find the whole affair extraordinarily exciting. But what does your young friend think?"

*What the so-called spatial arts have
long succeeded in expressing, what
even the time-bound art of music has
gloriously achieved in the harmonies
of polyphony, the phenomenon of
many simultaneous dimensions
which helps drama to its climax, does
not, unfortunately, occur in the world
of verbal didactic expression.
|Paul Klee, 1924|*

The poet tried to protect me. "He's not as young as he looks, countess; I'm afraid he's rather diffident on the subject."

The countess turns to me: "Speak for yourself, please."

I stammer, I thought a revolution was the transfer of power from one group to another. That certainly isn't happening. My guess is the specter of civil war will be used only to entrench the king. . . .

"My dear fellow," the countess interrupted me, "one gets the revolutionaries one deserves. . . ."

After tea, the Countess proposes an excursion to the Renault factory at Bouilly-Billiancourt. The students have mounted a march to express their solidarity at the gates of the factory in which the workers have locked themselves. Rumor has it there is intense division inside between the younger workers and union officials. The Rolls is brought round.

"We shall come back and eat here," the countess announces. I excuse myself and sneak a last look at the Klees, pleading a previous engagement.

Even a voyeur must have some scruples.

Some of our contemporaries in their yearning for 'initiation,' have gone as far as inventing new rites, if not new cults altogether. We dream of being 'initiated,' of managing to decipher the occult meaning of all this destruction of artistic languages, all of these 'original' experiments which seem, at first sight, to have nothing left in common with art . . . on one hand, we have an impression of 'initiation' . . . on the other, we display clearly to those others, *the crowd, our adherence to a secret minority; not any more, to an 'aristocracy' (modern elites are leftward looking) but to a gnosis, which has the merit of being both spiritual and secular, by being in opposition not only to official values but to the traditional Churches. . . .*
|Mercia Eliade|

In a bar on the rue de Bac, a student is chiding an elegant elderly man about his class-consciousness. The older man holds his brandy aloft, as if in quasi-toast, announcing, "I'll have you know, sir, that I am a member of the class which produced Karl Marx and Sigmund Freud, Albert Einstein and Vincent Van Gogh, Nikolai Lenin and Fidel Castro, Thomas Mann and Marcel Proust, Mahatma Gandhi and Igor Stravinsky, and, sir, I will be a traitor to that class in my own time and fashion."

Gasoline is restored and the city surges towards the Toilet of Triumph honking/weeping for *Mon Général.*

One of the more celebrated student leaders takes his Citroën to be gassed up—the attendants recognize him and smash the car to pieces with tire irons—"And how do you like *your* car destroyed, Monsieur? *Tant pis!*"

Friends take me to a château in the Loire for asparagus as thick as your wrist. As much as I detest their Louis Quatorze fixation, the French succeed as no other people in misinterpreting their past, since they know it is not real, and therefore have no qualms about prettifying it. The château, for example, in the spirit of the best *trompe-l'oeil,* does not attempt to faithfully duplicate the eighteenth century, but our fantasy about what we would have done in the eighteenth century. Other countries imitate other cultures better, but none imitate themselves as well as the French. The chapel has been converted into four double bedrooms, and the crypt below into a discothèque; our rich mixed drinks are served on the previous owner's sarcophagus. Another revolution has been screened and pronounced fit for its modern audience.

I went to see an old friend, a philosopher-recluse who has lived in Paris in the same *quartier* since he emigrated from Central Europe in 1938. His apartment has the strangest view I've ever seen. Once the servants' quarters of a great Parisian house, it is on a level with adjacent rooftops so that you are aware of nothing save the conjunction of the roofs with the sky. The bottom half, mineral-encrusted alloy; the top, a pure rectangle of air. If one looks very carefully in the left-hand corner, one can just make out the tip of Notre Dame's steeple, jutting out like a piling of a washed-out bridge in the trough of a wave. Somewhere he has written, "Parisians don't know of *what* to die." I ask him if he thinks anything has changed. "Well," he says, "soldiers have replaced the *clochards* under the Seine bridges, for one thing."

And they will soon be replaced in turn by American adolescents, I add. "All I know is, for some reason, they have chosen models for their revolt which are furthest from their actual circumstances. That is the first indication of their lack of seriousness. Ho Chi Minh was a pastry cook here, you know. What if he had taken Napoleonic military maneuvers back home with him as *his* lesson? If you demand a cause, however, I can give you as good as any. It is the students in the *liberal arts* who revolt, who hate themsleves. They have no future, you see, except as geniuses. Any *job* they accept will seem a compromise. They have been taught that anything less than tortured hermeticism or graceful fame is unworthy. Perhaps even dishonest. Few of us can live on that. Only the ones like myself who had no choice. There are *ten thousand* young people in Paris studying literature. What do you expect? On their own terms, measured against their work, they can do nothing but fail. For that I love them, but I cannot take their revenge seriously. Any *littéra-teur* knows that any literature worth the name is larger than politics, though he cannot publicly admit it. It may well be, in fact, that he would rather have the politics. What is a book, after all? A hole in the air! You know, the cultural attaché of my country came to me here in the Second World War; he was a brigadier general in the reserves. He told me that I must return and defend my homeland. I refused. In the first year, eighty-five thousand of my countrymen were lost on the Russian front alone. In the second year, he came to me and said that it was now mandatory that I return. I refused. Eventually I had to go into hiding. I kept myself alive and ten years later I began to write. My books have nothing to do with those soldiers lost forever, they are not about them, they are not for them, because they are dead and I am alive. But they would not have been written without them. That is all. And I mistrust any politics which has as its central strategy the exposé of those indecent impulses which have been collectively sublimated in the interests of harmony. Any man over thirty is vulnerable to the charge that he has wasted his life. You will not reorient any society with that challenge. Spontaneity is no antidote to sublimation. And willful spontaneity is the most corrupt of all. I need no one to heighten my own contradictions in order to raise my consciousness. My contradictions are quite palpable without assistance, were at an unbearable pitch long before these *enragés* were conceived, and I have experienced more intense anger than they will ever imagine. There are only unhappy lands and unpleasant ones. France falls in the former category. A month ago, I was eating alone up here and turned on the radio. A journalist friend of mine was talking about my latest book, and described me as wasting away for literature, always struggling, never having much to eat. I had before me at the time an organic chicken, a cold osso bucco, filet of Dover sole and a white Bordeaux. Put no faith in contingencies, my friend, nor in transitions. I despise transition in paragraphs, operas and in regimes. I have seen the best literary minds of my generation wasted on political polemic, and a morbid fascination with the sort of person they could never be. . . ."

I left him and walked up the rue Napoléon to see another friend who lives on the Place de l'Odéon. I still feel exhilarated by what has happened. The students have managed, after all, to identify their grievances with the whole of the country, and though that in itself denies much of the Marxist analysis which they so eagerly brought to it, it remains a unique phenomenon in postwar history. Their demands have humiliated the state, and the *phlegmatisme* of the city has been dissipated for a brief moment. The severity of the Latin Quarter intellectual pose gave way for a brief moment to a kind of joyousness which was, I guess, a kind of deference in the face of unexpected success.

I was soon caught up in a crowd of students crying, "On to the Luxembourg!" there to confront the Senate, that most innocuous of all upper houses of parliament, meeting apparently in the Luxembourg Palace. This seemed a very good idea, and my spirits were high. I was terribly excited, not through that usual upsurge of violence that I feel when a natural enemy could be confronted, but with the knowledge that despite the pitched ritualistic battles, not one person has been killed.

Unfortunately, the police assigned to protect the Senate in this instance were a grumpy lot—carbines and submachine guns in evidence for the first time, and even a few civil guards, horsed, plumed and sabered, providing a distinct operatic flavor—static like Berlioz, then redundantly busy like Glinka. The students subsided and broke almost at once.

CRIME IS THE HIGHEST FORM OF SENSUALITY.
|ON DA WALL|

|99|

Things were untethered. I retire to a restaurant which I cannot afford. I eat sparely. Across the square, a group of students "take over" the Odéon theater; "Ex-Théâtre de France" is scrawled across the façade. Red and black flags are hung from the gallery. "Imagination has taken over at the theater of France."

But this is not quite so. The crowd turned back from the moribund Senate had only decided upon a contingency evening at the Living Theater. They chose it because they had failed in their first objective, because it was proximate to that objective, and because it was unprotected. They did not storm the Rothschild bank or the Ministry of Culture or the Chamber of Deputies or even American Express. They chose l'Odéon because it was nearest and because there was no penalty in doing so. Merely a chance to bust up that proscenium once and for all, a little surrogate machismo.

The audience swarms the stage, turning spotlights upon the balconies where the "reviewers" sit, not wishing to miss a trick. A spontaneous discussion ensues as various speakers denounce the "bourgeois art of the theater," how it reflects decadent capitalist society which has nothing to offer. The modern American dance troupe which has been scheduled reports through an intermediary that the cancellation of this tour may be the end of them financially.

"Every man's an actor," someone screams. "Every man is an artist." For the first time, I am actually angry. That smarmy cry of our time. It's one thing to have free access to the theater. Quite another to have free access to the stage.

"The theater is for the people, not a repressive instrument of the state!" That, even in France, is an injustice. The director of the theater, M. Jean-Louis Barrault, in much too histrionic a pose for his own good, tries to argue with them—far from being a supporter of the state, he insists, the theater has an international reputation for the avant garde and is not even subsidized by the state. But he is not allowed to use the microphone. In any case, it is a bad argument. He could have simply insisted upon the theater's right to be a theater. What he's saying, implicitly, is that they should be allowed to proceed because their aesthetics serve politics to the left of the regime. In the end, he mumbles some-

A Propos de l'ex-Théâtre de France
The Committee for Revolutionary Action (C.A.R.) together with the militants of the revolutionary student movement, has occupied the ex-theatre of France and transformed it into a permanent meeting place for all. During the night of May 16, it transferred the responsibility for the unlimited occupation of places to a Committee of Occupation made up of actors, students and workers whose political position is in line with their own. The goals of the occupation remain the same:
—The sabotage of all that is "cultural": theatre, art, literature, etc. (right-wing, left-wing, governmental or "avant-garde") and the maintenance of the political struggle in highest priority.
—The systematic sabotage of the cultural industry, especially the industry of show business, in order to make room for true collective creation.
—The concentration of all energy on political objectives such as the expansion of the revolutionary movement, the struggle in the streets against State Power, and the reinforcement of the union of revolutionary workers, revolutionary students, and revolutionary artists.
—The extension of direct action: for example, by the occupation of the greatest possible number of places of work, of communications, of decisions.
The C.A.R. feels that it accomplished its goal by occupying the Odéon, ex-Theatre of France, when its political objective was clearly and publicly achieved: the government press (Paris-Presse) recognized, moreover, that the occupation

thing which has been variously reported, but I made it out as, "This theater is dead. Barrault is dead." [He is at least prescient. Malraux sacks him later.]

It struck me that in this performance we are witnessing the absolute impossibility of our own renewal. That utterly random free flow from the seats to the stage, that reversal of the elements, is to no purpose save reversal itself. What has happened is precisely the opposite of its avowed aesthetic invention—rather than create a new dynamism, new relationships, the scene has been frozen hard, indelibly so; even the volunteer performers with their pronounced lack of officiousness, their gentleness, do not make up for it. They are only a reverse negative of their enemies.

As I walk out, an extraordinary thing happens. In the lobby, a young girl is doing a series of solemn pirouettes and tight *fouettés*. I have no idea where she came from, but her accented French is heavy with a more guttural language. Someone yells from the balcony, "Dance for the revolution. . . ."

"*Mais non,* Monsieur," she replies, "I am not dancing for *this* house. I am dancing for the dance."

I take a last look back through the lobby. A rebel is smoking under a No Smoking sign. The girl slips, falters on the marble of the foyer, but nevertheless regains her balance. So in the end, ungainly, she remains exemplary; proud and unique despite the occupation of her house.

If my politics are suspect, it is only with regard to leaving her to dance alone.

of the ex-Theatre of France and certain workshops in the Renault factory at Cleon has provoked a drop in the Paris stock market. Today, this irreversible movement must be extended and reinforced. In regard to theatre, the slightest corporatist activity, the slightest intramural and organized entertainment, the slightest relaxation of revolutionary agitation, would be a betrayal of the élan which was revealed on the barricades and which must not diminish but increase and fortify at all costs. Never again must a single ticket be sold at the ex-Theatre of France; its free status must be maintained. The theatrical act of occupation was, under the circumstances, a political act:

—It laid siege to one of the bastions of Gaullist power.

—It revealed the collusion between certain counter-revolutionary trade-union elements and Management allied to the State (i.e., goons).

The C.A.R. has decided to move on to other things in other places. The C.A.R. expresses its solidarity and its sympathy with the Committee of Occupation of the ex-Theatre of France and remains at its disposal to aid in rejecting all attempts by the state to reoccupy these places, to prevent all reconversion of places back into theatres.

The only theatre is guerrilla theatre. REVOLUTIONARY ART IS MADE IN THE STREETS.—Comité d'Action Révolutionaire de l'ex-Théâtre de France, 17 May 1968

The plaque appears on one of the columns of the Odéon, the steps from which Stendhal watched the 1830 "revolution." I wonder if Phillipe knew any more about what he was doing than these *enragés?* Was his rage purer, his courage greater? Is not this grotesque foolery a matter of survival as well? Or are the profundity of our politics, the consequences of our resistance, always defined by the nature of our enemy?

Phillipe Girrére, Etudiant âgé de 20 ans, tué par le gestapo le 20 août 1944

This morning, someone across the street burned up in bed. I sat on the balcony smoking, watching the traffic just like unborn generations of insomniacal French dialecticians. Before light, they brought the body out and below my croissants they reassemble his gutted door, his mattress now so much blackened jelly, personal flammable effects, watch, jewelry and radio. *Les pompiers* in the silver helmets of Roman legionnaires flood the wreckage; it will smolder all day. Then after a fine lunch, they rake out the singed wallet, the identification moulted in plastic, and *Le Chef* exclaims, *"Voilà,"* and flings a glistening ashtray upon the curbing. All Cartesian cause and effect, he turns to his *confrères:* "We'd never have gotten the hose up those stairs anyway." It's all so sad. Time to move on.

But consider the Paris Commune. . . . In essence, it's all the same Rousseau and the dream of recreating the world anew through reason and experience (positivism). They desire the happiness of man and stop at Rousseau's definition of the word 'happiness,' i.e. at fantasy, not even justified by experience. The conflagration of Paris is a monstrosity. 'It didn't succeed, so perish the world, for the Commune is above the happiness of the world and France.' However, to them (yes, and to many), this delirium does not seem a monstrosity, but, on the contrary, beauty. And so the aesthetic idea has become muddled in the new humanity. *In the West they have lost Christ (through the fault of Catholicism) and therefore the West is collapsing, solely because of this. The ideal has been altered, and how clear this is!* |Dostoevsky, Letter to Strakhov, May 18, 1871|

ime to get the hell out again. Did I always associate growing up with running away? In the Jura, the last unspoiled part of France, I'm always going a little too fast, the cycle not really under control. The frost is on the snail, cows clog the foggy road. As the owner of a château appears on his front steps, thirty mastiffs in his kennel rear up on their hind legs and eye his progress through the arcade of Lombardy poplars.

There have been bombings here too, in these ravines and cliffs and falling streams; violences a little less subtle than in the capital. What's up? I ask around. They would rather be Swiss than fight. Well, what the hell, at this point I may as well be Swiss too. It's not hard to believe in a demography uncontested by armies for 800 years. My motorcycle is German, but I will never go back to Germany. I too am conditioned by World War II, or rather the movies of World War II. Is that how our politics come to us? Even the train conductors in Germany terrify me. I always think Kurt Jurgens is going to come along, open the door of the compartment and heave me out into no man's land. I had never ridden a cycle until the day I bought it; the Bavarian salesman told me to take it over the Alps that afternoon on the theory that if I made it I would never be scared again. I was not afraid to take a motorcycle over the Alps. I was afraid to take a train into Germany to pick it up. Three decades of late-night insomniacal gestapo festschrifts have made those one-dimensional villains of my infancy too real for this boy.

Is that how our politics come to us? Once in the fourth grade, my class was taken on a field trip to a cookie factory. And in this cookie factory there was a juncture of two conveyor belts which didn't mesh properly, and at this juncture stood an old woman who turned each cookie box a quarter turn so that it would be aligned properly for the new track. Now half the class thought this obscene—that an old woman would have to do what was obviously a machine's mute task. The other half felt it marvelously efficient problem-solving—that someone so obviously unskilled should have the opportunity to put bread on the table and look everyone in the eye. It would seem, Doctor, that our predispositions in these matters are formed quite early. The first is not so much a moral as an aesthetic judgment, and the second suggests that politics for the

|103|

RESSENTIMENT

Several admirable and noteworthy things in Europe are more recent than the crusades . . . my plan does not include them,—that is all, and you can find out everything you need to know about them without my telling you. |Grant Allen, The European Tour, 1899|

American is neither a technology nor telos, but a yet unnamed stage of infantile personality development. From the minotaur motorcyclist's point of view, each generation has a speed at which it finds it most comfortable to think. Direction, destination are relatively less important—surface and vehicular weight more so, landscape overrated, just a marker to know you're moving, what gets you *out* of yourself. A proper speed for reflection, is all that a man can ask. Myself, I find about 45 on a hard-surfaced, tree-lined winding road is about perfect. No doubt others have their preferences, that's why we have the party system. On such a road, I become a 30-year-old, 45 mile-an-hour, bearded palimpsest. And there's nothing I can't imagine. Except History.

When at 19 I first took this road, I was not heading for Switzerland, nor for the Channel, but for those endless graveyards. We hide, disguise our dead. The French flaunt them. And before my cycle, there appeared a white Buick, white as diluted Pernod, the nuclear American family with a New Jersey sticker. Man and wife, two kids in the back, together with a nodding black and white styrene electric puppy whose red eyes ignited if they were stopping fast, going left or right. I blew my 450 CC by them, skirted them, roared at them, farted at them, took cursory side roads, changed course, intention, direction, ran only at night, ran like a black wombat out of hell, and yet at Meuse and at Verdun and Chateau-Thierry and at Chalons, I would suddenly come upon them again, ubiquitous as they were unextraordinary, cresting a rise, peering into the vortex of those chestnut-lined roads against which so many of France's finest dash their brains. I would once again overtake them, be rid of them, and the large pleasant pink man always in the same plaid jacket and striped tie would nod, and his expertly coiffed wife would smile, the 2.7 blonde kids pound on the glass on either side of their nodding, incandescent directional-signaled styrene puppy. In one town, a girl seated upon a high wall threw a rose to me, but I had a schedule to keep, and a supernumerous Buick to beat.

In my goggled peripheral vision, the remnants of the Maginot line came into view. I ate and slept in cemeteries. Not in the wheat or corn or leeks, nor in those magnificently redundant battlements where they are now growing mushrooms. For us, we got 40 acres, your sidearms

. . . the character of the scenery is always the same. Mile after mile of stunted trees; some hewn down by the axe, some blown down by the wind, some half fallen and resting on their neighbors, many more logs half hidden in the swamp, others mouldered away to spongy chips. The very soil of the earth is made up of minute fragments such as these; each pool of stagnant water has its crust of vegetable rottenness; on every side there are the boughs, and trunks, and stumps of trees, in every possible stage of decay, composition and neglect. Now you emerge for a few brief minutes on an open country, glittering with some bright lake or pool, broad as many an English river, but so small here that it scarcely has a name; now catch hasty glimpses of a distant town, with its clean white houses and their cool piazzas, its prim New England church and schoolhouse; then whir-r-r-r! Almost before you have seen them, comes the same dark screen: the stunted trees, the stumps, the logs, the stagnant water—all so like the last that you seem to have been transported back again by magic. |Dickens, American Notes|

and a mule. For them, they got one used fort, some bacteria and a boar. A landscape of broken columns, stalled engines and cultivated craters gives me shelter . . . I read the names of the dead at each stile and village. Why does it take the names of long gone French boys to bring home war for me? They do not hide them as we do in our post offices, do not, as we do, disguise their cemeteries as a front garden. We should cast the names of our dead in the street, two-inch raised letters in the steel and bronze that killed them, so when you drive into town, 10, 20, 50 years later, you tear your tires to shreds. The lives of those we have wasted must respectfully cease our momentum.

Lord, how do our politics come to us? How do we hold both annihilation and daily strategy in our minds? Why is our patriotism and our intelligence always opposed? This good gray Buick, this tiger smile of a machine, is taking up too much of the road for its own good.

If the Europeans have lost their extensions, we have lost our inclusiveness, both our right to lead and our right to be left alone. It is our *future* Death, our *Dying,* not our dead, who are monumentalized at the crossroads. What would John Winthrop have thought if the hill upon which he was to build his city was honeycombed with cells for catastrophe? Why should he have left Europe at all? Will we end, then, known only for our admirable bunkers?

I do remember now! Shortly after my visit to the cookie factory, the people next door built a bomb shelter. The trucks and cement mixers rolled up and down the road, a mound of scalloped earth appeared, and, I thought, a patio, a sleeping porch, if I thought anything at all. Then one morning, an overalled workman came to the back door and asked equably, "Is this where they're building the bomb shelter?" I stepped back dumb, glanced for a panicky moment at our neighbor's house, shouted back into the face: Certainly not, I said and slammed the door. I passed the rest of the day searching out the root of that insult, and the next morning, I got up early and went over to view my neighbor's handiwork. There was nothing to be seen, of course, only a few scraps of wood and a fresh patch in the asphalt driveway. They had dug there, I assumed, reinforced the basement beneath the garage, and as I stood there in the lonely suburban air, upon that still resilient patch of tar with that pure chamber beneath me, I again behaved unaccountably. "What *right*," I thought, "has he to do this!" Like most Americans, when pressed, I revert to natural law. I went home and, though the day had started, got back into bed. It was a threat more real than any invasion.

To be honest, I had to admit that I did not fear nuclear war; that I could no longer use it as a convenient excuse for paralysis or action. It had no *causality*. What I was really afraid of was living in a society defined by and driven by a dream war which was simply unthinkable, a putative, metaphysical war which we so carefully disguised in the fifties by the guerrilla warfare we carried out against ourselves every day.

So in the end, I found my neighbor had something after all—though perhaps for the wrong reasons. It was hardly a matter of survival; I for one have no interest in surviving a nuclear war. My tastes are complex if not subtle, and I live for civilization as I have come to it. When the flash appears, I shall go to the cemetery and copulate as during the plagues. So the time had come to build *our* Maginot line; to illustrate precisely our precariousness by the absurdest commodity of all—another middle-class appurtenance, equipped no doubt with early American furnishings for new humble beginnings.

From that day on, I ceased to be a Manichaean. It was not a question of adapting to the fact of tunneling, but to the principle. Such shelters will surely pose no ecological problem—in our cities and suburbs, on our highways, we have adjusted to far more hideous devices. It was, of course, the metaphor of tunneling which concerned me; how the American Mind would work in the cellar. To learn how to live on several levels at once. To accept the appurtenances of holocaust, to face up to them, so that we might go about our business again. Why did we learn nothing as a nation from this? Why did we choose, once again, not to live with ourselves, our vast silence? Freud, our Marx, outlined the international situation as the personal (he did not live to see them indistinguishable); that is, the eternal competition between the life and death instincts. He saw individual activity, as we tended to see world activity, as a conflict between these two impulses, and the fusion of such extremes lay in aggression, which *solved* the conflict by replacing the desire to die with the desire to kill. Why did we believe that, since it was no longer possible to kill without dying? Some think that with Vietnam we lost our virtue; the truth is we had not even reached puberty. Imagine that, in the fifties, we had made shelters mandatory, hollowed out and mined the entire continent, rather than projecting our fury upon the Orient. It would have given us the one thing we have never had—ruins. Ruins of a distinctly American type, of course, ruins of the future. A second city of *de*monuments, untombs, testifying not to the past, the dead, nor even our resistance to death; but to the thin continuity of present and future, to that rare willingness to live with our rough selves, to the knowledge that there is always a mindless room in the mind, a white pre-cancerous cell, equipped with bottled water, bandages and cots, and no forgiveness. Perhaps it might have prevented the barricading, darkening of the entire estate. Simply a vast, empty windowless room to remind us of what is undone, and what we cannot do. . . .

And in this landscape, cleaved only by white Buicks and their imperishable cargoes, the road narrows, the fields become tank-tracked, the hedgerows are hazy with mustard gas, the cycle begins to wobble, the road hairpins through a small village, the asphalt suddenly becomes a single polished cobble, and the cycle slips out from under me as easily as a stool from a baby. . . . On my back, in the air, I can see the cycle spinning away from me, beginning to slant and skitter like a bronco, and as Coach always used to tell us, "Relax when falling, go limp and you'll never be hurt," I did, sliding marvelously along on my shoulder blades, the leather trenchcoat saving me even a burn at 45 mph.
The cycle smashes into a house and then topples back, the rear wheel spinning madly. I was afraid to move even though I wasn't even scratched. I lay on my back on the cool cobbles until a small French-

woman came to the door. She glanced at her dented wall, the still furious German machine, my prone body: "Que voulez-vous, Monsieur?" So goes the revolution.

June 5, 1968. But I was talking about becoming Swiss. Hydroptique Basel is getting on my nerves. No revolution here. Perhaps the Swiss are correct in believing that true civilization is possible in the modern world only within a culture without politics. I cannot tell the difference any more between my contempt for their sort of civilized riskless burgher life and the liberal's impulse to make a chaotic America more like them. Again, I've been politicized to no end. It is easy to despise the regulation of the easy earnest life, just come from a state of inane emergency. It's clear I despise the Swiss because they offer no antidote to the bourgeois life they have perfected; that is to say, *we* can learn nothing from them. They are only better bourgeois—more gentle, more uninteresting and more successful. Their probity is the mirror of our anxiety. They are the better part of our worst part.

I make the obligatory stop to buy a watch. I have not seen a newspaper for days. I am filthy, but I have Travelers' Cheques.

Give me watch.

The salesgirl brings out a velvet pad with all the time you need on it. As I pick one out and sign my Traveler's Cheque, she commiserates, "I'm so sorry for your Kennedy."

You stupid cunt, I think. I'm sick of this redundant patronizing. I know all about the cost of that. It's too painful to still believe that we all would have been better off had Jack Kennedy reached his second term, if his program had been allowed to degenerate on its own merits. If *he* had failed, then we would have been rid forever, not only of our banal conspiracy theories, our petty villains, perhaps we would have even turned to confront our paranoia instead of luxuriating in it. If there is an analogy which is appropriate, it is cirrhosis of the liver, in which the normal waste simply begins to accumulate, and the organ's connective tissue must assert itself, must relegate its function within

the system to that of simply keeping itself intact. So rather than ro-
manticizing it by saying we had our potential politics burned out of us
before we were thirty, let us just say that through the effort to keep
ourselves together, we ignored certain habitual functions which in the
end proved quite painful and embarrassing to the entire organism.
The salesgirl didn't have to remind me. I had already left speechwrit-
ing for teaching, since politics between election years seemed only so
much housekeeping. I was in the faculty lounge when the news came.
A medievalist staggered into the lounge shortly after 1:00 screaming,
"Oh fuck us, fuck us!" He had been listening to the ballgame when
the announcement was made. I knew immediately he wouldn't last the
day.
"God, let's pray it wasn't a Negro," another colleague muttered. I went
home like everyone else to be mesmerized by the media for three days,
meditate on the word "catafalque" and then, like at least two million
other people, I wrote a thousand-line elegy to that man, the first serious
poem I ever wrote, and the the last. It was absolutely awful, though not
as bad as others I've seen; but that was the legacy of our puerile politics, which ended as they were inaugurated, with a lousy epic poem. In
the end, we had nothing to fall back upon but our *literariness*, somewhere in which are still buried those idealistic impulses which will require an exemplary public act to exhume them. Is it any wonder that
we have had to find new forms of mourning? Whatever, the following
afternoon, the phone awakened me from a drunken sleep—a friend
from college whom I hadn't talked to in more than two years. He was
sobbing long distance.
"Charlie, Charlie, this is Benny."
Yeah. I know.
"Turn on your TV," he said.
I know, man, I know all about it.
"They got him."
I know, Benny.
"No, you don't understand. They got Oswald too."
I don't know what I said when I hung up. I had no visible or conscious
reaction for some time. I did not feel precisely cheated or hurt or para-

noid—as much as a victim of an incredible naiveté to which I had
thought I had grown immune. Was not public grief a literary idea? Was
it not, like being invaded, or being poor, somehow instructive? But I
was struck, not with despair, nausea, terror, eleventh-hour *Angst,* any
of that classy modernist stuff—but with only the petty grief of melo-
dramas, and the knowledge that we wear so brightly and tiresomely to
this very day: "Okay, keep yourself together baby, and when they try
and tell you something next time, tell 'em to fuck it." The trouble was,
I had known that at the age of five, and had only recently given it up
for the provisional government. I would have never come back from
Europe at all were it not for Kennedy.

At least a week later, on some expressway, I suddenly and inexplicably,
without cue, burst into tears, and my companion had to grab the wheel
to keep us from going off the road. Given this, is it really so hard to
comprehend the apathy of those fifteen years older or the hysteria of
those ten years younger at the time? Those for whom this was even
more pointless?

The salesgirl strapped on my watch, took my disdain and defensiveness
professionally. And then it came out. Wait a minute, I squeaked, *which*
Kennedy are you talking about?

"Don't you know . . . ?"

I ran out into the street surrounded by tape recorders and cameras, past
the newsstand, the chronometers and cuckoo clocks, past a museum
where the entire city had a referendum on whether to buy a Picasso.
Shit, not even *déjà vu.*

Even our terror has been programed; absurdity has become theater.
How many times can you turn your back on them and tell them to fuck
it? The rest of the world is absolutely right about us.

Today, I so envy the Swiss.

The archetypal American is a killer.
|D. H. Lawrence|

Got another letter from my best student today. Not making a go of it in a Canadian Commune, he wants a letter of recommendation to a writers' school. Wants to be a writer. At least he wants to live like one. I have never seen a word of his poetry, nor am I sure he has written any, but now he wants a degree in it. Well, what the hell can I say: join the army?

YOU'RE HAVING A VERY GOOD TIME, ISN'T IT?

And that my ego, bound by no outward force—Once a small child's before it became mine—Should now be strange to me, like a strange dog |Von Hofmannsthal|

How can I give advice to dropouts when I realize how both totally useless and all consuming my education was? Of the first eight grades at eight different private, parochial and public schools in almost every region of the country, which I attended with letter-perfect regularity, I can hardly remember anything. I certainly didn't learn anything except two different systems of subtraction which still confuse me. I read voraciously, out of boredom and self-preservation. I began reading, in fact, to drown out the teacher. I remember thinking, "If life's going to be like this I better read a lot." I read all the classics before the eighth grade, all the "great books" at an age when I could not possibly comprehend their "greatness." I cannot remember a single thing about them today, and I have not returned to them. They were, after all, my childhood, not books at all, so I cannot recall them in any literary terms. When I could have been learning how to sing, dance, type, fix TVs, anything, I existed only insofar as a few isolate minds had imagined the world for me. I believe in words because they kept me alive when there was no reason to be, and I write now basically because I believe that somewhere there is an unborn boy very much like myself who, in order to survive, must believe that I imagined him. There is the nexus of my aesthetics and my politics.

When I emerged periodically to a classroom consciousness, I was abstractly incorrigible and punished regularly. Most of my classes I watched indifferently through a window, banished to the heights of the jungle-gym. And I never once felt bad at being "outside." What was the difference? Through the window, the teacher's mouth flutters ghostly about her text.

|111|

The most interesting thing I can recall *knowing*, before girls came along, is that all information seemed to be of equal value, and the absorption and regurgitation of information required the same localized activity. In America, in school, everything was *truly equal:* spelling, singing, eating, deportment, multiplying, being quiet, running, poetry, push-pin, all experiences of equal duration and intensity. In order to disguise the fact I had preferences, I tried to be first in everything, desperately hoping I would not be caught out, and be forced to admit that some things made me happier than others. Between the ages of four and fourteen, I wrote a long paper on the importance of rice in the world, went to see Lincoln's tomb, cut out some Christmas decorations, wondered why Indians live in tepees, and made a clay brontosaurus. It was a heady time. The most useful thing I learned beyond fucking and driving was how to take 200 deep breaths in rapid succession, then hold my nose and faint. I did this with great skill and regularity, toppling over in the lunch line, falling over in the boys' room, my head banging down the fluted radiators in the gym. My chin is pure scar tissue from this activity, and I often regret very much that I did not keep my skills sharp, though I would be afraid to try it today, in order to be first again.

Had it not been for unceasing athletics between faints, I would surely have gone mad, and I frankly cannot see how anyone brought up in this country can possibly get through American adolescence without totally exhausting himself at least once a day. I used to wonder how the girls survived without such games. Indeed, I still do.

At any rate, in high school, I did learn a couple of things. One, that analyzing reading was different than living the reading. The word was not the thing, after all. I accepted this with equanimity, for I had had it both ways. Also, watching the teachers, it struck me for the first time that there was perhaps a possibility of making a livelihood doing something one liked and thought important; in short, there was the possibility of a true countervailing style and community buried somewhere in this unhappy society. It took me ten years to realize that this was only my idea about them, and that they had never once thought of themselves in this way. Of course, they were the last of the amateurs—

Everything that's happened in this goddamned country in the last fifty years, has happened in, on, around, with, or near a car. |Harry Crews|

"those who can't, teach," as one used to say. Teaching is a "profession" now, and it offers the most reasonable access to bourgeois life, without many of its attendant repressions, and thus attracts people who once might have done *anything* else. One of the enormous sadnesses of "progressive education" is not that it sold out Dewey, but that, as an alternative to middle-class apathy, it offered liberalism, i.e., a politics which is self-serving for one's class by making access to that class a reasonable reality for reasonably motivated people, and offering "welfare" to those for whom the reality was inapplicable or unattainable. Whatever its motives, and they are relatively decent as motives go, it's a lousy politics because nobody knows whether he is acting out of guilt or charity.

Once the Ford Foundation gave some money to send a bunch of us professors to Chicago inner city high schools for several days of inspection and talking to student teachers, We were then asked our recommendations. I was nonplussed. The only thing I could think of was (1) get them some breakfast, (2) buy some books, (3) clean out the urinals. I'm sure my colleagues thought I was being sophisticated—a kind of Matthew Arnoldian despairing profundity—but I was being literal. I did not have the honesty to confess that I hadn't the faintest idea what to tell them, except read, and that my reasons for suggesting *that* could never be articulated. I wouldn't admit that I had never paid any attention to anything that I was told in class, and that if they couldn't educate or even keep the attention of a "normal middle-class kid" like myself, then what to do with those kids whose hatred and/or apathy had much more specific and intense correlatives? I still wouldn't know what to say, for I neither feared nor loved those children; to take such people "seriously" amounts to just another way of keeping one's distance. And all I know is that if we were taught by the "losers" of the previous generation, it will be interesting to see what being taught by professionals will bring. I have this vision of one kid in an empty classroom looking *out* through a window at the rest of the class and the teacher, perched wordlessly upon a renovated, endless jungle-gym. . . .

In the university, I found out two more things: (1) that people could actually make a living doing what I did up to the eighth grade, reading

In the conditions of modern life the rule is absolute, the race which does not value trained intelligence is doomed. Not all your heroism, not all your social charm, not all your wit, not all your victories on land and sea, can move back the finger of fate. Today we maintain ourselves. Tomorrow science will have moved forward one more step, and there will be no appeal from the judgment which will then be pronounced upon the uneducated.
|Alfred North Whitehead|

the same books over and over, drowning out what was around you for the hell of it, because nothing else seemed worth the candle, and (2) I learned to quote Herbert Mueller, "In the last analysis, there is no last analysis." I had, of course, already known that. But now I had corroborative detail to add to my otherwise parochial and personal narrative. In the first month of college, we had Hume's *Ethics,* Freud's *Civilization and Its Discontents,* and Ayer's *Language, Truth and Logic.* It would seem from that point on both conventional bourgeois life and mysticism were out. Beyond this, our pragmatism was officially certified as cultural relativism. A large football player (good block, bad catch) stood up in a seminar and addressed the professor of history incredulously, "You mean you *can't* predict anything after all? Then what the hell are we here for?" I also realized for the first time that the only thing that really mattered to me were "the arts," but that they did not, as I had been told, make you a "better person"—indeed, if one had to generalize, it seemed rather the other way around. That is the crux of modernism and a notion which would lead, eventually, to political considerations. And yet, despite the forced atheistic sophistication, it was clear that our current fears and confusions could be linked, even through the most cursory examination by a punk kid, to what had happened in the world in the last few hundred years. We *were* part of a history, and if reason and history were not the same, our mean condition was nevertheless explicable. We had *not* sprung fully armed from the womb of the void after all. I would have liked to have written home about that, would have wished at least one ancestor of mine could have survived to estimate my wonder. Given this glimpse of seamlessness if not the sense of things as they are, it is difficult for me to understand people who do not take delight in being able to walk into a good library, totally ignorant of a subject, and in half an hour have within physical reach a good portion of what better men than you have thought about it. And more, to assimilate this and come to your own conclusion, *to produce a tentative order,* gave me, at least, a physical sensation equal to that of competitive sports or uncompetitive sex. It was a prelude, I suppose, to the first complexion of what used to be called "aesthetic bliss," which means, I think, that range of feeling when producing and consuming becomes an undifferentiated activity, when you are *in* time, not simply defined by it.

I did not understand the importance of this activity—beyond the pleasure it gave me—until so many of my friends went mad by definition (i.e., were unable to write another word) in various graduate schools. Far from providing an equilibrium, the critical method, if it is pursued honestly, pushes one to a consideration of the metapossibilities of language, insists upon the creation of one's own voice *beyond* a proven methodology and acceptable style. And one inevitably faces the choice of whether to transmit and evaluate culture or to break it up, and make it over again, I'm afraid, in one's own image. This is not simply personalism vs. objectivity, but the recognition of two superficially opposed truths: the first, that criticism as an *a priori* discipline, while fascinating in itself, is not often very helpful in producing that aesthetic consciousness which criticism proposes to examine. Yet on the other hand, the analytical critic pushes just far enough into non-discursive experience to realize that there is a language available to both isolate geniuses and the functionally illiterate, that places the critic's honest worry, training, hard work, restraint and scrupulousness in a severely reduced perspective. . . . We will not fully understand our time until a mind appears which can demonstrate, in critical terminology, the phenomenon of the critical method turning upon itself, frequently producing a mentalistic aberration directly at odds with the very values and perception it sees itself as preserving.

One of our problems is that you can walk through any university today and get the feeling that no one in a tenured position ever agonized over such questions. In a sense, this disguise is the intellectual counterpart of that of the successful businessman who lived though the Depression and would have us believe that his success is due strictly to rigorous and relentless application of sound procedures. . . .

Even if the society of knowledge should succeed in showing how the complete freedom of the knowing mind from the impact of particular group interests is possible, and what such freedom would mean, it would leave the epistemological question precisely where it was. A hypothetical "purified" mind could go on indefinitely asking itself the question whether, now that it is free of the distortions caused by the social milieu, it lives in conditions of "essential rationality"—and it would be powerless to resolve this question. . . . |Leszek Kolakowski|

The modern university, it seems to me, may be characterized by five interlocking functions: (1) an ivory tower in which ladies and gentlemen are certified, and pure research is taken on by a few pros; (2) a handmaiden to the industrial state, where engineers for a high consumption economy are turned out; (3) a sanctuary for active resistance against the industrial state; (4) an institution independent of the state, and actually of the culture as a whole, creating an adversary ideology or methodology to challenge the status quo; (5) a community of unlike minds pursuing, in a consensus of neutrality, highly individual truths. I can admit to no great enthusiasm for any of these as strict alternatives; a university can really do only one thing: provide familiarity with linear sequential logic in a variety of symbolic forms. It cannot in itself provide either an aesthetic or a politics. It cannot, of itself, convince anyone of *a priori* truths, it cannot, of itself, create an effective community or missionary force beyond itself in any context which doesn't play by its own rules. It cannot avoid the conflict of vocational training and pure research, between its avowed aims and the sort of people from whom it must get its money, and it should make fewer presumptions that it can. It *can* have two social functions beyond this: (1) to create a calculated hiatus in a culture which understands progress in the most crudely measurable way, and in which everyone is encouraged to find out what *in fact* is interesting to them; (2) to keep artists, scientists and engineers free from constraint, contingent with one another, and aware of the society which does not share their expertise and/or power. It is a sad fact that such a community, elitist and stratified as it may seem, can be achieved only through certain shared political assumptions. It is even sadder that in our present society, the university is the only institution which can provide this, and sadder still, that most don't even try. So while I would prefer the university to function like the medieval church, as a unifier and synthesizer of thought, the one I will have to support will be more of a 12th century church, providing dispensation to those in need, pardons to those who think they have strayed, and sanctuary for heretics.

Democracy, crudely understood, is based upon shared information made available equally. Modern experience shows us there is too much information for anyone to digest, let alone share. You can restrict information, but that's totalitarian, or you can let people fight for information, and that's anarchy, or you can let elitist institutions gather and interpret and disseminate this information, a kind of oligopoly. In this respect, universities have not become irrelevant. They have failed because they have become redundant. In other words, they are increasingly processing information which is available through other channels, and they do not even reconstitute the information; they only certify it. The university can recapture its social function only by concerning itself with alternative, *privileged* information. Methodology it can pass on, but, like the church, it will be ultimately judged on its alternative communication system, not on its peculiar expertise, but on the secrets, the mysteries it recognizes.

When I try to remember my own university experience apart from the insomnia and humiliation, the post cards which arrived informing me I was in the bottom 10% of my class in "intellectual skills" and urging me to report for "remedial attention," it makes me wonder today if my happiness at finally learning something only indicates a severe defect of character.

The only time I ever went to a psychiatrist I went to the Health Clinic and told the resident shrink I couldn't sleep. He told me to masturbate more. "But *that's* not the problem, Doctor," I tried to explain. He told me to come back. I went and bought a new bed.

The only time I went to see a religious man—to tell him I wanted a wider political involvement—I visited the university chaplain, notorious for both his CIA and civil-rights activism, and he tried to convince me of the necessity for believing in God as a predicate for moral action. I could only complain, "But don't you see, sir, I became a liberal precisely because I could no longer be a Christian."

And the only time I visited a writer for advice, a sheaf of manuscript in my hands, asking him how to get published, he pounded on the desk. "You gotta get up early and start writing, write all morning to lunch, don't eat too much, get back to your desk, write, write, you gotta think,

In place of the great historic movement arising from the conflict between the productive forces already acquired by men in their social relations, which no longer correspond to these productive forces . . . in place of the practical and violent action of the masses by which alone these conflicts can be resolved—in place of this vast, prolonged and complicated movement, M. Proudhon supplies the evacuating motion of his own head. |*Letter of December 28, 1846, from Marx to P. V. Annekov*|

eat, *live* writing . . ." and I took my poor manuscript and went away. What else could they say? They had their routines for impossible questions, just as I developed mine for the Ford Foundation. I bless them, as I do my teachers, for not allowing me for one minute to use them as models for living when I was most vulnerable. I worked hard for them because it fascinated me; I worked hard because I wanted their respect; I assumed that most of them knew more about their subjects than I did, and I was right to do so; when the regimentation seemed to outweigh the rewards, when I wanted to do more than imitate their methodologies, I got out. That this should seem at the least remarkable today strikes me as so heartbreaking I can hardly bear to contemplate it.

. . . the advantage of the new movement is that we do not want to anticipate the world dogmatically, but only to discover the new by way of the criticism of the old world. Until now, philosophers kept the solution of all mysteries inside their desks, and the stupid uneducated world merely had to open its mouth and the fried dove of absolute knowledge would fly in. Philosophy is now secular, for which the best proof is that philosophical consciousness itself feels the pain of the struggle not merely externally, but also internally. It is not our task to construct the future and to deal with everything once and for all, but it is clear what we have to do at present—I am thinking of the merciless criticism of everything that exists—*merciless criticism in the sense that it is not afraid of its findings, and just as little afraid of conflict with the existing powers. . . It will be found that what is involved is not to draw a large dash between past and future, but to* realize *the ideas of the past. . . it will be found that humanity does not start a new task, but consciously carries through the old.* |Marx to Ruge, 1843|

ncidentally, I had this professor my first year who said we ought to get out and meet the *proletariat*. The way he said it sounded very much like my mother when she spoke of the "common people," although she'd just as soon I stayed away from them. They were agreed in one respect however; that I couldn't handle them. As I look back on it now, I think the professor's vested interest in me oddly stronger. Because he was basically frightened (as opposed to my mother who merely suffered), he provided me with a surer principle of selection.

He was born on an Iowa farm, the high table gossip went; one of those guys who read all night after the chores were done, standing up "so's he could stamp 'is feet, keep warm." He still worked standing up when I knew him, at a stoolless accountant's desk, but I think more because of bad circulation than from habit. By the time he was twelve, so the story goes, he had read every single book in the village library, including the encyclopedias, mail order catalogs and train schedules. Blessed at birth with a photographic memory, he could recite entire Robert Ingersoll lectures at eight without a stutter. His spelling bees had the quality of a revival meeting. He could tell you today the time, destination and second-class fare of every train that left Ames, Iowa, between 1913 and 1922.

He was not withered by his brilliance largely as a result of his size, a stooped seven feet due to a pituitary as far ranging as his memory. He could fell a small-town dolt with either a quip or a fist. And I saw him many times in the University Post Office go through spectacular feats of coordination to retrieve his mail from a box, allotted on purpose, certainly, in the row six inches off the floor. His face was indented and his skin shingly. His hair more maroon than red, falling in half-hearted ringlets. His ears were enormous. He walked with his arms motionless and stooped over, like a pajamaed child in the morning trying to conceal an erection. For that we called him Mr. Pants.

The town banker, as a matter of personal and professional pride, had seen Mr. Pants through the State University, where he had taken a degree in Romance Languages in two years, and then like so many Americans who see their future all too clearly, who feel themselves trapped on an escalator even though it is ascending, willfully broke the inevitability of his progress, tried to find out more. He held the usual jobs; he worked for a year on a Ford assembly line, washed dishes, managed a YMCA locker room, boxed kangaroos at county fairs, punched cattle, sold encyclopedias door to door, dug graves, edited a radical journal (suppressed in the mails), rode the rods for a time, drove a stock car, painted a mural for the dining room of a Panamanian Hotel, stoked boilers on a freighter: that whole bit that qualifies you for dissent in this country, and which in the end only amounts to a book jacket blurb of occupations to certify your blighted sensitivity. "The whole world is easier to come by than any single part of it," he used to say.

Mr. Pants was not as hurt by the Depression as he was fascinated by it; the concept of failure engages us much more than the brute facts of failing—just as it is the idea of success and not its fruits which compels us. For analysis, he chose Marxism, admittedly because it was quicker.

Marxism, he told us once, failed not because of any perversion of the system, but was doomed from the first, since it misunderstood the nature of capitalism. The thing that one learned in the thirities was not particularly that the Soviets were corrupt, but that capitalism doesn't require prey as much as successive enemies. Without a feudal structure to attack, capitalism had become unchallenged and irresponsible—the Stalinists were not destroying capitalism; they were making possible its resurrection—justifying its relative tolerance and pluralism at the very moment it had broken down from within.

Sociological investigation bored him after a time, however, and around 1936, he went back to the farm to help. Things got better, but shortly after his return, on a foggy fall harvest evening, his father fell into a reaper and died without even jamming the mechanism. His mother had already died and his sisters married, so he went to New York to work simultaneously on degrees in law and medicine. Unfortunately or no, the Spanish Civil War soon cut those interests short. He recognized it immediately as "a state of affairs worth fighting for," purchased a pair of Beretta automatics with gutta-percha handles and showed up one night in a hotel on the Avenida José Antonio in Madrid, where several prominent American journalists were hoarding food. Shocked by this, he allowed himself to be goaded into a fight, subsequently breaking the arm of the largest and most belligerent of the journalists, who had to cancel his trip to the front and stayed in Madrid for the duration. Each time the shelling began, this now famous man would dash through the streets brandishing his damaged arm and crying, "Falangiste! Falangiste!" No one knew if he was cheering or cursing them.

Mr. Pants, who will remain nameless for security reasons (mine, not his), was, incidentally, a member of my secret fraternity. We had a house near the ocean, and once a year, without fail, he would come and tell us about his part in the Spanish War. There was neither nostalgia nor feigned dryness to his account. He just related what happened—about how difficult it was to choose which outfit to fight with, whether it was better to use good Soviet arms with the labor union front or obsolescent arms with the Trotskyites, things like that—but this was soon to be relieved by a sniper's bullet in the retreat from Toledo Alcazar. He was shot through the windpipe and saved himself by performing a self-tracheotomy with his fountain pen. He spent the duration in the hospital like the rest of them, writing gentle letters to the parents of those he had known in the Abraham Lincoln Brigade, furious letters to Roosevelt, doing neck exercises, and translating neglected Spanish poets. When he got back to the States, he found that the letters to the President had made him a security risk, and that, coupled with his injury, kept him out of the War he had anticipated and fought to prevent. He took a job as a male nurse during the day and worked the night shift in a munitions factory. He did this for four years, until Hiroshima, when he was among the first, in a long letter of denunciation to the *New York Times*, to protest the act. Later he was arrested for picketing the White House during a national emergency, spent the duration in a special detention camp in Vermont among Trotskyites, conscientious objectors, anarchists, a few Japanese truck gardeners, and a great many Nazi prisoners of war. Nevertheless, in the aftermath, suspicion gave way to the bull market—he was set free and found to his amazement that not only had his book of Spanish translations been awarded a prestigious prize, but his letters to Roosevelt had been clandestinely circulated by the Republican National Committee in areas of anti-Catholic sentiment. He made use of several foundation fellowships, took a position at some progressive women's college in the east, and then, at the height of the McCarthy scare, presented himself at the university with an agonizingly long list of his past indiscretions and dared them to hire him, which of course, they did.

"Irony always saves us from profundity," he used to say to close our secret fraternity meeting: "to stand firm in the middle is, I assure you, gentlemen, the most difficult of stances. But because it is the most difficult, you must not confuse it with the most moral. It is easy to see what is right; the difficulty is to attain the position from which being right matters. That is something I never achieved. Morality without power is meaningless, to reverse a political cliché (I assume you were aware it is a cliché), and quite possibly immoral as well. And our choice frequently seems to be between morality and humanity—those situations when it is preferable to be human than principled. There are other times when a single human being or perhaps a single idea must be protected from civilization itself. That's morality. If you ever, gentlemen, see an occasion where the two are combined, don't pass it up." I often wonder what he would have thought of our hapless rage at our imperial politics, had he lived. He would have probably been reminding us of the atrocities of the Viet Cong.

Thursday evenings he always invited a group of us up to his apartment for spaghetti. There were such things as a special chair Mr. Pants had made for himself from seaman's rope and wrought iron, and when he sank into it, it sounded as if a mizzen mast was coming down out of the dark. He was also an amateur archaeologist, and along the length of his concrete block and pine plank bookcases glittered hundreds of arrowheads, amulets, pestles, coprolites and rare quartzes. Once, when I was going through an old *National Geographic* in the stacks, I came across a picture of him. He was on some expedition, Peru, I think, and the picture had been taken with him standing in an excavation to minimize his size in relation to his colleagues clustered about him. His name was in the credits although misspelled, but you knew it was him—even though he had a sombrero pulled over his face—by how tiny the pick hammer seemed in his hand. He dangled it between two fingers. Yet when I asked Mr. Pants about this, he denied ever having been to Peru.

Mr. Pants had married one of his graduate students, a full twenty years younger than himself, Jewish, bowlegged and beautiful like Egyptian queens from the long neck up. She looked as if she had just come in from throwing marbles under the cops' horses' feet at the Haymarket. They had two children when I last saw them, five-year-old boy twins with sharp dark Semitic features and Iowan dispositions. They sat like Roman wolves under his swollen legs the entire evening, saying nothing, playing half-heartedly with broken model autos and listening to the break and fall of conversation. I remember picking them up; they were always perfectly calm and affectionate, but there was nothing easy about them, they searched you out with their eyes and fingers—it was like picking up a miniature concert pianist or physicist. His wife, Katrin, usually stood in a corner with her arms folded, smiling, her head cocked to one side, listening to her husband put his students on. One time she evidently grew tired of this ritual, brought out a balalaika and sang some central European songs in a pure arching alto. When she was through, Mr. Pants disappeared for a moment and returned with a homemade single-string washtub bass viol to provide a resonant continuo. The first few times I went, I remember having a terrible compulsion to see their bed, and on the pretext of going to the bathroom I snuck into their bedroom. I was amazed to find only a bed of average size, not even a double, and realized that considering his bulk and the severity of his desires, she must have slept literally on top of him or not at all. The simplicity of this made a great impression on me at the time. I mentioned once, offhand, that one thing which dissuaded me from going into teaching was the general homeliness of faculty wives. Katrin was passing his chair at the time and he grabbed her by the waist, spinning her around to face me.

"You find my wife homely, Mr. What's-your-name?"

I stammered, saying I didn't mean *her;* that, in fact, I found her quite . . . disconcerting. But both of them just stood there and stared at me, and in the end, I had to get up and kiss her. It was the only way to get out of it.

I didn't see much of Mr. Pants my last few years. His care for us had its calculated effect. We withdrew more and more into our own confusions. I no longer had the time for a pleasant Thursday evening, busy with my own private versions of the Soviet-Nazi pact. He needed us, but it is to his credit that he never cultivated protégés.

The last time I saw him was during those first days of the Hungarian "Revolution." There was a rally on the steps of the library to raise money for refugees. Mr. Pants had been asked to speak in lieu of the president, who had canceled out at the last moment as a result of cancer. There were bonfires in the street, and he stood against the leaded casement windows casting his absurd shadow up into the arches. He made a short quiet speech in which he invoked Burke—you know, about "all that evil needs to triumph is that good men do nothing"—and after that, fire buckets were passed for contributions. Then one of the singing groups broke out banjos, guitars, and started yelling the good old songs, "Which Side Are You On?" "Row the Boat, Michael," "The Union Way," "This Land Is My Land." The same music, the same militance, now flip-flopped. Mr. Pants passed me in the crowd and I grabbed his coat sleeve . . . He winked balefully, stooped beneath a gothic arch and disappeared into the rare book room. . . .

The money collected brought three Hunky refugees to the university, fine high-cheekboned, very brilliant guys, and one was taken into our secret fraternity for a night to tell how he had pitched Molotov cocktails at tanks and the rest. We knew then that we would never have *our* Civil War, our "state of affairs worth fighting for." No, our little war would be one in which being principled *or* human was equally inconsequential.

The last I heard of Mr. Pants was from a newspaper clipping somebody forwarded to me. He evidently had been passed up for tenure and was out on the West Coast teaching at some big public university. He had caused an unprecedented furor there by flunking an entire class for plagiarism. They had all used the same fraternity file or something. He hadn't understood that it had been that way for years, that they knew exactly what they were doing. He thought by catching them up, he could shame them. And I remembered the last thing he said to us. "When you graduate, boys, you will go out in this world as the best prepared, most talented, most capable and intelligent youth this country has yet produced. You deserve to lead. But the problem is, the other people don't know that."

I gave much thought to this "proletariat." Who were they, those who **German Ideology** "would produce the material conditions of a new society out of the de- **German Ideology** clining accomplishments of the old," who would not allow their political **German Ideology** thought to obscure their *"social instinct"*—those who would be "forced by an ineluctable, irremediable and imperious *distress*—by practical *necessity*—to revolt against their *own* inhumanity?(!)" Were they the ones who live in towns that have "Join the U.S. Marines" in block letters on the movie marquees instead of a movie, the ones who squat a Jesus on their dashboards, the ones who wear nylon socks with a little arrow running up the anklebone, the ones who buy the jelly in gas station johns that either speeds you up or holds you back, the ones who buy suction pistols to remove blackheads, the ones who sell four thousand packages of garden seed for one set of china, the people who almost always have to say hello?

I can remember lying on the checkerboard linoleum floor of a kitchen looking up the legs of my grandmother's laundress. She washed, and I watched the mammoth pink Irish thighs caress each other. If she moved, I followed her along the floor, pushing myself on my back like a grasshopper. She always wore sweat socks and crepe-soled sandals. I followed underneath her for hours at a time and I can't remember her ever saying anything about it, or for that matter, my seeing anything of note.

When I was a little older, we moved to the suburbs where we had no basement or attic. That was fine with me as the maid's room could be approached on any one of a number of pretexts; I hid among the whining gas meters listening to Lena entertaining friends. They would drive for two hours from South Chicago, enormous mortgaged autos, pick her up, go all the way back to the city, get her back in time to fix breakfast. She was a lovely girl and a kind of genius. One night her apron caught fire and she just walked into the dining room ablaze and asked to be put out. My father tore a curtain down and rolled her up in it. In the summer, when she returned from those late dates, I used to climb out on the roof and listen to the Buicks and Mercurys and DeSotos ease her back. I watched the parked cars sway through the pneumatic summer night. And in the morning, at breakfast, I stared at her, amazed that anyone was capable of such savage rhythmic weight.

Her cure for the common cold was to spit it out, and she carried a coffee can with her for that purpose when she was ill, which was often. We used to watch the wrestling matches on TV with a can between us on the sofa. Occasionally, if I concentrated on the spot in the middle of my forehead, I could muster up enough juice to add to the pot.

"But it's fixed," I screamed at the late-night spectacle.

"Wouldn't pay a nickel to see a fair one," she said.

Or Jimmy Gene Ray? My mother said that he was "common." He had no mother, for one thing. His father drove a cab in town. They lived in the city, and the father brought his son out to play in the park while he worked. That's where I met him. In the rose garden. We used to sit in the latticework cupola of the garden and sing, picking things off the radio and harmonizing. And we weren't ashamed of it. You'd be surprised how many people are. People would stand around the cupola just to hear us. When we quit they would say things like, "This is certainly a nice way to spend a Sunday." Young girls would pinch their escorts' arm, gaze into his face, and he would straighten up and perhaps ask us if we knew their favorite. We never did. But there were other things we did too. Or rather Jimmy Gene did them, and I went along. One was to run along the walks, right there in the rose garden, and pull up ladies' Sunday dresses. Jimmy Gene would run in front, run as if I were chasing him, and then when we got near the appropriate couple, he would veer in, and with a grand swipe, send the lady's skirt above her midriff.

I never did any of the yanking myself. I ran along in front; at first the pretext, then the judge. I announced the extent of the attempt. "Legger!" I yelled if it were that, "Yowsa!" if there was a glimpse of those wonderful pastel triangles, and of course, "You gotit!" too. The thing was incomplete without me. Jimmy Gene *did* it, but *I* humiliated. So there was Jimmy Gene, stooped over at fifty miles an hour, the escort yelling, wild with helpless rage, his fine defenses outflanked, the lady locked in a swirl of her own devices, and then me, gliding by, noting the moment.

"Crotch-hopping," we called it. We got so good at it that we could run full speed bent close to the ground like Indian scouts and lift everything—crinolines, halfslips, knit wear, even shifts. And we were in dead earnest. We did it because it was better than singing in the cupola, because nothing like that had ever happened in the rose garden before, and because we left in our wake an astonishment.

Later we worked at a filling station together, me summers, he forever. I worked nightshift, cleaned the grease pits and lift, washed the pumps, closed the place down. Though he was off at four, Jimmy Gene always stayed.

Polish Rudy who ran the station had a knot in the back from a Jap bayonet and whenever he lifted anything the veins stood out in his arms like a road map. Every night when I came to relieve him and Jimmy Gene, he asked me good-naturedly, "Getting any ass lately, guy? Getting any on the side?" Then he would grin and take a mock swing at me, making a noise of destruction with his tongue.

Once he pulled it in front of a customer, some salesman in a Pontiac. "Hey punk," he yelled. I was washing the windshield while he got the gas. "Getting any on the side lately?"

But I was ready for him. After all, it was at least the hundredth time he had said it. And I went on wiping the window as I answered, "Oh, is there a place for it there too?"

Well, that was it. Again I had humiliated and got away clean. Polish Rudy's mouth dropped open, doubling up over the fender until the tank overflowed and gas cascaded over the Pontiac's trunk. The salesman didn't care, helplessly pointing a finger at Rudy, then at me, shaken in a noiseless rupturing guffaw. Rudy, soaked with gasoline and tears, limped around the car, holding himself, repeating that comeback over and over in the hisses between his laughs. "Is there a place . . . Hee . . . Is there a . . . Haa," and so on. Finally he disappeared down the ramp into the grease pit, shaking his head and still squeezing himself. I made change for the salesman, but he closed his hand around mine when I gave it to him.

"Keep it buddy," he said, "You've made my day." Then he put his hydromatic in gear and went.

"I would've given a million dollars to be able to have thought of that," Jimmy Gene said solemnly, then walked away.

I had gotten $1.35 clear and knew for the first time how Jimmy Gene felt about those strangely flattered ladies in the rose garden and *their* tips. Our lasting gifts come through such spontaneous humiliation. But spontaneity, if it is to work, must be deeply practiced. It's practice that makes a comeback to the hundredth repetition possible, the capacity to run at full speed close to the ground. And practicing to be spontaneous has a lot to do with commonness, "degradation conscious of its degradation," as old Hegel would have it.

At any rate, late that night when Rudy, the salesman and I had tired of surprising each other, and Jimmy Gene had gone home with his father, I was very depressed and felt like . . . driving. I didn't want to take the highway where I was liable, or leave the station open, so I just circled the pumps in second, tires hissing on the hot tar, cruising around until it was time to close. So I know what happens when you're common. I've done my espionage, and I had my labor theory of value at thirteen, though I was no worker. I mentioned this to Mr. Pants once.

"Christ, young man, who's the snob? You just reverse it, that's all. You don't accuse them; you just assume them. You take them for granted. You leave them alone. That's the final prejudice, you know. That's the last thing people want. To be left alone. The only *class* distinction I know of is between those people who prefer to be left alone when they're screwed up, and those who want to be comforted . . ."

It was odd. He ignored them but he liked them. I wanted to help them because I didn't like them. It reminded me of the time I had asked Jimmy one night as we were closing what he wanted out of life. "Well, it's simple what I want, " he said slowly, "What I want is to have a family and be able to take them to a good restaurant once a week. This restaurant has been around for a long time, always been run by another family. One of them is always there, overseeing things. On the inside, it has no music or pictures, just a lot of red wood—not redwood—but *real red wood.* It is one of the best restaurants in the world. They make their own ice cream, bread and chili. They put a dish of butter on the table, and you put it on your plate yourself. And the catsup is in its own unwiped bottle, instead of in a plastic gun with water. They ask you if you want seconds. In this restaurant there is a waiter, say named Herman, who isn't a member of the family, but has been there from the beginning anyway. He knows everyone's name, including mine; he knows my wife and kid on sight. Once a week we come in. I shake hands with Herman, he takes the wife's coat and tells the kid he's bigger. Then we all sit down in the booth and he tells me what's good today. We don't ask. He tells us. I maybe say, "My wife's not very hungry so she wants a small filet, the boy wants a hot fudge walnut sundae without the walnuts, and you know what I want." He takes the order and then comes back right away with two old John Jamisons on shaved ice and a cranberry cocktail for my kid. As we finish I call Herman over and mention that the kid is captain of his ball team and is currently hitting a hefty .527. Herman thinks this is terrific, and the kid jumps on me the rest of dinner for embarrassing him like that. When we're done Herman don't mention the overtips, and when Herman goes home to his bachelor flat, takes off his white coat and his big black shoes, he lies down on the bed and hopes my kid will keep his streak going so it won't be difficult to ask me about it next week. See, because if you can't have all that—you spend your whole goddamned life looking for it."

And I realized then that in America there can be no proletariat as long as everybody has their own, as long as everyone thinks "they" is somebody else.

So much for Jimmy Gene. I remember how he and I used to fish in the park duck pond after dusk. It was full of goldfish, some a foot long, bloated with bread thrown from shore. Whole loaves were thrown there. Kids slung them like discs. Slice after slice of miracle-whipped, sun-cracked, vitamin-enriched golden-crusted manna spiraled out over the water.

If a duck got to the bread first he would eat it this way: *down* with the eight-color head like a rocker arm, right through the center of the slice. He kept at it, hammering, squeezing the water from the pulp before he swallowed it, working from the center out, until there was nothing left but a circle of crust. Then with a single movement he broke the circle, dove beneath one tattered end, and leaning back swallowed it like a snake.

The carp, goldenfish, were both less efficient and more subtle. When they got there first, the slice would quaver, bob until, in a matter of minutes, its miracle fibers sufficiently punished, the bread simply separated like a cloud, broke into a film of particles which sank to orange blunt lipless mouths.

Either way they both got too fat. And we would lie in the shrubbery at night, Jimmy Gene and I, with a loaf of unsalable bread between us, and with a hooked string and sinker, pull those carp flopping and shimmying across the olive water like nothing at all.

We never ate them, of course, they were filthy fish. We just put them in a pile and let them strangle. They stank even before they died.

Once in a while, too, we got a duck. Unintentionally, of course. When a greedy bill swooped and swallowed in one motion there was nothing you could do. Or rather there were two things. With the hook gone smoothly to the gullet you could just yank and rip that duck right through the throat. The red bread would sink, the duck would scream, stand in the water, swim a spiral down. You'd rather kill fifty fish than one duck. It was bad publicity. We never recovered the body. Freed fish lose their mouths, 'scaped ducks their anuses.

That only happened a few times and usually we just let go of the string. Then the old bird would swing away, trailing twenty feet of twine from the corner of his mouth. He swallowed it slowly, I suppose, unconscious of it at first; only when it caught on some bottom snag and jerked him off course did he know. Gradually, the hook's legacy would be absorbed until it formed a compact sodden mass against the ribs, a false entangled heart next to the gaudy real one.

I did some research once to ascertain whether a duck's gullet is like that of the oyster or deer who make functional use of their cancers. But I found nothing. I would like to think that he has no such coating, no inner defenses, and that the hook, wound with string by the convulsions of his own chemistry, rests against his chest like a precious locket on the inside of a soldier's lapel. And that one day, while flying south for the winter, a shot will ring out and he will fall into the reeds. But before the dogs reach him, as in the movies, he will awake, and inspecting himself, find that the absorbed old wound has deflected the shot from softer regions, that he just has been dazed, that a *miracle* has saved his life!

So we lay in the bushes with bread, rolls of hemp, irreversible hooks, and the stench of inconsequential but still immoral death. Jimmy Gene the Carp, professor, and me the Duck.

So here's Italy again. How's it going to heal you this time? We no longer know the seasons; the American senses have atrophied; we believe too much in our eyes, our radical epistemological doubt invades both our ideas and our emotions. No wonder we fall back on lonely slick surfaces—blue haze, orange earth, brush fires almost indistinguishable from the natural umber and mocha fields. Lemon tree, cypress, acacia, wisteria, the crimson drooping St. Joseph vine, and in the dusk, the derelict aqueducts turn lavender with the hills. Nope. They won't get you back the world anymore. I look in my journal for 1962 in this same month in Italy—the same adjectives, the same nouns to document the pastoral, cypress, acacia, wisteria, etc. Also the following observation:

RISORGIMENTO

In the society of the period, in which everyone was worth for his intelligence and capacity, Humanism, which exalted the human personality, had a big reception. . . .
|The Renaissance: A Guide|

"During this interminable afternoon in early July, the large black Lancia of the carabinieri droned through the town. There had been an accident on the coastal highway. A crimson Bugatti had come over a rise to disintegrate in a hayrick drawn across the road; the driver had been thrown clear and killed instantly. He lay on his back beside the road in a white polo shirt, tight twill trousers and brilliantly polished boots. Entirely unmarked, his injury had been internal. The rick's driver sat alone on the other side of the road, hands clenched at his sides. The dead man's mistress had been sent for and she stood beside his corpse staring tearlessly up the hill he had died descending. A crowd of field hands looked at neither man nor machine, but also up the hill. Their eyes were following the pattern of his skid marks that decorated the road with a series of black whorls, undulating from one curb to the other: a perfectly equidistant transcript of his death-slide. It was apparent that, finding his brakes insufficient, he had used all his long-developed skill in throwing the car into lateral drifts no less than seven times before he had at last plunged into the rick. Dying in such a way allowed for his present unmarred condition; *a orglio calmo*—in pride relaxed, as an old man muttered. The carabinieri propped the man upright in the back of the Lancia, and with his mistress kneeling beside the body, returned him to his villa.

|128|

"I find myself curiously detached from the entire incident. I remember a similar accident which had taken the life of a powerful and respected man in the town of my youth. He had been found in the burned-out shell of his Cadillac with a woman to whom he was not married in a ravine along the main highway. The car had skidded for three hundred yards along an embankment before they had gone over. The woman turned out to be a widow working as a waitress in the next town, and the newspapers dwelt on little else for a month. The wife, after a peremptory breakdown, took her children and moved to New York. *And what is the difference between this Cadillac and this Bugatti, these two curious crowds, this mistress and waitress, those two lifeless princes . . .* one death finished in itself, the other relevant only in aftermath? I can make no sense of it, wondering why for them death was the last part of life, while for us it was a sin."

Quaint juxtaposition. And not just a beginner straining for contingencies. Because the possibility of our learning anything from each other has rapidly diminished over the last decade. They are becoming like us, and Italy becomes only the latest manifestation of pollution, of clogged space, of quintessential *crowdedness,* without purgative *mob.* Brigands are weighing ambush behind pyramids of beer cans. New ugly villas everywhere, on the peaks of this and that. Not a silent stretch north of Firenze. The catacombs are a positive relief, physically the nicest place to live in all Italy. Ah, those early Christians, they had it both ways. A secret hideout, where one can always be reached in an emergency. An infinite progression of caves in which to inscribe one's fantasies, your enemies snuffling unawares above you in the humidity, the knowledge that what you use for light to see will blacken out what you've written; all technology auto-destruct, your symbology a jelly-electric commentary on itself.

I know nothing about cinegraphic technicalities, but with good will, one can master it all. Life has already taught me to become a translator of poets, a literary critic, an author, a proofreader, a teacher, an editorial consultant, all things I knew nothing whatever about when I was twenty. I can learn this too. You'll have just as much to do: learning your lines, dancing, posing, speaking Italian. Until now, Italian-American collaboration has produced nothing worth while. . . . |Cesar Pavese to Constance Dowling, March 1950|

Florence is recovering from her flood. They are working fast to get the riverfront ready for the heaviest influx of tourists, and the work proceeds with little attention to detail or texture. Moorish and Palladian windows are replaced with picture windows sent in Care Packages from Scarsdale and Winnetka. Kangaroo skin key cases have gone up 20%. The height of the floodwaters is demarked by plaques on every wall. One more catastrophe absorbed, subsumed and cataloged. The arches and tiles on the rebuilt Ponte Vecchio have been chiseled from defunct American Winn-Dixie shopping centers. We who have barely one coat, and a borrowed sharp one at that, have set the tone for the Restoration. How does a nation lose *only one* of its senses so severely and so fast in just a few centuries? The grand villas gone under, the gardens overgrown, the Renaissance murals painted over with Victor Emmanuel's *trompe l'oeils* and the Po now resurfaced with real electronic waves, plastic trout, breasting a family-type restaurant with proto-Spanish decor. Their fear, their tragedies have taught them nothing. The view that Time cannot alter, the Chamber of Commerce can. Well, in any case, the clouds still congeal roseate over the Ponte San Trinitas at sunset. The tourists are now directed to what was destroyed, what is no longer there. The east facade of the Baptistry which is not there, the obliterated Fra Lippo Lippi which is not there, the volumes at the Biblioteca Nazionale which are no longer there. Down in their basement American students are trying to save Italian books, the books they cannot read, could not previously touch, the books which have come to them in decline, poring over them—not quite like Petrarch scanning, fondling the Homer he could not understand—soggy incunabula, putrescent artifacts, they piece them back together a page at a time for the posterity which is also no longer theirs. The Piazza del Signoria's copy of David, scum of the high water mark on his foul balls, the Duomo, its base now inscribed with the names of its latest donors in its greatest hour of need—no Medicis here—it has been put back together by the combined efforts of such as the Girl Scouts of The Netherlands, and the Jay-Cees of Cincinnati. And good old Perseus, my favorite, a lion with a lily in its mouth underfoot, raising the severed head of that not unlovely woman, the Victor who cannot understand his victory, his estimable

We shall limit ourselves to indicating works of universal and major importance. . . a thankless and difficult task. . . |Uffizzi Catalog|

At ten o'clock our time, we emerged from the Appenines and saw Florence lying in a broad valley which was amazingly cultivated and scattered with villas and houses as far as the eye could see. I took a quick walk through the city to see the Duomo and the Battistaro. Once more, a completely new world opened up before me, but I did not wish to stay long. The location of the Boboli gardens is marvelous. I hurried out of the city as quickly as I entered it. . . Around Florence, all the hill slopes are planted with olives and vines. In my opinion, they do not check the ivy enough; it does great damage to the olives and other trees, and it would be easy to destroy. There are no meadows anywhere. I was told that maize had exhausted the soil. Since it was introduced, their agriculture has declined in other ways. I believe this comes from using so little manure. . . . Other dreams hover before me. In my impatience to get on, I sleep in my clothes and can think of nothing more agreeable than to be roused before dawn, quickly take my seat in the carriage and travel dayward half asleep, letting dream images do what they like with me. . .
|Goethe, *Italian Journey, 1786*|

green calf now etched with the Peace Sign. I can no longer walk the Pitti or the Uffizi searching for the one small sepia etching of a man hung by his wrists, to give a handle to the indigestible whole, something on which to focus, but rather seek out the simplicity of San Miniato at Port Sante, San Miniato who, it is said, carried another severed head up there. His own. I would if I could. Well, Death is here at least terminal and not literary criticism.

"How would you like to get some girls?" a native painter friend Alessandro asks me this evening. "I've got one lined up; then we'll get you one." His wife and children are at the ocean for the summer.
We jump in his Fiat and take off to a nunnery in the hills where an American co-ed has been sequestered by her family for the summer. By day she takes the Renaissance, by night Alessandro. She is very beautiful except for that New York accent which makes Alessandro think she has a speech defect. It is darkening. We pick her up, after clanging upon the gate of our nunnery, and for some reason we drive all the way back into town, where, stopping in the Boboli gardens, they scramble down an embankment while I leaf through *Il Diario*. They emerge, presently, from between an urn and a Bacchus astride a Galapagos tortoise, Alessandro's seersucker slacks now grass stained at the knees, and then we careen back to the nunnery, all ahorn to make her mandatory Vespers.
"Okay, friend," he says, then we are back downtown, cruising the railway station and the Via Tornabuoni, "Now pick yourself out one."
Through the Fiat's windows the whores' hips are above our sightline. They veer on the sidewalk locked like that dead expert's Bugatti in a four wheel drift.
No thanks, I say.
He shrugs.
"You Americans are certainly puritanical."
I believe I am beginning to understand Uccello. One-dimensional plasticity.

|131|

Go die, Florentia, Judas—vanish
Beneath the ages' murky tide!
In love, I shall forget your image,
In death, shall not be by your side!

O, Bella, laugh at your misfortune,
Your beauty, once, has passed away!
Your features wear the wry
    contortion,
The sickly wrinkles of decay!

Cars wheezing, house on house more
    hideous . . .
—You heedless of your sacred trust,
Have sold your beauty to perfidious
All-European yellow dust!
|*Alexander Blok*, Firenze, 1909|

In three months, we will have been
abroad two years. In my opinion, it's
worse than being exiled in Siberia.
I'm speaking seriously without exag-
geration. If here one finds such a sun
and sky, and there such wonders of
art, unheard of and unimaginable,
quite literally, as you have here in
Florence, then in Siberia, when I
came out of prison, there were other
merits which do not exist here, and es-
pecially—Russians and the Mother-
land, without which I cannot live.
|*Dostoyevsky to his niece Ivanovna*
from Florence, January 1869|

So I ended up at the *Circo Americano*, at the bol-bol booth, where a pyramid of milk bottles has been set up, I cannot believe my eyes, only a dozen feet from our perimeter. A few gentlemen effeminately toss their three-for-cento lire, then, standing ten feet away from the booth's edge, I snakewhip three sidearm fastball strikes at the knees—the bottles explode, some landing outside the booth, the gathering crowd screams encouragement, the vendor is tearing his hair, and pays me off with three magnums of Asti-Spumanti for my victory, though it turns out to be vinegary. For me, the most marvelous building in all of Tuscany is that small cramped house where Dostoyevsky wrote *The Possessed,* and by hating rebels so profoundly incurred all unborn rebels' love.

In Venice, one sees many former American girlfriends in the Piazza San Marco with their kids and things. Also hirsute American youth sprawled in the parabolas of the vague arcade, desultory whines on their beggar's lips which would embarrass an Arab. Spare change? A Polish gentleman tells me in a different kind of whine, above the atrocious band, how one could come to Venice in the thirties and really meet people. Now, there's no one even worth escaping, he mutters. The city is stinking. The city is sinking. Peggy Guggenheim is pulling up stakes. The only way Venice can survive in its present form is to become a Summer Extension Institute of Ohio State University.
I take my old room which, though insufferably hot, has a balcony directly over the basilica, and a view of the piazza entire. The kitchen fans huff up at me, the oregano is not of best quality. Directly in my line of sight, big bronze blackamoors totter out of the *Torre dell' Orologio* to strike the hour. The basilica's floors are sunken and the visitors to the silvered appendages of past popes are fanatical, endless and unseeing. They wind up through the spires; across from the ducal palace gleams San Giorgio Maggiore. On the first open terrace of the basilica, the Italians carve their initials on the testicles of those horses which have already turned lysol green from the sulfuric acid created by the carcinogenous humidity.

What I am writing is a tendentious piece, I want to speak out rather more forcefully. Here the nihilists and the westernizers will begin howling about me that I'm a retrograde! Well, the hell with them, that I'll say everything to the last word! |Letter from Dostoyevsky to Markov, March 25, 1870—The murder of Ivanov occurred November 21, 1869|

I have been in this particular room many times. And I have been more depressed in this room than in any other. I used to come here to think, to take stock, to cut my mind away from self-concern and other stories, to step back and look at my head, this weird pulsing muscle. I paced the geometric patterns of the marble floor to make some now forgotten, irrelevant decision; I paced this huge marble room; while beneath me the German proprietor does his penance with unfailing politeness and good humor. In 1960, he claimed the new revanchism of Germany would soon plunge us into another war.

How do you know?

"Aha! I was in the SS, my friend."

And I, pacing above him, unable to locate my guilt, the adolescent furious to discover he has nothing, nothing to confess.

I have made love in this room many times, as the snatches of Mascagni coming up through the air shaft remind me; but it is a room made for pacing, a room totally without consequences, in which the contemplation of suicide turns upon itself until it becomes as meaningless as any reflective affirmation of living. Today, of course, I can only identify with the room, *its* problem, and how many times it must have been put upon by earnest, self-concious young men. No wonder the city is sinking. While this is my sixth stay in as many years in this room, it is only the second when I have seen the square awash with crowds and pigeons, and not in the dead of winter with the lagoon snowed over and all color gone. The last Christmas I was here I offered to cook a "dinner Americano" for some fisherman friends on one of the outer islands. I took the ferry with twenty pounds of groceries, the women and I made hamburgers stuffed with blue cheese and deviled ham, baked potatoes with sour cream and cherry pie. We all ate with relish, fell into a deep communal sleep in the one-room pink house, and then to celebrate, the men took me "fishing." We dragged the lagoon until dark, anchoring off the Isle of the Dead. It was warmer on the water than within the stone houses, but the nets produced nothing but a few dwarf scampi amidst the omnipresent cans and condoms. "There is nothing left," one of the younger men said, "not even garbage."

A faint peristalsis had begun even before they dropped me at the Fundamente Nuovo, and by the time I had wound halfway home, I was utterly faint from the hand of God upon my sphincter, grasping my intestines like a drowning man. I staggered into the lobby of some fancy hotel, a green uniformed attendant behind the desk rose up as I gasped, implored, "Dove il gabinetto, il gabinetto," but it was too late. Excrement coursed down both pantlegs, and I fainted upon the marble lobby in a pool of explosive Christmas offering.

Somehow they got me back to the pensione, where my fever so alarmed the German that he had two six-foot tanks of propane gas and a heater wheeled into the room, between which I awoke as from the dream sequence in *La Gioconda*. I never inquired as to whether my dinner companions suffered as I, but sometimes I reconjure the entire island running pell-mell for their boats, hiking up their long dresses, fumbling with their high rubber boots and suspenders, cursing the meat the boy had brought.

Yet another island lost to Communism.

That grossest of exhibitions the *Biennale* is being prevented from opening by the students. They mill about the park, march through the narrow alleys of the city, but they are no match for the inexorable tourists, who bog them down, defeat their maneuvers at every turn. They seem less intelligent than their Parisian counterparts—perhaps that is because I know the language less well, or more probably because they are chiefly art students.

It really doesn't have the style of Paris. The relative pastoral of the park doesn't permit guerrilla tactics, and everyone already seems tired, caught up in too familiar gesticulatory violence. At least one lady I overhear thinks it is all part of the annual opening ceremony, celebrating the defeat of the Moors or some such. The police, who for some reason seem much smaller than the students, also lack that certain elan. In Paris, it was clear that the police were defending something beyond the Sorbonne. But here it is quite clear that they have little interest in defending Bridget Riley's op art. The Doges' Palace, perhaps. One's blood could boil protecting that. There's real cultural authority. But Marisol? Doubt it. The few beatings are desultory, to say the least.

A painting should have copiousness and variety, young maidens, old women, youths, young boys, fowls, small dogs, birds, horses, sheep, buildings, provinces . . . there ought to be some nudes and others part nude and part clothed—but always make use of shame and modesty—the parts of the body that are ugly to see, and in the same way, others that give pleasure should be covered with draperies, a few fronds, or the hand . . . |Alberti|

|134|

Some paintings are slashed, protesting the "capitalistic exploitation of art" (rather an oblique strategy for getting at the capitalists responsible for the show), but I see something which I did not in Paris. For, unlike the anachronistic Sorbonne murals, these derivative abstracts and assaultive pop art in a sense invite mutilation, and it might even be considered appropriate had this audience, so long cowed by unexamined respect and consumership, not confused their violation of the proscenium with participation. It is an outrage made banal by the very coy passivity of the objects which are attacked. Of course, neither the insurance company nor the entrepreneur will lose here. Not even the artist will lose. It is this very demonstrative audience who loses most, those people who confuse the artist's ability to explore with their *reactionary* capacity, who cannot distinguish between that which is made and how it is marketed, who confuse the processes of managing and transforming human nature. They do not see the similar impulses between those who make their money from isolating art as a commodity and those who get their kicks from destroying art, having it without the price, so to speak, the ones who also want their love and toilets free. Marinetti wanted to pull down the Campanile of St. Mark's, an act which would be in this small tributary of the modernist tradition; to look at it for fifty years lying over there in the piazza on its side. It is mediocrity's greatest privilege to expend its major energies, not in creating new forms, but in making the past appear old. I guess he would have been here slashing up the abstracts and I will bet that this mock destruction of bourgeois values will, as in his time, chiefly benefit the Fascists. I also predict the advent of the newest reactionary aesthetic vogue of SLASH-ART as a *necessary* defiance of Abstractionism—preslash, postslash, spontaneous slash, slash/slash, softslash, neoslash, kinetic slash, psychedelic slash, decorative slash, heuristic slash, etc. Now it appears the genuine consumer must more than ever *possess* the work of art, capture reflective time as the present, thus somehow gaining a hedge on the future. How they love to run their fingers along the fluted columns and watch the dust accumulate at the pillar's base, to inscribe the air with their own flesh! No wonder that the artist wants to turn the viewer to stone, put him to work like a galley slave, possess

Futurism is a movement that is strictly artistic and ideological. It intervenes in political struggles only in hours of grave danger for the nation. We were the first among the first interventionists imprisoned for interventionism in Milan. We are issuing this manifesto of ruinous and incendiary violence by which we today are founding Futurism because we want to deliver Italy from its gangrene of professors, archaeologists, tourist guides and antiquaries. Italy has been too long the great secondhand market. We want to get rid of the innumerable museums which cover it with innumerable cemeteries. |F. T. Marinetti, A Futurist Manifesto|

him, offend him, punish him—whatever it takes. This is the basis of the new aesthetics—in which the beholder's totalitarianism merges with the artist's soft Fascism—and through mutual recognition of each other's isolation, mere possessiveness is transformed. It takes a little repression to remind us of this. Here at the Biennale, those artists in sympathy with the revolution have covered their works with newspaper, though most have left one side untaped so that the strongly motivated viewer can slide the paper away and peek in. This provides an immensely erotic effect and improves the paintings considerably; having one's solidarity and eating it too. The voyeur, the entrepreneur, the revolutionary, the consumer and the artist meet here—in the act of reopening in the name of simple curiosity what has been concealed in the name of commerce and/or ideology. And it is surprising how infrequently such a strategy of concealment is used. This of course is the secret of form—the secret of the artist—for those in this room this very day, those who even go so far as to slash the arras are not really trying to destroy the picture, but *prove* to their satisfaction there is *nothing behind it, after all*—for the moment the form is pierced, then the knife must go deeper, through the wall, through the museum, out to . . . what? This time it is the left that is slashing the paintings, in the long tradition of those moon-faced zealots who knocked the blocks (and pricks) off so many saints. But in art it is the same as politics; where the left breaches, the right will rush in. And because of this, the audience must no longer see itself as passive receptor, or even protected by a *cordon sanitaire*—they are defined between those who would destroy the art, and those who would inflate it, completing through its curators, impresarios, agents and critics what one bemused anarchist began with his pocket knife—the freezing of art and the emulsification of History itself.

Did you ever notice what goes off statues? Fanatics get your genitals; the elements, your nose; Time, your garments and texture; scholars, your vertebrae and limbs; and institutions, your torso or your head—though rarely both at once.

put your lover's phone number here
(   )

The logical result of Fascism is the introduction of aesthetics into politics . . . Mankind's self-alienation has reached such a degree that it can experience its own destruction as an aesthetic pleasure of the first order. |Walter Benjamin|

All this gratuitous action is driving me to enforced reflection, and all this enforced reflection is driving my literary concerns into my dream-life, which is not where I want them. I have a friend, for example, who once realized in his sleep that he had written enough stories to make a collection, and the rest of the dream was spent in rereading the stories, putting them into a particular order and choosing a title. When he awoke, he realized that he had not written a single story in his life. Another friend dreamed he saw his name in italics in a Borges story, and yet another dreamed he went to the laundromat and, through some switch, came home with a large supply of Norman Mailer's soiled underwear. And tonight, it struck me that Gustave von Aschenbach must have been in Venice about the same time Vladimir Nabokov and his father were emigrating from the Crimea on a boat loaded with oranges. Naturally, they would have stopped at the Lido after the voyage, and would have spoken in Polish in order to disguise their origins from *agents provocateurs.* Poor Aschenbach, unknowingly only a character observed in this charming, precocious fourteen-year-old Russian boy's journal, watching the old man sitting alone, curious about this highest product of the civilization to which they were now en route. Yes, Tadzio Nabokov, that anagrammatic code name, choosing his wardrobe with care to pique the old gentleman's curiosity, posing before him on the beach, feigning brawls, leading him on exhausting excursions through the twisting streets, having to look over his shoulder to be sure the old man had the strength to keep up, and then after a captivating narcissistic smile, leaving Von Aschenbach to his nap, while he returned to his room—where, in Cyrillic, he would consign to his journal his observations of an old voyeur, and observe through this his own awakening sexuality, the prospects of life after the plague. . . .

. . . puerile, perishable poems, which, by the time the next were printed, would have been certain to wither as had withered one after the other all the previous ones written down in the black exercise book; but no matter: at this moment, I trust the ravishing promises of the still-breathing, still-revolving verse, my face is wet with tears, my heart is bursting with happiness, and I know that this happiness is the greatest thing existing on earth. |Vladimir Nabokov, Berlin, 1935|

Tonight, after the open air bare bones recital in the courtyard of San Giorgio, I realized the difference between the 19th century novel and the sort that we must write now. And that is, simply, between a production of an opera with its traditional full complement and that of a

stripped concert performance. Both derive from necessity, overblown
economics in the musical case; overblown psychology in the literary. In
the concert performance, the new novel, the singers are placed oratorio
style before the orchestra, all costumed as they are in the same bland
evening clothes, for the story must derive from their faces, how they get
out of their chairs, how they fondle their scores, what they do with the
text when they are *not* singing. In the old style—plot, setting, motive,
costume and entertainment are emphasized; in the latter, it is voice, the
moment, technique, inflection—not the integration of existing elements, but the creation of a cutting edge out of pure air. The former is
hopelessly allegorical, admitting of *everything*—three-dimensional illusion. Our art is to be oblique, contrapuntal and uncompromisingly
multi-dimensional. The orchestra and the chorus are in full sight, in
fact take most of the space. And thus, our characters must strain, must
develop vast and unnatural command to become distinguishable, since
everyone concerned is *always* on stage. One is done in a box, ours in a
continuum. And if we make a gesture, it counts—even if it is a throw-
away gesture, as most are. A furrow on the brow of a melomanical
soloist is more than a brace of chariots driven on the stage at full gallop,
or even a real camel under blue light. You do not have to know where
you are in the story to love it, nor do the characters necessarily have to
know what's happening to them. They are not related through arche-
type costume or class; only because they are now proximate. (The rumor is they've been flown in especially for this evening and will be
gone in the morning.) Still, they rarely look at each other. The program, perhaps, is telling the audience a story, even a good one, but it
bears little relation to this stripped-down, souped-up version. The program is only a paraphrase of the past. And our conductor/narrator, *precisely because* he couldn't see very well from the pit in the old format,
is now *on* the stage, accidentally obliterating some of the principals
with his gesticulating; he must exercise extreme peripheral vision and
the desperate motions of a back stroker to keep on cue, not to mention
his very equilibrium. Despite this, he is clearly in command, though he
is still constrained not to turn around in an inappropriate place. Although once perhaps, once in a lifetime, reaching backward to steady

himself, he will miss the handy restraining bar and, grasping in terror the shoulder of the nearest enormous soprano, prevent himself from falling from the podium as she tries manfully in the midst of a low tremolo to ignore his gaffe.

He has finally created characters who have a reaction time beyond his immediate touch, who can sustain themselves not only beyond him, but in spite of him.

And for this he will walk off while the others step forward individually for applause, and when he returns, assuming he can make it, he will thread his way through the anonymous orchestra, and signal everybody to rise—everyone to rise for one another in that silence which makes possible the languages to come.

With the designation experiment, the avant-garde excludes its results, takes back, as it were, its "actions," and unloads all responsibility on the receiver. . . . Every boldness suits the avant-garde perfectly as long as it itself remains safe. The concept of the experiment is to insure it against the risk of all esthetic production. It serves both as trademark and as camouflage. . . What is to be chalked up against today's avant-garde is not that it has gone too far but that it keeps the back doors open for itself, that it seeks support in doctrines and collectives, and that it does not become aware of its own aporias, long since disposed of by history. It deals in a future that does not belong to it. Its movement is regression. The avant-garde has become its opposite; anachronism. That inconspicuous, limitless risk, of which the artists' future lives—it cannot sustain it. |Hans Magnus Enzensberger|

Crossing the border to Hungary at the main checkpoint, Hegyeshalom, proves to be a mistake. An hour's wait in a long line of cars. The mime fear. The movie fear. The guards look a little like Germans used to. But perhaps we all do. The minefield, bounded by an electrified fence, stretches across the fields to both horizons, a swath of anti-powerline cut through the farms and forest. The Austro-Hungarian farmers plow up to the edges of their otherwise indistinguishable fields and then at the fence turn about-face, for a single moment, stooped reverse images of one another. One is ploughed to ingest seed; in the other field, the earth is turned to reveal footprints. How could this banal plain ever be considered an empire? But then, the stretch between Akron and Toledo, or Lvov and Kiev, tells us as little of its power. A gray sentry with a dog the color of spoiled meat is examining some suspicious thistles in the distance.

The enlisted men, 18 at the most, handsome in their Russian style blouses, jackboots and Czech Sten guns, laugh as each car is passed in its turn beneath the raised gate-pole and the machine gun tower. The gate is the thickest oak from the Royal Forest. Do they know we're using telephone poles and railroad ties and other creosoted impermeables of our very last forest to shore up Japanese-type gardens in our vacation homesites?

To the north, the American army is dug in on the German border in their starched hopelessly tapered fatigues, zeroed in on the chest, their heavy guts maggoty parentheses of flesh between the buttons, crotch tight as a drum. Another nondescript business suit, another corporate identity; they seem no match for this virile peasant army, if not Germanic, then fierce Goths. Nope. Rid yourself of all allegories and dialectics, my friend. All conscripts in the world are from places called Midland, Texas, or perhaps Satoraljauhely. And this is a land where *this* is never quite *that,* a nation where ellipses are the only enduring metaphor, the land for which Tuberculosis was named—Morbus Hungaricus.

A Hungarian intelligence officer, a doctor on weekend reserve duty, sporting several mysterious decorations, crawls beneath the car to check the crankcase for jewels or something. He is not very good-na-

LETTER FROM THE FIRST AND EVERLASTING THIRD WORLD

Make all blanks legible . . .
|Hungarian visa application|

The fact is, that since the day more than a thousand years ago, when Arpad first entered Hungary, the Magyars have done much harm and little good in Europe. |Harold Nicolson|

tured. I'm nervous because I carry certain technological items to which I am personally indifferent for the delectation of my friends here. Transistor radios, nylons, contraceptives, vitamins, bits of ribbon, Philip Roth. Nothing illegal, but I still fear they will misinterpret and confiscate my suitcase of manuscript, my journal, the writing pad on the dashboard which secretly I assume amounts to an international conspiracy. I give him a hard stiff time. He yells at me that he's just doing his job, that he's not the Secret Police. As the car is searched, he beckons me to a long, dark hall. Now I'm sure I've had it. The jig's up. I'm going to be arrested, given an enema, and if I should shit a diamond I'll be put away for life. Or perhaps I'm just going to be liquidated right there. He has a conference with a higher ranking officer in a cubicle and returns with my indictment. Now my executioner is before me, the light is in my eyes, the final interrogation has begun. I am the smallest of his lies.

He asks me sinisterly if I have any *Playboys.*

I shake my head proudly.

But he will pay me well for them.

It suddenly occurs to me that Kafka's heroes *are* guilty because they *assume* their guilt. They may question the court's method of justice, but the only form of expression their innocence can take is indignation, and every indignation only seems to certify their culpability.

According to my precious note pad, still intact upon the dashboard, the scenery changes automatically once we're over the swath. The hills are pocketed with quarries; inexplicable clots of mist issue from ravines, neither combustion nor condensation. The language thickens and turns upon itself. The fields are not coiffed. Geese strut and shimmy before the pastel houses. A polite and handsome people are eating well under acacia trees. They have been fleeing the east for more than a millennium—their church, their law, their culture are western from their origins, yet the east has always remained one step ahead of them in different guises: Tartary, Turks, the poop and drag of the Austrian secession,

GYOR, ESTERGOM, TATA, SZEKESFEHERVAR, ERD, BUDAPEST.

for whom they were both police and prisoner, to Soviet hegemony.
"We are surrounded by Slavs, Slavs and Germans and a few Rumanian
dinye (melon-heads)," an old peasant tells me. "We have been in every
major European war since the 10th century, but have not won one
since 1440. We are a miracle!"

A country of mutual and systematic betrayal as well as that cunning
and virility which I so envy, and which apparently gets you absolutely
nowhere. A language impossible to translate, their great incense and
defense, which has kept them alive during successive invasions, yet
denied them their due appreciation and cultural influence in western
Europe.

A writer tells me, "Oh, I could write in French. My French is perfect.
But it is such an unmusical language. And after all, you can make so
few puns. It is really not a language at all, ours. It is an instrument of
delight which in spite of itself occasionally doubles as a
communications medium. We have no space here—for *anything*. We
export our overproduction of intellectuals, our expertise, our temperament, our souls. All those Hungarian symphony conductors and
atomic physicists would be teaching secondary school had they remained. The one thing we would wish to export, our language, we cannot. No amplitude for us except in bed, at the table and in the codes of
language. Did you know we have more poets per capita than any nation
in the world? In Budapest alone there are 500 writers. And this in a
country of ten million, of which half are functionally illiterate. Yes, it is
the poets, only the poets, who *must* stay, who have no choice, and who
deliver us to ourselves. We are not, you see, composers or ballerinas."

This lack of space, a true and refined claustrophobia, is made endurable
only by the strange symbiotic relationship with the soil, retained by
even the most urban sophisticate, despite his open disdain for "country
people." It is still an agricultural country, and nowhere in the world
can one eat so well for so little. At its best, Hungarian cuisine has the

Nuthin like us ever was

LEGESLEGMEGENGESZTELHETETLENEBEITEKNEK
(to the most irreconcilable ones)

*My blind Hungarians, in battle you
    are strong,
Like a tornado, to the fight you tear
    along.
But here at home the old internal
    hates are rife,
You'll be destroyed by the poison of
    this strife.*

*Vitezi nepem, te elvakult magyar . . .
Csatan oly gyozve gyozol, mint a
    szelvihar . . .
De itthon szethuzasnak osi merge rag:
A regi partutes vegveszelybe rant!*

|*Josef Katona*, Bank Ban|

structural rigor of French cookery, the flavor complexity of Mexican, and the dialectical texture, both visual and oral, of the Japanese—cold apple soup, paprika salami, truffles stuffed with cold puree of goose liver in *gelée* of red wine, duck with wild cherries, venison and kohlrabi, squash and lentils in sour cream dill sauce, wild boar, onion souffle, chestnut puree, Turkish coffee. The rumor is that after Kadar dismantled the Secret Police in 1956, like the shrewd politician he is, former AVO officers were given jobs as managers of hotels and restaurants. It is a tactic for us to consider. It certainly won't hurt the food, and our general surveillance might improve. Imagine a city where it is not uncommon for an average couple to go out for a good dinner and then take their choice of ten theaters or concerts several times a week. Stuff your hands in your ranchero pockets, America, and cry. Now this is an old question, and frankly since it was asked already by John Adams and Washington Irving, I do not see why I have to inquire after one hundred and fifty years, why a Chicago of seven million capitalists, with a real personal per capita income ten times greater than their Budapest benighted commie counterparts, cannot offer those few material pleasures which are presumably the highest achievements of bourgeois culture: decent restaurants, cafes, theaters, bookstores, that elemental margin which justifies cities in the first place? And this is no strict Marxist nor even European phenomenon—for Budapest as a functioning metropolis barely antedates Chicago, no matter how fond they are of pointing out that there were human settlements in caves of castle hill 2,000 years before America was discovered. Is it because we lost our turn-of-the-century excitement with urban life very suddenly, and somehow never recovered it? Here it persists, albeit in a crude and diminished form. Is it because Central European Communism consolidates the virtues of the urban bourgeoisie while destroying those of the rural bourgeoisie? Or is it simply perhaps impossible for us, after living in an environment in which everything is always getting bigger, to understand the phenomenology of a *shrinking* civilization with a declining population, a society which does not live within its means so much as on the bitter-sweet admission that is has no *means*, a country where on the cans of their most popular export, paprika, the map of the origi-

The English menu translations make the food even better; fried leg of fog, posh eggs savar, Paisant ham, crowfish cocktail, pleasant rice bashed, chateau of a potatoe, stromberry whipped creme, Flambed porkollop of the spring, noodled loins in bull's blood, sheatfish good woman style, braised stag leg with hips, cillops froed in breadcrups, watered melon, bottled peach, barmy cucumber, the magnificent two-personner-on-wooden-plate, and the ubiquitous Russian salad which is here called French.

nal empire is emblazoned in red—from Rijeka, to Belgrade, to Brasov, to Bratislava, Slovakia—and the present reduced state in white, shaped rather like the left ventricle of the heart within a putrescent corpse, borders which do not follow natural ethnogeographical outline, nor even geopolitical realities, so much as the calculated indifference of distant, opposed powers. There is a tincture of revenge, a modicum of exploitation in this newest Balkanization, but essentially, Central Europe is an unrealized fantasy of fatigue, defined first by our Colonel House, then solidified by Russo-American distended psyches, a mutual agreement that those crazy inconsequential little fuckers are not going to get us all killed all over again. These are politics created out of a larger forgetfulness. Once making history far out of proportion to their influence, they are now consigned to ahistoricality, a vacuum, a buffer. A no man's land of hyperthyroids.

This situation determines the Hungarian team's tactical aim at the match against Norway: to score as many times as possible, and keep the Norwegian side from scoring, if possible. |Budapest Times|

Jakab B. lives with his wife and three children in a single room which I measure as 16 by 18 feet. There is cold running water and a gas stove in an alcove, a toilet for the entire floor of the apartment building. He is a steelworker, his wife a pastry cook. His son is studying violin, his two daughters are studying literature. The boy's practicing gets on the girls' nerves when they try to do their homework. It was worse when their father-in-law was alive and lived with them. Hardly a slum; these people are not poor. The room has often been redecorated; there is no dirt and sufficient heat. They certainly have enough money to live on, their children have free education and medical care. What they lack is precisely what we, of course, have exaggerated beyond their usefulness: space and mobility. There is no place for them *to go*, except out, and "out" is still *in*. At night when someone wishes to enter or leave the room, someone else must get out of bed. I lie on their couch listening to the floor's populace pace around the lavatory. The cherry brandy is not strong enough. The sugar salves the alcohol. I'm being energized when all I want is release.

Across the courtyard from this apartment lives a young couple in a single room with three high windows. I am still working when they retire. They have no drapes. When they go to sleep they pull the bed to the center of the room, taking their refuge, their love, behind the yard-wide machine-gun-stitched pillars which separate their windows. Occasionally an orgasmic arm or leg protrudes, as if the pillars had suddenly sprouted an appendage, a statue come to life. Their privacy is wholly imagined and does not suffer from all that. But it suffers from its own defiance.

Just as when I first saw the hurricane green of Provence and understood how the impressionists were also realists, just as when I realized how myopia or perhaps glaucoma turned Van Gogh into an expressionist, the *realistic* second-sight for him, just as when I finally realized how Turner was becoming a 20th century realist with those immense abstractionist waves gradually taking over the canvas and finally obliterating the 18th century picnickers in the lower left-hand corner, now it is clear just how much Kafka and Ionesco are realists in their own tradition. The world as both concrete and unattributable at the same moment. . . .

Jakab B. blames his lot on not being a party member, in which he takes pride. "I would have left in '56," he mutters. "I should have left then. We're too old now"—a common enough complaint. Everyone has his own excuse for not emigrating, just as everyone suppresses his own circumstances of survival. They are guilty about *not* leaving, guilty about the cost of staying. History both as revisionism and as *re*-vision becomes totally privatized, and nothing gets passed on except cunning. Yet that is precisely what is so attractive about them as people, for the presumption seems to be that as everyone has had to severely compromise themselves in the past, humanity exerts itself in a very fundamental way. No one expects you to be perfect here . . .

What would happen if you went down to party headquarters tomorrow, I say, admit you had seen the light and wanted to join up? "Ah, they would send me to my local chapter. They would query me and, in the end, I would be refused."

A neighbor, later, freely offers the information that Jakab B. is just

*Couldn't you have died
or at least bled,
instead of pacing the floor
stunned with despair?
You kept clear of the trouble:—
bullets, armoured track emblazoned
girls' screams. Not for you broken
wheels, scattering rooftiles,
grim gangs of working lads,
and soot-brindled petals.
You did not spill one drop
of blood, and when it stopped,
you had only gone grey and mad.*

*In usual winter weather
you stand here; no other
but yourself, and wide awake,
squared by walls that echo
a cough like raking
gunfire. It's not merely
your flesh that's cold;
mind and heart are frozen,—crowned
by knives of ice.
You are ashamed of your melting
    phrases;
as if you had lost the right
to think of spring
and lilacs,—the lung-like trees
    blossoming.
What agony for a Lord of Life!
Yet, deep in the secret places
of your being, furtive with guilt
you are breathing on the frosted pane,
that you may look out at the world
    again.*

|Laslo Nagy, *from* Squared by Walls|

lazy, that with his dependents he could get another flat if he really wanted to. Who is to know? "*I* should have left," Jakab goes on bitterly: he does not use *we*, as his family listens intently.

I tell him of the Hungarian-Americans I know—those few millionaires in Canada and the one rich wheat farmer in Pennsylvania, the couple who ended up with a jewelry store on the Ponte Vecchio and screw every nationality equally, but also of the older enclaves in Pittsburgh, Chicago, New York; the 65-year-old woman with phlebitis enduring a daily 45-minute stand-up subway ride to the garment district; she has no medical insurance, is terrified to go out in the street after dark, and, ten years after emigration, does not speak English and has never been to a restaurant or the theater in New York. And of the second generation bourgeoisie in Chicago, whose pointless ethnocentricity is directed now primarily towards the blacks, and who praise the lost monarchy at their banquets, America as End of the Road. The *émigrés* lie about what they were—"In Budapest I could speak Greek; in Budapest I was Director of the Opera"; the generation left behind lies about how it survived. "Yes, I am on the black list, yes, I am anti-Communist because I was anti-Fascist"—but the second American generation, apart from their scandalous parochialism, have nothing worth lying about. I would guess, I said, if you are a gypsy violinist or a serious intellectual with a salable skill and enormous personal charm, or are pretty and are under 25 and have no future here, then maybe you ought to try it. Actually, Vienna would be far better for most. But if you are none of these things, then it is not worth it to leave.

"America," Jakab B. says, pursing his lips defiantly, "is the most wonderful and free country in the world! Chicago, Al Capone," he grins, then sighs dolefully. "In Hungary we have no gangsters . . . In Hungary you *must* work. I have a sister in South Orange, New Jersey. Do you know it? It must be so beautiful. . . ."

I tell him of the disaster that is South Orange, New Jersey, but he will not hear a word against it, and looks at his shoes.

Frankly, I said, If I were you I'd join the party and try to get something out of them. That's the American way.

All the things that take the traveller's breath away in the first days of his stay in America resemble what one reads with youthful imagination in a fairy-tale. The faces, the garments, the customs and the language, religion and laws, the products and open nature—all this makes one fully conscious of the new world. Even more surprising is the fact that all the many appearances and forms which we believe are essential to our life in Europe, have no trace here anywhere. A foreigner will try in vain to find people of high rank, powerful magistrates, officials—all these persons are merely simple citizens! He looks in vain for better-class families, for a higher or lower nobility—they are merely simple citizens! The clergy and the military, the police and the judges, the scientists and bankers— they are merely simple citizens, exactly like each other. Even more incomprehensible to a foreigner is what he sees about religion, that among the 48 religions none is the ruling one, and all possess the same rights! That the clergy does not constitute an order, and that there is no regular army! There are no privileges, there is no nobility! There are no titles, medals, guilds or secret police! How important are all these things, one by one, to a foreigner! |Belonyi Farkas, 1843|

"Too late for that," he said. "It's too competitive now."

He looks up at me and pours some cherry brandy.

"Now listen. There is an old man who lives down the hall. You will see him shuffling by occasionally to go to the toilet. He lives with his son and his wife in an apartment even smaller than this. The children want the apartment to themselves. They are literally trying to kill him. They beat him terribly when they are drunk. I want you to understand something. They are killing this man next door, and there is nothing I can do about it. As long as they do not create an enormous disturbance, the police will not interfere. The son is a party man, you see, and I cannot report him. I am afraid. It may not be like the fear of the past, but I'm still afraid. The father is old and will die soon anyway . . ."

But that could certainly happen in New York, I interrupt. People are killed every day while others literally stand by and do nothing. It is simply murder over different commodities. . . .

"You don't understand, it's that your hoodlums are *below* you socially, perhaps you believe they are not even to blame. It's one thing to be hit over the head, and another to be told that a new vision of man will come out of it. You must understand, my friend, that we are a violent, autocratic nation. This has nothing to do with Communism. We have chosen wrong in every war. I do not join the party because it is a compromise with the future—hardly—but because it reminds me of everything we have done so stupidly in the past. The history of our traitors is nearly as illustrious as that of our *émigrés,* and I will live out my life resisting both alternatives. I will neither emigrate, nor resist, but I will remain somehow ungoverned in my own land."

"The boy has to practice now, Jakab," his wife says with some annoyance. "All this is just expresso talk."

In my eyes grief dissolves;
I ran like a deer;
Tree-gnawing wolves
In my heart followed near.

I left my antlers
A long time ago;
Broken from my temples
They swing on a bough.

Such I was myself:
A deer I used to be.
I shall be a wolf:
That is what troubles me.

A fine wolf I'm becoming.
Struck by magic, while
All my pack-wolves are foaming
I stop, and try to smile.

I prick up my ears
As a doe gives her call;
Try to sleep; on my shoulders
Dark mulberry leaves fall.

|Attila Josef, Grief|

Active cynicism is a luxury and is healthy only when the stakes are high. When one doubts the power of one's cynicism, when one is cynical about cynicism itself, when it becomes state-subsidized, then it turns inward and can sustain at best only reasonably dignified melancholia. The streets of Budapest are suffused with this gradual strangulation of fury, which accounts partially for the most rapacious urge for consumer goods I have ever seen, a commodity fetish of metaphysical proportions. This is not so much the greed or wonder of an underdeveloped nation, nor even the scarcity mentality of the war years, but akin, in a reverse image, to the pathetic attempt to prove you exist by purchase, by expenditure, since the notion of *reinvestment*, both economically and psychologically, is denied. And mark, part of its motive force is that by *owning* certain things, one gives evidence of *beating*, not corroborating, the system; in a word, proprietorship becomes a *political* act, which, incidentally, Dubcek has divined clearly. How many of them would burn a *car* out of defiance, when *having* a car is the most obvious defiance? There certainly can be no Internationale without taking these different attitudes towards possessions into account. The very day I entered Budapest, it was announced that Coca-Cola is building a factory in Hungary to general rejoicing. "And now," exclaims a girl, her face flushed with incredible beauty, "now all we need is a Fiat factory!" Today I bought an East German radio for a friend—and the appliance store which has no customers fills immediately with curious passers-by, *watching* me buy it, experiencing the purchase vicariously. On the street I am offered a fortune for my Italian pants. My French car, lately escaped from the revolution, is surrounded and patted in its parking place. Several times I come out to find it washed, a mark of respect for Monsieur Peugeot, or occasionally someone writes "wash it" in the grime on the fender, and so I am admired for what I care least about in my own culture. Better to be despised simply for one's cash, as in western Europe—here my own repudiation of the priorityless affluence of America is taken as a genuine perversity, a lack of deference, an inexplicable sourness. I complain about the new Intercontinental Hotel, Waldorf-on-the-Danube, another extension of the American corridor, amiable American tourists and their sullen children sealed off from yet another culture; while on the periphery, in the cafe of the hotel, lurk the leaders of Hungarian hippiedom, who in their tie-dyed shirts and flared hair play the gypsies *their* fathers despised and mistreated, ape the pseudo-anarchism of their American counterparts.

The "Golden" Doctor,
If someone has everything but wants more, we use the word greedy. It may sound funny, but greedy persons do not live off our superficiality, imperfection and negligence. One of those we are talking about is Dr. _____. His circle of acquaintances is unexpectedly large. Though he knows few people at the hospital where he works, his circle of friends in private practice from five to seven daily is almost countless. His patients are not only from Budapest, but also those who with foreign currency add to this extraordinarily high honorarium. So, indeed, the doctor has an unusually high income, not to mention the fact that his wife is also a well-to-do doctor. One cannot believe that such a family should have any financial problems whatsoever. Incidentally, this is the same man who in 1942 sent an invitation to Hermann Goering to come falcon hunting in Hungary. He was a respected and devoted "falcon fan" to the end of his days. But let us assume his financial situation was bad, so to make ends meet he applied for his visa and left for Italy which naturally in itself is not against the law. But he did know that to be granted another travel visa within the next three years would be almost unheard of. He arrived in Italy with a six carat diamond in his pocket. The seller, by the way, an old insurance agent crony from the past, knew the value of the gem and told him 150,000 forints wouldn't be too much for it, because he could sell it in the west for seven or eight thousand dollars. He sold it for seven thousand dollars without any difficulty. With this, he bought six thousand dollars worth of sixteen carat gold and, with the remaining money, had a copy made of Hungarian official stamps for his passport. The sum was well worth it as he would no longer have to wait another three years if he wished to travel. The thirteen pounds of gold he had smuggled successfully into the country. At that time, he knew that had he invested the money, it would be worth eight times as much, so he found a way to sell it legally. The national pawn shop will pay 150 to 160 forints for a gram of gold, if the merchandise carries the stamps of

|148|

In every land, the same drama: guilty middle-class fathers subsidizing their sons' token opposition, sitting on opposite sides of the grand terrace, glaring at each other's clothes; only smugness and vulgarity pass between them. "Well, if something has to be creeping, let it be Americanism," a friend says. What can I say to him? If I am too guilty about my own government to tell him how much I despise his own, how can I warn him about those very commodities with which we surfeit ourselves, and to which he certainly has a "right"? Is it not instructive that we always assume that it is the poorest cultures which are responsible for developing a morality not based on money? The most suspicious thing about this most superficially sinister of people remains their open admiration and affection for America.

The genuine dilemma is shown by the reaction of a Hungarian writer just returned from a year in the States which shook him considerably. "I'm as anti-regime as anyone; I never went to jail, but they held up my books for a decade. But when I have seen in America how we are becoming Americanized, I went to a 'Socialist contact' immediately upon my return, and asked him to pass on my thoughts to Kadar. The horrible thing is, you see, that under Rakosi people valued their culture, they knew *what* to choose from the West—duress somehow causes people to seek out quality, and now all the moral corruption and opportunism of two centuries have been given a renewed focus and momentum by consumership—and my impulse was to tell Kadar, for God's sake, stop this, assert your authority, or we will have lost everything. But then I realize that these men, whether cynical or convinced communists, don't know how to do this any more than I do. Only under Mao is such a thing possible. And then not only do I feel the helplessness of the leaders I laugh at, I realize that if they really clamp down again, the sort of cultural revolution that I fantasized about when I was afraid to go outside at night in America, a fear for which even Stalin could not adequately prepare me, I saw that the effect of denying

the National Metal Institute which charges three forints to do so per gram, no custom papers or other identification required. Gradually, he began asking his friends (patients) to exchange the gold for him in this way as a small friendly favor. Everything went just swell. By this time, he had already begun to think about his next business venture, and he called the hospital stating he was ill and needed to be in a sanitorium at Szeged. In the meantime, he had purchased another diamond of one and a half carats. Without even stopping in Szeged, he proceeded through Yugoslavia for Italy. There he sold the diamond for $1500, bought four pounds of cheap gold. After returning, he went through the same procedure as before, and the national pawn shop paid 240,000 forints for the gold. Plus, he also collected the health insurance money for the time he had presumably spent in Szeged. Unfortunately, his passport is now missing, so he is in jail. Who knows how many times he made this trip, carrying the false stamp of Hungarian authority! Whose fault was it that all this could happen so simply? The National Metal Institute? The national pawn shop?—or those who made it possible for him to do this—namely, his patients and friends? |Nepsabazdag|

people their cars, their trashy films, would in the end also deny me my foreign library, my dialogue with the world . . . so there you are. It is for me, now, a hopeless question . . . if you installed multi-party democracy and complete political self-determination tomorrow, I do not know to whom I would turn as an alternative, nor what I would expect them to do. . . . Opening the border would only mean that we would grow fatter off West German vacationists and East German escapees, fatter and stupider. . . ."

Curiously enough, rather than patting itself on the back for increasing productivity, the regime still maintains, somewhat unconsciously I think, a wartime psychology. Every morning when I go to buy fresh bread, there are unruly queues, fighting and pushing, though there is more than plenty in the store. It is a scarcity consciousness encouraged by the state, just as some of the war damage in the city is, I believe, somehow left purposefully intact. It still looks as if it had been shelled recently; machine gun and mortar holes stitched across facades and broken cornices. The Communist Party Headquarters (Budapest Branch) is one of the few buildings which has been repaired totally, these holes courtesy of the '56 affair. But it has been strangely patched with a limed cement, a far different color than the gray stucco, and it has not weathered. Surely this is not unintentional. For each hole, each blow, though now flattened and filled, is preserved as if the building had broken out with the pox; an architecture of scar tissue. Today when I park, an old man, a parking lot attendant, comes up to me and addresses me in perfect Sorbonne French. He inquires about my reactions to the city.

Most beautiful, I say.

"It is not beautiful, it is a disaster. I'm no fool, young man. The coal smoke, Monsieur, surely you can smell it. You cannot see it now, but in the winter a black cloud hangs over the city. We have the most polluted city outside of Tokyo in the world. I have seen the figures myself!" His civic disparagement is the index of his personal integrity. The implica-

Freedom in the West, in order to manifest itself, requires a void—and succumbs to it. The condition which determines it is the very one which annihilates it. This freedom lacks foundation; the more complete it is, the more it overhangs an abyss, for everything threatens it, down to the principles from which it derives. Man is so little made to endure or deserve it, that the very benefits he receives from it crush him, and freedom ultimately brings him to the point where he prefers, to its excesses, those of terror. To these disadvantages are added others: a liberal society, eliminating mystery, the absolute, order, and possessing a true metaphysic no more than a true police, casts the individual back upon himself, while dividing him from what he is, from his own depths . . . Imagine a society overpopulated with doubt, in which, with the exception of a few strays, no one adheres utterly to anything; in which unscathed by superstition, certainties, everyone pays lip service to freedom and no one respects the form of government which defends and incarnates it . . . You are disappointed after promises which could not be kept; we, by a lack of any promises at all . . . |E. M. Cioran|

tion is clear and constant: "Don't diddle with me, my friend, I've been bullshitted by experts."

And what will you do about the pollution? I ask him.

"What will we do about it? We will die from it."

The rudest people in the entire city (outside of the lady police magistrates) are the ubiquitous cash register women who sit in their enclosed turrets in officious blue smocks. In one sense, they have replaced the informers and the soldiers patrolling the streets with Sten guns. They are everywhere, a constant post-Stalinist reminder of *who* dispenses the goods. Every time they hit a button on the register, it says, "It can be cut off any time, comrades." This too is unconscious. Everything which normally can be written off to inefficiency takes on the grandeur of conspiracy. If you walk into a store and buy a postage stamp, and they give you a bag large enough for a liter of wine, and then you buy a dozen eggs in another and they give you a piece of string, you start to wonder.

If my attitude towards the commodities I take for granted is suspect, then my own interpretation of their "revolution" is also met with polite disbelief. Too young to absorb McCarthy and the Rosenbergs, bemused by Korea as a kind of late-night re-run of a horror movie, their '56 was for me the final indication that our foreign policy was not merely rhetorically bellicose, the subject for fatigued amusement, but actually death-dealing in its ineffectiveness. It would take another half a generation for our government to be despised for saying it wasn't doing what it was; we merely hated it for not doing what it said it would, i.e., liberate oppressed peoples who generated their own revolution. I don't remember any of our intellectuals opposing our putative support of the Nagy regime as "military adventurism," and I am sick to recall how many of us 18-year-olds would have run down to enlist had Dulles decided to intervene, once again to search in that pocket of the European continent for some kind of camaraderie, once again to prove our courage and unselfishness—for the remembrance of most of us was that World War II was the only vital experience which our parents had been permitted, the only possible antidote to a nation's psyche destroyed by self-delusion and the Depression, of which the fifties were only a desul-

The counter-revolutionary rebellion in Hungary in 1956 was a case of reactionaries inside a socialist country, in league with the imperialists, attempting to achieve their conspiratorial aims by taking advantage of contradictions among the people to foment dissension and stir up disorder. This lesson of the Hungarian events merits attention. |"The Correct Handling of Contradictions Among the People," Chairman Mao's Red Book|

tory aftermath. Our invasion of Hungary would have delivered us likewise from our adolescence, from our boredom and inertia, from the
petty violences we inflicted on each other every day. As intellectuals,
we could have had *our* thirties, had *our* Fascists, our very own initiation—and become instant veterans. It would take another war,
against a less conventional foe in a different scenario to burn that naiveté out—so when I tell them that *their* revolution disabused us of *our*
self-esteem, and was really the beginning of our despair over our un-
wieldy power, they can only laugh politely, and when I say that the
proof of our ignorance was that we could not even see that the crucial
issue had been Suez, and not Hungary at all, they become almost as
sad as I.

Refer to marginalia on page 17

"I still cannot forgive you," my friend says. "I still wish you had inter-
vened," he insists.
But Gabor, I plead, then we'd both be dead now.
"I listened myself to Radio Free Europe's instructions on how to make
Molotov cocktails, and our 20,000 dead are partially your responsi-
bility. We are a tragedy . . ." Then he sighs, "But a small tragedy.
Nothing compared to Biafra, or Pakistan, or . . ." Then he chokes on
something.

On one of the Buda hills, I am told, there is a hotel for former aristocrats who live in splendor on money sent from relatives in Europe and
America. It doesn't matter whether it exists or not, for I cannot help
wondering why we could not accomplish our revolution, not through
electoral change or liquidation, but by simply offering all our top execu-
tives, Senators and chairmen of the committees, a free lifetime of isolate splendor and early retirement if they would only give up their
power.

At the most distinguished Hotel Gellert, the outdoor cafe is filled with American businessmen with their wives and Hungarian high party officials with their mistresses. They are one. The waiters come and go. A single *New York Times* offered at $1.25. One is put on a list. And among this high officialdom, this conspiracy of the status quo, the result of the Cardinals-Mets game is passed like a state secret from table to table. We are informed there are no foreign papers left today.

I ask them where I can get an American paper.

The young clerk tells me, "Try the Sabostag."

The what?

"Freedom, my friend. Hotel Freedom. Sabostag!"

And then he laughs ruefully, a forced laugh from deep in his throat. My friend whispers as we leave, "You see, you have no idea how much better things are. The way we can talk! Did you hear that! In the Gellert!" Then he mutters, "It's those goddamn Czechs. That's why there're no papers."

A younger intellectual I know, self-described as a "cultural bureaucrat," tells me the revolution was definitely not a mistake, because it meant substantial reforms with relatively little loss of life. "We live in an accursed quadrant of the earth; that quadrant is defined by the birthplaces of both Freud and Stalin. We never have had Anglo-Saxon freedom here. It was decided at Yalta who we are. We are *their* Guatemala. You have never been used to anything in the left save masturbation. Look at what happened in Paris. Your ideology is confused, and you lack physical courage. I must say that we have finally caught up with the West at least in that respect. This generation, our younger generation, will never mount a revolution. Why? Well, occasionally things still do happen. One morning, for example, I took a picture of my wife on the balcony of our apartment. In less than an hour, the police arrived and searched the house thoroughly, wanting to know why I was taking pictures out the window. No one seems to know who reported me or why. They confiscated the film. I asked them for the pictures of my wife, and they replied only that they have extremely good photo de-velopers working for them. I never heard another thing about it. We simply have a bureaucracy without professional bureaucrats. They were all replaced with the new regime. As a result, no one knows what is go-ing on—whether you're being "investigated" or whether you are the victims of inertia pure and simple. As for my own generation—those who did not leave—we are no longer discredited since the amnesty, and at least we were not killed. From a legal point of view, they had every right to do so. I have given up, in a word, but I have not dishonored myself. I have never informed, and that is more than I can say for most of my colleagues. I will die here. And in the meantime, I will try to ad-vance the truly remarkable achievements of our culture. The state and I have done more than reach an agreement; we have become symbiotic, and of course the suspicion is that we deserve each other. Nevertheless, for my own part, I would like to see the young take more risks. I con-fess it. They seem to be interested only in their clothes and cars. I think, you see, that we're closer to the generation of our fathers than we are to them. We *know*. We have created our own invisible line of self-censorship, we know precisely the parameters of our life. You are bored by your freedom. But mine is not a dull life. Every word that I choose is related to my survival. I must decide at every moment just *who* it is that I am talking to. As long as I can get my hands on every-thing I need to read. . . . But I was saying, my grandfather was a *real* Communist. I mean before World War II when it was dangerous, and he went to jail several times. Now my brother is the party leader for an entire county. He works sixteen hours a day, an utterly devoted man and gentle as well. During the revolution when every other bureaucrat had fled, the peasants came to the city hall with torches, axes and pitch-forks demanding his head. He walked out on the balcony and faced them. He told them, how do you say, that they had never had it so good and that they shouldn't give up their progress because a few crazy in-tellectuals in Budapest had inflamed susceptible college boys. He held that region together, and it's one of the most affluent in the country. He has never used any gestapo tactics that I know of. He couldn't get away with it now. You see, the bastards really believe that they are doing the

|154|

best for the people, and perhaps they are. Don't forget, my friend, the things that matter to people like us don't mean anything to most. Freedom of the Press? What does this mean, really? To have one's intelligence insulted every day? Perhaps it is not so different in America? All of us are ruled by Manicheans; but there are good and bad Manicheans, yes? Ha ha. But anyway, after '56, my grandfather, the pure Communist, who made his wife clean his boots and hit his kids if they picked grapes off his arbor or bothered his doves, the old man literally spit on his son for his acts, and they never spoke again, not even when grandfather died. A week after he was buried, his wife had electricity installed in the house. He would have never permitted it. When I get depressed or self-loathing, I do not think of my son, no; I think of my grandfather. And I do not find that reactionary in the least."

As I turn to go, he stops me. "One more thing. Do not exaggerate *your* repressions. You might bring on a real one, yes?"

I examine his face carefully. It has neither the wisdom of the peasant nor that toughness of party men—it has some of the defeat and consternation one sees in low-echelon American businessmen and academics, except in their case it is a defeat by immensity, by odds which they cannot fathom, where my friend's defeat is one which he understands precisely, an *unnecessary* defeat not by inexplicable fate, but by a few thoughtless actions of unimaginative men with total power who confused social revolution with the destruction of normal intellect.

The Czech business is heating up, though it is difficult to follow since it is still nearly impossible to get any foreign newspapers. One man, a gas station attendant, thinks he can get me one from a friend at the railroad station when the train comes in from Vienna. He explains that he is a party man *and* in the militia, a volunteer policeman, who donates eight hours a week without pay to help direct traffic in a congested part of town. The purpose of the militia is to protect people from counter-revolutionaries, "like in '56," he says. "Did you hear about that?"
I had heard, yes.

Question: *Why are the same people who demonstrated for the Fascists last week demonstrating for the Communists now?*

Answer: *This is a small country. We have only one mob.*

|155|

"And of course, that's what's happening right now in Czechoslovakia. They may be on us at any moment."
No paper on the train.

Walking down Nepkoztarsasag Avenue (Street of the People's Republic), previously the Street of Hungarian Youth, previously Stalin Avenue, previously Hitler St. on Mussolini Square, formerly . . . and tonight, I see the unbelievable, a brand new tomato red Cadillac Eldorado convertible making its way among the traffic. At a stoplight, the fat driver waves to me and says in heavily accented English, "I'll bet you're an American?"
Yep.
"Well, I'm an American too. Left in '56. Pretty nice car, isn't it? Look at 'em gawk."
It's a nice car, I allowed.
"I do this every summer. It costs me hell, but I buy a new Caddy and I ship it over to Antwerp, and then I get in and drive it over to Hungary, and then I drive down this fucking street and watch 'em look, and then I go back home. Every year for the last five years."
And through my inarticulate disdain, I recall with what pleasure I drive down from the Buda hills into the city each morning and immediately find a parking place. For the pastoral dream for the American is not to get the machine out of the garden, but to have the *only* machine in the garden.

Every *intellectual* I've talked to seems to think that Dubcek is going to make it. Imre Nagy made two mistakes in '56, they say. He threatened military alliances with the West. When things got tough, he trusted the Russians and gave up asylum in the Yugoslav embassy. Moreover, Dubcek has a local power base in Slovakia; he can threaten civil unrest rather than spies from the West. There's no way they can take him out now. I write all my friends that things look good for Dubcek.

Foreign newspapers are cut off. The Hungarian news agencies follow the events closely and accurately. Everybody laughs at my paranoia, but my reaction time, for all my coddling, seems quicker. I go buy another East German radio, a month's wages for a worker, to find out what in the hell is going on. The clerk recognizes me in utter disbelief. But the Bratislava conference seems to bear out their optimism. I feel ridiculous depending on Radio Free Europe for my only source of information.

This evening, a doctor friend leaves in the middle of the night. He has been called up to his reserve unit. I turn on the radio—Vienna and Stuttgart are jammed. I race down the hall to tell my friend. He can't believe it. Then, after listening to the static for a moment, he snaps his fingers, puts his ear to the wall and grins.
You mean we're bugged too?
"No. And we are not jammed either. It happens only that your neighbor is shaving with an electric razor."

At the Venice Biennale, the most impressive works I saw were bronze miniatures by a Hungarian sculptor. I call him up and ask if I can visit his studio. He is a charming man, as is his studio, on the outskirts of Budapest. He has just come back from six months in Italy. At the violence in Venice, he can only tremble with rage. "What self-indulgence. They are nothing but young hoodlums with too much time and money on their hands. Would-be artists. A new lumpenproletariat of the upper classes. Who would have thought it possible? They should have a little taste of Rakosi."
In the rear of his large studio is a beautiful wild quarter-acre of garden. It is the only such space accessible to a private individual that I've seen. He makes his living doing monuments for the state, and turns out these wonderful miniatures, at the most a foot high, which gain him a good reputation and a very good price in the West. He says they will soon be taking his studio away from him for a housing project. They've already offered him a modern apartment with all the conveniences.
"What am I going to do with a modern apartment?" he wails. "I can't

sculpt there. Here I have three large unheated rooms and a garden. But fifty families could live here. How can I argue?"

He constructs his models out of styrofoam, life size, then sends them off to be cast. He cannot afford the basic materials, even clay. They stand in the garden, white porous shapes against the greenery, kept from toppling by guy wires. "We are a nation of craftsmen with no raw materials." The monuments just meet the Socialist realism requirements, as far as I can tell. One is a state monument for Lake Balaton, an arch to be put on a hillside in which a little girl is standing with her arms spread.

"Not bad for a monument to health, eh?" he says, coughing. "You know, they are moving the country people into these housing developments. In one of the provincial towns, I understand you can have your choice with your new apartment, either electricity or a pig. I'm not sure of the significance of that, but I like it. And I am glad that those people will not be displaced, though it will make my work harder than ever. I don't mean physically so much; rather it will, how do you say, *zuruckgezogen,* "interiorize" it even more. I wonder if I can work *that* small. Ha ha. Oh well, let me show you the miniatures which were *not* displayed in Venice. I'm allowed to display in the West only with the *most* capitalist of artists."

More abstract and intricate than those at the Biennale, they depict men in agony, imprisoned in transparent cubes, caught between a series of doors, men on collapsing chairs, women staring through a series of panels, each of them not quite wide enough to allow entry, and lastly, a series of heads staring through bars.

"Marisol is absolutely brilliant," he says, "did you see her? And that American, Frank Gallo, his women in those wonderful collapsing chairs."

They aren't collapsing, I explain. Those are sling chairs. Actually very popular. Everyone has one. That is simply how you look when you sit in them. Gallo is also a realist!

"For polyurethane, for *plastic,* I would give up ten years of my life. Now the state will even provide me with as much bronze and iron as I need, even gold, for the finished product at any rate. But I will never be

a contemporary artist until I can use plastic, and the new materials."
I look at the heads in their cages and ask if there is no political aspect
to his work. Utterly straightfaced, he replies, "No," tapping one of the
bars, "this is pure aesthetics. A low aesthetics, perhaps, but a pure
one."
I laugh, but he does not reciprocate.
"I mean exactly what I say," he said. "You must have some of this
Johnny Red scotch. Remember also, my friend, that the artist is limited
by his audience as much as the authorities."

Behind the Museum of Fine Arts and the enormous pedestal on the parade ground where Stalin used to stand, I run my laps among the children sailing their boats—and the lovers, older men with the younger
women, the classy old cockers with burgeoning chicks—they use each
other so well—I run my vain western mile to keep in shape, for Lord
knows what. Once while doing pushups in the high grass, I am tapped
by a woman with her cane who tells me in Hoch Deutsch that the grass
was not put there for such a purpose and that I will soon wear it out.
The children also laugh at my plodding rounds. So at last, I go to the
magnificent Turkish baths, copper sulphate now obliterating the mosaics, a tier of rosewood lockers leading off to twenty different pools
and temperatures. My knees and back and throwing elbow, true victims of violent American games and the American Medical Association, never felt better than in that soak. I buy the best, a quarter's
worth of a three-hundred-pound Turk who kneads the very shit out of
me. He hurts my knees terribly, but I cannot cry out, and wouldn't
know what to say had I throat enough. In the baths of Budapest, men
are equally morose in the steam, sighing into the thick waters, groans
signifying neither ecstasy nor pain. I remember Big Sur.
Upon the marble slab next to me, a distinguished-looking corpulent
functionary is getting the callouses of his considerable feet pared by an
earnest thick-wristed young man. My Hunky Turk Suma-wrestler
speaks to me in what sounds like Italian—given respectability by Ger-

man and Russian gutturals—somehow he knows the grammar and inflection but none of the names for things. His adverbs are Russian, his verbs high German though always in the present tense, but the sentence somehow comes out Italianate.

"Deutsch? " he queries.

No.

"Finnish?"

No.

"Austrian? "

No.

"Not Czech? "

Not on your life.

"Ah ha, Slovak."

Nope.

"Not Russki? "

No.

"English? "

Sorry.

"Are you certain you're not Finnish? "

Nope.

"What, then? "

A*mer-ican.*

His fingers stop, the podiatrist as well.

"Is it true that the . . . *Schwarze* are treated as badly as your papers say? That they are actually murdered! "

Yes. Not murdered, exactly, in the same sense that you understand it, but things are every bit as shameful, I would guess, as you've heard.

"But what do you mean," he relents with his fingers slightly, *"not exactly killed,* then what? "

I mean, not *liquidated.* But, how do you say, *lelkileg elnyomott,* "psychologically oppressed."

The very distinguished man speaks up at that point. "Such counts for very little if they are not hungry. Are they hungry, sir? "

Yes, some are hungry, but it's a hunger that's a function of something else beyond . . .

The masseur interrupts, "I never sar a *noir* until I saw the Mongolian soldiers in '56. They thought they were in Berlin. They kept running around yelling 'Where are the Nazis?' . . ."

The distinguished man interrupts violently at this point. "Give me a concrete example. A racial comparison."

I think for a while. Well, the only one I can think of that would be at all close would maybe be your gypsies. I mean, from what I can see, their culture is tolerated only in the most paternalistic way. Their poverty is ascribed to a matter of their own indifference, and is thus self-perpetuating. So when they do break community and make it in the city, their occupations are possible only in terms of the myth you have created for them. There is not a single restaurant in this city without its gypsy band. They will always be entertainers; and in this sense you deny them the possibility of equal competition. . . . In socialist or capitalist nations, that amounts to the same thing . . .

The distinguished man again interrupts.

"This is not a true comparison at all. First of all, we do not 'compete' in such a vulgar way. And in any case, a gypsy can go as high and as far as he wants."

The masseur chimes in, "And since '56, it is *easier* for them than for full-blooded Hungarians! " He purses his lips. "They are very loyal to the party, they are paid off, they are like the Jews in the Horthy regime. They get special treatment and the hard-working people get nothing."

OK, let's forget it.

The distinguished man continues calmly now in French. "That which you have just heard is not true. The party gives equal power to all the people." And then he breaks out apoplectically, "No one here wants for medical care! Nor education. Everyone has a vacation! Every school child goes to Lake Balaton for at least two weeks in the summer."

At this, the young podiatrist jumps up. He seems about thirty. "Oh sir, they do, do they? Well, I did not go to the Balaton when I was a child and I do not go now. Where did my Balaton vacation go, Mister Fonctionnaire? Where is *my* Balaton vacation, sir? Where is the free medical care for my dead mother? Where is my diploma? What happened with my generation, comrade? "

The Hungarian press has today listed the agreements reached at the Bratislava conference. Reports of Swoboda's stubbornness begin to trickle in, and there is a kind of general rejoicing. "If Dubcek can hold on, it will be good for all of us"; that is the general consensus—though this is shot through with the proviso that the Czechs are incredible clods, without guts, and that they are inconceivably lucky in this matter. A party member confides to me, "Actually, the only brave Czechs are the ones who live on what should be Hungarian soil." Again, I am to depend on the American Seventh Army Radio for the objective side of things.

My friends are urging me to go to Prague immediately. "There are great things happening. This can have momentous consequences." I'm going, I'm going, already. But I want to see what the *Herald Tribune* says before I take my ass over that border. Then a rumor that a cache of American arms has been found. Oh, the bloody CIA, I think. I pray to God that the CIA will keep their hands off this. "Are they really that powerful? " a friend asks me.
I have no idea anymore, I said.
"Well," he consoles me, patting me on the back, "Maybe they're not that powerful. Maybe they're just stupid, eh?"
In any case, it appears that I am the man to go, since I am the man with mobility, who has his space and eats it too, the heavy breath of America, checking out the Czechs for the honorable Hungarian opposition in the interest of international good will. They do not understand *our* kind of mobility, however, the conditions of our acceleration—for the European, movement is transcultural, panlinguistic—from one historical epoch, one climate, one culture to another, across the richest, most diverse and blessed territory on earth. For us, however, and, incidentally, for the Russians, whose real intent I am charged with divining, *our* common impulse is ahistorical, anti-cultural, challenging neither history nor time, not even language, but space and nature itself; the Russkis and us, doomed to meet repeatedly on the opposite sides of some Central European river, glaring across the rapids with enormous field-

glasses at one another—without the faintest idea of the many lands and peoples we have passed through. . . .

On the way, I spend the night with friends at the great Danube bend. We are at the tip of a long island in the midst of the river. I swim half-way across, and the current is so strong that I'm half a mile back to-wards Budapest before I even look up, and another half mile before I can get back to shore. The hydrofoil from Vienna breezes by. My friend laments the lack of fish in the river. Apparently there is a new sulphate plant upstream. He has given up fishing the Danube entirely, except for sturgeon, catfish and other bottom feeders, and even the feeder streams near mountain spas are apparently no good any more. It's the fertilizer. "If I come to America," he says, "Will you take me fishing? "
Not listening, I reply, Well, if you come, we ought to really go to Canada or Mexico. He cannot understand this. "There are no fish in America?" he says. I wave at the how-now-brown Danube. Sort of like this, is all I can say.
He drops the point and gestures across to the dense eastern bank capped by a ruined fort. "There are still stag and boar in that forest," he says. "Khrushchev came here to hunt once." On the prime frontage, however, ugly plastic A-frames, with pseudo-Swiss trappings, are being constructed. "Villas for famous Budapest actors," he explains. "One queer opera singer has a swimming pool lined with Herendi porcelain." It's Beverly Hills all over again, Socialist Commercial, International eclectic atavism. A mile downstream, a new spa has just been finished, furnished with patched-up art nouveau and chinoiserie, bad paintings of the Munkacsy school, Biedermeier china, confiscated from minor aristocrats with furiously eclectic taste, an estate populated exclusively by heavily armed German dentists, who, thank God, through their sheer natural offensiveness, have alone displaced us as the most hated visitors to the old world.
The orchards, fields and vineyards which sweep down to the river from the peninsula are in total disrepair. A woman complains, "We can't get help. You can't pay anyone to work with the earth anymore, no matter

what you offer." A peasant woman talking like a Scarsdale housewife. In one field there is a swath as if a tank had turned around. "The boar," she explains.

Down the main drag of the peninsula at 5:00 PM sharp, here come the cows. Each one knows which house to turn into. They peel off like Pontiacs going off the cloverleaf at Scarsdale, each to his own garage, bells going like All Saints' Day. . . . You can hear them mooing, "No help any more, nobody to pick up the cowshit. . . ."

At the extreme tip of the peninsula is a public campground, filled with Czechs. The mountains are turning purple. The light is more Veronese than Venice. Small kettles are brought out and goulash or fish soup is prepared. But space again. Where is the space? It is a Provincetown in miniature, a more casual Carmel in August. It differs only in the intensity of consumership, the fewer pounds of disposable waste per person, and the manners developed out of always living in close quarters. For the American, camping is associated with the conquering or the simulation of space. Yet here, with their tents right up against one another, as the steaming kettles turn the peninsula into an ocean liner of night, here a new mobile middle class is being formed, beautifully mindless, taking the air over their barbecue; a second city, a trailer camp without cars, is their reward. They are beginning to spend their money like everyone else in the world.

"You give people money, and they will *all* do the same thing with it," my friend says. "That's the only hope of the world," he sighs.

The only difference is the miniaturization, the tiny cars, the Czech tents, even the volleyball at dusk seems smaller, the net lower than ours, the not unenviable simplicity of a new bourgeois holiday, of getting away from it all. . . . Do they know, can these brinksmasters possibly know what they are now on the brink *of*?

August 22, 1968: Off before dawn, heading for Prague by a side road, towards what I have been told is the least busy of the checkpoints. We are not stopped on the road, and I'm surprised that no patrols have crossed our way. Again, I think about my notes being confiscated; paranoia has its erotic side, never doubt it. To think that all I have to smuggle in is whatever articulateness I can muster; small piece of change that. I've been practicing not being scared for a little too long.

Then, as the sun breaks out of the mountains, in a field to my left, I see a column of Hungarian tanks, advancing angularly towards the deserted checkpoint. The striped gate-pole is up. Machine-gun tower unmanned. As part of the invasion force, my residual curiosity quickly evaporates, and I take a U-turn. "Well, how about Yugoslavia this year?" my friend says.

Yes indeed, there is a stone table in western Czechoslovakia marking the geographic center of the continent! It may be said that you will receive a "heart-warming" welcome from its friendly people. You will be greeted with "Prejeme si abyste se citili jako doma." (We hope you think of our home as your home.) |Brochure of Czechoslovak Airlines found at Border Station.|

Back in Budapest, two days spent in seclusion as if I were to blame. Are we never going to have any kind of honorable confrontation with authoritarianism with any odds at all? And now I see the difference between my cynicism and real melancholia, hatred and self-hatred, guilt and impotence, being apolitical by choice and being depoliticized by events. The worst question one can ask oneself is not what would happen if one were a braver man, but even if one *were* a braver man, what in hell would one do then? Why have I involved myself in this? Misled, on the losing side once again—denied in the end even the luxury of self-loathing. Even our stupidities robbed of character. All that hard-won irony and pragmatism, appropriate only to self-defense, and never to the survival of what one cares about beyond oneself. One cannot "give up" any more programmatically than one could help "succeeding." One cannot blame oneself any more than one once refused to blame history, and the worth, if not the cost, of such knowledge remains the most open of questions. . . .

|165|

In Budapest, among the intelligentsia who were once so hopeful, there is some fear that the Czechs have brought the house down on everyone. Lukács is reported to have said, "It is the end of the first dream of Socialism."

Kadar seems strangely respected for his handling of the situation—there is a rumor he made *18* trips to Moscow during the course of the crisis in order to try and mediate. Even among the most anti-party intellectuals there is respect for Kadar, this soft-spoken man whose nails were torn out by Stalinists—respect not for his office but for his personal integrity. Now, can you imagine that? A country in which the people detest their leader's *office*, while respecting him for the sort of human being he is. Reverse image again. This is getting very complicated, America. I wonder sometimes if I wouldn't give up some of my personal freedom simply to be governed by men I could respect as human beings.

It's felt, ironically enough, that the presence of the large Russian garrison will insure the status quo, and counter the domestic repression. "No one in opposition would dare to move openly now," one intellectual says. "If we're smart, we can play on the crisis and consolidate a few more reforms."

Another shakes his head. "Dubcek will get what Nagy got. I cannot understand it. My God, why didn't they fight? They had everything going for them. Why did Swoboda cave in? "

"To save lives, of course."

I'm asked if the Americans would have intervened.

Are you kidding? If I were a Czech, I certainly wouldn't want them to.

"You just don't know the Czechs," one man finally slaps his knee. "They are chickenshits. But still, it just proves that we *were* wrong in '56. You see, this proves there is *no way* we can get out of this."

A Hungarian who has been vacationing in Prague cries out, "They spit on me. They spit on me right in the street."

What do you expect? I said.

|166|

Our cultural policy ought to have this single aim: to be in harmony with the endeavours of avant-garde writers and artists in general. Here, of course, arises a whole complex of questions around the autonomy of culture, as it is being discussed in the West; in Italy for instance. But beware of those discussions. Let us not forget that the Italian or French communists are in opposition, and that we have in mind an autonomy of culture inside this revolutionary opposition, apart from which there is a further wide cultural area arising from different ideas. Nor do we want in our country to see communist ideology dissolving itself in a multitude of views; it should be developed within itself and should keep its integrity. But our situation differs from that of the communists in capitalist countries in this, that we, as a ruling force, are and must be simultaneously the guardians of freedom for a different view, or even an opposite one. *The moment we forget this, we have forgotten a very essential premise of socialism. Where, then, are the boundaries: I should say that these stand at private ownership of the means of production and the exploitation of one man by the other. This is where the dividing line lies, but beyond it there is, on our side as well, plenty of room for widely differing views.* |Laco Novomesky, Czech poet and politician, 1966|

"I am not the minister of war," he wails.

Ah, I say, you must learn to live with your responsibilities for maintaining the balance of power. We are beginning to understand one another.

A couple arrives from Rumania. A mother and her middle-aged daughter. They say they were searched for eight hours at the border, including free vaginal inspections.

"We were searched by our *own* police," the woman coughs, "and me with a bad heart. I spent five years in a concentration camp and now I'm searched eight hours on my own border."

Well, I interjected, trying to ease things, it looks as though Ceausescu is now the most liberal leader in central Europe.

"He is a pig," the older woman declares flatly.

It seems that they have come for an abortion. The population rate in Rumania is also declining; there is little birth control, and they are trying to encourage children by giving large family allowances. Apparently, a woman can't leave the country without a certificate stating that she is not pregnant, and this is what resulted in their search.

The middle-aged daughter looks tired.

"If he were not a pig, he would not let women suffer like this. In return for foreign policy, we get Stalinism at home. I already take care of two of hers. Imagine, a 45-year-old woman getting pregnant. It's disgusting."

Later that evening, I announce my intention to leave for Yugoslavia.

"Ah," the pregnant lady says, "yes, we won the lottery once and went there. It is very beautiful. It is *another world. . . .*"

Today, I sit in the hills of Buda, gliders in the haze overhead and, below, the Danube, no longer blue if it ever was, and I see that this is the mirror I have so long searched for—not the England of my intellectual antecedents, nor the France of my forebears, nor even the Russia of my putative enemies, whom I can finally despise, not for their anti-Ameri-

|167|

canism, nor even for what they have so needlessly done to this remarkable people, but because they have not afforded, in any sense, an alternative to America.

When I ask my friends why the most reasonable reforms cannot be undertaken, when they pose no threat to the party's hegemony, they can only shrug—"Because we cannot be different, we just cannot appear *different.*"

How strange for an American of this time to be in a country where even the most libertarian personalities are largely thankful for a few years of quiet, bland, gradualistic progress, where increased production of any sort is a source of pride, where to be a liberal is to be both humanist *and* cunning, where every act of the imagination is defined and frequently sharpened immediately by official resistance, where survival is the primary aesthetic, and where the daily insults to one's intelligence make a mordant wit the norm. They know how *their* establishment works. I see just how irrelevant my individualism is, when transferred to a milieu where power is never diffuse, hierarchy never unbroken, even for an instant. All one's maneuvering and posturing, even the better anarchistic gestures, one's subtle indifferences and contempt, are on a different scale with different consequences, one's integrity becomes not a weapon or a tool, but merely its own subject. I wouldn't last a week here if I were not granted a certain immunity. And I realize how much further I must go in analyzing and dealing with the peculiar unique sort of repression which is my lot at home. For what would instantly destroy you here would be effortlessly absorbed by the American establishment. Yet we continue to dignify our obstreperousness, by reference to those who suffered a great deal more from the consequences of similar actions. This doesn't mean we should accept ours as a relatively better lot, but it does mean we had better begin to fathom the real sources of our paranoia; in a word, make it instructive.

I remember suddenly that I was born in the spring of 1938, as the Spanish Civil War, the Munich Conference and the Moscow Purges closed out each other, the year it could be said that old Europe committed suicide. And now I have watched it, grown up with it, repeat-

When knowing becomes an object for itself it can justify itself in its empirical procedure only by relating itself to the conditions of its origin and to the ways in which it has functioned. |Leszek Kolakowski|

edly fled to it, only to watch it resurrect itself in the image of my own country. Yet in Hungary, the adhesions of the year of my birth are not, were never closed, and I feel again in touch with the history denied me, denied for reasons which are still not at all clear. It is hardly a pleasant feeling, but it is real. And it occurs to me that the best argument against totalitarianism is simply that human nature is basically revisionist; we re-vision all our experience if we are to survive, and if this is so, then to institutionalize such revision is *prima facie* inhuman and a lie.

And here in the stuffy crawl-space between Fascist and Communist temperaments, what does it mean to be "a leftist in an American context"? It means a lot of laughs for Hungarians, for the cost of their survival is not to take Marxism seriously. "America is a big, rich country," they say, "it can afford Marxism." In fact, one would guess that Marxism will never have any relevance for Hungary, even for the generation which did not experience Rakosi. It will have no relevance until its rhetoric will cease to subsume day-to-day reality—and so Marx becomes useful only as a mirror-image for Western smugness, not for its anti-capitalism as much as an antidote to an overdose of Freud, voluntaristic philosophy, of *modernism* itself, which Lukács characterizes as that "vulgar and cynical laughter which is its own subject and has no effect." But there is more to it than that, for precisely in opposition to American reformers who yearn for fresh theory (and explain their failures by the lack of such), Hungarians have dismissed theory completely—for not only is theory itself associated with corruption, but their new pragmatism is the confirmation of whatever independence they are developing. And when theory goes out the window, everything goes—Lukács goes out with the worst party hack; indeed, apart from a few disciples who have inherited only their master's opacity, Hungarians admire Lukács not for his analytic rigor, his power of synthesis, but only for his ability to land on his feet (and the fact that he is admired in the West). And so, even posthumously, the greatest Marxist conceptual thinker of this century remains unread in socialist countries, but alive and well at MIT—yet another export.

"America is now the home, the new Germany, of theory," my friend says, "the theory of the novel, the theory of resistance, the theory of the occult and mystical," and the implication again is that only we can afford it. They are quite perceptive, of course—to my right, on Gellert Hill, stands a monument originally commissioned for the son of Hitler's ally, regent and admiral Horthy, to celebrate the defeat of the "Scourge of Bolshevism," only to be chosen from the sculptor's studio by General Voroshilov of the occupying Red Army to stand as the Soviet War Memorial. To my left, on the site of Roman ruins stands the most hideous public housing development imaginable, wreathed in fumes and anonymity, rubble upon rubble. So if history is a seamless absurdity, then the moment, the decision on the spot, is what delivers one from Time itself. Hungarians would call themselves professional existentialists, if that were not also a theory.

There is nevertheless a deluding aspect to this cagy realism, for in spite of their hatred for the Soviets, they will not easily admit that those national characteristics usually associated with Hungary were destroyed when the class of country gentry was liquidated, and what remains of their culture is increasingly only a commodity to be trotted out for tourists, another *export* for hard currency, while at home the state tries to kill off interest in the operetta as a remnant of petit-bourgeois decadence, and buys up *Love Story*.

Having once been obsessed with Fascism, Irredentism, Imperialism, Communism, and Anti-Communism, Hungarians are now obsessed with being reasonable. As one friend is at pains to remind me, "It does no good to be a champion sprinter in a swimming pool. What would you have us do? " But there is one thing the American knows better than his more sophisticated Hungarian counterpart, and that is the cost of privatizing history, of taking pride in pragmatism as a total *identity* as well as an attitude and technique. We know how the Stalinists came to power; but we know much less about those who rule as a result of surviving Stalinism. And in this sense, the official line is self-defeating not because it is simple-minded nor jargon, but because it curiously coincides with Western establishment rhetoric, proclaiming itself thusly: "The revolution has been made, our enemies defeated, the major suffering over, and so as inheritors of this unparalleled grappling

Neken egyaltalan nem felel meg.

Nem vagyok meg-elegedve (vele).

Nagyon kellemetlen (itt).
(Nagyon) rossz [szornyu, remes, undorito]!
Pech. (Pechem van.)

Figyelmetztetni akarom.
Viselkedjek (viselkegy-gyek) rendesen!

Vigyazzon!

Tiltakozom!
Nem ezt mondom. (Nem ugy ertem.)
En nem ezt monodtam.
En semmi ilyet nem mondtam.
Felreertette, amit mondtam.
Ezt nem teheti meg.
Hogy mereszel?
Ez nem illik
Ez nem fair.
Ezt nem turom el.
Panaszt akarok tenni . . . ellen.
Irasban akarok panaszi tenni.

with History, your task is to refine and consolidate the mechanism.
. . ." It will backfire on them as on us, not with another spontaneous
revolt, but with sullen youngsters swilling barbiturates in suburban
cemeteries, as they have already begun to do here. Our government excuses itself by protecting the world from the Communist Menace; the
Hungarian government blames its deficiencies on the residual psychology of capitalism. And in both cases, the only political prisoners are
those left of the party in power.

So what do you make of a socialism which has established itself precisely because it has not changed *any* of the social relations of the
society, a socialism in which the people who make it are precisely those
who practice the most bourgeois virtues? "Ah," my cynical ex-populist
friend says, "we live under *compulsory* bourgeoisdom; the ideal society
is one in which you can get a few of the benefits of the consumer
society while not being a bourgeois."

But the only question for me, I insist, is the one you never ask your-
selves: what would socialism be like, were it not for the Russians?
"There would be none."

And would you be better off, in the long run?

"Of course, don't be an idiot. We will have our capitalism as you have
your socialism. By default, under other names. But the rhetoric, it will
always remain. We will buy our economic freedom by selling our foreign policy, which unfortunately bureaucrats confuse also with cultural
policy. . . ."

Below me on a hilltop, the prime minister of this country and its most
famous poet live next door to each other, each in unpretentious and indistinguishable villas. They have been rewarded for their expertise by
the two most scarce items in the country—interior space and a view.
Their lifestyles appear rather similar—one has a dog, the other a body-
guard. They differ radically only in the way each perceives and reconstitutes the world. And that of course remains, in spite of everything, the dream of socialism, not so much equity of power or position,

|171|

It doesn't suit me
    (at all).
I am not satisfied
    (with it).
I am not very happy
    (about it).
It's very unpleasant
    (here).
(Too) bad [awful,
    horrible, disgusting].

Bad luck!
I'm up against it!
I want to warn you.
Please behave yourself.

Look out!
Be careful!
Take care!

I protest!
No, I don't mean that.
No, I didn't say that.
No, I didn't say
    anything of the sort
You've misinterpreted
    what I said.
You can't do that.
How dare you?
It's not done.
    (It's not proper.)
It's not fair.
I won't put up with it
    [that].
I wish (am going) to
    complain against . . .
I wish (am going)
    to make a written
    complaint.

|*How to Say It in Hungarian*|

but that men would be differentiated by the way their minds work, and that their minds would be given work which would be both intrinsically meaningful and organically related to the community. It does not matter whether, as it turns out, the poet's house is the inheritance of his wife. With his reputation and his ego, he would have had it one way or the other. But only poets and geniuses create their *own* work. Otherwise, freedom is gained in conscious association. That was once a revolutionary idea. Now it seems rather a simple, sadly unrealized fact. Is there no way to bring about the proximity of the prime minister and the poet without force and repression?

Below me, also in the square, is the mushroom tester—a penultimate holdover from the petit bourgeois of old Europe, now an "official body," a man who will tell you for a fee, when you descend from the hills with your mushrooms, which are poisonous. We could use such a man in America, many of his kind; a man who can show you how not to poison yourself. But he will not be here much longer; no longer than the bootmaker next to him whose son will not apprentice himself to his father, even though he would make three times the money that he will in his new white collar job. As with what little interesting architecture remains, these artisans are tolerated not because of their value, but because the state is still too poor and preoccupied to displace them with its version of the modern. And next to the bootmaker, the bookseller, which involves that most unique of Socialist measures, unique to this country—the Trash Tax—a tax upon "popular entertainment" to subsidize "recognized culture." For example, an Agatha Christie mystery costs much more than a Victor Hugo novel, and, as a result, any poor person may build up quite an impressive library of classics for practically nothing, subsidized, and properly so, by popular entertainment. The question is an open one; can the Trash Tax save the Taste Tester? Can the Trash-tester, through a Taste Tax, save the Protester?

Their children will let them know—if not this generation, then the next. To separate revolution, consolidation and transcendence into historical stages is a Marxist compounding of the Freudian division of consciousness, and no one can live his life if he is repeatedly told he is locked into a categorical imperative, since both open protest and acquiescence in such a case are equally self-defeating. And the single benefit of Communist-Capitalist competition for the last twenty years is that the value of work can no longer be defined by either Freudian *or* Marxist mythology—in terms of isolated self-knowledge, or the good of the community, in terms of the marketplace—whether "free" or "planned." As the protagonist of a contemporary Hungarian play, as yet not allowed to be published, observes:

I don't want to be split into bits any longer, nor to hear my name together with lots of other people . . .

What, then, is so admirable about these people—if the stupidities of our respective ruling classes cancel each other out at every remove? For one thing, they have re-found, as they have so many times in the past, what we have so recently lost—self-esteem. In other words, despite the absurdity of their history, the full share of culpability for what has befallen them, at the same moment they refused to blame history for their lot, they ceased hating themselves. They know what impulsiveness and revolutionary romanticism are worth, for they have experienced both home-grown and imported varieties. They are unhappily a colony without a colonial mentality—just as we are imperialist without a true imperial certitude—they know that their own nightmare is now the world's—and if they continue to look west while being tied to the east, they know that to be Europeanized now means to be Americanized. They have, in short, learned the basic rule of survival in the modern world. That is: to live with full consciousness of the irony of your situation without allowing irony to be your sole response to it. They have thrown off, then, programmatic despair, feeling sorry for themselves. They have discovered they can deal with oppression in a number of ways, between the suicidal dialectic of violent revolution and apathy, and that such resistance is temperamental before it is ideological. And finally, they have learned that there is no model, particularly a foreign one, for coming to terms with one's own repression. All repressive families are different. Given their place on the earth, politics may still be fate, but fate is, surprisingly enough, not all there is to life; or to quote a new American radical:

Politics is not a position on an issue . . . politics is how you live your life. |T. Gitlin|

So the instructive thing about Hungary is not that it lies between Germanic and Mediterranean culture, between the Capitalist-Communist ideological struggle, between State Capitalism and Incentive Socialism, between western Europe and the Third World, between a society of scarcity and one of affluence, though all of these are true—the interesting thing is that it lies between a 19th century pastoral illusion common to all Western cultures, and an America almost already destroyed by its wastes and stimulants, between a discontent with parochial tradition and an unexamined faith in new technology. They are on the make once again, and if the increasing uninhabitability of London and New York is due to greed and lack of planning, then to what does one attribute precisely the same encroaching ugliness in a socialist society? If a socialist state, with its established control over the rhythms of daily life, and its pretense to collective priorities, cannot at least teach the world how to deal with basic contradictions of production and consumption, then, given the enormous suffering it has already caused, the socialist experiment will truly be consigned to perdition. The left will have lost the claim to expertise, as it has already that to righteousness, and all of us will be the poorer. . . .

So it is. They are impossibilists because they were not allowed to become; while we have become what we thought impossible.

I asked my cynical ex-populist friend this morning, could I not, before I left, meet at least one Communist, one committed revolutionary? "Why certainly," he sneered, and an hour south of Budapest, we leave the shallow Danube and cut into mud country. He explains that we are going to visit a town comprised solely of Greek Partisans who fled in 1948 after their Civil War.

The road narrows, becomes gravel, then ruts out. We arrive after dark; the town consists of barracks-like buildings, a small textile factory, and beneath a single streetlight in a dirt square, a cafe. Inside, we are in Greece, all men, mostly old, mustachioed, fingering their worry beads,

THE LAST REVOLUTIONARIES

"Here are your *real* revolutionaries," my friend says softly. "Look at that man over there," gesturing to the oldest and most dignified of the lot. "He would have been near fifty-five when he took up his rifle and went into the mountains."

We are in Greece, it is true, and Greek is spoken; but it is a cafe without banter, without song or dance, without ouzo, baklava or Turkish coffee, without questions, without even air, it seems. The stale torte and headless Egyptian beer turn to stone in our mouths. Suddenly Hungary is very heavy. Insupportable. They look at us as if we were crazy. In Greece, we would have already been bought a drink, and a man who was in Chicago in 1920 sought out to interpret. But this is not *theirs;* there is nothing for them to offer.

After some time, my friend gets one of the younger men to loosen up. As he speaks, the others turn and their faces unfold like camellias, their hard bright eyes and teeth emerge.

"No, there is nothing Greek here. If you came on Friday evening, perhaps the folk-dance ensemble would be practicing. And once a year we roast a lamb, but on *their* Easter. There is not one of us who would not go back if we could. Even with the colonels. But imagine, if old Papadoupoulos would not grant us immunity . . . that man over there, for example," pointing to the patriarch again, "he killed a priest . . . and he . . ."

Suddenly the room freezes; a Hungarian policeman is in the doorway, his arms folded, jackboots astomp, mustache aflame, a theatrical parody of the lost Monarchy. "I will," he announces, "be requesting your identity papers!" He comes to us first, and after one glance at the foreign passport, suddenly drops the *Verbunkash* authority, and slips into a schizoid servility, saluting, bowing, admonishing us to enjoy ourselves, then loses himself among the Greeks, still minuscule in their enormous Hungarian felt overcoats, slapping them on the shoulders, making little bad jokes. The worry beads reappear and the low conversation recommences.

What's up?

"Oh," my friend smiles, "He was curious as to who we were, and he just didn't know any other way to ask."

|175|

HUNGARIAN PEASANT WEDDING

Members of the tour will have the chance to take part in a real Hungarian peasant wedding. They will attend the different phases of the ceremony from the dressing of the bride to the wedding preparations. They will take part in the bridal procession, sipping fiery wines with the wedding-guests. After this a Hungarian-type nuptial dinner follows and, the highlight of the day, the dance with the bride. The programme starts at 5:30 every Tuesday and Saturday in front of the Mezokovesd Matyo-house.

Rate (including dinner and wine-tasting): US $6.50   Ft. 195.00

You would think, I interrupt, that for the bravest of partisans, a socialist state might at least import some ouzo?

"My God, you are naive. They lost the Civil War because they were Stalinists. They were defeated because Tito closed his border, as much as by any American aid. And here they are hated because they were *convinced* Communists: Under Rakosi, they were used as jailers, and to enforce collectivization . . ."

The policeman has come back to see if we have enough to drink.

"They made the mistake of being old-fashioned," my friend goes on. "They murdered one by one, they knew and hated their victims personally, and so they are remembered. They are the last terrorists with faces."

The killers are all smiling at us now—positively beatific. The Hungarian bargirl is laughing at us. The policeman is in the back getting smashed. The single neon streetlight throws urine-colored streaks of synthetic light across the square. In the corner, there is a plane tree in a tub. On the wall, a profile of a man drinking wine, made from coathanger wire—straight from the Holiday Inn at Lebanon, Indiana. They invite us to come back as we leave. The octogenarian touches me on the wrist, then makes a friendly fist—signifying what, I do not know. Perhaps he simply cannot undo his fingers anymore.

On the way back, we stop for dinner and mention to the waiter we have been to Beloiannis.

"My God," he starts, "you went out there? You're lucky to come out in one piece! They're murderers, you know."

The land flattens immediately out on the Puszta, that indefensible great plain, the thatch-roofed cottages becoming pink, ochre, blue pastel, as one nears Rumania. The roads at night are impossible—unlit bicycles, ox carts crossing without warning from hidden side roads. Cross a small bridge dedicated to eleven Communists massacred during the White Terror of '21. And then we pass through the more theatrical aspects of the Hungarian wild west, the cowboys, the brandy, the vineyards, the blooded horses, the shepherds draped with long-haired sheep cloaks like vultures. As in the midwest, the land gets down to business rapidly. The languid rivers, so lethal in the flood season, lined now with willow and cedar. You know where the rivers are by the trees; a line of trees on the horizon does not mean a windbreak, but a stream. Wells like Ls on their side, fields of glittering rye and glowing saffron, Calvinist and Catholic churches, Italianate clouds; the sky appears about four feet off the ground, leaving room only for the ubiquitous geese which scatter so calmly.

Then, on a side road, within sight of the Rumanian border, 40 kilometers from the nearest town, where I could quite conceivably be the first American ever, I swing round a curve, and see on the wall of a grange in letters four feet high, imprinted in English: **PEACE IN VIETNAM**

I find my friends outside the next town.

PORTRAIT OF AN EX-KULAK

Palinkas, now 69, inherited a fifth of his father's farm as did each of two brothers and sisters. Two meandering streams make it exceptionally fertile land. The peppers and vegetables were in such demand before the war that they were shipped throughout Europe. Each farm has a sturdy mud and dung whitewashed house over 100 years old, walls two feet thick, retaining coolness in the summer and warmth in the winter. One large bedroom, a kitchen without running water, and a large cool storage room. It is thoroughly idyllic, surrounded by poplars, lindens and views in all directions across the fields. Palinkas keeps his own pigs and chickens, grows his own vegetables and obviously eats and drinks very well. His patriarchy (which he does not take very seriously) seems serene, jovial, not wanting for any necessity.

Palinkas does not recall exactly when the farms were collectivized; only that he went to work for them as a tractor operator. Apparently he was so well esteemed that the collective's management retired his tractor with him. It now lies in his barnyard in dinosaurian disrepair, his name stenciled on its loins. After collectivization, the families were given a small settlement and allowed to keep their houses as well as something less than an acre of land for their own gardening.

Over breakfast of raw green pepper, which when hulled is as sweet as a Carolina apple, the best salami in the world, and a plum brandy which makes even the best coffee seem like urine, we get down to cases and discuss the unamusing century he has spanned. Nothing has obviously made any particular impression, even the salutory fact of his survival. "Don't talk to me about ideology," he says. "There is only one thing that corrupts, and that is unequal barter. Russia is bleeding us. They always have. I'll tell you how it works: we buy clay from them with which we make clay midgets, we sell the midgets to Yugoslavia for piglets, which we fatten and sell to Russia for more clay. It doesn't make a damn bit of difference. We're just having the shit cheated out of us and we can't do a damn thing about it. No, don't talk to me about Communism. I'm not in the party, but there's nothing so wrong with Communism except the Russians. May God drive his peter through their brain."

No young man will ever take over the farm, and only a few among the sons of this man's colleagues will go to work for the collective. "Nobody but a fool or a widow will work for them." Palinkas's son, on the next farm over, has been working for the railroad for twenty years. Yet, on his acre, from two yearly crops of vegetables made possible by a hand pump irrigation system and sold on the private market, he earns more than his gross annual salary with the railroad. The few pigs are a luxury. He fattens them only for friends. He has no help nor mechanization, though occasionally he steals some fertilizer from the collective.

No one else in the family will stay near the farms. Palinkas himself will sell out to the collective shortly and move into an apartment in town. It's getting too cold for him out there. And in any case, his children and grandchildren all work in town, mostly in the stocking factory where a nephew is a foreman. His grandchildren do not like to visit the farm particularly. "For what, then, should I stay?" he complains.

I insist in a furor that he must *hold on* to the farm—for his family—for his country! I am blurting now, and even with the plum brandy it is hardly justifiable. I tell him that his grandchildren, his great grandchildren will honor him for it. And more, he will be unhappy in a tiny apartment in town, electric heat or not.

He smiles at me thinly. "But I have been on the list for an apartment for fifteen years!"

For the life of me, I cannot figure out what I am defending. Private property? No. Forty acres and a mule? No. Pastoralism? Hardly. Primogeniture? Not likely. The notion of a true peasantry? Who needs it. Certainly not the spirit of collective sacrifice. For unlike us, with our subsidies, the Hungarians are at least forthright about the death of subsistence farming. Collectivization does not mean sharing, nor even the liquidation of private property, but simply the establishment of oligopoly, the application of big market muscle. Across the field, 15,000 Rhode Island reds lately arrived from America, en route to Russia, cluck desultorily. Palinkas denies that his children will be better off than his father was.

"How do they know? He spent his days hunting, his evenings with his doves. His wife never addressed him in the affectionate form of 'you.' He read the Bible at meals interminably. But it was certainly better to work for him than the cuntfaced tartar who manages the collective. . . . Oh no, progress is the ability to keep your problems to yourself. You don't have to believe things are getting better to live like a man."

I try to account for the source of my bemused nostalgia, and it occurs to me that my relationship to the Middle West is based on the myth of a very peculiar relationship between labor and leisure: for the Trans-Mississippi, between the terms of Jackson and Lincoln, remains the locus of the middle-class dream of a middle ground where freedom and security do not conflict. Situated between the *real* prairie, that howling wasteland where Indians really got mean, and the cutting edge of inexorably advancing industrialism, *that* midwest may be seen as a kind of switchyard in American fantasy life, between healing dream and nightmare, a still point in the peristalsis of advance and consolidation, ruled by the admirable desire to have it both ways. It was here that emphasis upon the values of work, production and adventure met those of leisure, reflection and security, and the self-sustaining family unit exemplified the original meaning of subsistence—that is, work which is not valued for its own sake, but only insofar as it can provide leisure for more important and pleasurable activities. It was an Arcadian hiatus in the progress of escapism and/or empire, a place of the mind which required neither Noble Savage nor General Custer. A land capitalism to be sure, but one without the bank-controlled technology and Puritanism of the east, the slave labor and hierarchy of the south, or the bitter all-consuming struggle and loneliness of the "wild" west. An area, then, where common defense and trade were to be provided voluntarily and democratically, a territory, in short, neither anarchistic nor institutional. Dickens, for one, saw us through the lens of European posterity and grandeur:

The prairie at sunset left nothing to the imagination, tamed it down and trampled its interest. . . . It was lonely and wild, but oppressive in its barren monotony . . . it is not a scene to be forgotten, but it is scarcely one, I think (at all events, as I saw it), to remember with much pleasure, or to covet the looking on again, in afterlife. |Dickens, American Notes|

But the point is precisely that one did not come to see the prairie and die, but to live on it, achieving a commonsensical balance of natural and cultural forces. Not the best of all possible worlds; just the best of this one.

So this is what I have superimposed upon Palinkas's Puszta—and I see that he knows what we are just beginning to suspect; that technology is the overriding factor, that the only thing collectivization means to him is that his compost heap is closer to his house than ever, that the "advantages" his children have are not due to a new vision of the world, but would have been afforded by the normal advance in technology, whatever political system was in force.

The family is growing uncomfortable. They have no idea what we're talking about. Evening arrives abruptly; we eat again. Palinkas brings out the plum brandy and the eldest son apologizes that he cannot drink with me, because he must take his motorcycle back to the village. If he is stopped by the police, he explains, one breathalyzer test and he loses his motorcycle for a year, and if he loses his motorcycle, he's lost his job.

Can't you bribe them? I ask.

"Not *them*."

I offer to go back with him, since he passes the farm where I will be sleeping. As we leave, the youngest son takes my hand and whispers to me that "whatever happens," he is not going to be "a worker." He had written me in Budapest, in fact, telling me that he wished to go to the university to study literature, since he was too sickly to do farm work and enjoyed reading. Would I bring him something to read? Would I! I tried to buy him continental or American fiction throughout Budapest. The best I could do was *Monte Cristo, Count of; Twist, Oliver; Quixote, Don;* de Maupassant, Salinger, early Brecht, very early Steinbeck, ubiquitous Jack London, very late Hemingway, *The Scarlet Letter, Moby Dick* abridged. I bought them all up cursing the shopkeepers, the state. "Where are the surrealists, the symbolists, where is Proust and Joyce, where, for God's sake, is Sinclair Lewis, *The Wizard of Oz?* Where, sir, the Transcendentalists?"

The books make a pile on the dirt floor of that farmhouse: the largest personal library of a 12-year-old in the history of the province. The boy fondles, rearranges, catalogs them each night, patting their bindings like pets. When he gets in bed with his brother at the foot of his parents' bed, the fire glows on the books like sheet lightning. God knows what they think of this manic American Cousin, who in the space of an afternoon ransacked every bookshop in the capital of their country of every "foreign classic," spending the equivalent of half a year of Palinkas's salary, impulsively berating the clerks, demanding why Melville has been abridged, now demanding that they *stay* on the farm—and read—as he would.

And approaching the end of the novel in his mind as he sat there with his wife sleeping alone in the next room he could feel that something unusual had happened. Something had grown up in his life dearer than—It, as the end. The words from long practice had come to be leaves, trees, the corners of his house—such was the end. He had progressed leaving the others behind him. |W. C. Williams, The Great American Novel|

|181|

The head of the collective farm, a dapper man in jodhpurs and a mustache, impersonating Walter Pidgeon, insists on taking this foreign visitor on a tour, having heard of his amateur interest in horticulture. The flower garden is magnificent—bordered with specimens of some kind of wild dill, I think, though it is the size and strength of a small evergreen. "An annual," he says and gives me some seeds to take home. There are also enormous poppies, altheas the size of softballs, split at the seams after lying in a rainy outfield for a month.

After this, I am taken by ox cart to see the "money crop." Three miles out in the fields, he drops me off in an infinity of rotting tomato vines. '68 has not been a vintage year for tomatoes either. I want to yell out in the field those Hungarian menus that I have memorized, an onomatopoeia of smell. But the dray draws away, leaving me to ponder the collective's enterprise. I watch the dray merge into the horizon, then I watch the tomatoes for an hour, walking their rows disconsolate. Eventually, I come in sight of some peasants who are harvesting; they spy me among the rows half a mile away. One grizzled old man breaks away, approaches me with long, loping strides and, upon squatting down, asks me where I'm from.

America.

"Bet you don't have tomatoes like this in America." I shrug aimlessly. He takes three putrescent green ones from the vine and swallows them down.

I decline his offer.

"You like it here in Hungary? "

I like it better than I've liked anything in a long time.

"Why don't you come to live here then? "

Oh, too expensive.

"How much does it cost to get here? " I estimate for him round trip high-season New York/Budapest air fare in forints.

"A lifetime's wages," he mutters. Then, "OK, you can have some tomatoes since you've come all this way, but take only the green ones." His cadre is screaming at him to get back on the job. They wave empty packing crates menacingly.

I ask him, what do you make from these?

He frowns.

You know; juice, canned tomatoes, what?

"Tomatoes," he sweeps his hands to all horizons. "This year tomatoes, next year, *not* tomatoes. Too watery . . . Communismus! " He shakes his fist, then turns his thumbs down. The sun is right on the treetops. After two hours, the dray is coming back. I have seen the tomatoes undiminished. He flips me a green one before going back on the job.

On the perimeter of those penultimate tomatoes sits a large fort with V-shaped crenellations built either by or against the Ottomans, and these battlements have been brilliantly restored into an outdoor theater, for the edification of this provincial town. Surrounding this is a new cooperative spa; all of this the remains of some count's estate. A lagoon for sailing has been dredged from the moats; a cafeteria installed beneath his grape arbors; and the skeleton of a highrise for those foreigners who will come to use the baths now dominates the park. It consists of perhaps a thousand landscaped acres, woods and fields—occasional kiosks selling fresh hot bread and unpasteurized cold beer, and thirty different pools of varying temperatures and medicinal content, some Olympic-size for swimming. The water which comes from the renowned springs is of a uniform color, a sulphurous dark brown, yellow when roiled. But it is pure, absolutely without sediment or chemical. Your joints become as molasses within its lubricity.

It is nothing less than a singular triumph of socialism. The state's usurpation of our privileged private property for public benefit—totally unpretentious, functional, non-commercial and utterly democratic. Gnarled gypsy women and party dignitaries eat sausage at the same table, paring their fruit with large hunting knives. Old women with coronaries and kidney ailments sit in the same 105° bath with their three-year-old grandchildren. I am put up in a motel with bunk beds, built on the edge of a stream with the same brown magical water. "You must," says the manager, "relax here. No one will expect anything of you." Repose.

|183|

Most restful is the fact there is no conflict, programmatic or otherwise, between the young and old here. Perhaps this is because the state lies to everyone equally and does not attempt to blame public confusion upon "the generations." They don't get in each other's way. No one raises his voice except to laugh, though in Budapest the scream is the norm. Here their leisure, their games and their ailments bind them together. In Budapest, the classlessness would have not been so perfect, and, in any case, class differentiation in Hungary is not based on socialist ethics as much as the fact that there have been so many shifts in power that those *in* have a respect for those deposed—being "on top" is seen as arbitrary. It is clear that the party people have more privileges, if not money. But there are fewer ways for them to flaunt them openly. And certainly in a more exclusive spa at Balaton relations would be less democratic. Nevertheless, people are sent here from all over the country regardless of cost, and it is said with realistic pride that the skyscraper will be reserved for the enormous German tourists, the income from whom will pay for more amputees and arthritic gypsy women. It costs practically nothing, even in Hungarian terms; the poor gain access upon medical prescription. It is not a reward for hard work, with its attendant hysteria; it is for whoever *needs* it. And for one moment, in this improbable swale situated so unpropitiously in central Europe, a group of willful patients, with a little help from their enemies, have created a kind of paradise possible only in the modern world—an environment both democratic *and* uncommercial, where consumers understand how to take their leisure because they believe it belongs to all of them. No need to invoke natural law, assert their rights, show the color of their money. They are here not to demonstrate success, but because they need rest. It has the kind of serenity which no American last resort will ever have, and which, I suspect, few Westerners have experienced; a communal, a shared privacy. Repose.

In the evening there is a performance in the fort—concert stars and ballet dancers brought from Budapest to give an eclectic program of ex-

WELCOME IN HUNGARY!
Only information considered to be of a certain importance is to be found hereunder.

Hungary—land of hospitality, polyglot guides and 10.3 million hosts . . . the site of magic Budapest was chosen by the primitive caveman but with very good taste, and if Hungary is the Queen of the Danube, then Budapest is the crown of the Queen . . . there is a very witty definition according to which Budapest is not only the capital of Hungary but the capital of Hungarian gastronomy as well . . . within the strong walls of a one-time fortress one will find most peculiar restaurants . . . where the Hungarian cook radiates gastronomic pleasures and the leader of the gypsy band can find the very tunes to his heart . . . Alexander the Great, Julius Caesar and Napoleon together couldn't conquer so many people as Hungarian cuisine has done . . . eat and drink as much as you can—Budapest can provide you with 35 liters of medicinal water a day . . . or visit magic Lake Balaton where sunshine gives a uniform tanning as it is reflected by the lake. And the frequency of rainy days is uniform . . . it is like the first lover that you could leave but never forget . . . where the science of sailing means the art of setting up sails, recognizing the different winds and also making use of them . . . the tourist will not miss the National Museum (200,000 different coins) or Badascony, an extinct volcano, a masterpiece of nature, Szigliget with its famous alley and old mouldering castle . . . the most romantic place, however, is magic Tihany with its homely manor-house facing the stables . . . Whether in Budapest where New Hungarian plays are performed August 15th to 16th, or in the magic Puszta, an unspoiled ancient landscape and hotel rooms supplied with running water, your stay will be the experience of a lifetime . . . Hungary will be the venue where modern technology is confronted by the exotic, where the sciences are faced by the arts, and where the basic forces of nature will be as well represented as the refinements of the present civilization of mankind.

cerpts, a kind of rural WPA theater program. Some are clearly over the hill, some have sung the same song too often. There is a male dancer, however, who has danced in every major European capital. He is one of the two or three best in the world and he knows it. The stage is bad, the orchestra's *tempi* hesitant, the audience easily pleased—he does the *Corsair* perfectly but perfunctorily. His disdain for his audience, their provincialism is obvious. For this, I hate his guts quite as much as I loved the girl who danced against the revolution in *l'Odéon.* Damn him. He does not know what he has: an appreciative audience. Moreover, an audience who knows who *they* are as much as they know who he is. He does not know about my country, which trains the best singers and dancers in the world and then leaves them to rot, no place to perform, leaves them no hope except the big New York dollar or a degree in education. And for his Danubian villa, his apartment in Budapest, his traveling abroad, his free training, his facilities, why should he not go to the provinces and dance? Why should he not perform for the people who paid to develop his talent? Why should he not dance for those who otherwise would not see him? How many of us would give up everything to reach *those who otherwise would not.* My country is made up of Melville's Bartlebys who believe that free will is simply to say "I prefer not. . . ." Moreover, by this link with the people who cannot dance, cannot sing, he has an audience which few American artists know beyond guilt-edged white faces, those same faces at every performance in every city. As much as this indifferent male lead needs New York and London, he needs this fort, this casual, elementary respect. Repose.

Many thousands of people . . . will certainly share the opinion—irrespective of their nationality, or which country they come from—that the closer we get to nature the closer we will get to ourselves . . . Hungary! stormy past, peaceful present, where many ancient cultures followed each other—"The laid table of Europe—Hungary!" |Pastiche of Ibusz promotional brochures|

Our former Count's magnificent residence, a yellow and cream palladian villa, is now an orphanage, supported by the gate fees to the park. If you don't have enough money for entrance, you can bring a toy for the orphanage.
A peasant woman who has refused an administrative job with the collective and a chance to be sent to school in Budapest because she wants

to be with her children, shows me around.

What happened to the fellow who owned this place, I ask.

"No one knows."

When did they kick him out?

"Who knows? "

Was he a good man? A tyrant? What did he *do*?

"Who cares? "

Where did he go?

"Ah. America."

On second thought, I suppose it would be the same if an American were to inquire of his neighbors, upon moving into a new subdivision, the history, ethics and whereabouts of those who previously inhabited this thin-walled house with curtains in the garage windows. Or perhaps, everyone knows, everyone cares, but they just won't tell me.

One of the towel girls choruses, "Of course. He went to America."

"Well, who knows," the peasant woman continues. "Let's get on with it."

She guides me into an enormous baroque building, longer then a football field, four stories high with a gabled, beamed cathedral roof which covers an Olympic-size pool. "The only thing we know about the Graf," she says, "is that this is where he rode his horses when it rained."

She then gives me an explanation of how the collective was started. Every worker on the collective was assessed an annual percentage of his wages, through the regional party committee, to capitalize the spa. In return, they received vouchers or actual cash interest, a kind of profit sharing.

Sounds like Capitalism, I murmured.

"Well," she said smiling, "it wasn't exactly voluntary, you see."

Still sounds like Capitalism, I laughed.

She grins. "Ah," and then laughs very long. "Different dog, same leash."

And we exit from the former Count's former stables, arm in arm.

ON THE NEW ECONOMIC MECHANISM

|186|

The news comes that Dubcek *et al.* have been spirited away. The last hidden transmitters have been located. A few young Czechs have been shot in Wenceslas Square. Hungarian armored divisions have secured the southern frontier. They are rioting at the Democratic convention, they say. The Chicago police are beating everyone in the streets. Impossible, I say, not in public, they wouldn't dare. I tell them I'm going to Yugoslavia for the sun or something. I've had my revolutions for the year.

We go out for dinner, I load the car, then my good friend, a machinist in the stocking factory, comes forward with a package. He is crying and we kiss like Frenchmen in a documentary. I unwrap yards of tissue paper. It is a bayonet, polished to brilliance, with a sandalwood handle. "I found that when I was about six," he says. "There was also a grenade. You know how kids are."

He twists his face to show me the piece of shrapnel embedded like an insect in amber in his walleye.

Which army? I mumble. Austrian, Serbian, German, Russian, Bulgarian?

He shrugs. His walleye glows.

"This is the eye that kept me out of the Hungarian Army," he says proudly.

When I was six and the war was on for us too, I used to dig in the Georgia soil for bayonets which weren't there. My father was stationed outside of Atlanta at the Naval Air Station before he shipped out to the Philippines, and we lived in a large stone house in the country, requisitioned, I suppose, for officers. I have no idea who lived there previously, but in the considerable acreage which surrounded that house there perched, a hundred feet up in a live oak, an incredible hideaway constructed from the ball turrets of some gutted bomber. It had a full complement of leaded-up machine guns, plexiglass, radio equipment, and even a bullet hole. I sat there for the duration, blasting Zeros and Fokk-Wolffs from the sky, and one day, seeing what was actually in my sights for once, I discovered in the ridge, directly in the sightline of those fixed machine guns, a camouflaged bunker. I clambered down the tree, crossed a deep ravine, and located a slit trench with a reinforced bunker dug ten feet back into the hillside. Directly across the ravine, the glistering turret was trained upon us. What industrious knowledgeable children had preceded me! We will never see their like again. But there were no "children" now, only a gang who would occasionally catch me away from the house, surprise me sliding down the muddy banks of the creek and there make me perform acts such as the drinking of my own urine. Perhaps I could have befriended them by showing them the turret and the bunker, but after such meanness, I kept these to myself, playing one side and then the other; one redoubt occupied, the other always empty. It was a stand-off. I had no preferences.

Along that creek there were many dull-witted snakes, mostly water moccasins as thick as my arm, and each morning, I would go down to the creek in nothing but shorts to wade on the sandbars as the snakes crawled out on the overhanging willows to sun themselves. Then, with carefully chosen stones, flat and heavy as silver dollars, I would blast those snakes into the current . . . I never went back up the hill until I had knocked every snake I could see into the stream. When I hit them good, just beyond their grin, they would strike at themselves, the pain or humiliation was so great, and when I found a stone which fit my fingers perfectly, their heads would explode in a profusion of blood.

It is a curious motion, this American throwing, the most unnatural movement of the human body, it is said, and for this reason, perhaps, it is remarkably lethal. It is something like the motion of an aging relief pitcher who has torn a shoulder and can no longer come over the top. The wrist is cocked behind the buttocks and the arm swung around exactly like a flail. As the elbow passes the hip, the forearm drops, the wrist is cocked precisely as in a benediction, and the index finger guides the stone as the wrist snaps completely through. The stone appears to have been shot from your groin. Your hand should end at eye level, fingers limp as those on the Sistine ceiling. Throwing, words, and guilt: these are what set us apart from snakes and other species.

In our large garage, there is a bomb. A blue four-finned bomb, robin's egg blue, tall as I, a 500 pounder without its load. My father carries a photograph of me cradling this souvenir in my long skinny arms, the right one already beginning to swell like a jai alai player's, from stoning the snakes.

In our house, in a basement room, lives a strange young woman whose husband is also at war, but already gone, and with whom we must share our quarters. She "sits" with me while my mother is at various sociomilitary functions, at which my father, for some reason, is to wear a dress sword. He giggles as he straps it on. It is a large house, as I've said, and she could live in any of its rooms, but she prefers this small dark low one with a cool flagstone floor where chameleons appear on the screen door. One evening, while we are "sitting," and she has prepared her usual meal by throwing some carrots into an electric blender for a broth—she brings out what she introduces as her husband's leather jacket. It is beautiful black shining leather, and as she puts it on, her little fists are lost near its elbows, her collarbone breaks the massive shoulderline only a third of the way to the outer seam. "It's as strong as iron," she says. "Here, I'll show you." And going to the kitchen drawer, she takes out a large butcher knife and hands it to me, handle first. "Throw it at me," she says, "go on," and turns her back and spreads her arms. The coat balloons on her. "Go on," she says, "it won't hurt." I demur. I demur again. She insists. I shrug and throw. The knife strikes flat, bladewise, against her back, the black leather, and slides, as she predicted, harmlessly to the floor.

Don't tell my parents.

"Why should I? Just throw it. Harder."

It never sticks.

Another evening. I have checked out my twin opposed fortifications. I am in the ravine between them. No action tonight. The snakes and gang are downstream. All our enemies are eating now. From the house I can hear her blender start up dinner. The light is failing. The long stone walk which winds through the rock garden up to the front door is perforated with wasp nests; wasps attack mercilessly as it gets cooler. I walk to the rear of the house where there is a small stand of yellow jackpines, where I can see the sun go down, as well as the only neighboring house in view. It is a gloomy house with its drapes always drawn. The people in it are old, their car is old, they have no children, no uniforms. They never go out, their lawn is overgrown. They are not at war.

They are spies. I know this because one of these jackpines is a secret telephone. With my pen knife I bore into the heart of the tree. The wood is spongy and closes about my blade. I cut a little deeper each day, as I come up to check on the spies at dusk. The pine's marrow is gray, then yellow, and finally I find the secret, the cord, the connection; it's first black but then oozes a translucent red. I have cut into their communications system, and if I hug the tree very tightly, pressing my lobe just below the oozing pitch, I can hear the guttural German or effeminate Jap, sinister instructions of which I can understand only the intent.

So it is for the duration; these are my days without end. I'm a child without toys or friends, but all outdoors, as my grandfather says. A child, no doubt, luckier than those in Europe, as my mother constantly reminds me, those children who I must bless in my bedtime prayers, and who, from my black bed, from my bunker and turret trained upon one another, I so envy. I see now that I was irrevocably pointed back here from that time on.

And Lord knows, I *did* pray for them:

Oh, children of Europe, come fill my empty fortresses, you who know what to do with them. You, whose food I have eaten this evening. I will show you how to throw and together we will take on the gang, force them to eat their own excrement. I will show you the magical telephone I have discovered to listen in on your worst part, bubbling in spite of massive defensive measures, through the trees of America. And we will go down to the basement, once you have learned to throw correctly, to meet the thin woman who eats so many carrots, whose husband is, who knows, this very moment delivering you from our enemies; the knife will fly to the floor and lie there forever. And my father will appear at the head of the driveway, the rim of the ravine, all in officer's white and gold, laughing at the sword at his side. . . .

|190|

My friend from the stocking factory is advancing upon me with the brilliant bayonet. Others are now beginning to cry with us. I race the engine, the lethal edge turns in his hands, and holding it by the blade he offers me the handle. Though his face is a foot from mine, his stare veers off. I can never meet that walleyed gaze, no matter how obliquely I position myself.

"You see, dear friend," he says, "we are really brothers now."

Of course.

"No, no," he says. "You don't understand. You think I am being polite. No, now we are *really* brothers—because we both live in countries in which a revolution against the state is no longer possible."

Question: Can one leave Hungary only by towns with names beginning with ''K''?

Answer: Keskemet, Kunszenmarton, Kiskunfelegyhaza, Kiskoros, Kalocsca, Kecel, Kiskunhalas, Kistelek.

On the way out, I will tell you why I turned around at the Czech border, curbed my usual impulsiveness.

Before I left Oxford to find out what my new nervousness was good for, it occurred to me that as long as I was halfway around the world, I might as well briefly go the *whole* way, i.e., to Moscow. After all, I had still to live up to the pledge on my original application—to carry the antecedents of English social thought into Russo-American *Lebensphilosophie* and somehow come up with the common synapse—locate that nameless station on some *mitteleuropäische* frontier where the different gauge railroad tracks meet so spuriously, and the entire load is suddenly, effortlessly, transferred to a new train. I was sick of being "sensitive," that "powerless, feeling young man," whose "secret hurt" was so secret that it had been kept even from himself. It was time to become astute. And I thought that Russia might well toughen me for the great ideological debates which the New Frontier would doubtless inspire.

As I could hardly afford such a trip, it seemed reasonable to make application for the World Youth Festival, but I found that the Russians had progressively moved the affair from Vienna to Bucharest and finally that year to Moscow, claiming that our National Student Association had been quite rude at the Vienna conference, which was, moreover, infiltrated by the CIA. I recalled the NSA, those fresh-faced petty politicians from the midwest and Texas trying to consolidate the gains of their penultimate high school student council election, and could hardly imagine them threatening the hard-core "youth" of the Soviet Union—the only representatives of which I knew were uniformly 35, tri-lingual, with important-looking medals in the lapel and eyes like Svidrigialov's.

I went to the American Embassy where I was similarly discouraged, the fat attaché telling me that I had already been "out of the country" too long. After I worked my way up a few levels, a *chargé d'affaires* asked me why I wanted to go to *that* conference. I said because it was free. Apparently, he interpreted this as a political remark.

It was when I discovered that even the American Friends Service Committee had been sufficiently discouraged from sending a delegation, however, that my annoyance spilled over. Take away an American's mobility? The only thing he's really good at? So I took matters into my

|192|

An anarchist, conservative and Christian, he had no motive or duty but to attain the end; and to hasten it, he was bound to accelerate progress; to concentrate energy; to accumulate power; to multiply and intensify forces; to reduce friction, increase velocity and magnify momentum, partly because this was the mechanical law of the universe; but partly also in order to get done with the present which artists and some others complained of; and finally—and chiefly—because a rigorous philosophy required it, in order to penetrate the beyond, and satisfy man's destiny by reaching the largest synthesis in its ultimate contradiction.
|*Henry Adams*, An Education|

own hands, went to an English stationer, and had a letterhead made up. I only needed two sheets and an envelope, I said.

The English clerk didn't even flinch. Another insane American. I tried to explain.

You see I only need to write one letter, but I might make a typo so I need two sheets.

Not a twitch.

"Certainly, sir."

It was magnificent stationery, mottled watermarked paper headed with *Americans Abroad for International Understanding* which was the best front I could think of, and a fake Board of Directors, including my high school basketball coach, Leon Csongloz, and Walter Mitty; listing myself as chairman. I mailed it off to Moscow with a carbon to the Russian Embassy, and after three months of silence during which I entirely forgot the matter, I received a telegram from the Russian Embassy telling me to report the next day. I didn't flunk *that* interview, sparing them the details of my new synthesis research project, and the next day was put aboard an Ilyushin jet with interior mahogany trim, caviar and champagne. As I got off the plane in Moscow, blushing girls in peasant blouses threw roses at my feet, and Lord, the birch woods came right to the edge of the runway, like a tidal wave.

It was a strange and obviously carefully chosen delegation. No socialists or pacifists, no Trotskyites or bohemians, no NSA finks or Ayn Rand Republicans, simply three young couples, the deflected progeny of some tired New York City Communists: Martha and Joe, Jewish; Ike and Ruth, not Jewish; Ralph and Helen, a mixed couple, the black girl a little ill at ease with her husband's tone (you don't have to be so mean when you argue, Ralph); good old Bill, a black Maoist protégé of Robert Williams, then at large after a North Carolina kidnapping charge—and me. Bill was there to talk with the Chinese about smuggling weapons into North Carolina. No kidding, I said. He laughed, "Sure man." The others were suitably impressed.

|193|

Now that was the very sort of thing I'd come to hear. I wanted to know how Bill was going to maintain his supply lines, and so that evening when the discussion switched to literary topics, I was disappointed. Faulkner was a racist capitalist who sold out to Hollywood, Fitzgerald the dupe of the industrial conspiracy ("a lapse of moral vision") and Hemingway, while his early things were promising, had ultimately perverted the great tradition of Jack London in American literature.

I mean, don't you see any difference *between* them? I stammered. I mean, for instance, don't you think that Hemingway is say a . . . a *more important* writer than Jack London?

They all looked up.

Look, Hemingway probably perverted just about everything, *except* Jack London. And I added, it seems to me that Faulkner didn't sell out to Hollywood as you suggest. Quite the opposite. And Fitzgerald, don't you remember Nick Carraway saying that Gatsby represented "everything for which he had an unaffected scorn . . . "?

There was a dead silence; through lit crit I had blown my cover, and again fingered myself as the fink.

We were put up at the Hotel Ukraine, the lobby floor strewn with flower petals, welcoming "international youth" from all over the world, given meal vouchers and rubles. The elevators seldom worked and there were no stairs. The women in charge of keys who sat at a desk on each floor appeared to be the same ones who had kept me from sneaking girls into my room at the Hotel Biltmore. Why am I the youngest youth? I kept asking myself.

My roomy turned out to be good old Bill. As I began to unpack, he gave me a stern lecture on four hundred years of superannuated profits.

Look Bill, we're going to be together for a couple of weeks now. I admit your central point. You've been fucked over forever. You're perfectly correct in wanting to cut my balls off and all that, but please, spare us the rhetoric.

His enormous heavy-lidded eyes flicked open, he laughed long, kissed

However, does not an excess of solidarity, as the Nietzscheans fear, threaten to degenerate man into a sentimental, passive herd animal? Not at all. The powerful force of competition which, in bourgeois society, has the character of market competition, will not disappear in a Socialist society, but, to use the language of psycho-analysis, will be sublimated, that is, will assume a higher and more fertile form. There will be the struggle for one's opinion, for one's project, for one's taste. In the measure in which political struggles will be eliminated—and in a society where there will be no classes, there will be no such struggles—the liberated passions will be channelized into technique, into construction which also includes art. Art then will become more general, will mature, will become tempered, and will become the most perfect method of the progressive building of life in every field. It will not be merely "pretty" without relation to anything else . . . Art, therefore, will not suffer the lack of any such collective psychic impulses which make for the creation of new artistic tendencies and for changes in style. . . . In a struggle so disinterested and tense, which will take place in a culture whose foundations are steadily rising, the human personality, with its invaluable basic trait of continual discontent, will grow and become polished at all its points. In truth, we have no reason to fear that there will be a decline of individuality or an impoverishment of art in a Socialist society . . . |Trotsky, 1924|

me and went off to the Chinese Embassy for a party.

My interpreter turned out to be a kid my own age, straw shock of blond hair, clear plastic glasses, by the name of Bunin.

Bunin what?

"Just Bunin."

Okay.

"You play soccer?" he said.

Nope. I throw.

"Too bad. It's going to be a long conference."

These first days were spent getting oriented or, as Bunin put it, "marinated." We walked around the Kremlin walls; promenaded the embankment of the Volga. One evening, after dinner, he shuffled me in great secrecy away to the embankment. "We cannot talk here," he said. "You see that drunk beneath the streetlight?"

I nodded, somewhat confused, since at night everyone in Msocow seemed to be drunk.

"He's an informer," Bunin said. "Do not say anything."

All right, I said. Let's talk about literature. That should send him packing soon. Which American authors do you like best?

"Jack London."

Why not.

So we talked a little again about Jack London.

"You don't seem to have very good recollection," he said.

I haven't read him since I was eight, after all.

"All right then," he said, looking at his watch, "we can go now."

Then we slunk off to an ice cream parlor in the middle of town where everyone seemed to be eating three banana splits at four rubles a throw. After we ordered, several people, each in their own turn, sidled to the table—all of them turned out to be religious fanatics of some kind. One man, an exact replica of Maxim Gorky, introduced himself by saying, "I am a Christian." I looked up from my banana split. He was more than crestfallen when Bunin translated that I was an agnostic, and replied, "If all Western youths are like you, then we are indeed lost."

I assured him that at least as far as agnosticism went, that was the case. But this was in 1962.

|195|

Then he said, "I will give you this beautiful balalaika," which he did. "In exchange," he went on, "send me a good crucifix."

What?

"That is all," he continued, "send it without a return address in brown paper to me at this postal address."

He gave me the name of a Moscow suburb and disappeared.

Bunin, I pleaded, what the hell is this?

He smiled and shrugged.

"You are not being tested?"

By this time another character had seated himself and wanted to know about my "religious experiences." I told him that on the outskirts of Moscow I had seen an Orthodox church, surrounded by an enormous iron fence, through which peasant women in black kept crawling to kiss the feet of a torn and rusted icon. And how, in the great rotting onion dome of St. Peter's across from the Kremlin, now a graffitied museum for the Revolution, I felt for the first time the sentiment of religious defacement. Having grown up in a country in which every street corner sported a new church indistinguishable from gas stations or banks, I had always assumed the Soviets had done precisely what I would if I could: take away their money, their lands, and turn the churches into museums. That in itself, I used to think, would turn our country around. I liked myself for this small totalitarianism, and wish I could have kept the impulse pure.

I talked with Bunin and our Witness about this. I tried to make them understand that if I were Russian, I might have been able to take my Christianity, apart from my *Protest*antism, more seriously. Religion, like radical politics, requires an articulate resistance. Had I only been born behind the Dnieper, I could have appreciated this ice cream bar, full of Gogolian standbys wolfing up the butterscotch, and been able to confess . . . what?

"But when did you first know God?" my interlocutor insisted.

I admitted the only "legitimate" experience which could be called religious occurred on my 13th birthday when the State Legislature threatened to raise the legal driver's age to 15. I prayed mightily then, making a pact with God that if he would disabuse the people's

|196|

representatives of this notion, I would not only read the Bible carefully, but read it in the original Greek! But he did not keep his end of what still seems to me a most flattering bargain, and I did not drive until much later—though I made up with a vengeance for lost time.

"Ah ha," Bunin interrupted. "You could not become a Communist because you could not remain a Christian." Which was astute, I thought.

Our general or plenary sessions were held in the Palace of Culture, naturally, and like all such conferences were formally, pointlessly, translated into six languages. I pressed the various buttons on my earphone and found English the most opaque of all. I was in much demand, I think, because of my Leninist beard, then somewhat unique, and just as Bill's color gained him *entrée*, I had my interviews. A little Russian lady from a magazine, "like your *Life* magazine," desired my impressions.

But I wouldn't be interviewed by *my Life* magazine, I plead.

"Please?" she says. "Just what do you think of our Moscow?"

I think it's just fine.

"Do you find it beautiful?"

Oh yes.

"Is it as beautiful as your American cities?"

American cities are, by and large, very ugly.

"But you like it here?"

Oh, I like it very much.

"So how is it, say, compared to your Washington?"

You mean architecturally?

"That too."

Well, they seem rather the same.

"Can't you say something more specific?"

Well, as in Washington, the new buildings are just horrible and the old buildings are quite wonderful in a silly way. That's all I can think of.

"Can't you say something beautiful?" she asks.

You mean like the birches at the airport?

"Is that all?"

End of interview, madam.

How much I would have liked to please her.

Bill came back very drunk from the Chinese Embassy one night.

How's the gun running going?

"Oh, great, man. They all cool cats."

You think you could get me in?

"An American, yes, a bourgeois democrat possibly, a white man, no."

Bill, honestly, how the hell are you going to get those guns in?

"Why should I tell you?"

You can trust me.

"They're Czech guns too, man," he snarled. "Good stuff. None of that Chink shit." He turned around and examined me quizzically. "How would *you* get them in?"

Well, if I were you, I'd just land 'em in a big steamer trunk or two from a submarine on some beach, take 'em to the nearest train station or United Parcel and have them delivered to your home.

"You think we could get away with that?!"

I don't see why not. How many guns you think you're gonna need?

"As many as we can get. We are organized and we are ready to die."

Bill?

"What?"

Do you know how to shoot?

He looked at the floor.

Have you ever fired a rifle?

There was a long silence. He was sitting on the edge of his bed in his T-shirt and jockey underwear, which he changed twice a day, his thin chest drawn across his collarbone like a drum skin.

"Hey man," he whispered.

Bill?

"Will you let me make love to you?"

My first thought, of course, was that it all had been prearranged. Sure, they run in with a flash camera and send your picture being buggered to the *N. Y. Times*. The following conversation is pretty much verbatim and demonstrates why we cannot pass off such little daily epiphanies as plausible fiction.

"Why not?" he was whining.

Because I'm not a homosexual.

"No it isn't. It's because I'm black, isn't it?"

Bill, that's not true and you know it.

"It's because I'm ugly then."

As far as I'm concerned, you're not ugly. I just don't want to.

"Please," he stammered, "I'll do anything you want me to."

Look, I said, look goddamit, I'm just not about to go to bed with a black Maoist queer who's threatened to kill all my kind in a bugged Moscow hotel room. That's all. Okay?

Bunin came to our room the next day, "simply to talk." I had been sick from the heavy food and hadn't gone out much. He told me of his duty as a medic with the Red Army in Siberia, how proud he was to be in the party at his age. He had many friends who had genuinely wanted to be in the party but who had been rejected solely on the grounds of training and intelligence, he insisted. He was proud of his elitism, and I was proud of him for it.

He was now trying to gain admission to the State Archives in order to read American newspapers, on the pretext of improving his English. It was remarkable how little he knew. He didn't know, for example, about Khrushchev taking his shoe off, etc., and his speech at the UN. No one I talked to the entire time, in fact, claimed any knowledge of this bellicosity.

I asked him if he ever thought he would be able to travel.

"Oh yes, when my English is better. We will see the world together, yes. Would you like that?"

Sure, Bunin, that would be really fine. Tell me when you want to go.

A few days later I asked him: Bunin, I want you to do a favor for me.

"Certainly."

I want you to get us permission to take the Trans-Siberian railway to Irkutsk; I know it's closed area beyond that. But I want to see Lake Baikal and then get on to Japan somehow. I'd rather not have to go through China, but I will if that's the only way. Maybe they would let me do that if you came with me, at least to the border.

"I'll see what I can do."

He did not come back for several days, and then I was informed a new interpreter had been assigned to me: a nervous dark girl, Lydia, who dogged me whenever I emerged into the lobby. That evening, one of the wives of our delegation asked me with a faint smile how I liked my new interpreter. They had ceased their discussions when either Bill or I came near. They were clearly frightened of us, afraid that either his impulsiveness or my lack of seriousness would embarrass their solidarity, or perhaps worse.

One afternoon, as I was sitting on the massive front steps of the Ukraine, a blade-faced American correspondent whose visage has since flickered across my TV screen more than once, stopped before me with a portable tape recorder. I recognized him from the network news.

"Hi," he said cheerily, "having a good time?"

Uh-hum.

"Well, I guess you're part of the American delegation."

I'm one of the Americans here.

"Well, I suppose you're a Communist." He was joyful.

Nope. Kennedy Democrat.

"Oh," he said disappointed, "What are you doing here? I thought the State Department . . ."

I'm here on my own.

"What are the affiliations of the other people in your group?"

Beats me.

"Well, how do you find Moscow?"

The subways are marvelous. Particularly those mosaics of Lenin instructing the little children . . .

"Well, I understand. I guess you aren't free to talk . . ."

This sort of simpering foolishness, however, together with the incredible boredom of the conferences, and my fear of Lydia, had made my paranoia, my ego, and my liberal idealism all of a redundant piece. And a day or so later, when a correspondent from the other major network approached me in a more sophisticated way, treating me as something more than an ideological oddity and buying me the first decent meal I'd had, I submitted to an interview. Oh, I had a story to tell, all right. After lunch, he took me up to his suite in the Hotel Metropole, threw open the doors of a balcony which overlooked the Kremlin, the warped onion domes of St. Basil's—and as the TV camera, dragging its cable-like intestines, dollied in on us, I lost my integrity completely.

For there I was, Newman from the Anglo-Saxon, "newcomer or recent arrival," now bridger of cultures, breacher of the Iron Curtain; defiant of both the State Department and the Komisol, spanning time itself through the great medium of TV, bringing ideology to the home folks, independence of spirit to the enemy, confidant of a black queer Maoist, suspect by the indigenous old left, beloved by his humble Russian translator, now silhouetted against the Kremlin, a true pioneer with love for all men in his eyes and the hard Moscow sun glinting off his hair. . . .

We went through the old routine: not a Communist, a Kennedy Democrat. No, the organization didn't actually exist, I represented no one but myself, but if individuals could not participate in such confrontations, what would become of us? I wanted to talk with my Russian counterparts, and I had no respect for either of the governments which prevented me from doing this. I didn't want to die in a nuclear war, a limited nuclear war, a war of liberation, a war of self-defense, and I was damned if I was going to let anybody tell me to whom I could talk or where I could go.

"We need more young men of your caliber," the commentator assured me.

I marched back to the Ukraine as if it were the Finland station. It was an altogether unconscionable if exemplary performance, and if only I'd kept my mouth shut, I might have crossed Siberia with Bunin, seen the orange groves at Kazakstan, the lake where entire columns of tanks fell through the ice in the Russo-Japanese war, and where the last snowy egret lives.

As it was, however, I am sure that my Aunt Lena in Highland Park, Illinois, and the NKVD were equally surprised at my appearance on the early morning show the following day.

The next afternoon, still high as a kite, I attended a plenary session of the conference. The Cuban Delegation, overwhelming in their khaki uniforms and red scarves, marched in, ten representatives, color-graded perfectly from a stout coal-black West Indian athlete to a red-headed girl with skin and breasts from shampoo advertisements. I felt a furious pang of jealousy, then nausea. How long would it take for our youth to approach that kind of virility, not to mention militancy? (Well, at least we have the uniforms now.)

This brief charisma was not to last, however, as a spokesman for the group harangued the hall for two hours in a perfect imitation of Castro's manner and tone. His statistics were complex, lengthy and over-whelming. In the first year of the revolution, poverty, disease and illit-eracy had been totally wiped out. There were no longer political prison-ers. The arts were flourishing.

During a break in the simultaneous translation, I found myself on my feet, in my mind's eye still silhouetted against the Kremlin no doubt, at first choked up, then calm as I was recognized.

I would simply like the speaker and his delegation to know, I said, that his analysis of American foreign policy is most correct, but there are many of us, even those who are not necessarily Marxist-Leninists, who are utterly ashamed of what our country has done to the Cuban people, and that your revolution is very important to us. Because it is so impor-tant, and because of the solidarity so evident here, I would ask you not to falsify statistics for propaganda value, and tell us frankly, even per-sonally, how the revolution is going, what are the obstacles you face, and not cloud your considerable achievement by this rhetoric. Tell us what American sympathizers (the word caught in my throat) could do to help . . .

|202|

There is a mode of behavior imposed on the soul just as there is on the body: man must learn to submit to it. This is an old truth, I know; but it seems to me that in our country it still has the value of novelty. One of the worst features of our peculiar civ-ilization is that we have not yet dis-covered truths that have elsewhere be-come truisms, even among nations that in many respects are far less ad-vanced than we are. It is the result of our never having walked hand in hand with other nations; we belong to none of the great families of man-kind; we are neither of the West nor of the East, and we possess the tradi-tions of neither. Somehow divorced from time and space, the universal education of mankind has not touched upon us . . .

Every nation has its period of stormy agitation, of passionate unease, of hasty activities. In such a period men become wanderers over the world, both in body and spirit. This is an epoch of strong emotions, great under-takings, great national passions. At such times nations toss about violently, without any apparent ob-ject, but not without benefit for future generations. All communities have gone through such a phase. Such a period provides them with their most vivid memories, their legends, their poetry, their greatest and most pro-ductive ideas; such a period repre-sents the necessary basis of every society. Otherwise, they would have nothing valuable or cherished in memories; they would cherish only the

In the few moments it took to complete the translation, the hall became deathly quiet. Hands fluttered about earphones; then an explosion of a dozen languages. A hand grabbed me by my belt and pulled me to my seat. It was the wife of the Jack London fan, and my delegation's eyes were full of hatred. At least I had satisfied *their* suspicions. I was afraid I would cry, so moved was I by my inarticulateness, that leaden pedantic self-deprecation which was simply a pathetic cry for communion, which I would never have allowed myself in less hostile quarters. Then a large, gray man, head of the Young Communists, moved to gavel. A few heads turned, the pretty redheaded Cuban girl looked through me with disdain, and the bearded Castroite resumed his harangue as if nothing had happened, which was true. . . .

Back at the Ukraine in a daze, I found Bill waiting for me, commiserating:
"You didn't have to do that, man. I mean, what did you think you were doing?"
Then a call from Bunin apologizing for being out of touch. Bill left in the middle of the conversation for yet another Chinese dinner.
"Let's go out to a good restaurant," Bunin said. "No vouchers. My favorite place."
Bunin, I said, let's go get shitfaced.
He arrived fifteen minutes later in a taxi, and we drove to the outskirts of Moscow, a restaurant on a marvelous stretch of the river. The Oarsmen's Club.
A bottle of vodka was placed on the table. "Champagne and duck will come," he said.
Did you go to the plenary session today? I asked innocently.
"No, my wife, you know. I haven't been home at all since the Congress started, and finally these last few days she put her foot down."
He seemed pale and nervous, his flesh-colored glasses nearly indistinguishable from his skin.
Bunin, I pushed him, any word about the Siberian trip?
"There *is* a problem, you see; you know it's *military* . . . from Lake Baikal west."

dust of the earth they inhabit. This fascinating phase of the history of nations represents their adolescence, the age when their faculties develop most vigorously, and whose remembrance brings both joy and wisdom to their maturity. But we Russians, we are devoid of all this. At first brutal barbarism, then crude superstition, then cruel and humiliating foreign domination, the spirit of which was later inherited by our national rulers—such is the sad history of our youth. We had none of that period of exuberant activity, of the fervent turmoil of the moral forces of nations. Our period of social life which corresponds to this age was filled with a dull and gloomy existence, lacking in force and energy, with nothing to brighten it but crime, nothing to mitigate it but servitude. There are no charming remembrances, no graceful images in the people's memory; our national tradition is devoid of any powerful teaching. Cast a look upon the many centuries in our past, upon the expanse of soil we inhabit, and you will find no endearing reminiscence, no venerable memorial to speak to you powerfully of the past, and to reproduce it for you in a vivid and colorful manner. We live only in the narrowest of presents, without past and without future, in the midst of a flat calm. And if we happen to bestir ourselves from time to time, it is not in the hope, nor in the desire, of some common good, but in the childish frivolousness of the infant, who raises himself and stretches his hands to-

I shrugged cynically.

"And the Chinese, you know," he blurted, "you would not be safe going through China. It's you and us against them."

Do you really believe that? I mean do you believe that we would help you if they invaded Russia?

"Of course. Wouldn't you? "

I wouldn't bet on it, Bunin. It would be fun to serve in the Red Army in China, though. Just think Bunin, you and me, The Red and the Black.

He looked at me sadly. "Did I tell you my father was in Spain? He was an aviator. He was killed."

He was Stendhalian. We're closer to Jack London—you're right about that.

"You don't understand me, Charles. I have no politics. In the party there is no need to have a politics."

Are you being ironic or what?

"I work for my family and for the building of my society. That is not a political question."

I think you'd get some argument on that.

"You have no politics either, Charles. That is why you can stand up and make a fool of yourself at the plenary session. And that is why we can talk and indulge each other. My father was not the only one 'to die in Spain.' All of our fathers left their better parts on the German front. Or some such front."

I don't like this self-indulgence, Bunin, I've been at it all day.

Bunin was becoming drunk and melancholy. The lights had begun to hurt my eyes extraordinarily. We had been there an hour and though Bunin had presumably ordered, there was still no food. I asked him about this and he spoke angrily to a waitress who fairly sprinted from the table. They he poured two more wine glasses of vodka for a toast. After the revolution, Bunin, the food will be on time. I would like to be Minister of Restaurants. I could make the state a lot of money. I said this weakly and, though I had not drunk much, was slurring.

"What do *you* know about revolution?" he grinned.

Not much.

ward the rattle which his nurse presents to him.

So long as life has not become more regulated, more easy, more gentle than in the midst of the uncertainties of its earliest age, the true development of mankind in society has not yet begun. So long as societies waver about without convictions and without rules even for daily life, so long as that life has no form, how can the seeds of good ripen in them? This is the state of chaotic fermentation of the things of the moral world, similar to the revolutions of the earth which preceded the present state of our planet. We are still at that stage.

I don't know whether one can draw any universal conclusion from what I have just said, but one can certainly see how the strange situation of a people which cannot connect its thought with any succession of ideas that have been progressively developed in society and devolved slowly one from the other, which has taken no part in the general progress of the human spirit save by blind, superficial and often very awkward imitation of other nations, must powerfully influence the mind of every individual within it....

I ask you, is it not absurd to suppose, as is generally done in our country, that we can appropriate in one stroke this progress of the peoples of Europe, made so slowly through the direct action of a unique moral force, and to suppose that we can do this without even trying to find out how it developed?... |Peter Yakolevich Chaadayev, Necropolis, 1829|

"You should know a bit," he snapped, "after all, you fought in ours. Remember Murmansk! " He lifted his glass in a mock toast.

You're paranoid. The whole goddamn country's paranoid. From the worst monarchy to the worst democracy. By God, the only thing that saves us both is our capacity for work!

"Charles," he suddenly brightened, "could you arrange for me to visit America, when you leave? "

What the hell do you think I am, an agent or something? I tell you I represent no one save myself.

"We know you are an agent. But it makes no difference to me."

I was angry.

"Would you like to stay on here then? " he continued.

What do you mean, *on*?

"For a long time."

No, I said. I don't want to go back. But I couldn't live here. No.

"Why not? " he thundered.

There's nothing for me to do here. That's all.

"But from what you've said, you may not be able to do what you want in your own . . ."

True enough, I said. My feeling now is we have one last chance.

"Ah," he groaned, burying his face in his hands, "I can never leave Russia. I cannot leave my country. I mean I *would* not."

I envy you that, Bunin, at the very least.

There was still no food. I was becoming suspicious as I could pack away a fifth of American vodka and still retain a certain dogged comprehension. But now I had a burning sensation in my bladder and my eyes refused to track. I excused myself and staggered to the men's room, a crowded stinking pissoir at the bottom of a spiral stair. A number of people watched me while I tried to undo my fly. They didn't seem to be there to piss. Only when *I* couldn't piss, couldn't even direct my cock, did it occur to me that I'd been drugged. There was a numbness in all my extremities. My head was clear, but the motor control was going. In the mirror, I saw my pupils begin to encroach upon my corneas. Someone grabbed me. "With your beard, sir, you look like a young Lenin," he said as he helped me up the spiral stair. My mind and

|205|

my hearing were still lucid as my body was drained of all sensation. But I couldn't speak.

I was guided outside into the parking lot, a favor, I thought, since I might vomit, and I began again to fuddle with my fly in the bushes. I saw then, however, that I was surrounded by five or six short stocky men in brown uniforms and red arm bands, the People's Militia. The first one tried to kick me, and I got him a good one alongside the head, but my right cross missed by two feet, and, the momentum of the punch carried me to the ground.

They didn't really beat me as badly as they might have. They had no weapons. I recall it as an official, resigned pummel. They broke my glasses and a couple of teeth, but I might have done that as I fell, and it wasn't until they had me handcuffed in the back seat of a sedan, that I saw Bunin rolling around with three of them in the gravel. This particular unit was not the elite of the People's Militia, and Bunin was uniformly kicking the shit out of all three of them. In the moonlight, I could see he had an oarsman's back, and he fought terribly—but paunch and weight endure, and ultimately he was in the front seat, his wrists manacled to his ankles, and as we sped off along the river. I was too astonished to be scared then; as a matter of fact, I remember distinctly thinking it was just like a gangster movie. I could tell we were headed back into central Moscow, but it seemed to me as if we drove for hours, and I couldn't possibly keep track of the route. Finally, we arrived at a police station, a façade of logs, a kind of big Aunt Jemima cabin in the middle of Moscow.

Naturally, with the Westerner's flare for the anticlimactic, I thought I'd had it. It was now only a question of maintaining my dignity, not wetting my pants. The policemen in the station were as phlegmatic and businesslike as the People's Militia. It was as if—the horrifying thought had more than once crossed my mind—I actually *was* drunk and had legitimately been arrested for some *gaucherie*. Then there was a scream and Bunin was at the throats of his guards again, taking two of them to the floor. As soon as they had removed his handcuffs, he had begun to fight; finally, they hit him in the back of the neck with a rubber club, which stunned him temporarily until they could get the cuffs back on.

Let life itself patiently and naturally round off and smooth out what was begun in storm and violence. Don't meddle with its transformations. Don't hinder it. [Because not a single war has ever taken away the evil it was supposedly started against; the evil has always been strengthened and perpetuated.]*.

But here was a country where people, pure in heart as children, did not trifle with their words. They took everything seriously, and words were laws for them; they considered that if something was said, it had to be done. And they plunged recklessly, without thinking twice, into the maelstrom of their (and—mainly—your) theories. They achieved the new political maturity you had proclaimed, and they alone in all the world have passed through it. What had been so long planned, prepared and postponed, came to pass. Thank us that this is done; that it is behind us.

And thank us for this too. Our revolution set the tone for yours, however great the difference between them; it filled this century with sense and meaning. Not only we, and our younger generation—even your banker's son is not the same as his father and grandfather were before him. He may be more cynical and less well-educated than they were, but he is simpler and less long-winded, his spirit is wiser and closer to the truth. He no longer believes in the divine

*Deleted in Russian original.

I sat quietly through all of this, partly because it was so absurd, but also because I figured it was all an act. After all, the bastard had arranged the whole thing, he'd gotten me into it, and now I was not about to applaud his dramatics.

On the other hand, I had also begun to have doubts. Why go through all the trouble of fighting, this ritual, to keep him "clean" for me? Obviously, I wouldn't trust him anymore. Yet what was I to make of Bunin's mouth and nose, which now were pulp? Well, maybe he'd erred. Maybe I was supposed to be liquidated or something. Or maybe *he* was actually drunk. Or maybe I didn't get enough of the drug, did not create sufficient incident, enough cause for arrest? But again, why go through it all? Who were they trying to kid? Perhaps I was drunk. But no, that wouldn't explain never getting our food. And I had never lost motor control from liquor before . . .

They dragged Bunin off somewhere and stripped me, itemizing the contents of my wallet and presenting me with a copiously detailed receipt in Cyrillic, for which I bowed in recognition. Now they were all laughing in their brown shirts, and again I thought, maybe I'm just drunk, caused some scene for which Bunin will have to pay . . .

I was given a smock and led to a large basement room, two stories high with small semi-circular windows at the very top, through which the moon occasionally appeared, and through which a man might crawl if he could somehow scale the wall. The only furnishings were a number of what seemed to be gothic operating tables, about thirty in all, spread about the room. On each was a recumbent form, either undergoing some wild paroxysm, or limp unto death. I was led to an empty table; across from me, prone, Bunin was staring at me.

Our dinner still hasn't come, Bunin.

He looked at the floor.

Did you arrange this as well?

"Believe me . . ."

"You didn't know anything about it, you say? A little hard of hearing over there . . .?

"I was given money and instructed to take you to dinner—that's all."

I don't believe you.

"What can it matter now? "

origin of property, nor thinks that with his savings he can conquer death. He enters life unencumbered, as a man should; he comes as a guest to the feast of existence, and knows that what matters is not how much he inherits but how he behaves at the feast, and what people remember and love him for.

Thank us then for this new man, even in your old society; thank us that he is livelier, finer-witted and more gifted than his heavy and pompous predecessors; for this child of the century was delivered in the maternity home called Russia.

So should we not rather peacefully exchange good wishes for the coming New Year, and hope that no echoes of warlike thunder mingle with the popping of corks as it comes in, nor are heard later in the course of it, or in succeeding years.

But if fate has decreed a disaster, then remember the events that formed us, and what a severe hardening school they were. There is no one more desperate than we, no one more prepared to do the impossible and unbelievable; and any challenge to war will turn us all into so many heroes, as our recent ordeal has shown. |Boris Pasternak, "To Friends in East and West: A New Year's Greeting", 1956|

You still want to stay in your beloved mother Russia, Bunin? I said cruelly, and then we were silent for some time. Later I asked, what's going to happen to us?

"I don't know." He pulled his smock over his head, writhed on the table. "I know nothing," he said, "I am nothing."

Again, I began to feel like a character in a bad novel, and had begun to shiver uncontrollably, though I maintained a strange, stoic lucidity; perhaps the drug, maybe simple masochism, or hopefully just the knowledge that I brought all this on myself and had no cause to whimper. I couldn't control my body, however, and finally, with exquisite relief, I shit, pissed and vomited convulsively. I no longer saw the situation in terms of Poe, Kafka, Dostoyevsky, or even Norman Mailer. Bunin had passed out. The prick. Had I feeling enough in my fingers, I would have strangled him. A crew of babushkaed women moved in to clean up below me. I had seen them moving among the motionless forms, taking their pulse and temperature. Then, extraordinarily, one took my hot head in her cool hand, and rubbing my temples, actually began to sing to me. Moussorgsky. I stiffened from her touch and pushed the old woman from me. She shrugged and left me to my own devices. All right, I resolved, if this is the way it's going to be, I'm not going to show the slightest fear. And that's the way I'll go. I'll show the fucking bastards, and if they start to torture me, I'll kill myself. Having fire-squadded myself, made my noble preparations, I glanced over at Bunin. He was asleep, his mouth agape, curled like a baby on his pallet. I was proud and stiff, already liquidated, taking it like a man, a real Protestant all the way. Mom would have been proud of me. How my countrymen would admire me when the news of my decease in the name of free speech reached them. I had achieved the perfect literary response to an otherwise lonely and undistinguished death in a foreign land. I kept thinking of that phrase of Chris Newman's: "I may be dangerous, but I am not wicked; no, I am not wicked."

There was a light at the high window, a light bright as noon. Some of the older men were now being taken out one by one. I waited stoically, relaxed. A babushkaed nurse grinned at me, her mouth all gold, a map of Tartary upon each cheek. Then she made a swinging motion, mimicking a drunk swigging from a fifth, and shook her finger mischievously at me.

Then it became quite clear that I was not relating to reality at all, and that this no longer had anything to do with the drug. Indeed, I saw that my *political* strategy, that curious alienation which makes a liberal out of a middle-class apathetic, an intellectual out of a bourgeois, was in fact literary and aesthetic at base, and that my current reaction to this dangerous situation was to *savor* it—it was a test not of survival, even of principles, but of the validity of my aesthetics—I was watching myself imagine myself. Will he break? What good is his pride now? What price glory? And while this was understandable, perhaps even enviable, in an adolescent, I realized I was well on my way to a stylish masochism of the literary left, a moral sectarianism which would prevent any real confrontations, an abstracted curiosity always at one remove from the problem of changing reality. Here I was in jail, perhaps near death for all I knew, and rather than acknowledge my fear—in other words, consider how to escape—I busied myself, incredibly enough, preparing for my demise—how to go out in style, with appropriate gesture and text. No wonder I was attracted to Kennedy. I was simply going through the familiar routine of the literary intellectual in politics, the Menshevik unwilling to keep his mouth shut, but unable to get his hands (words) dirty, always exacerbating and never winning—and from that time on, I swore I would never again confuse literary attitudes and political action, or squander my manhood in such a frivolous way.

So that is what I learned in *my* Russian campaign. "It's better to be afraid," a character of mine says, "than always figuring out how to be brave. It's reasons, not conditions, that will make a man of you." And I knew then what Vietnam has forever confirmed, that it is not literature which is dead, nor the left; only literary leftism.

As my self-disgust mounted, it also became clear that I was not in a dungeon of the Kremlin, awaiting execution for my high-minded, articulate attack upon the state—I was simply in a drunk tank, a high class one at that, and my companions, who I had originally assumed to be in terminal stages of Orwellian tortures, were merely those I had seen so often, teetering, careening along the river embankment.

They were given their clothes and a lecture. I was sent into a private office with a very tired ununiformed official, given back my clothes and wallet, each of its contents enumerated on a checklist, fined 50 rubles and presented with a long statement in Cyrillic to sign.

"If you sign this, you may go," he said in German.

What does it say? I can't read your alphabet, but if you'll read it out loud, slowly, I can get most of the sense.

"If I read each statement to each prisoner, we would never have the time to free anyone," he said. "It is simply a document that you have received your property back and that you plead guilty."

What's the charge?

"Drunk and disorderly. You are a guest of the Soviet Union. You should be ashamed of yourself!"

I was not drunk, I said firmly. I was drugged.

"You are in an alcoholic ward. You are a drunk."

Do you generally beat up your drunks?

He shrugged. He was very tired.

So if I sign this, I get out, right?

"Most certainly."

I signed it with some flourish.

There's an awful lot of words here just saying I was drunk. I suppose you've defined me as an enemy of the state.

The official's eyes were almost closed. "You are simply a highly strung and foolish young man. Believe me, things could have been much worse."

Bunin was waiting for me, already dressed, outside the dock. I refused to talk to him. He followed me out into the bright sunlight; his face was very puffy; split lip, black eye, some purple antiseptic on his lesions.

"Where are you going now?" he asked mournfully.

I don't know. Get the hell away from me.

"I didn't know, Charles. You must believe me."

Fuck you. Get lost.

"Let's take a cab. You won't be able to find your way back from here."

I've had enough of private transportation, thanks.

"Then we will take the streetcar."

I resisted no further since, in fact, I had no idea where I was. I was learning. My only thought was to get to the American Embassy as fast as possible. We walked a long time until a streetcar came, and as it turned out, we were only about fifteen minutes from the Ukraine.

On the steps of the hotel, Bunin said, "You should leave the country as soon as you can. But please do not forget me." Then he took out his wallet. "I want to give you a picture of me," which he did; the same staring goggle-eyed sincere man on the party card who now stood before me blinking like a prizefighter. "I will also give you my address. But you must never write me here. Please understand. I give it to you only to show that you could get me in trouble if you wanted to, but that I trust you not to. And one day, perhaps, you will believe that I had nothing to do with this." He wrote an address on the back of the picture and handed it to me. "If you will give me your address in America, I will write to you," he said.

Not on your life, baby.

Then I shook hands with him firmly with a glare I'd been practicing in the opaque streetcar window.

Of course, I would never know how much he knew, any more than I would know to what extent my politics and protestations coincided, precisely what had offended exactly whom, why they were not rougher with me . . . it may well be that my guest monologue on TV saved me from a jail term. During the same week, I subsequently discovered, there had been several similar arrests, including a Fulbright student picked up in Leningrad for allegedly taking photographs of military installations. He remained for seven years. As soon as Bunin was out of sight, I took a cab to the Embassy. The driver accepted the tip sullenly.

As I reread this, I note a certain unsteadiness of tone, which if this were fiction, I would correct. It is unclear, for example, whether the "narrator" wants to be taken as larky or grim, searching or glib, confused or wrongheaded, a relatively decent young man, or an arrogant prick. I do know this is how I acted then, but cannot to this day know whether to attribute my redundant cruelty to a temporary paranoia, a deficiency of character or experience. And at that, I must leave it.

|211|

A Marine took me to a presumably debugged room where they shut three doors behind us and I told my "story" to a sympathetic attaché. In the telling, it became clear we had been there, not overnight, but two entire days. They gave me a physical, found traces of knockout drops in my urine, the Navy doctor laughing all the time, "Oh, they're really bastards, aren't they? Really bastards!"

The attaché told me a few horror stories about Americans who had suffered worse fates than I, and told me to make arrangements through "them" to leave as soon as possible. "Stick close to the hotel," he said; "if for some reason they won't give you transportation out, we'll make arrangements to get you out of the country."

Feeling safe, my curiosity peaked again. Just what sort of "arrangements" could they make to get me out of the country? A sealed train, perhaps? And as I walked back to the hotel, the old insane Calvinist stubbornness welled up in me; now that I'd survived, why should I get out? Now that the embassy knew, they wouldn't dare touch me. I'd simply keep my mouth shut, be as affable as hell, with everybody thinking I was the youngest, the most cool agent the CIA ever had.

I went back to the room and Bill.

"Where have you been, man?"

Informing on you, you dirty Maoist.

"Comes the Revolution, Charles, we're going to make you Minister of Culture."

Don't think I won't take it.

Nevertheless, I was poorly prepared, lacked the necessary resiliency for what was to follow. My paranoia and my stubbornness canceled one another out, and I began to see what an odd and precarious thing it is to be an American, to advertise as historyless.

The harassment began with phone calls in the night; either no answer or quite unreasonable Russian voices giving commands which I could not decipher. But the switchboard of the hotel was so loused up that these might well have been routine mistakes. Bill thought each call was a confirmation of his weapon order.

"Who was it?" he asked as I would hang up on the heavy breathing. Chou En-lai. He wants to know if you want thirty-second or minute fuses on your grenades.

One can bed down just as comfortably on the idea of tragedy as on the idea of eternal salvation. |Leszek Kolakowski|

"You think I'm kidding about this, don't you?" he said.

I'm just not afraid of you, Bill. That's all.

I often wonder today if Bill ever learned how to shoot or whether he lived to see Detroit or Newark. And I wonder when he found out he could go downtown or pick up a mail order catalog and buy as much weaponry as he would ever need.

The next day I resolved to stop going to the sessions, after meeting several instances of unpleasant hostility as well as unremitting boredom— "Comrades, now we will hear from the Argentine delegation on the International Organization of Children's Summer Villages"—and began to take long walks, trying to get a sense of the city. Having overexposed myself politically, I might as well get some culture, right? So I watched the heavy women in their white coats mop up the glistening subway stations, and wondered how anyone in the 19th century could possibly miss predicting, with Henry Adams, the hundred year interregnum of entropy co-sponsored by Russia and America.

Occasionally, on these walks, I would notice a large ZIV limousine cruising behind me, but could never determine whether I was actually being followed, since such limousines were so common, and the traffic so desultory. Nevertheless, when I couldn't shake one during a walk in the outskirts, I would finally lose my nerve, jog back to a main thoroughfare and a protective crowd. Here, the most common encounters took on surreal import; *stilyagi* began to approach me, offering to buy dollars at triple the black market rate; or "50 rubles for your dacron socks, sir."

It is a very curious thing to watch one's mind close up with fear, and to see oneself, rather than existing in a heady vacuum, the object of an elaborate plot, the pointlessness of which was almost erotic in its effect. Finally, after a week, I stopped even my walks, stayed in the room on the pretext of the flu, holding on just to see if I could take it without going mad. The furthest I would venture was the perimeter of benches surrounding the Ukraine, where one afternoon the prettiest girl in Russia showed up, walking up and down before my bench in a smart western suit, legs like a javelin thrower, hair like the dome of St. Peter's, golden in the sun. I was terribly horny, as we used to say, but I kept envisioning those photographers breaking in on us, the pictures flooding the wire service of a repressed America—and then I knew I'd had it, would soon have to leave, for I was in profound trouble if I could not act on so obvious an impulse. What did I have to lose—what exposure did I have to fear from this Ludmilla? Clearly she had been sent for some sinister purpose; why not turn it to my advantage? She'd probably stab me at orgasm, I remember thinking.

And so I began to take cautious circuitous walks again, as by this time my contact with the Congress and our delegation had almost ceased completely. I ate none of the prearranged voucher meals, avoided their curious stares in the lobby, their invitations to attend various working sessions to iron out the problems of the Cold War. Bill also became less friendly, made defensive perhaps by my reclusiveness, though I am sure he would have disclosed the highest Chinese state secrets to me had I only asked. Almost overnight, however, I had developed from a somewhat naive, energetic and manic youth to a dangling man without resource, and more, accepted this with equanimity as a kind of natural state of affairs.

So I awaited the peremptory calls at night, smoking black Russian cigarettes in bed, spinning around suddenly in the streets to see who was following. I still wanted to see if I could give my terrorized condition some aspect of routine, some useful perspective. But in trying to remember from the movies how to ditch a tail, my gait itself became unconvincing, my smallest gestures pointlessly dramatic; I was in fact taking on the coloration of a pushy, émigré stereotype. I had accepted my guilt, as well as my accusers. I wore my alienation like a Dewey button.

A day or two later, outside the Ukraine, I was amazed to recognize my friend the Scot from Oxford. He seemed delighted to see me and sensed my nervousness at once.

"What's happened to you, old man?"

I found myself blurting, My room's bugged, I'm being followed all the time . . .

It was clear that he thought I was, in my charming parochial American way, simply manifesting my residual anti-Communism.

Look, when you leave, I went on hurriedly, I want to make reservations on the same flight with you and if I don't show up, you must call the American Embassy at once.

"Sorry old man, I'm off to Tashkent to see the power stations. Then on to Siberia, actually. I can imagine how an American might feel that way here. Well, don't let their Slav manners get to you. They're quite a lovely people if you give them a chance, actually. Very much like Americans I should say . . . Look here, come round this after and I'll introduce you to some Russian friends . . ."

I headed back to my room in a kind of terminal depression. As I turned for the elevator, however, an old woman dressed in something out of a Glinka ballet, face blotched with birthmarks, leaped in front of me, beating her arms and screaming. The only word I could make out was *Americanski,* and I could not tell whether she was imploring or threatening me. An unfriendly crowd began to gather as she became increasingly hysterical. I couldn't believe it to be an act, but how had she singled me out as an American, particularly in that crowd of conferees? I stood transfixed before her for perhaps a half-minute as she advanced and the crowd thickened. Then I ran to the other end of the enormous lobby, stopping abruptly when I realized how suspicious it would seem. Out on the front steps, I breathed deeply, fought back the tears, and squeezed my triceps. Ten minutes later I re-entered and she was gone; the lobby strewn as always with the dead, crushed petals of an infinitude of welcomings.

In the elevator, I met the black girl of our delegation, easily the least assuming of them all, and the only one who had shown any tolerance for me. I was too reticent and in any case too mentally constipated to explain my predicament, and so we talked for a while about how "illuminating" the conference had been.

"And just think," she sighed, "in three days, it will be over, and I'll be back at work."

Finally, I pulled myself together and asked her if she would do me a favor. She looked suspicious immediately. I explained that I should like to call on them when I returned to New York, and that if I *didn't* call before a certain date, perhaps she could notify the State Department.

"The *State* Department?" she asked incredulously.

You don't have to tell them who you are, I said, just tell them that a member of the delegation did not return. Give them my name. Tell them that you expected to see me in New York and that you are worried . . .

"But what would you want to see *us* for?" I could only say that I promised not to bother her, but that it would be a great favor. What could I say? That I feared for my life?

While it was clear she wanted to help as she put her hand on my arm, her eyes read fink and shill. And in the end, after some niceties, she refused almost tearfully to give me their address.

I kissed her on the cheek and went back to the room. Bill was gone. On his bureau I noticed four different kinds of deodorant. Then the phone rang. A long, high-pitched scream. That was it.

I went down to the Aeroflot office in the lobby and told them that, due to a death in the family, I had to leave immediately. They seemed a little disconcerted, but soon had a flight for Vienna confirmed for that evening. I grinned like an idiot.

As I was packing and humming old Slavonic ballads, the phone rang again. I answered it with a cheery scream. The Aeroflot office informed me petulantly that a car would be available to take me to the airport.

I'll just get my own cab, thanks.

"There are no cabs available," was the curt reply. "You will be escorted."

After leaving a note for Bill in much the same spirit as Bunin had given me his address, I sat in the lobby strumming my balalaika. The limousine arrived promptly two hours before the flight. In the back was Lydia the interpreter.

This really isn't necessary, I said weakly.

"Of course, it's my job after all. I was so sorry to hear about your death. Perhaps it was no one close?"

My father . . . and mother, I stammered crazily.

There was a silence as the driver put my suitcase in the trunk.

It was a plane crash, you see, I parenthesized hopelessly.

"Of course," she said sadly, "you have so many plane crashes in your country." Then, "We must hurry now."

As the car pulled away, the streetlights were turned on, and Lydia's face suddenly shone cadaverous; sweat beaded on her upper lip, her English became strangely guttural and hesitant. I spoke to her in French but she insisted, "I am an interpreter. I will speak to you in your own language."

After a time, I noticed we were not on the expressway to the airport by which we had entered Moscow. I inquired about this.

"The old route is quicker now. It's the second shift and the workers go home now."'

There wasn't another car in sight, Lydia was deathly pale. The car sped and slowed. My tongue was swelling in my throat. The driver seemed to be hesitating at each intersection, as if he wasn't sure where he was. Lydia was giving him directions under her breath. Then the car slowed and Lydia lurched to the window and vomited profusely into the dusk. Probably her first murder, I thought. No more stoicism for this boy. No more literary defenses. I resolved to leap from the car as soon as it slowed again—for indeed we were now accelerating. I'd mash the driver with my balalaika, leap from the car and make for sanctuary at the embassy. Lydia rolled up the stained window, dabbed her lips with a hankie, and we rode on in silence, she refusing to meet my all too credulous stare.

But the car did not slow again, and, as a matter of fact, arrived smartly at the airport by its detour in good time. Lydia was abashed. "I'm terribly sorry," she said. "I'm with child and I've had no rest the entire conference."

I commiserated and, after submitting to a perfunctory search, boarded the plane for Vienna. I could see Lydia through the window, a tiny figure in the night against the neon birches, waving sadly to me, thinking no doubt of all those airliners plunging into America.

I sat next to the wife of the American ambassador to Poland and told her of my little adventure. "Oh, they're really bastards, aren't they?" she laughed. "Oh boy, are they ever bastards."

When I arrived in Vienna I wrote my parents a letter, letting them

The school of Lenin is a school of peace . . .
Don't pin Lenin's name to him
Who plots his progress on a pile of bones
Turning half a planet to scorched earth.
|Andrei Voznesensky|

know I was okay and, after a résumé of events, added a few gratuitous remarks about "trusting the Russians." I should not have been surprised some eight years later, when I casually announced to my parents that I would go to jail before going to Vietnam, that my father the veteran produced that very letter from his files, and asked me what had changed. I could have made the usual pithy argument that the logistics and politics of the situation were not comparable, or argued historically, morally, whatever. But I chose to say nothing. For if my analysis of Soviet intentions was perhaps correct in the broadest sense, I could no longer live my life by such self-evident analysis; or rather, I could no longer afford to be afraid in that way—which meant I would no longer *die bravely.* I felt prouder being devious and devoted to the question of my survival—less stylish and exemplary, perhaps, than my projected series of noble expirations—but now I would enlist against my own paranoia before I would kill, and for my own good would try harder to distinguish insult from real threat.

So while I am less of a pacifist than I ever was, carry a revolver in the rural south and a billy in New York City, I am no longer ashamed of my fear, because I know that I am not dangerous; only sometimes very wicked.

I went back home soon to work in Washington, where my first official act was to buy a crucifix at a local Catholic supply store and send it to my interlocutor of the ice cream parlor. It was more embarrassing than when I purchased my first contraceptives. Shortly thereafter, I was visited by a CIA man.

"We handle extraterritorial affairs," he explained.

Is it true that you guys have to submit to sodium pentathol once a month?

He laughed and reminisced about serving in the Philippines during World War II. "That's where your father was, wasn't it?"

The letters were postmarked from there, I said cagily. I was six then.

"We understand you had some trouble behind the Iron Curtain."

|218|

Now listen, this is what I've planned and decided. If I run away, even with money and a passport, and even to America, I should be cheered up by the thought that I am not running away for pleasure, not for happiness, but to another exile as bad perhaps as Siberia. I hate that America, damn it already . . . as soon as I arrive there with Grusha, we will set to work at once on the land, in solitude, somewhere very remote, with wild bears . . . and there we'll tackle the grammar at once. Work and grammar—that's how we'll spend three years. And by that time we shall speak English like any Englishman. And as soon as we've learned it—goodbye to America! We'll run here to Russia as American citizens. I daresay they won't recognize us . . . I'll make up as an . . . American all my life. But we shall die on our own soil. |Epilogue, The Brothers Karamazov|

As I had no furniture, we sat cross-legged on the floor, his attaché case between us like a parlor game. I rehearsed my adventure for him, both of us laughing at my ineptitude.

He wanted to know the location of the back stairs and the fire escape in the Hotel Ukraine, the approximate thickness of the doors and a floor plan of the level where I stayed.

I told him that these details had somehow escaped my attention. He asked me how, and I patiently explained the two schools of contemporary realism—that I didn't belong to the one which stressed memory or concrete detail.

He wrote this out in painful longhand on his pad. As he flipped the pages I noted that he had been given an intensive course in cursive writing during his formative years.

Finally he wanted to know Bunin's address. I had stupidly mentioned the photo incident while trying to impress upon him that what was *important*, tragic about the whole affair was the fact that neither Bunin nor I would ever know what the other was really up to. In retrospect, it is still hard for me to believe that I could have possibly learned so little—here I was, in terminal ludicrousness, trying to explain to a petty clerk spy that the nature of terror in our time lay not in conspiracy nor totalitarian methods, but the fact that it was no longer possible to attribute motives.

He batted his large eyes, replying that no pressure would be brought to bear upon Bunin, he would only have a "permanent dossier" referring to it as if it were some kind of routine promotion.

I went back to the bedroom and got out my files. I was speech-writing for a senatorial campaign (one of those four liberals who would gain us the kingdom) and was beginning to fear my recalcitrance might compromise our candidate. Bunin stared up at me, his glasses frames nearly invisible in the poor positive print, determined Slavic lips pursed so strangely, his address in a script as childish as that of my interrogator reversed out across his face.

I closed his file and went back to the cross-legged crosseyed agent, with a cross about his neck.

Look, I said, I could tell you I've lost it, but I won't. But I'm not going

"You are courageous," I am often
   told.
It is untrue. I never was
   courageous.
To share the cowardice of my
   colleagues
I simply found unworthy and
   degrading.
I ridiculed what seemed inflated,
   false,
But never shook proverbial
   foundations.
I tried to say the very things I
   thought.
I wrote. I did not write denunciations.
Yes, I defended decent men all round,
And branded mediocrity and
   bleating.
To do so one is surely duty-bound,
Yet "courage" is the word they are
   repeating.
O, with a sense of bitter, burning
   shame
Will our descendants—with the
   vileness dealing—
Think of time—so strange—when men
   were feeling
That simple honesty and courage
   were—the same.
|Evgeny Evtushenko|

to give it to you either. I have no idea how much he knew, and I have no idea what you'll do with it. We've all got enough problems as it is. He was crestfallen. "But it's just for the *record,* I don't understand." I don't live by the record anymore.

"Christ, they beat the shit out of you, didn't they?"

There's no way that I can get at the pricks *over there.* Bunin and I were kind of accomplices. I want the record to show that I am withholding information. Frankly, I only wish I had *more* to hide . . . this is the only sensible thing I've done throughout this whole business.

"You should have been older when your dad and I were sweating our asses in the Philippines," he said grumpily.

I actually felt sorrier for him than I did for myself.

When he left I went to the bedroom and reopened the Bunin file. I burned his photo in the ashtray. Who knows when in another, weaker moment . . . ?

As his face curled and carbonized in the flame, I thought seriously of saluting him.

I am not *funny. I love everyone, and there is nothing ridiculous in loving everyone. I know you. You have feeling. You do not like things that are not calm, because you have weak nerves. I on the other hand have strong nerves. I am not trying to start a campaign for the extermination of nervous people. [But] I do not like propaganda. |The Diary of Vaslav Nijinsky|*

All I want now is a little unambivalence. No literature, no politics. Just constant, controlled movement. A separate peace. We slide from the last of the Hungarian plain where the border guards, armed to the teeth, subject us to intensive search. After the two iron gates are cranked up, I am turned loose from my Janus-faced brothers.

I stop dutifully at the Yugoslav border station, but no one comes out. A few casually uniformed unarmed guards are dozing in chairs at the rear of the station. After a honk, finally one glances up and wearily waves me through. We are in the Mediterranean again, where indifference itself has been the best defense against invasion. At an enormous gas station, a frantic attendant begins with the windshield, then wipes the entire car as the tank fills up, and penultimately, as he gives me my change, produces from a leather pouch a can of aerosol deodorant and sprays the interior of the car. I raise my arms. The best in the west.

I want now only to get lost—surfaces and sensations. An out-of-print English guidebook suggests an itinerary for a raft trip down the rapids of the Drina, near Visegrad. That's for me. The guidebook is divided into sections and indexed by Castles, Caves, Churches, Defiles, Islands, Lakes, Monasteries, Monuments, Mountains, Passes, Rivers, Spas and Waterfalls—which is how, Duncan Swine, a nation ought to be categorized.

There appear to be more tourists in Yugoslavia than even Spain, and among them the ubiquitous Czechs are starting to crack. Each time a Czech passes, he invariably shakes a clenched fist, and we give him back, God knows, all we have, the peace sign, blink our lights, honk our horn . . . our pathetic *symbolic* solidarity. But as we approach Belgrade, the lights and horns and fists diminish as the Czechs begin to estimate the cost of their vacation, begin to ponder the terms of their return.

It is either too early or too late to identify with them, make another metaphor of the month, and that's why I badly want some wildness. I go from tourist agency to agency in Belgrade to find out about the raft trips. No one knows anything about them.

"Ah, you must go to Banja Luka to find out about that," a large Serb reiterates; "that is very wild indeed. But I would not go there if I were you. Perhaps you won't find it. Yes? Instead, you should go hunting and fishing."

He hands over the list: one bear – $200; one elk – $350; one wild kat – $150; on down to the partridge, trout and grouse at $10 to $25 each. They will make the reservations. The guide is included.

How much is a krazy kat? I ask.

Utterly straightfaced, he replies, "Ah, you will find them only near Albania." Then he smiles, "Don't shoot unless you're *loaded.*" Later I'm told they cage the animals and the guide drives them upon you. "We got the idea from an American chap."

I want those rapids, to lose myself in that blast of bright water.

At the State Hunting Agency, I'm again offered a trip to Albania.

No thanks, just came from Czechoslovakia.

"Ah, but Albania is the *wildest* part of Europe left."

It's also restricted on my passport . . . and this isn't the best time to visit Albania, I would guess.

"Well, you don't actually go *into* Albania," the official says.

Oh?

"You take a bus to the border, you see, have lunch, look at Albania and return. It is truly a beautiful view."

I see.

"Many Americans have taken it and enjoyed it thoroughly," he insists.

I want to take big raft on white water, I said in my best Hemingway, and he knew how to play.

"Then you must go and find yourself."

Tito is on every wall here; his cherubic visage in every office, so unlike the somber Kadar, Gomulka, Ulbrecht. He is ubiquitous but somehow unassuming, and that makes all the difference, I suppose. Mostly, they are casual shots. There are only a very few photos left of the young beady-eyed stable boy in a marshal's uniform. The president fishing in a white linen suit, hooking a trout, and as he brings the fish from the wavelet, fish and fisherman's eyes pop at one another. Their Chief-of-State is actually enjoying himself. Sometimes he is fondling a flintlock. The shrewd peasant and gentleman at once—that cunning again, that animal, virile cunning which we so lack in our politicians. One wants to run up to Humpson or Niphrey and shake him by the lapels. "Do anything you want, but for Christ's sake, be a man about it, be a man!" Belgrade is neither socialist drab in style nor vulgar capitalist, though it proliferates with consumer goods which would stop a Hungarian in his tracks, a city which takes its character from the fact it has been bombed to the ground twice in my lifetime. For some appropriate reason, the large state buildings are not like the underground jails of Hungary nor the vast vulgar skyscrapers of Moscow, monolithic to be sure, but *horizontal*, skyscrapers on their side, not higher than the other buildings but longer, as if to suggest the metaphor of the party extending horizontally through the five cultures of the country.

Tito Marsala Tito has been remarkable again—while Johnson and De Gaulle overreact to student unrest, Tito steps directly into his student rebellion, accedes to their demands for change in curriculum, and fires the head of the secret police. The students respect him, but say he's just too old. But the actual *respect*, that's what's unique. Instead of a snotty communiqué from Rumania, or a referral letter from the Department of Health, Education and Welfare, Tito merely says, "If I can't run the country, I will get out"—or at least this is how it is reported in the Western press. The tense is mistranslated, however. What he actually says is, "If I can't run the country, I *ought* to get out." But the effect is the same. He confronts them like a man. He is not uptight and he sees their impulses not as a threat to his authority, or a mark of disrespect, but coextensive with his own efforts of a lifetime. It occurs to me that the American people have spent the last twenty years trying to make their leaders believe we don't really threaten them.

Tito is not only the last leader of his generation, but in many ways the most remarkable—the best of the authoritarian tradition—and perhaps the most exemplary in the sense that he has accommodated intense internal heterogeneity with a foreign policy of extremely subtle and conflicting interests. Most importantly, he has avoided maintaining a wartime psychology, nor does he trade publicly off his war record. It is a country which, in its day-to-day relations between people, appears as democratic as the Scandinavian countries, and is also in some ways as boring. The students tell me that the secret police have been infiltrating their opposition movements, but that they are so obviously identifiable that they are not really "secret." One pretty much knows *who* is a policeman here. It's the *police* who aren't sure who a policeman is. And that is the beginning of modern civilization. But what a man, this Tito. He has created the only Socialist country with a "normal" cultural policy. The only small country to defy both Russia and the United States. The only tourist country which has not lost its identity or integrity in a rush for foreign exchange. And when you think about it, he probably has less blood on his hands than any leader of his generation, or since.

So I'm off for Banja Luka by back roads, through what is clearly the last unspoiled and most beautiful part of Western civilization—Switzerland without chalets and watches and ski lifts, sub-Alpine but still real mountains, not post-card mirages which take your breath away, but strange and wild enough to give it back.

"Don't take the yellow roads," they say, "and when a *Yugoslav* says the road is bad, then you know you're crazy to take it." But I stick to the yellow roads exclusively, heading toward Titovo Uzice, the first "liberated" area in War II, on what is called, rather euphemistically, "poor macadam." Five hours to go sixty miles. The road is one long dry fissure, crossed at fifty-yard intervals by wet fissures. Every quarter of a mile the road disappears completely. Suddenly, around a turn, an enormous truck loaded with logs roars by; he forces me off the road, I brake a foot from plunging into a gorge, while his longest log whip-

lashes, smashing the windshield. The truck does not slow in its careen
down the mountain. I get out and throw stones at the bastard as he
emerges on the turn below.

Once on a plateau, the forest is stunted because of the rock underlay,
pines with a quill-like feather every three feet up the trunk, like a back-
drop of false trees in the old believer scenes of Russian opera, a pseudo-
steppe. It is a land which needs no composer, no poet, no painter—only
a sculptor or an engineer could deal with it. No road for the holiday
maker, not even the Czechs will camp here. Our speed is reduced to no
more than 10 mph. No speed for taking the air, nor does it suit my 45
mph reflective, peripheral haste.

Streams which must be forded accumulate. The few goats ignore/adore
you. There are no people, though certainly there are occasional houses
along the road, family cemeteries in the front yard, Turkish headstones
like so many circumsized penises off plumb. Death taking the only
loam around which isn't flooded or rocky, the houses themselves indistinguishable from their vineyards, and minarets stuck about like lost
javelins in the forest.

We're alone in here where there's no we're.

Then a remarkable thing: at the convergence of several tributaries, the
Drina begins to widen and deepen, the road becomes its flange. No
more gravel bars, eddies, rapids . . . these are gone; simply a gray,
opaque sheet moving like molten steel in a trough.
I turn the car engine off.

absolute silence

I throw a stick in the Drina and it disappears to stage left like an arrow. Total ineluctable silence, but noiselessness is not peace; nature abhors a vacuum because it is one.

So here is the desired oasis, my destination for eight months in all its mindless serenity, where all the senses exist coexistensive with their stimuli, where history is simply geography, where all signs are their own essences—you touch yourself, but you are not there, you hear what you can't see, see what you can't hear, and there is nothing on which to use speech, nothing to *name,* and the body cancels out its signals for recognition simultaneously as it renews itself in the void.
The news here is that no explanation is required. Ever. The peace not of life nor death, but of the hinge between.
The reader will note this mote of silence lies somewhere between Loznick and Ljubovija in the midst of a most un-American dream. For suddenly *at one* with nature, without notions of either conquering or submitting to it, one's uniqueness and will are reduced to mere physicality within an infinite perspective, and the old terror returns—what to *do,* where to *go*—I must maintain my *progress,* my momentum, my motion—I put the car in gear in the fear that I will never catch up with my own mind.
As soon as possible I leave the yellow ribbons for the main red road. It's back then to 45 mph, to the notebook, to my allies the Czechs, who also have nowhere to go, yet can never stop.

This evening in Sarajevo, the light turns the minarets to maize and ochre. On the Gavril Princip Bridge, they are listening, on Japanese portable radios, to the news of the five-pronged strike into Czechoslovakia. Tito has sent tanks to the Hungarian frontier, making a point of routing them through Belgrade; in the streets of Sarajevo the militia is armed, and an old anarchist of the Franz Josef assassination conspiracy says in a newspaper interview he'd do it all over again.

|226|

We could go somewhere else as we had always had the right to go somewhere else and as we had always gone . . . Hemingway. We could go somewhere else as we had always had the right to go somewhere else and as we had always gone . . . Hemingway. We could go somewhere else as we had always had the right to go somewhere else and as we had always gone . . . Hemingway. We could go somewhere else as we had always had the right to go somewhere else and as we had always gone . . . Hemingway. We could go somewhere else as we had always had the right to go somewhere else and as we had always gone . . . Hemingway. We could go somewhere else as we had always had the right to go somewhere else and as we had always gone . . . Hemingway. We could go somewhere else as we had always had the right to go somewhere else and as we had always gone . . . Hemingway. We could go somewhere else as we had always had the right to go somewhere else and as we had always gone . . . Hemingway. We could go somewhere else as we had always had the right to go somewhere else and as we had always gone . . . Hemingway. We could go somewhere else as we had always had the right to go somewhere else and as we had always gone . . . Hemingway. We could go somewhere else as we had always had the right to go somewhere else and as we had always gone . . . Hemingway. We could go somewhere else as we had always had the right to go somewhere else and as we had always gone . . . Hemingway.

In Sarajevo where the evening light turns the minarets maize and ochre, and the coppersmiths repeat their 101,749th ashtray of their lives, the populace packs an open air cinema-urinal to watch John Wayne blow up some Japs. A partisan, an old man in pantaloons and slippers, whispers, "a true partisan." So it is that we romanticize each other's wars. While we fantasize our heroes, Dubcek, that ultimate symbol of playing the game straight, the supremely rational man, liberal of liberals, has been abducted without so much as a struggle. Can an entire nation fail one man? My own anti-libertarian feeling is that John Wayne should not be allowed in the bazaar at this time. In this last center of mercantile handicrafts, and the memory of total heroic resistance against totalitarianism, how can you permit this buffoon, this hack, trading on the most vicious intersection of patriotism, puffy masculinity and commercialism, to enact his personal dismemberment of the Orient? But the Commissars are right—they know what corrupts the state and what does not. Wayne is as good as the next man in this context, his violence just as programmatic and just as entertaining. They give us these monotonous yet somehow unique copper trays, testimony that you can't copy *anything exactly,* no matter how hard you try; they give us inlaid teak and polished cherry, capes of ram's wool, goblets of horn, goat cheese, cabbages, venison; we give them John Wayne. And yet, in an instant they would willingly trade their expertise with the mallet for a movie. They could never be persuaded that, as barters go, once again they are getting the short end of the stick.

After the nature of the Czechoslovakian "resistance" becomes clear, I get very drunk and watch Yugoslavian TV for eight hours straight. I hate myself for my contempt for the Czechs—for the need of a model courage which can mitigate the pseudo-resistances of Frisco and Paris, for the need of an instant of both heroic and effective rebellion, so that I can believe again in the reality of my own oblique opposition. On the single channel, a man and a woman take turns fly casting into a river rather like the Drina, singing neo-Turkish arias to it. It is incredibly monotonous, they don't catch anything, but the song goes on, just like

the river. Maybe that's the point? The river's a stone which can't be scratched; and these people are neither alienated from nature as we are, nor like the Hungarian, futilely attached to his scrap of land; they are simply content to be part of the horizon. Like that jar in Tennessee, they stand, or rather lean, against it. I think for a minute, with a kind of primitive vengeance, how the Tuscan hills, the Chianti valley, or the Appalachians of North Carolina must have looked before they were settled and eroded. Then it occurs to me that there is no aesthetic reason at all to prefer this—that I have only politicized my visual sense to no end. Here we go again. While the image of that trout leaping into Tito's mouth would be surreal for us, it is perfectly fitting here, for they truly take their land for granted, in the best sense. But if you should ask them to show you what is remarkable about their country, like all governments they will show you the modern copper mill, the Tomb of Basha Bella Jamin, interesting fortifications, the hydroelectric, priceless frescoes, a good restaurant . . .
And suddenly I can no longer bear my third-class hotel in Sarajevo, in my TV landscape to hear of a Czech, and crazily turning the car around, head back into the interior for that peace which I also cannot bear. So begins the zigzag, and our movement, once reflective, has become a careen.

Turbulent history, lovely verdure, magnificent position, owing to its location it suffered frequent destruction genial climate, much entertainment, relaxation and education. Rule of the road, keep to the right. Under no circumstances leave the country without your car. |*Official Guide Book*|

The Czechs are no longer moving; they sit by the side of the road in their Skodas and Trabants, their Mockbas and Wartburgs, and they no longer blink their lights or wave, and we choose not to encourage any further hapless, gratuitous response . . . Their hopelessness has become, finally, appropriate.

Now, I am again among the wild asparagus of minarets, the mushrooms of Ottoman graves, rattling the yellow roads, and snug in the lee of

CHAMOIS   STAG   ROE   BEAR   AND   BOAR

Arrive at Visegrad at dusk. And the bridge which Andric celebrates, erected in 1574 by the Grand Vizier Mehmed Sokolovic. It is the most extraordinary structure I have seen in all Europe, making the aqueducts of Spain and southern France seem officious and even clumsy by comparison, for it does not span the gorge as much as it holds the mountains apart. While the current is very strong at this point, the bridge, which appears to be constructed entirely of chilled cubits of rose wine, makes the river itself seem almost febrile.

And next to it, wonder of wonders, a stone house proclaims *Timber Raft Excursions* "all the way to Bajzina Basta." The windows are plastered with photos of the long raft of lashed logs crashing in the rapids, a tiny Bosnian grimacing at the tiller and four or five terrified passengers holding each other. Through a crack in the posters, I see a delightful young lady working late and implore her to open the door and put me on that river.

She explains patiently that in fact there has been no trip for five years; the reason, a new hydroelectric plant and a dam. There are no longer any rapids, she explains, and even if there were, you couldn't get through. Then laughing at my utter disappointment, "Perhaps you don't understand? We need the power for our people more than the beauty. We have more than enough beauty, yes? Sad but necessary. You must have many great beautiful rivers in your country, since you do not need the power, yes?"

I know the story, and I'm through crying. But why are the signs still up, and why was she still around if the trips had been discontinued? "Ah," she purred, "you would be disappointed if you came all the way to Visegrad and found no one to speak to you of our famous raft trips, no?"

That is what comes of always being on the move . . .

So, back to the coast for some sun?

The King of the Road game has finalized into a pathetic, unennobling routine. The Czech borders are closed and Czechs encamp by the thousands, squatting among the German tourists like so many pale elves,

I remained there an hour and got a complete impression; the place was perfectly soundless, and for the time at least, lonely; the splendid afternoon had begun to fade and there was a fascination in the object I had come to see. It came to pass at the same time I discovered in it a certain stupidity, a vague brutality. That element is rarely absent from great Roman work which is wanting in the nice adaptation of the means to the end. The means are always exaggerated; the end is so much more than attained . . . and I suppose a race which could do nothing small is as defective as a race which could do nothing great . . . |Henry James, A Little Tour in France—*upon seeing the Pont du Garde|*

DRINKING GRK ON THE BAY OF KRK

still sporting their genteel black-power salutes in solitary walks upon the beach. The refugee camps are being refurbished. Even the Germans now make way for these fey, high-foreheaded people of the final compromise.

Jews and Germans have much in common. They are industrious, efficient, diligent, and basically hated by others. |Franz Kafka, 1909|

The Nerevta delta opens up toward the sea. We take the ferry to Orebig on the peninsula, drive across it, losing the entire exhaust system from the manifold down, and with the engine going like all Le Mans, we descend for the second ferry to Korcula, the traditional retirement place for sea captains. This island of Marco Polo's birthplace is all of . . . well, stone. Stone breakwater, stone streets, stone churches, stone walls, stone ground, stone cliffs and defiles, the boats are all of stone; the people, food, the local wine, Grk, are flinty. They have been invaded too many times.

Their lobsters feed in the naval yards. They taste more like game than fish. I wouldn't be surprised if the lobsters they are losing in Maine are swimming to Korcula. If you were a lobster, wouldn't you rather be from Peljesac than Bar Harbor? But here the waters are too warm, too clean, too clear. It is more like heavy air than otherness. I suppose I prefer fog to repose. We can see you, lobster, on the bottom, see you, lobster, through ten fathoms where it's really too warm to crawl, the medium too idyllic to displace. The poor Dalmatians cannot adjust to being a *resort*. They have not the welcoming graces. Any more than we do.

Across the straits, the shore is filling with villas. The pines—short and wind-warped as they are—are coming down. From this perspective it appears that the Adriatic will become yet another Geneva, Balaton, another Lauderdale—the test of this state will not be whether it can rescue the poor, those unequipped to compete, from a life of misery—but whether they will be able to resist the stupefaction of affluence resulting from a hedge in natural competition.

The town of Korcula has all the perfection and aridity of a model. Perhaps it has paid too much for its endurance; its perfect medieval streets, equidistant stone arches, computerized serial ramparts. It exudes the illusory permanency of a people who have known mostly piracy and occupation—the thrust of the ubiquitous lion of Venice from the rock belies itself. An open-mawed and soundless roar. They are as quick to stoicism as we are to calculated amiability. And they cast over their land the illusion of homogeneity—just as we with our mass production create the chimera of variety—strategies which have only their desperation in common.

Atop Marco Polo's house, a study/observatory overlooks the series of bays which lead to the open sea, each strip of bright water converging to a dot. It is exactly as if one were at the still hub of a wheel. All force here is centrifugal, Balkan exhaust. No wonder that he left to round the world, or that he would end his days gazing twenty feet across one of the darkest interior canals of Venice at the encrusted paint and elaborately barred windows of an opposing house. No distance, no perspective, and the only light a diagonal bar descending like a guillotine once a day. Microcosm was what he wanted. An end to endless view. Peace is, in the end, always a wall. With a door.

Some English friends arrive who have never been fishing so I have arranged a trip into the rich waters. A girl at the butcher shop says that her father is the finest fisherman on the island, and will take care of everything. At dawn, we file out along a long jetty of cubed boulders to meet his small launch, then cruise out into the warm, shallow Adriatic which is now like slate. There is only a small wrinkle at the prow, we trail neither a bubble, nor fleck of foam. Finally I know what *ply* means.

It turns out that this magnificent fisherman lived for eight years in New York in the twenties.

I'll bet you were glad to get back.

"Not really. My wife didn't want me to be a sailor anymore, that's all."

I look over the equipment, hoping it is relatively simple for the uninitiated guests, who now sit in the bow holding each other's hands tightly, staring fixedly ahead of them, waiting, no doubt, for a spume or fin.

Our fisherman takes a coil of matted string from his back pocket, takes half an hour to disentangle it, ties on a rusty hook with a double half hitch, cuts a putrid mullet into strips, baits the hook and lowers it hand over hand until the lightness of the line telegraphs the bottom.

An hour passes. We three are attentive. He is watching his line. We converse in Franco-German with Italian verbs we cannot conjugate.

After a while, the guests ask me, "Are we fishing now?"

I nod. We are watching him fish.

What are we going for? I ask him.

He shrugs. "Big, small, whatever." He gestures like an accordion.

Two hours later, he puts on a fresh strip of rotting mullet, and works the other side of the boat, the end of the twine wrapped about his knee. I presume we are not going for the big one.

The sun hits noon with a ratchet click. We have already been out six hours. He moves the boat to the shoals on the leeward side of a bald igneous island.

Do you have an extra line or two? I ask timidly.

"Oh, this one is strong enough," he says.

2:00 PM. He is becoming grumpy and we move back into the center of the channel. Somehow the sun is not moving. My guests have begun to perspire heavily. They eat their picnic lunch. Their hands against their salami sandwiches are the color of lobsters.

3:30. He heaves a sigh of what seems to be relief, pulls up his line, coils it back in his pocket, goes forward and drags a large cork trimmed net from the hatch. He feeds this out for about 75 yards and we watch the bobbers surface.

5:00 PM. He takes the net in. There is one six-inch fish with horns all over it.

He takes it by the tail and smashes its head a dozen times against the gunwhale. My friends cringe and watch, the girl covers her face with her garish hands.

The fisherman looks up and shrugs. "No worse than what you're doing in Vietnam, is it?"

Back in Belgrade, tired of Chebob Chichi and Razna Chichi, ashes on a skewer, I go on a tip to what is supposed to be the most authentic restaurant in town, a soccer club on the outskirts. During dinner, a soldier eating alone invites me to his table. He is a Major in the Yugoslav army. After a supper of carp soup and baklava, we take a bottle of Montastirka, that plum brandy smoother than the best scotch, and go out to the soccer field, bathed now in a full moon.

We sit in the nets of the soccer goal watching the moon grow brighter and brighter through our dilated corneas. We discuss Tito's move of sending tanks to the border. I mention that I don't see how the Russians could possibly think of invading this country, given its terrain and the partisan spirit. They would lose entire divisions.

At this he laughed uproariously. "You are so naive. You are crazy. I am telling you, I am a military man for life, and I know these things. It is only you and Russia now. If you wished, you could be in Hanoi in a week. Of course, you would have insuperable problems in governing, and that is the only reason you are not there. It is also true, from a military point of view, that you could have bombed them into submission had you not been concerned about civilians. Had you bombed them as you bombed the Germans, as you bombed Belgrade, they would have had to capitulate. As it is, they are far more crippled, I know this from our intelligence, than you would imagine. I am not talking about atomic weapons. They are not necessary. World War II weaponry is perfectly satisfactory to destroy any nation now—in fact, much more effective for most. No, you could have not only bombed them into submission, you could have taken over easily with the troops that you have there, had you chosen to invade. I only say this not to embarrass you, to shock your obviously fine sense of morality, but as a way of telling you that the Russians could be on our Adriatic coast in three days. I am not exaggerating. It is simple military logistics. Likewise, they would have insuperable problems of governing and a loss of prestige. But believe me, if we fought to the last man, and we would, we could not stop them. Yes, they would have their headquarters in Diocletian's palace in Split, a submarine base in Dubrovnik before you snap your fingers . . . the only thing that could save us would be *your* intervention—and I do not mean just a blockade of the Bosporus . . ."

We then discuss those particular "objective conditions" which have resulted in this country's unique fortune. Like most Yugoslavs, he has nothing but disdain for the new left, though he also claims to be anti-Tito, left of him. The partisan heritage in even the most intense anti-Titoism seems to recognize that mono-party politics are the only alternative in divided and underdeveloped countries. He goes on to say that there are two reasons for their success. The first is simply the heterogeneity of the five-state, multilingual country which helps to insure decentralization and discourages the worst aberrations of state capitalism and/or Stalinism. The opposition of Djilas, for example, can be understood better as pro-Montenegrin and conservative than as anti-Communist and opportunistic; that is to say, his opposition is essentially patriotic. "And the man serves his time, he paid for it," he says, "unlike your rebels!"

The second is tourist income—a way to get capitalist dollars and foreign exchange value without being capitalist. "We can attract investment and expertise without creating a capitalist reactionary class within the country."

You mean, I say, you can create a revolutionary proletariat without their becoming merely the new bourgeois?

He grins and literally beats his chest. "We are the only Socialism which has not been produced at the point of a bayonet!"

The Major has nothing but scorn for Castro—he could have had it both ways, he says, and from both sides. "Now he's stuck with an unfair exchange. He is dependent on a medieval barter system. Cuba will become the Czechoslovakia of the Caribbean."

Would he argue that Latin Americans are more corruptible than Slavs?

"Ah, I assure you we are quite as corruptible. Look at those men over there"—he points to two enormous mustachioed men in Western sharkskin suits in the parking lot of the restaurant emerging from, of all things, a '68 Plymouth Fury. "They are party men, and they are Slavs. They are our, how do you say, 'traveling salesmen.' They are mindless pigs, but they have energy and they make our economy function, they move the goods. You see, Spain and Greece could have done the same thing as we—every country has such men—but they are additionally burdened with a corrupt philosophy."

|234|

In my country now, I replied, it is those very men who are most reactionary. For it is they who have most to lose.

"I know, I know. Essentially, you see, we are lazy. It has been our salvation. Our secret police are as lazy as our counter-revolutionaries. Because we are lazy, because we are patient, we have been able to rehabilitate our Stalinists, and avoid liquidating our democratic reformers. It's a beginning, yes?"

We're lazy too, I said, but we're not patient.

"Well, you must stay then," and he insists that I buy land in Yugoslavia. "I can arrange it," he says. "You need not worry. Soon we will be as stable as Switzerland."

That's just the point. I admire your politics, your landscape. But your culture bores me. I still prefer Greece or Spain.

"Yes, yes, of course you are right. Our cunning has finally made us dull; we are losing our manhood along with our terrorists."

The brandy is making me sentimental again.

Do you think the Russians really had much to fear from Dubcek?

"What would America have done if it were suddenly discovered that the West German Bundeswehr supported a coup d'etat?"

But why didn't they fight? As you would?

"Swoboda was the key. He chose to save lives. 'Better the King die than the country.' Had they resisted they would have been annihilated. The Czechs are cleverer than we. Only a basically unintellectual people can be democratic for long. Too much reflection on natural rights impedes the construction of humane institutions. . . . Constitutions have never meant much in this part of the world."

What you're saying is that America is lost.

"Ah, too much self-hatred, young man. Just think, you may well be the first *people* in history to end a war perpetrated by their own government. Because when it stops, it will because of pressure from the people, people without direct political power. If not the general will, then the general nausea. This could not happen here, yet. Nor, I think, in any other country, even England. Despite your corrupt philosophy, you have found reserves that you had not imagined. And *without* being invaded. It is really quite remarkable. You have lost your virginity, but asserted your basic nobility, and yet you express only despair . . ."

I was nothing but a baleful stare.

"Oh, there is another fact of life which will no doubt infuriate you. Tito will pass from the scene sooner than you think. And he will try to leave behind a legacy of decentralization—both for egotistical reasons—there will never be another Tito, etc.—as well as profoundly reasonable ones. We will become more suspect by our comrades to the east as we become even more democratic domestically, and if conditions become serious—internal civil war—we may well have to turn to America for—not intervention—let us say, 'support.' And because we are not only the 'key to the Balkans,' but also own access to the Mediterranean, we will no doubt get your support. And America will preserve us—for the wrong reasons perhaps, and without a true philosophy—but she will make us *possible*, again . . ."

As he drove me back to the hotel, I had the terrible premonition that I would enlist in such a war, that the year had taught me nothing.

Another shock this morning. While having a haircut I pick up a *Life* Magazine, and in a photo of a demonstration at Harvard against McNamara, I see that boy I knew at Oxford, that prodigy through whose window I stared daily and took such strength from his writer's block. Now seven years later, this same young man is bald, his face distorted by pure but unreferenced rage, spending his voice shouting down an arrogant fool, an expletive no doubt for every logistical statistic; Harvard aestheticism turned in fury against Harvard Business School . . . The same Harvard which so involuted his mind has now engineered the nation into a total loss of self-esteem. He is identified in the caption as an "occasional graduate student." How many blocked prodigies we have! The air is inscribed with the clots of their silence, and I take back my glee, every ounce!

The modern democratic state is therefore no bright and rational creation of the new day, the political form under which great people are to live healthfully and freely in the modern world, but the last decrepit scion of an ancient and hoary stock, which has become so exhausted it scarcely recognizes its own ancestor. It does in fact repudiate him while it clings tenaciously to the archaic and irrelevant spirit that made that ancestor powerful . . . the whole era has been spiritually wasted, the farmers were apathetic, the small businessmen and working men are still apathetic toward the war. The election was a vote of confidence of these latter classes in a president who would keep the faith of neutrality. The intellectuals, in other words, have identified themselves with the least democratic forces in American life. They have assumed the leadership for war of those very classes whom the American democracy has been immemorially fighting. Only in a world where irony was dead could an intellectual class enter war with the head of such illiberal cohorts in the avowed cause of world liberalism and world democracy. |Randolph Bourne, Unfinished Fragment on the State, 1918|

In Novi Sad, I meet up with the Yugoslav poet I met in San Francisco.
He shows me his review of the new book of the remarkable poet
Vasko Popa.

At first glance he seems like a surrealist who has spent one summer
too long on Black Mountain. But as this poet retranslates the bad English version into his own, it becomes finally clear what the aesthetics of
dialectical materialism mean. For these are poems which purge themselves of more than rhetoric—our purist movement, imagism, was essentially aesthetic, but Popa is not only throwing off bad poetry, but
bad history as well—minimalist poetry perhaps, but not the cynical
minimalism of the West which so blandly accepts the death and brutali-
zation of sensibility.

Our last evening together, the poet and I walked back through the
town of Novi Sad, and again, the general tranquillity, the sufficiency
of consumer goods, compared with the dreariness of Hungarian
cities—as well as the cleanliness and intelligent planning, compared
with an average American suburb—make me rage. It is a pride given
concrete form—rather than being repressed, as in Hungary, or overblown, as in America. The city is surrounded by hills, and across the
Danube, the Petrovaradin fortress rises from the cliffs, now given over
to an immense sculpture garden and artists' studios.

The poet's wife sighs, "Lord it's good to be home. America is so tir-
ing."

I ask him if he wants to go back.

"Yes, of course," he said, "I'm writing a book about you."

His thesis seems to be this: that America's confusion is doubly terrifying because its best people are confused. This manifests itself in its
revolutionary "re-action" or *cult of the deed.*

"I believe," he says drily, "you can appreciate my distrust of action
for its own sake. Our passions have preserved our nation, yet the opposition to Nazism springs from the same perverted energy which be-

Dandelion

On the edge of the sidewalk
At the world's end
Solitude's yellow eye

Blind feet
Knock his neck
Into his rocky belly
Underground elbows
Drive his roots
Into heaven's dark soil
A dog's raised leg
Mocks him
With a boiled shower
His only joy is
The walker's homeless glance
That rests in his corolla
Overnight
And so
The butt is burning out
On frustration's lower lip
At the world's end

|*Vasko Popa from* Inventory|

gan World War I. A nation should always discount its strengths. What I cannot understand about Americans is they do not seem to know the difference between avant-garde art, radical politics and bohemian lifestyle. Each acts as a code for the other, and so the cost and consequences of each are hopelessly confused. They are very different things, you know."

Near dusk we drive into the mountains above Novi Sad to see the Partisans' Monument, as fine a piece of socialist realism as I've ever seen. From the mountain top there is forest to infinity, 360°.
"The Germans cut down every tree as far as you can see," he says distantly, "so that the Partisans would have no cover . . . and, pointing down the Danube, he relates the same story he did in the bar where Jack Spicer died.
"You see out there where the bend is? The Hungarians were in charge of administering Serbia under the Axis. One evening they marched a thousand Serbs out onto the ice, poured gasoline on the ice, and . . . well . . . my father was among them. They could have at least shot them before. The Hungarians have short memories. They should know what it is to lose their freedom, since they denied it to others for so long. It is good for them to be able to visit here occasionally."
But what about your . . . *hatred?* I ask meekly.
"I am a poet," he replies, "hatred is a luxury for a poet. As a citizen, I have my pride. Eventually pride displaces hatred. That is only dialectic which concerns me."
We drive back down, across to an island in the Danube, where at the far end there is a marvelous restaurant. It seems incredible, but save for the restaurant, the island is almost wild. We discuss the possibility of publishing his work in American periodicals.
"But not the ones," he says, "with a professional history of anti-Communism, the ones who snap up journalists like Mihajlov and pass them off as either great literature or indicative of the repressed Yugoslav artistic spirit, neither of which is true."

OK, you've told me about the hatred. Now what about the fear? If you did publish in *The New Leader,* say, would you be afraid of . . . repression?

He thought very carefully for some time. "No, I am not afraid. I am cautious, it is true, but that is more a cultural than a political phenomenon. This has always been an authoritarian part of the world. I'm not going to hold a press conference denouncing the regime; on the other hand, I'm never going to win the Lenin Prize either. It is all a matter of degree. I suppose it is about the same degree of fear as an American professor waiting for tenure . . . Look, I care about my livelihood, the people I love, and my work. One has not compromised the others as yet. And I do not live my life at the expense of my countrymen, nor other peoples . . ."

We eat fish soup and he walks me back to my hotel. I tell him I can't believe how much better river-fish soup is than bouillabaisse. I can't believe how much better they live than the Hungarians. It is meant to be a gratuitous, affectionate remark. . . .

"Yes," he sighs, "You know, I now feel the same way about Americans as I did about Hungarians. I mean, they both work so hard and neither gets what they deserve. They both get so very little for their efforts."

Everywhere I meet the hope, so curiously and earnestly expressed, that we will be well again.

November 1, 1968. I have gone to Rome to . . . vote. And to pick up the mail. Another letter from my best student. He has discovered that "all writing is pigshit" and encloses a recommendation form for Law School. In one summer he has enacted the circular adolescent ritual which used to take years; the Grand Tour is no doubt speeding up. And, in fact, in a single year we seemed to have re-rehearsed the scenario of 1848–1917.

The form stresses that the applicant be in the top ten per cent of my acquaintances in intelligence and character. Well, I don't know about him, but I'm not the man I was, to make such distinctions. If we are to take our soldiers, our Presidents, by lottery, why not our lawyers? His letter signs off, "We are the unhappiest people on the face of the earth."

I stand in the ornate hallway of our Embassy and fill out the form as my ballot—dutifully, respectfully, hopelessly.

Now there are riots in Rome. The police huddle and giggle among us, pressed against the wall of the Piazza Navona while a student mob shakes a Fiat to pieces. Over in the church, they play the complete *Messiah* in forty-five minutes. It has been discovered that the leaning tower of Pisa was built that way on purpose. We're already at third re-move. . . .

Question: *Who put the last six bullets in Mussolini?*

Answer: *One hundred Italian sharp-shooters.*

A SHORT HISTORY OF THE ROYAL FAMILY

Of Rome we shall say only that it is reminiscent of Chicago. A similar beast runs wild in its salubric center, a small and pliant beast with spinning eyes and hairless snout who eats/excretes in the same marvelous instant. When your eyes water unaccountably and your sinuses rebel, he cannot be far. "They are Arabs," my landlady says of her scuttling, careening countrymen, Arabs without a quarter, Arabs without Araby, not even Arabesque. She equates them with the beast. The Appian Way is lined with Gelati wrappers and Campari bottles left behind by brigands. The beast is partial to pistachio Gelati. Inasmuch as his olfactory glands atrophied in the 18th century, and despite his canine origins, he has recently developed color vision. He sees better than he thinks. He eats what looks best. He chooses what is easier. He is not dangerous, merely wicked.

As for the Arabs who prize his flesh, those who each day so cunningly appear without apparent effort in the elaborate disguise of Roman citizens, pretending to be that severe, extinct people—they have outsmarted themselves. That is why we are so partial to *them.* They really love being too much of a good thing. From surfeit, they do not suffer.

It is these very Arabs who prize the beast's flesh, and in the fall of the year, in the *Ottobrichi,* they unsheath their long curved knives and corner their prey, one by one, in the piazzas; those grandiose traps for light become weirs for beasts. They cut their throats with a single short stroke and the beast's rare bark ends as a gurgle of a motorscooter plunging into a lagoon.

It is for this reason, as well as the rich food, that when in Rome, I exercise. Violent gratuitous exercise if that's what's available, though I would prefer a conventional body-building routine with set repetitions and labeled weights. It's all a question of nerves, I suppose, the natural inclination to ride against the current of my metabolism which operates increasingly without a scorecard. But is it not foolish to be concerned at this point with what is *natural?* I no longer know which my "natural" instincts are. "No natural sensations, no ideas without consequences," Philippians says, hedging his bets. I know only which are my best instincts, and be they conditioned, repressed or pure genetic jelly, I intend to preserve them. This is why, while I might pursue the beast if invited, I would not eat of his flesh. Of course, that's easy to say, for I have neither knife nor dog, that high-prancing four-gaited white mastiff bred for hunting the beast. Older than Rome itself, their curiously prehistoric hindquarters slightly higher than their head, one occasionally sees their predecessors on a pedestal locked in some insensate allegorical struggle with a serpent or bird; one also sees them at cocktail parties, so sweet they'll break your heart, shaking your hand at the door, bracing their buttocks against a velour sofa, raising an enormous fen-resistant paw which once defended nobility from boars and boors. He hates only the beast. They are said to share a common ancestor.

I shall not live in the center of this city. The Spanish Steps are littered with the young knifelike bodies of my wildeyed countrymen. They sprawl insolently among the easels of the palateless Arabs, disguised in this quarter as Italian *Kleinmeisters,* and who, inspired by the pastels of Cello Campari and Giaocomo Gelati, recreate the banal late-night hallucinations of my brothers and sisters who await the long, cursive American mail. My brothers and sisters believe they are dead. I know otherwise. They just need some exercise, that's all. Soon they will be selling aluminum siding, and setting new records doing it.
So I have taken it upon myself to find space in this city of the beast, space where we may renew our bodies. Such facilities remain a premium. There is a YMCA, for example, which has a large reading room with foreign newspapers, discussion environments, billiards and bowling, but only a small airless cubicle where a pair of dumbbells without end lugs lie in desuetude, so that the weights, once lifted, will slide off and break your toes. And while our embassy flies-in movies of professional football games, it has no advice or counsel for less vicarious activities, unless you count absentee voting. One day I come across a villa with a decent-sized pool, the residence of a former American, of course. The water is green with scum, striped with sediment, and down the middle lane, for some reason, in a black corset and orange bathing cap, comes a nun doing the breast stroke. The water roils from her wake and slops over the edge. The drains, it seems, have been plugged, a servant explains effusively, with the dead litters of the beast whose proclivity for reproducing its kind is matched only by its ability to manufacture dung, of which a healthy male will produce some thirty pounds or more in a week. So, within this endless vault of fountains, pools and the sewer Tiber, it became clear that I could only jog.

I have rented a place, north of the city proper, on a hill in an "exclusive" suburb, where at night one can hear the beast roaming below. As his legs are foreshortened he cannot negotiate the hills, slipping as he does in his own excrement. They are not exactly pellets. It is said that the white mastiff has no trouble tracking him. Indeed, his method seems to be to head him off.
Through some oversight, civil or architectural, we have no sidewalks in our section of town. My building is brand new but as cold as a Venetian loggia at Christmas, my room always twenty degrees cooler than outside, and despite the thirty-foot expanse of window, the sun never enters. Could one have calculated this? From what I can tell, there are mostly diplomats around here. Their rough wives and timid dogs step across the mud to reach their pretty cars.

|242|

The first thing to do in Rome is set up a proper schedule. I shall work for six hours in my cold sublet, exercise for two, drink for two, eat for one, work for two, walk for one, read for three, eat and sleep the rest. In my dreams I trail the beast peremptorily. Then with Respighi in a background beneath the massive Piranesi arch, I watch myself club him to death with a lyre-backed Victor Emmanuel salon chair. It never fails to break me up, though I've never had a dream that I didn't know was one before it ended.

But we were speaking of getting back in shape. I always carry my work clothes in my backpack—gray baggy pantaloons, rubberized hooded parka, the faded numerals still upon it, and my Chuck Taylor All-Star Converse white basketball shoes with red laces, pink soles. They leave a complex ribbed track which would baffle the beast itself. He who follows the mottled octagonal imprint of a Chuck Taylor gym shoe has only himself to blame.

And I set off in the early afternoons, while they are absorbed with their long Arabian luncheons—couscous disguised in so many lovely ways, semolina baked into long strands, butterfly wings, tiny sandwiches, yes they do—as I pad into the endless autumn, taking my *ottobrichi* at a trot, forsaking all ruins, arms pumping ominously across my numerals, getting the decade's morning out of my lungs.

I run down my hill, as the steel corrugated shutters snap down for surrogate naps, dash beneath the curve of the expressway, and out beyond the Olympic Park where no Arab has ever ventured, running on my toes, in my gray peaked novice's hood. The road gradually becomes more deserted, the open fields blackened with burning trash. Smoke is always rising from these far fields; sometimes you can make out a scavenger policing the area among the coils of smoke, but mostly it's just the Arabs, with their gay two-suiters, come to honor the beast, or perhaps his absence, each in his own way.

In the middle of the day, I came to a dark woods where the paved road was lost. Totally winded, I fell upon the moss and needles. In the distance, the fields of garbage were burning listlessly. A rectangular haze floated toward Hadrian's tomb. My heart slowed, I rolled on my back. My hood was damp and limp about my face. Even my shoes were heated up from all those hills' macadam. And then as the wind abated, I heard an imperceptible metallic rhythmic thumping issue from the forest.

I raised myself up and split the screen of pines at a lope. Before me, an enormous pink and ochre stucco wall rose up, large blotches of brick admitting its decay. It undulated across the hill as far as I could see, its edge inset with the emerald of broken wine bottles. And in its shadow lay perhaps half a dozen Fiats, parked diagonally, the last of these swaying like a little poppet.

I ran a deliberate, closing circle about the company. Occasionally a large pair of buttocks would kiss and kiss a windshield. The tiny cars shook furiously like a herd of chihuahuas drying themselves after fording a creek. I was utterly silent, on my tiptoes in the pine needles. The diplomats were taking lunch, *ora casa.* The clearing was denatured as more cars arrived; larger ones now, Alfas, even one large Chocolate Lancia.

The couples stared at me, jogging in place despite the unevenness of the terrain. I stared at the wall. There was no breach. Too high to clamber with all that broken glass to grope, I ran along the wall for a mile according to my pedometer, finally coming to a well-made corner. Then exhausted, I made my way home, giving wide berth to the secret clearing, the sacred grove.

It took me several days to jog the wall's circumference. I conserved my energy; this was no time for shin splints. But there was no place low enough to vault. The weather was clear and I could feel my stamina returning. This was not leisure. Had I a car, a secretary, a lunch hour, a real leather bucket seat, things might have been different—such elaborate luncheons, such huge bodies, such small vehicles, these things make you reflective, and reflection tends to make you celibate, and celibacy requires the retention . . . of one's freshest hours to think . . . and thinking clearly demands a rigorous, disciplined bodily exercise, and such bodily exercise makes one exquisitely tired; one sleeps the perfect sleep in which one dreams of those wonderful lunches, large bodies floating in their little glass and metal carapaces—only inches to spare!—ah, we have given ourselves back to each other, like tonsils, like specimen organs, two to a package. "No ideas without consequences . . ." I wonder if the course of world history would have been different if Kant and Kierkegaard had jogged instead of walked.

One day I discovered a small handmade hole about shoulder height and looked through the wall. There was a great ravine, an impenetrable thicket. I then understood why this forest seemed so foreign. For when the leaves fall here, there are so many pines and evergreens that the skeletal pin oaks and poplars simply disappear into the green fastness. Their deciduous bodies become indistinguishable from the soporific interminable neon green; in other words, in fall, it is more green than when there were leaves. Visually speaking, it could stand a little snow.

The following day, nevertheless, I came upon a gate which I had apparently overrun in my initial survey, a massive interwoven iron structure twice again as high as the wall, dragon's teeth atop. Through the bars, I could make out a cypress-lined drive, ill-kempt but graded exquisitely to create views as much as catch them, and in the upper righthand corner, truffling in a grassy ditch, two boar. So I assumed an asylum, a sanitarium, perhaps the Italian CIA, where they take off their sharp suits and delicate gloves, their French knit underpants and Norwegian flo-through T shirts, their angora sweaters and Borsalinos, their crucifix decoders and pointy shoes, and sitting around in burnooses and djaballas, finally comfortable, sitting around and trading loose anticlimactic Arabian anecdotes, plot the strategy for the next foray of the Italian navy while lunch is prepared—stuffing a camel with a young camel, the young camel with a sheep, the sheep with a goat, the goat with a lambkin, the lambkin with ducks, ducks with pigeons, the pigeons with quail, and in each quail, the jellied egg of a sea tortoise trained for microfilm dispatch.

In the distance, the unmistakable bark of the white mastiff.

I am perhaps overly cautious about trespass. Once, in the north woods of my youth, I came over a ridge to a shallow lake and resolved to swim its length. About halfway across I noticed spumes of water before me. It was a flotilla of wood duck, and it wasn't until I was upon them that I connected the flashes of water, not with the antics of their young, but with the dull powp of a rifle. One duck was already gone, his many-colored head blown away, body listing, kept afloat only by the spasmodic thrusts of the left foot. Why they didn't fly I have no idea to this day—perhaps the death of the male, the incapacity of the young, the in-competence of the mother—perhaps this is what Philippians was talking about—in any case, we were to-gether. I waved my arms frantically and screamed at the shore. There was a very large house up there with a long green lawn sweeping down to the lake, and in the middle of the lawn at a white wrought-iron patio table, in an ice cream chair, sat a little bent cross-legged man with his rifle. He waved violently, cursed me off his frontage and then another wood duck disintegrated to my left. He had started with the furthermost vertebrate, as in a carnival gallery. I dove for the bottom as fast as I could and occasionally bellying up to breathe, left the ducks marooned in their habitat . . . and this is why I went directly to the Biblioteca Na-zionale before entering the villa.

Unfortunately, my suburb was outside the city limits proper, the known or natural range of the beast, and was therefore not included in any of the official maps, much less the innumerable "Walks in Rome"— indeed, it appeared that the northernmost limits of such walks, from the 18th century on, were the gardens of the Villa Borghese, which had become so clotted with bad statuary, Americans finding themselves, and enormous perambulators that even the beast itself avoided them—and we were a good half-hour drive be-yond that. I did find, however, in a 1904 edition of *Famous Foyers,* the oblique floor plans of several untitled villas of no particular interest, except one foldout of "Rome and Environs," in which a cross-hatched section bore sufficient spatial relation to the property I had under surveillance to make my heart leap up. . . . Apart from this, my only clue was an engraving from the Counter-Reformation, in which Rome appeared as a series of walls and hills, and my hill was beyond the furthest wall and oddly treeless— that most curious of Italian topographical phenomena, a swampy mountain.

But I'm not much for research. I jog through books too. I leave the library in search of a boat shop for a small anchor, or perhaps an Alpine outfitter for pitons and such. I end up with a stepladder and a ball peen hammer, and in the night, I trot with these down the hill, the aluminum ladder balanced easily on my shoulders, my head between the rungs. If they stop me, I'll tell them I'm changing burned out streetlights. I'm myopic, I confess it. Just below the sacred grove, I hide the ladder in a thicket, bury the hammer in moss.

And the next afternoon, sticking meticulously to schedule, I lean the ladder against the wall, climb to the top, bust the glass teeth to powder with the hammer. Entire sections of the old stucco crumble, a civilization of ants is uncovered. Leaping quietly to the other side, I leave a rope in the bushes to get back.

See me run. Run without stepping in the shit of the diplomats' dogs, the mud of their cheapjack prosperity, without being run over by another Italianate driver. Once through the scrub, a massy field, certain vistas open up. I am on a ridge; to my left through calculated gaps in the forest, I can make out the cypress-lined drive below, and through these same alleys, deer feeding. The trees make one interested again in one's body. Not the body that sits in the cold dark apartment watching the garbage pyres on the *campagna*. Not the body of the collapsing lungs, the body searching for synonyms, equivalency, contingency, the body which would make the everyday surreal forever real. Not the body upon which all but exercise is lost. Not the body which can't resist the hated allegory. But the body which is now sunned and in full stride against a wilderness so calculated—ballooned and stretched in all dimensions—an English garden gotten out of hand, the formal fury of those older, purer decadents who loved objects for themselves and themselves as objects.

At the center of this large arena, up a rough and winding road, I came upon the ruin of a cottage from which one could see all of Rome, where St. Peter's loomed like a polyethylene mammary. Only the walls of the cottage remained, its burned timbers like huge Roman numerals fallen against one another; in the midst, a hemispherical three-chambered brick bread oven. Beyond, a large villa twice-walled, six-terraced, with a laundry-strung parapet, the statuary and the urns on its cobbled approach slightly shattered for effect, and not by Visigoths.

I could run further in that compound without thinking than anywhere in my life. I could really wind myself. I let my hood down and felt the late sun on my neck.

One day I returned earlier than usual to my escape rope, coiled like a krait in a thorny patch. Clearing the scrub, I quickly dropped back into cover. A short thick man, in highly polished riding boots, velour vest and lemon driving gloves, was staring directly into the wall.

Totally absorbed, he carried with him, at considerable effort, a circular library stair, upon which he deliberately heaved his shortness to a higher point on the wall. It soon became clear that he was not searching for hieroglyphs, but was rather observing that flurry of little autos through a series of small, handmade, exquisitely proportioned portholes, of various heights, perspectives and prosceniums. He moved slowly among our diplomats taking their luncheons for perhaps an hour, and then, showing no emotion, backed off the library steps, and disappeared thoughtfully into the brush. When he was gone, I mounted the library steps and stared down through the windshield of a shuddering gray Topolino, where a young couple, the boy's knees on the floor, the gal's left leg crooked about the gearshift (they were in second, and red-lined), were making the beast with two backs. I got down, climbed my rope, ran back to the apartment, for some reason quite frightened. That evening I went to the opera. It didn't help.

Nearly a week later, on a gray sulphurous day, I was running the top of the ridge, still too timorous to go near the drive, dreaming of being run down by a Bugatti touring car. As I topped a rise, I saw him again. He was standing in a small swale, with a brace of setters and a shotgun. While he did not look up, it was clear that he had heard me coming, so I broke stride only for an instant, and then padded on down the slope, looking as unconcerned as a totally dedicated amateur athlete should.

He stepped into my path and released the setters, who began to run a closing pattern behind me. He broke open the gun as if to put me at my ease, and I slowed and stopped before him. The barrel was inlaid with golden arabesques, the stock was silver, with a large chestnut pommel. An Arab's weapon. A woodcock hung from his belt.

We ascertained my nationality. He spoke English with an Oxbridge accent.

"My name is, of course, Umberto," he said.

I had to admit it wasn't the first time I'd trespassed.

"I know. I have seen your tracks." He looked away, indifferent.

Good hunting in here? I asked ingenuously.

He laughed long: pointlessly, deservedly.

"The best. The only. The wall is not to keep out the likes of you, 44," he said, referring to my faded numerals, "but to keep the game in, you see."

Do you . . . is it all . . . yours?

"The State's, alas," he murmured. "I was the king of Italy, you see."

Terrific, I'm the pope.

He laughed shyly, not allowing his eyes to meet my stare. I still like that kind of dignity. He would have been handsome were it not for his stoutness. A bust of him would have been positively heroic. Well, yer pays yer money . . .

"And your profession?"

A writer.

"A poet?"

Shit no.

"And here? You are writing about this villa?"

I'm no journalist either.

"What then?"

I'm just . . . I thought I would say . . . exercising.

He still had not looked up.

"Well," he said abruptly, "you are, I suppose, welcome. But I advise you not to run too near the villa at the top of this hill."

The one near the ruin?

"The very one. My dear sister's husband is quite mad and will shoot you in a moment from one of his large windows. He has already shattered most of our statuary in an attempt to extinct the starlings. He is a very bad shot, to be sure, but it is only a matter of time before he will hit something."

I nodded as deferentially as I ever will.

"Incidentally," he said as he turned into the brush, "how did you manage to get in here?"

Just jumped, I lied.

"You must show me that some time," he said, and then he was gone.

I came across him a few days later as I was circling through the woods near his villa. It was a magnificent house, though poorly maintained—white marble sanded over with yellow shell grit, sprinkled with cumrebar to reduce the dazzle, and surrounded by a number of sagging latticework pergolas and overgrown summerhouses. He was posed on a bench, reading a thin volume of poetry—Rossetti, probably—but I remember mostly the marbled endpapers. Behind him a petite Bacchus bestrode a turtle, whose discolored beak was once a fountain. I was to learn later that the entire fountain system had been paralyzed since an artillery barrage in 1942.

"Ah ha, 44, you are covering more ground. You are becoming stronger. How are you finding our place?"

I said nothing. What did he know of the terrors of solitude? Of exercise without release? It was clear he didn't realize what I might do to stay here. I was alone, getting stronger every day, and prepared to intimidate the king himself. My talent he could have; I would take *his* leisure.

He continued to look at me quizzically and closed the book.

"Would it be an impertinence to continue my insistence in asking you which *genre* precisely you as an artist are presently most partial to?"

I am at work on *A History of the Royal Family.*

He laughed, delightfully as always.

"I suppose you'll expect a commission."

My interest in the subject does not require a patron, Sir. I mean Sire.

I wasn't going to be pushed around.

"Then what compensation would you expect?"

If you would allow me, Sire, I would restore your burned-out bakery and live there . . . where I would have the run of the grounds and be free to write what I please.

"And living here, what would you write about? Or rather, for whom would you write? Your Italian, incidentally, is atrocious."

I can assure you I would not betray any confidences.

"You did not answer my question. For *whom* would you write?" There was a long silence.

"You will not . . ." then he stopped short. "Do not suppose," he said, very severely, "you will find us an enigma." His mind was evidently wandering, "Our exile has made us gentle but it has also required of us a certain banal frankness. We are, you see, exemplary . . . only in our lack of an alternative."

I'm not a bad gardener, either, I blurted apropos of nothing. He looked at me steadily.

"It would be amusing, no, to . . . 'flesh me out'? That is the phrase, I believe."

My mouth was open but I could say nothing.

"I will think about it nonetheless," he said and turned with a suddenness that belied both his age and stature.

"Come, I want to show you something very interesting."

We walked on silently for perhaps half an hour, sometimes on the drive, sometimes breasting the high grasses to either side, the dogs running a zigzag pattern ahead of us, never once breaking out of their perfect trot.

I asked if he had trained the dogs himself.

"They obey me."

When I saw we were approaching the observation portion of the wall, I feared for his dignity and said:

If you mean . . . the cars . . . I've seen them.

"No matter."

He climbed his ladder and put his eye to one of the larger holes. I sat down in the brittle trampled grass to wait for him.

"Don't you care to have a look?"

I've seen them, I repeated, not without disdain.

"From up here as well?"

|249|

It's all the same.

He descended. "I see," he said, "you prefer to watch *me* watching *them!*"

I nodded imperceptibly, shamefully.

"Being an amateur athlete must be a complicated business."

I see *that* every day, I retorted, I don't have to come in here for *that.*

"And what, dear 44, *do* you find interesting in *here?*"

I didn't come to see the king.

"Neither did he."

I don't need *material* is what I mean . . . I stammered, I need a place . . . you know, repose? The word decorum also occurred to me, but it seemed presumptuous.

"What you want, my son, is a people. Your interest in me is only how I have survived losing one." Then he waved at the wall.

"That is all I am trying to show you."

I avoided his immediate grounds for some time thereafter.

Frankly, I was becoming bored with the city and even more with my exercise. My work was going badly; it needed some adventitious obstacle. I considered returning to the Biblioteca Nazionale to complete my researches on the villa. There were obviously records somewhere. But as a matter of fact, I was never again to enter Rome proper, never again encounter the beast. A casual friend, who dropped in one evening without invitation, driveled that one King Umberto had been assassinated by an anarchist in 1900 and I confirmed this through the concierge. My neighbors were of uniformly no help, however, with reference to what they called "The Parco," pleading diplomatic immunity. I am beginning to think my solitariness makes people distrust me. It used to be the opposite.

I stopped running altogether, preferring to walk the trails of the estate, though still dressed in my uniform and sneakers. It's true, I saw more this way. One afternoon I came to a mysterious series of large hummocks just off a path I had run many times before. One of the hummocks sported a small inscribed tablet. As I bent over to read it, however, something was shoved through my thighs and I was thrown to the ground. I lay terrified between two of the hummocks, as the pressure increased between my buttocks. It seemed to be neither a weapon nor human, and for a moment I could not bring myself to face my attacker. Finally, I lunged over on my back, and with an upraised fist found myself facing a white mastiff. A perfect specimen, he withdrew his pinkish nose from my parts, and extended a paw in solicitude. His yellow eyes were pooled with love, his ovulate lower lip, mark of distinguished ancestry, gleamed with spittle. Had he mistaken me for the beast, or was it a pretext?

Suddenly Umberto rambled out of the brambles, ignoring a brace of squirrels mating in a stunted pine. He carried an old but ugly Mauser 30.06.

"So, 44, where have you been? You must be more careful. I thought old Renaldo had discovered an *authentic* thief."

I'm just exploring. I'm sick of myself and my work. What are these mounds?

He ignored me completely. "If you do leave, you must tell me, yes? We will go hunting one day, you and I—not here, but in Sicily or perhaps Croatia."

Let's go right now. Or, I said sinisterly, do you prefer the beast?

"I warned you," he went on severely, "that you would become bored. It is just as I thought. That is why I did not give you license. Come, it is time to go to the house. We must bring this little drama to its conclusion. The beast, incidentally, has not been seen within these walls since they were built."

And when was that?

"How should I know? I did not choose to live here."

We approached the house through a corridor of pines; it was clear he did not wish to enter by the main drive. High on a large veranda, a handsome woman in an Empire gown entered my vision; she walked quite deliberately, as if the floors were slanted or slippery, only her torso visible along the railing webbed with ivy, and without once breaking her profile.

"That is my cousin, Gabriella," Umberto muttered. "She is the handsomest of us, but she knows nothing. She is so stupid she does not even know it. Like the owl who asks the sparrow why it has such big ears. You will waste your time with her. Still, she is statuesque. Yes? No?"

I confessed my myopia. How she, from that distance, could only reconstitute herself in my eyes as a wash of pastels and glints, chrysoprase and porphyry.

"My wife will be having tea on the front portico," he said mysteriously. "For today, we shall avoid her, yes? No?"

You may count on my discretion.

"It is not a question of manners," he said abruptly. "Behavior pure and simple counts for very little here."

The formal garden had gone to seed, the borders irregular with a pachysandra silver-edge, the variegated ivy strangulating the terra-cotta urns, broken not by time but with a precise, muffled mallet by some retired Czech stonecutter. Only a vaguely triangular spreading yew retained any shape. Above us, in a large and badly placed romanesque window, behind a large bronze grill of double crucifixes, a uniformed servant stood with his arms folded in front of him, shoulders hunched.

The king was speaking very fast now.

"I know many things which will be of interest to you in your researches: inside political talk, the affairs and perversions of illustrious personages, all quite banal when experienced daily, but nevertheless perhaps fascinating to the outsider . . ."

I'm not interested in history, exactly.

"This is not history. This is the truth of the matter."

I'm not interested in the truth exactly either.

What I meant to say was that all I needed was that lady walking from stage left and passing through my field of vision—creation of my own astigmatism and made real precisely by the absence of inside info. That was quite enough. For all I know of truth, of history, she might have been a wood duck.

"It shouldn't take you long to comprehend," he was going on. "You are amiable enough. You will be patient with the protocol . . . in the end, however, to learn, you must be loved. It is difficult to find out anything if one is merely respected. I should know."

His boots had begun to snap upon the graveled, penultimate terrace of the gardens. In my sneakers it was as if I wasn't there at all. There was no backing out now. Thus it was that we entered the palace at dusk.

"You will find your room somewhat cold, but certainly commodious. It will not be necessary to attend all meals. I realize that such a schedule could be a burden to an artist . . ."

His footsteps were ringing off the marble walls. I squeaked malevolently. No servants were visible. The villa yawned upon us. We were not up to it.

I can't, I stammered, live *with* you.

He had stopped short, nearly come to officer's attention. His past footsteps echoed up ahead of us and faded out of earshot.

If only you would let me restore the bakery, I pleaded, I would do it at my own expense. I'm not a bad handyman at all. And the meals I wouldn't mind coming to.

He was humorless now. Utter silence except for an occasional yelp from the distant kennels.

And if I'm not . . . lovable . . . then what? Anyway, I don't need love to find out what I need . . . you know the old song . . .

"There are people," he began apoplectically, "who would do anything—*anything*—you catch my meaning?—to live in this house!"

You must not think me presumptuous, I said as calmly as possible. Keep your secrets from me by all means. A few occasional details will do me nicely. And some walking around. There's no point in unburdening oneself . . .

The king patted his palm with a limp riding crop. He was not amused.

"You defecate beneath my window then rap on the glass for paper . . ."

I shrugged and began to jog in place. In a large paneled mirror at an intersection in the hallway, I could see the last of the sun caught in a network of plane trees.

"I would have expected . . . if not admiration . . . at least fundamental decency." He had lowered his head.

King, I whispered: King, let me use you as I wish.

We were silent for a long time. The double stairway rose above us. He shook his head but drew himself straight.

"I do not understand. You care not for *that,*" he waved his hand preciously, as if signaling beyond the walls, "yet you refuse *mon hospitalité!* One must have preferences . . . pretexts . . . you have lost nothing . . . you have nothing . . . how do you live . . . ?"

He searched my eyes; I received and took note of his. Tiny slivers of blue broke the bronze irises—a crazy dog's eye, the brushed but unplucked brows moving like antennae, an old movie-set Indian's eye, gone bad in the glare of the spots, now trained on the desert. Too much savvy, not enough surprise, a gland without tissue or awe.

As the king ascended the lefthand stair, slapping his crop softly against his thigh, there were hesitant, dainty footsteps on the landing above. And I could also make out a strange noise which I immediately recognized as the staccato shot of a master chef chopping vegetables upon an oaken cutting board.

The crop flicked imperceptibly again. Both of us were breathing heavily. He stared into my eyes. What could he have hoped to find there? At last, I turned abruptly and began to jog back down the hallway toward the dim semicircle of light, taking care not to be too hasty, nor show fear of any kind, as if I were about to emerge into the Coliseum itself.

"Ecco!"

It echoed behind me.

I went back only to prove to myself that I was not afraid; a very poor reason, incidentally, to do anything. I was accompanied, however, by a small Beretta .32 which I concealed in my handwarmer pouch, and kept exclusively to the perimeter of the wall, occasionally coming across broken spigots and altars, and in this way, I avoided Umberto utterly. Once I heard the dogs and a shot or two, but it was now as if I, who had blown the chance to be biographer-in-residence, the ultimate omniscient inside-dopester, was now a minor character, a gorgeous walk-on in some music hall rendition of a vicar-translated Boccaccio tale. A personage with neither mind nor sense nor place, only a disembodied voice, an instant of functional no-color in the mottling forest. How perfectly, then, I understood all those half-baked characters, those *ficelles* who have been created solely in order to throw some clumsy allegory into clearer relief. How much

I loved every man who has been endowed by his creator as a sacrifice to the intelligibility of an idea, as a linchpin in some absurd notion of cause and effect. And I knew then my little destiny would soon be upon me, that my irony and comic self-relief would give way to inexorable dry heaves of the conventional wisdom of Mr. Philippians.

So when I saw two gardeners, one short, one tall, one with shears, one with a hoe, come round the bend to intercept me, perhaps only fifty yards from my escape route, I recognized the time had come for appropriate resolution and, as a matter of fact, for resignation and relinquishment. It goes without saying I could have written their lines for them.

"His Excellency wishes you to leave immediately," the taller one said, a black spade against his hip.

"And not to use the premises again," the smaller one added, not without a trace of pedantry.

"The boar are mating, you see," the larger one repeated, the smaller unable to mask a snigger, "It could be dangerous."

"It makes no difference to us personally, of course."

I pulled the drawstrings of my hood to a perfect circle about my face and ran off with an impressive stride. My stubbornness, my piety, and not a little petty vengeance were activated, and I was, of course, over the wall the next day in advance of my usual schedule, running flatfooted along the most exposed path. My legs never felt better. My breath surged from my mouth in the frost like the twin exhausts of a touring car. And I heard the chorus of dogs *a capella* even sooner than I expected.

It was clear that the entire kennel had been turned out. Through one of the pine alleys, I saw a liver-colored mastiff twice as large as the white species gleefully rooting about my trail of the day before, and then I heard the shots—the Mauser unequivocally—the whoosh and whine of large cartridges, fired deliberately at three-second intervals, as in a salute, a cortege. For all its predictability, its cheap theatrics, it had its own deadly seriousness. What an enviable spectacle it would have been were there anyone else to watch it. It struck me how easily I could assassinate him, had I been willing to give myself up to the dogs. But the pretext, the oblique provocation, like the glimpse of Gabriella, was sufficient. After all, there were only two possible endings.

However unmanly, I was never less curious as I sprinted for the wall. For some reason, the thickets perhaps, some banal luck, or simply ingrained habit, the dogs kept to the drive as I kept to the ridge, and so, while their falsetto baying gained upon me absolutely, we remained on parallel courses, and I reached the wall with a bit to spare. Using the king's peepholes for footholds, I launched myself to the top where, squatting carefully, an inch of Chuck Taylor's pride beneath my haunches and the shards of glass, my ears filled with my heart. To my right, I could make out the lead hound bolting up the narrow path beside the wall. And then a shot, far over my head, clinked into the pines.

I looked down to jump. But directly below, within a magenta Fiat convertible, a pair of enormous buttocks, trousers bumbled about the calves like some felled Napoleonic irregular, scrotum swinging like a demolition crane against his luncheon mate, blocked my escape.

No cry. The car itself manufactured their banal, popular and unsyncopated rhythm. Of his love, one could make out only the slivers of her white calves, tiny doubled fists, the top half of her small head eclipsed by his black slicked skull.

Her slitted eyes widened darkly as I came into view, so like a gargoyle. She beat upon her lover's back with both fists, her fearful hips thrusting him off balance with what he must have considered excessive passion as I dropped beside them silently as an Arab, and another shot whistled overhead.

Already she was screaming; *"Aiuto Dio, spicciatedi veditore, guardare . . ."*

("Help, God, look at that voyeur, looking. . . .")

*Inadvertently, long about page 247, this became fiction. It won't happen again.

I must quit playing off this nostalgia for a past, not for roots but for earth itself, for a sense of time which is more than motion. There are a few facts, a few lasting impressions which must be documented. But the question is not whether it is possible to overcome one's origins, or even whether we are actually determined by them. It is whether we can make the revolutionary leap to believe we had an origin at all. It is a time for a little research.

Faulkner makes man a sum total without a future. At every moment, one draws a line, since the present is nothing but a chaotic din, a future that is past. His vision of the world can be compared to that of a man sitting in an open car and looking backwards. At every moment, formless shadows, flickering faint tremblings and patches of light rise up on either side of him, and only afterwards, when he has a little perspective, do they become trees and men in cars. The past takes on a sort of super reality; its contours are hard and clear, unchangeable. The present, nameless and fleeting, is helpless before it. It is full of gaps, things of the past, fixed motionless and silent as judges or glances come to invade it. The present is not; it becomes. Everything was.
|J. P. Sartre|

ON BEING AHISTORICAL

Most Americans hate their predecessors for being too rich or poor, too successful or not enough so, for what they imagine to be indebtedness or some accursed privilege, passed on to haunt. I do not despise mine in the usual way, their random ups and downs, bouncing off the parameters of upper middle and lower middle classes, refusing to acknowledge either their defeats or their accomplishments, that endurance which seems so problematical today. No, what I despise is their alacrity to adapt, their unwillingness to override their successors, their refusal of both praise and blame, and their supreme indifference to having *their* own story passed on intact, to resisting the velocity of the last two hundred years which undid them of time, place and personality, to providing any continuity which would make us accountable. For as different as these lives are, one senses only one common trait within the enormously conflicting evidence—the willed refusal to impose one's accumulated knowledge upon the future. The secret of survival was something to be won individually, but never shared. For example, my grandfather once told me that one of our ancestors was a member of the original Lewis and Clark expedition, but of this man's expertise all we know is that he was "whipped and sent home." And he remains the least opaque of my forebears.

Given their supreme reticence and the speed with which we were removed from one another—I myself lived in more states, more "places," before I reached puberty than all three of my ancestors' generations put together—I came to resent the lack of any visible past, not that impulse to trace one's lineage or to determine which genes were uncancelable, but simply to know whether they had been censored, or whether they really believed that *nothing* of their life, save for certain tangible property, could be of any use to anyone a decade beyond their death. And so for them, History was loss, revision, infliction, progress, but never repetition. For me, History is a half-dream into which I have constantly, and with predictably pathetic results, tried to insert myself.

Of my grandparents, those personages so uniformly likable, I believe I loved my paternal grandfather best since I never knew him; he died when my own father was twelve. Judging from a small and badly exe-

Universal history is the history of the different intonations given a handful of metaphors. |Borges|

cuted oil, I bear his high forehead, his small-boned wiriness, as well as his speech patterns and quirky heart. Like most of my ancestors, he shared a hardy disdain for the significance of hereditary characteristics. And while he died of a stroke and insisted to my father that his bad heart was a product of a childhood injury, and could therefore not be inherited, my father now wears a battery in his chest cavity, and I was told at thirteen by a fulsome pediatrician that a heart murmur would prevent me from doing anything strenuous the rest of my life. Despite the grossest abuse, my heart has not missed a beat since; but I look forward to the day when, toppling over in thundering apoplexy, I gasp to my son that he has inherited nothing, least of all a bad heart.

Of Grandfather's behavior we have only one anecdote, which perhaps serves well enough. One Christmas, my grandmother presented him with a beautiful meerschaum pipe, and his seven children gathered around to watch him enjoy it. He lit up, puffed a bit and set the pipe down on the table when satisfied. Because of its round bowl, however, it rolled, and the ashes spilled out upon the table. Everyone tried to ignore this, even my grandmother who ordinarily would have raced for a coal shovel. Grandfather tried this twice more and then, after the new pipe had tipped and spilled for the third time, he calmly picked it up, walked to the front door, and threw the pipe far into the night.

He was a surgeon, born in the first year of the Civil War, and after studying in England, Paris and Vienna, returned to St. Louis a confirmed bachelor. He did not suffer fools and drove a brace of gaited chestnut mares about the city at breakneck speed. One day while making a house call, he heard a woman playing the piano, and after treating the patient, introduced himself and announced that he would marry her. He was forty-seven, she thirty-eight.

Her demands were (1) that the children not be raised Catholic, (2) that he get his teeth fixed. To both of which he acceded. In the fourth decade of their lives, they produced seven children, of whom my father was the youngest. This royalist Catholic and proud Huguenot had personally resolved the conflict which had torn Western civilization apart for five centuries, through the symbolic medium of a dentist. Our family has had no religious problems (and no religion) since. As much as I appreciate that, I still would have preferred to know how they brought it off. Only in America, as they say, or, Congregationalists triumphant. In any case, grandfather, weakened by malaria contracted in the Canal Zone, suffered *his* stroke at 58 and was bedridden for his last seven years. As he lay dying, my grandmother called for a priest, who characteristically asked him if he wanted him to administer last rites and confession. My grandfather said no. What our priest could not know was that the stroke had immobilized the left side of his brain, and "no" was the only word he could say; in fact, he had said only "no" for the last seven years of his life—a handy paralysis which has been passed on, with his tricky heart, to me.

That Roman nose which my grandfather gave all of his seven children, but which has disappeared utterly in my generation in the course of my father's collision with my mother's cuter Anglo-Saxon, originated in all its magnificence in my *great* grandfather, Socrates. Clearly he is the source of our temperament and psychology, as well as a key figure in our history, had he only believed in it. His portrait is the better one, his whiskers finer, forehead higher, nose larger, eyes crueler than any of ours. While we have been diffused by America, he was, in his own deft way, softening her still while he lived. In our houses, even the pets had blue eyes.

Old Soc, as I would have loved to call him, was born in 1827 to that peculiar manic-depressive authoritarian streak which surfaces so often and engagingly in my family, and he is best remembered by my cousin (whom, typically, I have never met but once saw on a late night TV talk show) as terrorizing a barber in Punta Gorda, Florida, into shaving him on the veranda during a hurricane. *His* father had come to St. Louis when it was still a village of French and Spanish immigrants, by way of Pennsylvania, Kentucky and Maryland, only to perish in the cholera epidemic of 1849. A devout Catholic and a southern sympathizer, Soc closed his foundry business at the time of the Civil War, sent the family back to Paris, and went into fire insurance, clearly the better risk. The only documentation remains this blurb, which as it turns out, he paid for. (There is also a marvelous rumor that he also sold munitions to both sides, but this is too good to believe.)

Socrates' large house was usually filled with less productive members of the family, and he would moan regularly at the breakfast table that they were forcing him into bankruptcy. This was belied by his habit of renting an entire railroad car in the seventh month of each of his wife's pregnancies (a total of 11); filling it with liquor and friends, he set out for Florida to hunt and fish until after the blessed event had occurred, when he would return to his responsibilities.

In his dotage, he retired to a small farm in the Ozarks, which had been his father's. After dredging himself a lake, he became bored with the view, and, perhaps remembering happier days in Florida, imported an alligator to keep him company. As my cousin Edmond recalls, he then built himself an island in the middle of the lake to house the beast, and since it was impossible for it to live through the cold Missouri winters, he also built a small brick house for the animal, in the bottom of which there was always a coal fire. He is remembered as rising early on these cold winter mornings. Finding the fire gone out, he would curse his servants down to the edge of the lake where they would restoke the coals and apply hot bricks to the torporous beast to revive him. He has left me neither his nose nor his menagerie, only his stare, and the desire to have it both ways.

Of his Frenchness there can be no doubt, but of course no record. It is taken for granted that his ancestors fled the Huguenot persecutions of the 1700s, though his Catholicism would seem to be at odds with this; but it is not beyond our family to seize upon such an excuse. One can see them now, in Paris over a large dinner; "If the Protestants go, Pierre, you know who's next." (Didn't anyone ever just come over here for the hell of it?)

The father of Socrates Newman a native of Pennsylvania, arrived in this city when it was a little village of French and Spanish inhabitants, and he was among those who infused into the town a spirit of American enterprise and progress. He was a partner in the boat supply company and remained an active factor in the business life of the growing town until his death, both he and his wife being victims of the cholera epidemic of 1849 . . . In 1876, Socrates was appointed receiver for the St. Louis Gas Light Company during the period of contested litigation between the city and the company. About 1880, when matters had been adjusted, he was unanimously appointed Assistant Manager, for in his previous position, he had displayed the utmost tact, ability and careful management . . . he built the first office building in accordance with modern ideas in St. Louis—an iron and stone structure which his fellow townsmen who had much less prescience than he, termed "Newman's folly." He lived, however, to see his judgment justified in public opinion . . . in all the relations of his life, he manifested qualities of sterling manhood and stood foursquare to every wind that blows. Men came to respect him not *only* for the success which he achieved, but for the straightforward business policy he ever followed and for the genial, generous and kindly spirit he ever displayed in his relations with his fellow man. |*History of St. Louis, the Fourth City, 1764–1909*, Volume 3, illustrated|

His wife, known within the family as "Mamou," might have shed some light on their ancestry, but like most exceptional women of her time, she did not offer information readily. Her family had emigrated from France via Martinique, but of their life there we know nothing except that they did not share Socrates' interest in hurricanes. "Mamou," apparently indifferent to her husband's eccentricities, retired to her bed in her forty-third year with what was diagnosed as "a fatal woman's disease," but did not leave the world for thirty more years, and in the meantime served as the largest repository of French culture in the Trans-Missippi—a strategy which more American housewives might adopt. My father's father, the surgeon, her son, had lunch with her literally every day, but my father can remember only a tiny woman in an enormous bed, with Balzac and Zola piled to the ceiling about her. My only contact with these estimables was a few years ago when I visited Mamou's eldest daughter who, blind and at the age of ninety-two, was about to embark upon her annual trip to Paris. In an hour or two of talk, we drank a fifth of bourbon between us.

Of course, to be a real American, one must assume prior as well as ongoing persecution, and as the Catholic royalist side of the family seems rather to have been bored into emigration, one must trace the Huguenot lineage for more interesting and instructive ambivalencies. Through the assiduous work of my paternal grandmother, who after the doctor's death, busied herself with our genealogy for the Daughters of the American Revolution, one finds that her family first came to this country about 1700, where in Manikintown, Virginia, an Englishman, Bryan, married a Huguenot woman, LeFèvre, and the English name somehow became frenchified in his son's generation to Briant and later to Bryant. Sometime soldier of the revolution, James Bryant had the good sense to enlist only in the last six months of our struggle for independence, just in time to qualify for his pension, and with this and land warrants in hand, set off down the Monongahela on a flatboat. We have no idea how he portaged the Ohio falls, but in Kentucky they stopped

Will of James Bryant, Jr:

In the name of God—Amen. I, James Bryant of the County of Powhatan being of sound mind and memory, do write this my last will and testament in the manner following. ITEM: I lend to my beloved wife Jane Bryant during her natural life in lieu of her dower (after the payment of my debts) all my lands in the County of Powhatan (except such part as may be discovered to contain coal and what I shall annex to my mill seat) with the use of the following negroes, to-wit, Sam, Cesar, Patt, Mariah, Frank and Kitty and there future increase with all my household and kitchen furniture, except such parts there of as I shall hereafter otherwise dispose of, all my plantation utensils, one half of my stock of every kind with as much Indian corn and wheat as may be necessary to support her family until she can make a crop. ITEM: Having already given to my son John Bryant moity of my land in the State of Kentucky, one negro man named Prince, one horse and saddle, one feather bed and furniture all of which I hereby bequeath and affirm to him my

off at Bryant's Fort, just long enough to name it apparently, and thence to Indiana where they owned farms and presumably were farmers, and finally, in 1855, on to Missouri.

The only existing description of Bryant's descendents is the following letter, apparently a remembrance for posterity written by an unidentified grandaughter:

"His house sat back from Main Street and had an iron grill fence across the front. It was covered with rambler roses. There was a front porch across the front of the house, and he sat there in a swivel chair for hours at a time. He was not a judge, and our name was Bryant, but everyone called him 'Judge Smart.' When Mr. Snope came to Kansas City he was a young and active real estate man and persuaded Grandpa Smart to divide his property into lots and sell them, which he did but he always said, 'I want to hold all corners.' He didn't, though."

It is not surprising, then, to find these ancestors, so startlingly unstoppable, finally relocated on a farm which is now downtown Kansas City, and to discover they sold it for a song, either because, as one story has it, the Pony Express had relocated its office in Independence, Mo., and they speculated that the action was going to be there—or the other version, that they were afraid their three daughters would be married for their land. In any case, John Bryant's will may be found in the Harvard Law Casebook series as the classic example of how not to write one. It is not as elegant as James Jr.'s catalog.

How tempting to see them denied the final fruits of their quest in the malarial heartland of America, this proprietorship of the still center of the universe, screwed out of their century-long quest for both place and estate by a single lapse of judgment, a shyster's advice or one last gasp of residual Calvinism—and above all, to wonder how they reacted to this first awareness of a fate, a stasis operating apart from their will: the discovery that they were not, after all, contiguous with history and that History was not just Progress.

But this is not the case—indeed, there seems to be an unconscious but nevertheless calculated refusal to *settle*, to resent their losses, any more than they advertised their profits, or to round out or justify one's existence. As both the Anglo-Saxon derivation of Newman (Newcomer) and

said John and his heirs forever. ITEM: I give and bequeath to my daughter, Salle Locket and her heirs, two negroes to-wit, Amy and Patt, and their future increase, one horse and saddle, and two feather beds and furniture all of which have already been delivered to her. I also give and bequeath to my said daughter (Sallie Locket) the sum of two hundred pounds to be paid by my executors out of my estate. ITEM: Having already given to my son William Bryant, one moity of my land in the State of Kentucky, one negro man named David, one horse and saddle, one feather bed and furniture all of which I hereby advise and bequeath and confirm to him my said son and his heirs forever.

 ITEM: I give and bequeath to my daughter Jane Martin and her heirs, two negroes to-wit, Eva and Sam, and all their increase, one horse and saddle, two feather beds and furniture all of which have been delivered to her, I also give and bequeath to my daughter Jane Martin the sum of two hundred pounds to be paid by my executors out of my estate. ITEM: I give and bequeath to my son Stephen Bryant and his heirs, one negro man named Bristol, one horse and saddle, one feather bed and furniture, all of which have already been delivered to him. ITEM: I give and bequeath to my son Silas Bryant, one negro man named Ned, one horse and saddle of which have already been delivered to him. I also give and bequeath to my said son Silas at my decrease two feather beds and furniture. ITEM: I give and bequeath to my daughter Polly Bryant and her heirs, at my decrease three negroes, to-wit Little Sam, Sylva, and child called Alice, with their future increase, one good riding horse, saddle and bridle, two feather beds and furniture, and the sum of two hundred pounds, to be paid out of my estate by my executors. ITEM: I give and devise to my sons Stephen Bryant and Silas Bryant, and to their heirs for ever, respectively, all my lands which I have loaned my beloved wife during her natural life time, to be equally divided between them according to quantity and quality, (except such part of said lands as may contain a body of coal there on to be here-after disposed of

our coat of arms suggest—a swallow rising from a portcullis imperially crowned—no phoenix, no eagle, this little bird, not even a partridge, but both persistent and flighty—in a word, quick—the birdie who knows when to get off the Empire train, and that the completion of progress is death.

If Grandmother's historiography is accurate, one can trace them back to high positions in the army of William the Conqueror and the campaign of 1066, then fighting with "English generals" for 200 years in the Crusades; but at the same time, they seem also prominent in the wars of France, in defense of their church brethren under Henry the Second, and somehow they are lauded for their great deeds of patriotism by *both* the King of France and the English government. And one can only identify again with my dying grandfather, and as the paralysis sets in, and you are asked which side you are on, you can only say no, no, no. . . .

If the precise details of their exploits have been carefully hidden, and they are hidden all the way back to the tribes of Turkestan, one primary cost is that the villains, the crazies, the failures are never mentioned. There is one Uncle Will, who keeps turning up asking for money, known as "The Black Sheep"—one presumes for drinking, though given the history of the family, that could hardly be considered cause. And there is my paternal grandmother's first husband, of whom only two things are known: (1) that he was the "handsomest thing on two feet" and (2) that he shot himself in an upstairs bedroom when he was twenty-four. No one recalls why, except that his problems were either "fiscal" or "tubercular." And so I am denied not only the secret of their malleability, the methodology of their cleverness, their enormous appetite for survival, but also any notion of the defeats and deprivation which are also the history of my people. Their bodies, too, have been kept off the street for charity. I have been spared not only whatever pride I cared to muster, but worse, the possibility of becoming, like the Cardinal who bears my name, a great hater.

Given this opaque ancestry, which seemed to be constructed precisely to free me from any possible notion of cause and effect, I looked closely to my maternal grandfather, the only one of my grandparents I was

in different manner) and said son Stephen Bryant to have that part of my said land adjoining to that on which he has built his dwelling house. ITEM: All the residue of my estate heretofore lent to my beloved wife during her natural life, (except the land) I desire may be at her decease, equally divided among all of my children or their legal representatives, and as I have reasons to believe there are large bodies of coal in the land given to my said beloved wife during her natural life, and after her death divided or devised) Stephen and Silas Bryant and their heirs should there be coal discovered in any part of my land (excepting the three acres below the mill) and annex to the same and except also what the said mill may cover or overflow at a common height in the winter then and therein that case I give and divide to all my children and their heirs respective an equal interest and property in the said coal or coal mines with my sons Stephen and Silas Bryant, after they shall respectively pay to my last mention sons their legal representative, their equal proportions of the just value of the land or soil, which may be rendered unfit for cultivation by the sinking of coal pits there-on, either in search of coal or working the mines after the coal shall be discovered and to prevent dispute or controversy among my said children concerning the premises of my said two sons, Stephen and Silas Bryant and their legal representatives shall have sole and exclusive right in pointing out the place or places where coal is to be dug or searched for, provided nevertheless that neither of said children or the representatives of them shall have the right to search or dig for coal in the garden or orchard or so near to any house or houses as to endanger said house or houses or to make it inconvenient to pass to or from the same unless the privilege of so doing be had and obtained from my said beloved wife, in writing, and attested by three creditable witnesses. In witness hereof I have here unto set my hand and fixed my seal this twenty-first day of March in the year of Christ One Thousand eight hundred and seven. James Bryant, Jr. (SEAL)

ever around, for some better clue. I remember getting into bed with him in the early mornings during War II; he would wake up, sit erect and stare stolidly out the frosted windows, rolling his own Lucky Strikes, cursing the newspaper, which he read, still folded, six feet away at the end of his bed. Had he only let me, I would have held the *News* for him to read aloud. I must learn to read to myself, he said. My father in the Philippines might not come back.

Physically he was my opposite: short, stocky, with the hands of a laborer; yet I bear his shape, and as I age, I can see his Welsh rocky physiognomy, the veined temples, the undershot jaw coming out from France in the mirror. I would have preferred the Roman nose of Socrates, I have his body at any rate; I would have been totally French, delicate, detached and noble, but I will settle, in the end of our days, for his counterpart's Welsh feistiness; that clear craziness held in restraint.

He took pleasure from nothing save his own independence and his family, and while obviously brilliant in financial and legal matters, as well as an amateur historian, he took great pains to conceal his intelligence, as if it were, like a derringer, something to be displayed only when threatened intimately. I remember him telling me in that bed, as the war's atrocities mounted, that this would be a totally different country after the war, and he would have little use for it. And then he made me promise never to feel sorry for myself.

He had been thrown out of the University of Illinois for picketing—no one, of course, can recall what the issue was—and had gone out to Oklahoma where he rode the circuit as a judge, handling Indian cases in particular. Subsequently, he bought land in Oklahoma and Texas, upon which oil was discovered. His first son was killed by fumes from his oil well. He was never the same thereafter. When he died suddenly of heart failure, his last instructions to my grandmother were that she must outlive him by ten years so something would be left from the inheritance taxes. Despite Parkinson's disease, she survived him by eleven. Had they known of one John Bryant of Kansas City?

His wife was his childhood sweetheart. On her side of the family, the only records are medical—a long history of serious illness in childhood in every generation, the congenital melancholia of Pennsylvania Dutch

They were descendents of the Wends, who conquered the Roman Empire. It is remarkable that the Flints, Fosters, Bryants, Selbys and Terrys have for a thousand years kept together and participated in the greatest events of history. Each of these families have attained the highest honors in war, science, medicine, commerce, the ministry, law, literature, statesmanship, and the arts. If there were no other evidence, this fact alone would prove that they were of the same race. |The Huguenot, *1920*|

stock, originally from Trier, Germany, which they left also during the "persecutions" of the 1700s.

They too have managed to leave only a single document: a certificate of parentage in German with a notation scrawled over it, "the said heretofore is to remain in the dwelling house until he has a place to go to." And appended to this with wax is the following note:

"The Derrs were natives of the Palatine. After that they moved to the Irish settlement and after they had been living there a while they moved near to where the zinc mines are, on Mr. Hollenstein's farm. They did live there until Mr. Jacob Grim got the farm into his hands. Carl Derr and his wife Sibella were our grandparents and they had seven grown-up children. Three sons, Daniel, David and John. David and John died single, Daniel got married to Magtolena Greater and they were our parents, and we were their grown-up children, Charles, Samuel, David, Elizabeth and Leah. Grandfather Carl had two brothers, Christian and Henry, but of Henry nothing is known. Christian got married, died and left three sons as orphan children. After they became of age one of them went to Maryland and one to North Carolina but what became of them is not known to us.

> Given by Aunt
> Magalena, a sister to our father
> Deceased April 25, 1863
> written by Charles Derr

And this, my fellow Americans, is in no sense marginal.

In any case, suddenly a great grandfather, her father, crops up to complement entrepreneurial Socrates—a boy who runs away at 13 to be a drummer in the Civil War, is shot clean through the left thigh, limps west via Ohio and finally surfaces at Virden, Illinois, where he becomes mayor, principal of the school, owner of the hardware store and undertaker. Of *his* parents all that is known is that they went around the Horn to California and either didn't make it or didn't call. Of this branch of the family the frontier would take its merciless toll; numerous young schoolmasters, poor clergy, country doctors and failed ship captains are defined by nothing save illness, sporadic warfare and infant mortality. Of their origins there remains only a single document to equal (cancel?) James Bryant's will, recorded only because he, the great great grandfather, is wrongly thought to be the first settler in Illinois, defined by his Indians as James Bryant was by his slaves. They had, it seems, neither friends nor enemies, only mute chattels and hysterical savages.

Enter a man on horseback, broad-shouldered, rough and rugged, a rifle slung across the pommel of his saddle, a hand shading his eyes, which gaze across an expanse of prairie that ends at the horizon. What Canada's famous mounted police have been to the lonely vastness of British Columbia and Hudson's Bay country, the Rangers were to Illinois one hundred years and more ago. When the Federal government was unable to send troops to protect the settlers in Illinois from Indian atrocities, encouraged by the British during the War of 1812, the settlers themselves organized as rangers. "For several years," says Clement L. Clapp, in his history of Green County, "these brave, determined men rode over the bare and silent prairies for hundreds of miles, now chasing a band of fleeing savages, now hurrying to the defense of a threatened settlement. They were almost constantly in the saddle, rarely slept under a roof, were independent of civilization for food or comforts, and exercised almost superhuman vigilance in keeping the red men at bay. They were familiar with every feature of Indian warfare and their deeds of daring and endurance have been made the theme of many a thrilling poem or romantic tale [*sic.*] In these expeditions against the Indians the Rangers probably became the first white men to pass over the territory that is now Green County. They saw what splendid opportunities it offered for settlement—or would offer when the Indians were finally driven out. To a pioneer, the ideal spot for staking his claim was one that afforded first of all, good water; second, timber for building his cabin, and third a situation at the edge of a prairie, to avoid unnecessary clearing for putting in crops. Proceeding northward from the Wood River settlement, the hardy adventurers found no such combination until they reached Macoupin creek. No less than a dozen or fifteen of these Rangers from Fort Russell came to, or crossed the Macoupin to build their cabins on the very frontier of civilization.

Three men stand out conspicuously in this band. They were *Samuel Thomas,* Thomas Carlin and Thomas Rattan.

Samuel Thomas was the grandfather of Congressman H. T. Rainey, who now represents the Twentieth congressional district at Washington. Born in South Carolina in 1794, he began a race with civilization when he was eight years old by going to Kentucky. In 1813 at the age of 19, he set out on horseback for Illinois. After he and his two companions crossed the Ohio river, they found that the settlers had deserted their cabins and fled from the Indians. They were not deterred from their purpose, however, and pushed on to Wood river. When they arrived there, Mr. Thomas purchased a rifle on credit, in order to join the rangers.

A few months later, while he was serving in Capt. Judy's company, the Wood river massacre occurred, and one of his sisters and her six children were slain by the Indians. In 1816 Mr. Thomas visited what is now Greene County, picked out the land on which he afterward settled, cut and stacked some hay and made other improvements. Then he returned to Wood River, and the Indians burned his haystacks and destroyed his improvements. For two years more he remained at Wood river, and then in August, 1818, his desire to be on the extreme edge of things led him northward again. He was accompanied by Thomas Carlin and John W. Huitt, a brother-in-law of Carlin. When they reached Macoupin Creek, Huitt was unwilling to put that barrier between himself and civilization, and he stopped on the south side, while the other two crossed the creek and went on. Three miles north of the creek Thomas arrived at the spot he had selected two years before. A beautiful grove and a clear spring of water had figured in his choice. It is recorded that—"here Mr. Thomas killed a deer, cut a bee tree and engraved his name on the bark of a monarch of the forest, to indicate that the land was claimed." Then he built a cabin, and returned for his wife and household goods. With these loaded on an ox cart, he arrived at his new home November 9, 1818, and thus became the first settler in Greene county north of the Macoupin.

|*Journal of the Illinois State Historical Society,* Volume 13, July, 1920, No. 2|

Is it any wonder we chose to be ruled not by King but Constitution? Not by human lineage but by *document?*

For this is all we have to hold: the massacre, the clear spring, initials on a bee tree, a new life. Any wonder they suspected history? Any wonder they kept their mouths shut? Could they have possibly *known* that all that would remain of their efforts, their "life story," would be vulgar popular narratives, unrealized fictions, prepaid advertisements, cinematic stereotypes, and a few stylish variations on the crudest literary theme?

The difference between dream and nightmare is not fear. A dream is an elaboration of an experience other than the dream, perhaps frightening, perhaps difficult to recognize. But a nightmare is fueled by the suspicion that what we are undergoing never happened before and can never be passed on. It is totally defined by its *presentness*, precisely as a document, torn from a tissue so immense and encrusted that it cannot be named, cannot be brought in, dead or alive.

America, you are better off
Than our old continent
You have no crumbling castles
And no basalts
You are not disturbed in your heart
While life pushes on
By unnecessary memories
And futile struggles
And if your children should
Take up literature
May a good fate save them
From crime and ghost stories
|Goethe, America|

We recross the Adriatic with a fisherman, head once more far into the interior of Yugoslavia, take two trout, bid the vacuum good-bye, then blame the cold for moving south. But I am more than cold.

I take the yellow roads to Greece, passing the souffle of Dubrovnik's roofs; then I am come to Macedonia.

In a bar in Graconice, a man with a mustache completely concealing his mouth comes up and introduces himself. He searches me out, he says, because I am a foreigner and because I look like an intellectual. Thanks a lot. (An intellectual in our time is one who dresses like a worker, lives like a bourgeois and doesn't know whether to act like a gangster or an aristocrat.)

He tells me about the "Macedonian problem"—he is apparently part of a group that is pressing to be ceded to Albania, as the latter demands. What are your grievances, I ask dully.

"Oh, the same, you know, as all over. Like the Jura problem, the East Germans, the Flemish-Belgians, the Catholic-Protestants, the French-Canadians, your Negroes, you know."

I allow that I can't see the immediate advantages of Albanian suzerainty.

"That is because," he says, "you are constantly meddling in affairs which are none of your business."

Eventually, across a blasted, desiccated landscape, Shell Oil welcomes us to the glory that was Greece.

It is part of the democratic attitude for our intellectuals to go about in disguise and not to attack (which is easy enough for anyone with a little wit) but to make something of a society which they must admit has its general advantages . . .
|*Claes Oldenburg*, Notebooks, 1961|

OUR BUDDIES, GREECE 'N SPAIN

Things are beginning to break up. I cross the border with the indefatigable Panzer corps of Bavarian campers. Some English dudes on their way through from Pakistan censor me for visiting Fascist Greece. I allow that perhaps their moral superiority is due in part to their restricted travel allowance.

They reply that Americans think they can buy anything and that they wouldn't go to Spain either.

I tell them of my plans for revisiting Iberia in the near future.

They pronounce this doubly villainous.

I stride to a map of the Western World on the wall of the customs house, where Greece and Spain are colored pink, and demand which nations deserve to be visited. We argue about Switzerland from a Neo-Marxist point of view, and finally settle on that axis of morally feasible vacation spots which stretches from Brussels to Oslo. I remind them that if I followed their logic, their rigorous standards, I couldn't go home either. You wouldn't want us loose in the world all the time, would you? Do you have any idea what we might do if we had to stay home all the time?

They are appalled. I offer to loan them money. They are disgusted. I announce my intention of embarking immediately for South Africa.

Well, here we are in martial law again. With this landscape, it's lucky the Greeks have their architecture. The Army's out for the day; somebody has thrown a bomb at the Colonel. Missed, of course. The soldiers ride about on their tanks; they grin and wave at me. Soldiers laughing make me nervous. Just like the Spanish Cadres.

In Madrid, the police rush the one pathetic sit-in in the university. They are laughing too, but they are powder blue and ruthless. There is no time for brutality or recriminations. They cut through the meager picket line like a laser. And in the province of Zarogoza, an American of my college class has, in his new Ferrari, run down and killed a family of seven walking beside the road at night. Our ambassador is pleading for clemency. It was dark, after all.

|270|

WHY DID THE REVOLUTION OF APRIL 21, 1967 TAKE PLACE?

The English tourist, Mrs. Ilin Smith, owner of big shops in Kend declaired: "Greece is an excellent place for holidays. No irregularity, no agitation; a goodhearted people willing to serve you. If I had not read the newspapers coming to your country, ignoring the events, I would have not realized that a Revolution had taken place."

HOW DO WE ACT DURIND MAY

The last month of the year:
—preparation to holidays after the examinations, organization of excursions maintain—the clubs during Summer, a month of excursions for studying organizations.

Those summary elements show the perfect organization of Communist party which worked and acted freely against country and its laws.
By this letter, the Communists arranged with a perfect method all about students as well as the work which had to be done, in order to attract as many of them as they could.
It has also been provised to continue the connection during the holidays, even for night schools.
From the above, the abandonment of National Education comes in sight.
The Nation was not interested in the education of students and this permitted communists to penetrate in Education causing terrible results against the Nation. |Junta Brochure|

The Greek Army is being adorable again. I wonder who decides which country gets which color on maps. In the customs house, Yugoslavia, Norway and Portugal are gray; Hungary, Switzerland and Sweden, puce; France, Turkey and Lichtenstein, green; Austria and Italy, orange; The Netherlands, Bulgaria and England, blue; Spain 'n' Greece are pink.

An Athenian friend takes us out to dance at the wine festival at Daphne. We dance, drink; the beautiful young boys simulate fornication with each other while a few American secretaries perform a hopelessly schematic Boogaloo. In the morning, we end up in a cafe in the Plaka, begin to drink again. The proprietor begs us to leave, he is terrified. "You have no idea what is going on in this country," he whispers. None of my Greek friends will talk politics either. At least two claim to have relatives in concentration camps in the islands—Yioura, Leros; all the nationals leave the bar; only foreigners remain. And our oracular proprietor's prophecy is fulfilled. We are arrested, six of us, and hustled off to jail.
For what?
"For your hair, your clothes, your appearance of immorality . . ."
The eldest of us, a 45-year-old bearded structural linguist from Iowa, his love beads swaying ominously over his paunch, screams, "They're fucking the bejesus out of themselves in public out at Daphne, and you're arresting *us* for our *appearance* . . ."
In the station house, we are searched for drugs, our money is counted, and an Army Captain tells us not to worry, that as soon as the American government supports the new regime unfortunate incidents will cease. "It is all so confusing," he sighs.

12:02 p.m. This is the moment to bicycle through gleaming white island villages. To find a beach all your own. And spend the day swimming, snorkling and sailing in the crystaline blue waters of the Agean.
7:35 a.m. This is the moment to see ancient temples glowing in the warm morning light. To dream of gods and heroes and history. To feel the past breathe again in the clear air of the present.
1:10 p.m. This is the moment to lunch under a shady olive tree. To relish fresh-baked crusty bread. Mouthwatering Greek olives and hors d'oeuvres. And sip a deliciously dry white wine.
1968. This is the moment. Your moment to discover Greece. |Greek National Tourist Office|

This evening, in the cell, I recall a similar night in Madrid eight years before, when I was arrested for using profanity on the Guardia Civil. And so it comes down to this; after surviving at least three failed revolutions, I have finally been arrested for the lack of a haircut in the cradle of democracy.

In a world of Prague and Chicago, San Francisco and Paris, what can it possibly matter whether I am in jail in Athens or Madrid? What can it possibly matter whether I am guilty or not? My selective perception has begun to blur, the decade has collapsed to a still point; these two poor pink peninsulas, which can be escaped to, but never from, just the opposite of my own country; these amputated legs upon which European civilization perches, most admirable residue of Mediterranean culture—now preserved for our increasingly pointless leisure, twin totalitarian vacation spots, each with a royal pretender and an American Nuke waiting in the wings . . .

The next day we are released; another friend tells me he must now show me something intriguing and drives me 100 kilometers down the coast—Lord, another temple, I think, more ruins, one more fucking column . . . the interest in ruins for Americans is similar to the Europeans' interest in our spacecraft; the penultimate question becomes—"Where do you suppose they shit?" But we arrive only at a series of caves where what he refers to as "young Americans" have taken up residence. But this is not funny either, no health food cum Nature jag—they suffer from scabrousness, malnutrition as well as boredom. They support themselves by hitchhiking to Athens and selling their blood—or so a girl from Shaker Heights tells me. She is none too clean or happy. She's here because her parents are "fuckin' pigs on a bummer." And she takes the food my friend brings without a word of thanks. Ah, those neo-debutantes; I should have killed them off when I could. Two of the boys clearly have hepatitis. One gives me a half-hour monologue on the uselessness of words. He will be a musician when he gets back. He plays his guitar for us. But he has trouble remembering the words. His hands are not strong enough to keep the chords from wavering. Perhaps it is all part of a larger technique? I beg my friend to get us out of there.

|272|

BECOMING A PREY TO THEIR TROUBLES

The generation after the war did not trust those people whose inspiration was expected in vain. They were standing unprepared before unundemanding people who tried to survive in a selfishness which had been established by science and materialism. The "Old Guard" gave them dusted ideas and worn out values, accompanied by theories repulsive in action. A lot of old ideals were dead and the others demanded continual efforts.

LACK OF GREEK IDEALS

There were no powerful persons during those difficult moments our youth faced. Those who had to help and lead them were absent . . .

THE REQUESTED RAISINGS OF DEPUTIES INVIOLABILITY, 1960–67

Delects	Total
Perjury	11
Slanderous Defamation and Slanderous Defamation by the press	110
Dispersion of False Informations	6
Deceits	4
False Accusations	1
Insult and Threat Against the Authority	150
Resistance to the Authority	5
Disobedience to the Authority	1
Offence Towards the King's Family	3
Body Damages Face Wounds Body Ill-Treatments	44
Homicides by Carelessness	7
Car Incidents	1
Cars without License	1
Distribution of Unlawful Printed Matter	2
Reaction Against the Law— Stealing	4
Disturbance of Public Peace	4
Defalcations	16
Ravishment Attempt Disturbance of Home Peace	1
Lawyer's Perfidy	1
Several Transgressions	98
Total	470

"Are they not wonderful?" he asks me on the way back. "The villagers are frightened of them because they believe witches once lived in the caves, but they are martyrs, truly. At the very moment we are losing our monasteries for lack of monks, God has sent these penitents."
I could've shit.

Witches of the world, our putrescent adolescence has the earth agog. We are envied for our masochism only slightly more than our affluence. They confuse our resistance to the world with unorthodoxy; unable to understand that our fear was forged in the *absence* of a worthy enemy.

In their primitivism, their determinism, their exhaustion, their pathetic politics, they are one—these two pink peninsulas washed by such kindly water, wasted by harsh winds—where nothing is bland except the tourists who fuel their obsessions. But there is no hope in trying to sort them out any longer; they are all the same to me, these islands with no history or those which reek of legend, where nothing ever happens except for the tourists who come to escape *their* history. "Ah ha," an old man tells me on Chios, "you think *you* are violent, you should have been a boy in Chicago as I was in the 1890s." Curious how the traditions of one culture are available only to others. The Germans, the Americans knew what to do with Greece, though not with their own countries. For Greece it would seem that their past is no longer a monument, but a black hole across which they must leap. These islands, lumps of lichened marble, afterthoughts between sky and water, islands the same color and consistency as the towns of the Catalonian plateau, always one *more* on the horizon, another mote of dust transmogrified. My friend the Greek insists that it is only a matter of time before the underground rises, the Junta is overthrown.
And then what will you do?
"We will bring back Papandreou and the others now in exile in America."

THAT'S WHY THE REVOLUTION OF APRIL 21, 1967 TOOK PLACE

The reader of this text, dedicated to the national conscience of Greek people, must have realized that everything has been written objectively, without passion and prejudices, with true elements, pictures, phototypes and controlled numbers about the mobocracy existing in the period before April 21st which was going to lead our country to chaos and disaster. In these pages the reader and the future historian will find precious elements which will enable them to come to safe and positive conclusions for the necessity of the National Revolution; they will completely justify the Arm forces of the Nation and the leaders of the Revolution who changed the Panhellenic desires of getting rid of unskillful politicians, to reality. Several months went by since the Revolution of April 21st. The Governors, faithful to their promises, proceed to the fulfilment of their historical mission.
A wind of change and purification is blowing throughout the country.
The economy of the State increased, as well as the investments of foreign capitals, while the cost of living is continuously reducing. The relations between the State and the citizens are in a very good condition.
There is a complete quietness and peace throughout the country and communist danger does not exist any more.
People show their trust toward the Government by saving their money and the ministers of National Government who visit all districts of the country in order to solve the problems of the inhabitants, are accepted with great enthusiasm.
All Greek people together, leaving their partial passions which separated them aside, proceed to the creation of a new Greece.
Greece of the uncertain yesterday belongs to the past. A smile of optimism is on everybody's lips and our guardian angel—the army—cares about anything.
Greece is immortal. The 21st of April 1967 and the conscience of all Greek people guarantee for it. |Junta Brochure|

And then?

"Wait for the next coup."

My friend the Catalan assures me that a new coalition of radical clerics, Basque separatists and pragmatists of the nobility will bring down the government upon Franco's death.

And then?

"America will intervene . . .?"

On the side of the Pretender, I interrupt.

His eyes become white as the quay at Mykonos. I cannot bear to tell them the liberal's dirty little secret, that I would trade, in an instant, our democratic institutions, our saccharine reasonableness, our ingenious technology, for their honest primitivism, for their corrupted dance, their *manners;* trade it all in for the indifference of a shepherd.

I have known "religion" only twice—once in El Escorial, where Philip II reaped the treasures of the New World in a thousand uniformly bleak rooms, and on the island of Patmos, in the monastery built above the cave where St. John saw the ends of the earth and the end of the world—that tunnel again, with light at both ends.

In the former, I discovered the spirit of those who really "discovered" America; not those prudent protestants with time on their hands, but the plunderers—the Pizarro who could not write his own name; the Columbus notable mainly for bringing slavery to the New World and venereal disease to the old—those who destroyed everything they touched *in order* to formally renounce it, those who struck out dumbly into the New World for treasure, yes, but also to escape the consequences of the very ideas in whose name they went forth!

And on Patmos, the other half of the world, I found the blank stares of those who *didn't* discover America, those island people who, as Homer said of Syra, are desirable precisely because they have never *lived,* are precious because they are outside of history, serene and inconsolable.

"Religion," then, is that sudden perception that the price of eternal peace is constant terror, and the medium of access for me was through the vitrines of the Escorial and Patmos, vitrines which house the illumi-

I sent out two men into the country to see if the king or any cities were to be found. These returned in three days, having discovered a great number of towns, but all of them small and without any government . . . throughout these islands there is no diversity in the appearance of the people, their manners or language, all the inhabitants understanding one another; a very favorable circumstance, in my opinion, to the design which I have no doubt is entertained by our king, namely to convert them to the holy Christian faith . . . |Christopher Columbus to Rafael Sanches while returning from his first voyage|

|274|

nated manuscripts from which this book takes its shape—those books annotated in the margins by generations of argument, counter-argument and commentary, recapitulated and revised history, contradictory assertions, a spiral unfolding into space, which must be read as it was written—from the inside out. They remain the highest collaboration of technology and personality, echo the most intense relationship between the tactile and the intellectual, the analytic and the celebratory—those manuscripts which themselves, like stelae, hold Time.

And though the marginalia here are mainly words of others, they are still mine, alas; self-referential, autodidactic, desperately appropriated, signed by my own hand. This is our world now—a world in which *this* is never *that,* and *it* only about *it*self; becoming . . .

Think of it! In what form does the impulse of the illuminated manuscript remain in our world? In the film script, no less—that fictive exercise in which the narrative substance is reduced to its lowest common denominator, and juxtaposed to the "dialogue" as mindless exhortations to some illiterate technician.

And literature, from the time it called itself that, has been spiraling inward, a cosmic involution disguised by our democratic revolutions, that confusion between shared information and community. We have lost annotation by either priest or public; we are underliners, check-off artists, and that commentary which once *paralleled* the text and gave it amplitude has been reduced and codified to a specialist's careerist shorthand—its plunge from the healthy haunch of the text to the footnote parallels our own fall. For the loss of the margin is the loss of space, and the loss of space is the loss of time, and time, as Blake knew, is the mercy of eternity. For God, in the beginning was the Word; for Man, in the beginning was the picture, the hieroglyh. When He gave directions, He talked in sounds. When we began to talk beyond ourselves, we scratched on the wall. God was a voice, man a calligrapher; literature is the oral written down. And as we lost the commentary, we also lost the image first integral to, then coextensive with, the text, the letter which *was* the serpent, the Greek for fish which is also Christ, each word its own thing; we lost the essence of the book which was its *unfolding,* each page its own event. A simple machine that. And yet, as

All the subsequent achievements in the field of scholarship sink into insignificance beside the labors of these men, who needed genius, enthusiasm and the sympathy of Europe for the accomplishment of their titanic task. Virgil was printed in 1470, Homer in 1488, Aristotle in 1498, Plato in 1512. They then became the inalienable heritage of mankind. But what vigils, what anxious expenditure of thought, what agonies of doubt and expectation, were endured by those heroes of humanizing human scholarship, whom we are apt to think of merely as pedants! Which of us now warms and thrills with emotion at hearing the name of Aldus Manutius or Henricus Stephanus or of Johannes Froben? Yet, this we surely ought to do; for to them we owe in great measure the freedom of our spirit, our stores of intellectual enjoyment, our command of the past, our certainty of the future of human culture. [Sic.] |John Addington Symonds, Renaissance in Italy, *1875|*

the commentary spirals down, God himself begins to speak *in quotes,* his literacy the beginning of our self-consciousness, and then, like the *Evening News* conking out, He loses, along with the sound and picture, His omniscience—and only the proscenium remains . . . only this frame of brightest light which collapses to a single dot, as at the end of a tunnel. And friends, it is not our bountiful technology which did this to us, it is how we chose to make use of our technology. For if it is God who speaks in quotes, who is that guy up in the third balcony pounding out the narrative? The guy who is not quoted but *speaks,* says *this is the beginning,* that MC who gets God off to a good start and asks for the house lights—who is it? Moses? Ezra? Some Aramaic book freak? It doesn't matter who gets the credit, who gets his name in lights. For light is just our most recent nothingness until it has something to illumine, a name to frame. Whoever—he stands for all of us, and God, when He begins his "dialogue," becomes but one of many voices in the narrative of how we came to be. And so, having finally reached zero, having reduced ourselves to the word, and the world to our enumeration of it, we begin from the still center, that little splotch of privacy we have created for ourselves, to flood the proscenium again until it bursts, in glory or apocalypse—begin the long way out. . . .

And while my Spanish/Greek friends insist on their coming "revolution," my mind goes microscopic and whole . . . I care more for the speculative model of Knossos—how it *was*—than its remaining walls and terraces, more for the artist's rendering of Gaudi's Holy Family Cathedral—how it *will* be—than what it is now. And with typical American tinkering, I make arrangements for the merging of these two cultures. The favoring winds and Catalan domes of Barcelona and Zaragoza shall be moved to the sharp mountains and defiles of Santorin and Chios; the village of Naxos and the stelae of Crete set down on the Catalan plain; the stairway of Phaistos which leads nowhere will go to Segovia in exchange for the aqueduct which will connect Paros and Delos, making them green again; the walnut choir of the Toledo cathedral, its dragons devouring one another in rococo indigestion, is to be set down upon open rock to weather, in exchange for the Gate of Apollo, which will glow like plankton in the cathedral's crypt; General Franco for Colonel Papadoupoulos; the Tunnel of Eupalinos for the Valley of the Fallen, poppies for poppies . . . I have put away my camera forever.

In Seville, in another vitrine there is a letter from Cervantes asking for a job in the New World, which, by the Grace of God, he was refused, lest he become the first American novelist. Across the letter, the Clerk of the Indies has scrawled, "Let him look for something nearer home." After pondering this, the vitrine smudged from my nose, fogged with my short breath, it occurred to me that the myth of Quexalcoatl is perhaps our most instructive legend: that civilization which exports its intellect, its pure Godhead, will receive it back in a different form—as an invader. This small, strange continent—not even that, this collection of pastel states washed by the Gulf Stream, which so frantically fought its way across the ocean for a newness against which to play out its obsessions, to recreate themselves in the void—now receives back its due: a race of giant children, bred for infinite consumption, tumbling amiably among the artifacts of a history now denied them precisely because they are the outcome. And Europe reacts with its historic formulae for survival—copy the invader, assimilate him, absorb his techniques, even his gods if necessary; so she is no longer fit for escape, for loss—only a miniaturized replica of ourselves. At the very moment America seems to have the strength, or at least the perspective, to question the most brutish and unfulfilling aspects of the life we've fashioned for ourselves, that very life becomes the object of veneration in the cultures from which we fled, and with a few minor technological adjustments, they make themselves over in our image; all our excuses are false starts prepackaged and fed back to us with a mixture of awe and contempt which makes the master/slave relationship positively civilized by comparison. This extraordinary land somehow gave us the wealth, the curiosity, the

Miguel Cervantes de Saavedra has served Your Majesty many years in journeys on land and sea that have been offered devotedly and two years as [unreadable] *particularly in the Naval Battle where he was given many wounds of which he lost a hand from an arquebus shot—and the next year he went to Haventino and afterwards to that* [battle] *of Tunis and to the schooner and coming to this court with letters from Sr. don Juan and from the Duke of Sesa in order that Your Majesty compensate him . . . Antonio de Guevara as shown by the information that he has and* [unreadable] *has not compensated him at all. He asks and begs humbly as much as he can that Your Majesty may be served to compensate him an office in the Indies of the three or four that at present are not occupied, one being the accountancy of the New Kingdom of Granada or the governing of the province of Soconusco in Guatemala or accountant of the galleys of Cartagena or corregidor of the city of La Paz, with any one of these offices Your Majesty would compensate him.* [unreadable] *because he is an able and sufficiently worthy man that Your Majesty may do him this grace because his desire is to continue always in Your Majesty's service and to finish his life as his ancestors would have done who in it* [unreadable] *very great advantage and grace.* |Madrid, June 6, 1590|

simple courage to travel to the ends of the earth like beggars—owing no one anything, discovering the enormity if not the beneficiary of our debt, discovering how little we can really effect, and, in the momentum of the past, we see only our own hostility, the ravages of our technology, and in History, only the reflection of our own swimming eye. Truly, we can invade only ourselves.

So we have returned. We have come full circle. Perhaps we ought simply to sit back and let them continue to plead the dream which created us, let them continue to dress us in the flames and blood of their diminished pride.
It is almost as if, bored silly by our lack of a past, we have begun to recapitulate scenarios of European history, and then become petulant when our enactments release no body of meanings. At the very moment we have become aware of our own breathing, we forfeit it. Unable to enjoy even our decadence, finding history either opaque or redundant, realizing we can never achieve civilization *this way*, we resolve to embark on a non-historical career, to appropriate the specious present—in order to announce *where it's at.* . . . Having tired of "finding ourselves," we calculate how to "get lost." Just as a man who must announce his authenticity each day is a noble bore, a society which is compelled to announce its progress annually is likewise insufferable. Our minds have hardly been "blown"—only relapsed from themselves. Yet it is easier to feel sorry for Europe than to pity ourselves. They copy our unborn bourgeoisie; we mimic their dead revolutionaries. We yearn for their past, they simulate our future. And the question is *already*—how shall we be remembered? Will we suffer the fate of those illustrious, aboriginal cultures whose sudden disappearance can only be explained by the fact that their imitators, their inferiors, their admirers, bored them back to the jungle? Like the Maya, will we end a magnificent and wholly uninstructive mystery? After working so diligently to disperse our gods, they will return demanding more human sacrifice, and even this will be somehow only coincidental to a profounder dec-

THERE IS NO SUCH PLACE AS AMERICA.

|278|

adence, self-inflicted though no more dignified for that, that monstrous effort by which we gave up on ourselves. And thus, we will become a phenomenon, a *period* by which contiguous cultures shall be measured and found wanting—and we shall be remembered not for how we lived our days, not for our rich language, our subtle laws, our great wealth, our unprecedented leisure, our startling obsession with Time, which perhaps will be seen only as an inexcusable indifference to history—but for our roads—above all, our roads—which come out of nowhere and lead to the sunset. Object of the most intense and redundant study, we shall yield nothing, our origins forgotten, our demise inexplicable. . . .

It is now about time to visit that most despised of all cultures, against which I'd been warned in every European capital, a culture which I hope will prove hopelessly opaque or utterly distracting, an aloof adversary which will permit me nothing, a true hiatus, before I must haul myself home for good. There is some kind of Holy Week going on as I cross the Straits to Tangiers—Moslem or Christian, I shall never know. I want to be pure tourist just once more.

A brochure boasts modestly of high luminosity, accredited insularity, and perhaps the third best beach in the world; but the city is in decline, free now from the dignity that only unmitigated vice can give, a tarnished wedge in the hindquarters of Africa, its free-port status and Humphrey Bogart gone. Dogs are no longer allowed on the streets unleashed, so they defecate in the large patios. Cattle wander the marsh grass of the low eroded foothills.

The airport magazine stand has only two books in English—the-Compendium-of-All-World-Knowledge-Series edition of John Locke ("His eye shoots like a dagger of skepticism into the Western mind," the jacket announces) and a tattered copy of *Walden,* billed the "apogee of

KNOW YOUR ARABY

individualism that is America. . . ." Armed upon such an apogee with a shooting dagger, I am well fortified to withstand a rival culture. Play it again, Sam.

Back from the crescent beach some two hundred yards, its weathered stucco splotched with tangerine shutters, stands *L'Incroyable,* the door a pastiche of invitation. The owners are in the back; Priscilla, a buxom English secretary who came to Tangiers for a vacation once and never went back, and Peter, her husband, Dutchman *déraciné,* who had worked for the Cirque d'Hollande and fought in New Guinea. She lounges on a bar stool in a formless blue evening dress—in full contempt of my desire for stasis; she makes her living off the tourists' weak infatuations, but she *lives* to mock their residual discipline. I ask what "Housey-Housey" is. Peter rinses glasses mechanically, reading a magazine propped on the bar, chin pneumatic as he scans the pages. In my dark shuttered room I lie down and turn on the radio—the dial is warped, revolving off-center so that the fragmented numbers scrape the plastic window then fall away into the red glow of its innards. Unindexed bands of Moslem plainsong and anti-Israeli battle chants alternate with the fluttering evidence of a continental fugue.

At the top of the hill looms the Sultan's palace, an abandoned flurry of turrets and crenellation, and around it swarms the Arab quarter—the whiteness of whiteness, an unyielding linearity, the lives of its occupants broken only by the fecund bulges of the mosques. *L'Incroyable* rests in the basin where the architecture is modern, native only in the Islamaniacal passion for geometrica. A leafy railway track runs along the periphery of the beach, where, I am told, one used to see smugglers heaving their sacks from train to the sand in the early twilight. But the beach blows over the rails now and the ties have been scavenged for firewood. Beyond the city ride the green mountains, absurdly green between the white facade of the city and the rumor of the Sahara. I shall not attempt to describe the sky for I could not avoid the trite—it is something from a very bad mezzotint souvenir—such a heaven could be

Open to ALL Tourists

Bar	—	Hotel
Darts	—	Ping-Pong
Checkers	—	Chess
Cards	—	Housey-Housey
WHAT YOU WILL!!		

conceived only with our most faulty and indolent faculties.

The sky has now shuddered through a sunset, the set being changed for "the lovers' secret meeting in the garden," and I walk up to the Casbah to eat. The restaurant seats eight on stools and a Jew passes skewers of roasted liver back from the brazier with one hand as he cooks with the other. The loudspeakers are screaming "Kill the Jews" in four languages. Occasionally, a taxi carrying an apprehensive tourist to the tearoom of the Sultan's palace crashes up the narrow street, scattering the populace. But they absorb the interruption effortlessly, knowing simply that these vehicles promise more gold than all the camel trains that ever blinked out of the desert.

The voice came first as I was looking in a shop window, following at a respectable pace until it finally said, "Be no afraid, just say hello," and to prevent insult I turned to find a young Moslem holding out his hand for shaking. Except for pointy shoes he was dressed in Western clothes—tight slacks, tattersall sportcoat and plaid tie, only a scarred and toothless mouth breaking the fraternity image.

"English, yes?"

No, American.

"Come, I practice English with you, my friend; you buy nothing." I walked with him further into the Casbah, which became darker but cleaner, a series of large intricately carved entranceways in which children played with miniature war planes of the Western powers.

"You want whore?" my guide asked.

I came here for a rest, I shrugged.

"I am called Absalom," he said.

Why not.

We walked on, the street deviously ascending the hill, gullies of water on either side of us. Men sat in their shops, smoking, while children tumbled in and out of doorways. In an arch, a baker stood shoulder deep in a blackened fire-pit, surrounded by heavy discs of dough and two huge drowsy dogs. A horn broke the murmur and we flattened ourselves against the wall with the children as a taxi heaved past. At the top of the hill we mounted a balustrade and followed a roofless, walled passage from which large sections of mosaic had been pried; then we crawled through a drain and the walls fell away to a secret balcony of the Sultan's palace, assaulted only by the stars, the sea breaking precociously against the ramparts. The wind was wet and the sea black as the sky. I had had a glimpse of where ships once fell off the edge of the world.

"You come," Absalom said, tugging at my sleeve almost immediately. Why? It's so lovely here.

"Come *with* me: if you want to see the sights, take taxi tour please." I followed him eagerly along the old wall of the city, his leather shoes utterly silent. At the end of the wall, worn tile stairs wound down the hill. The air was heavy with jasmine and the city fell like a cascade of sparks into the bay. Descending, eyes for the stairs only, I asked him where we were going—but he refused to talk—save for occasional opaque aphorisms.

"Once, each night," he shrugs, "some man wants lay; now the city slips into the sea."

Arriving at the edge of the Casbah he took my hand, and signaling his departure, asked to walk with me again the next evening. I told him to come to the hotel at eight.

"Promise?" he said.

Promise.

Then he let go of my hand and turned to go.

Absalom, I called out after him, what are the chances of there being a revolution *here?*

He paused, puzzled; then his face lit up and he turned, feet grinding on the stones for the first time.

"Don't ask questions about politics, religion or girls," he said, articulating the words carefully. "An American told me that." Then he was gone.

The hotel was blazing with lights when I returned and Peter was preparing a daiquiri for Priscilla. She was sitting crosslegged on a stool and murmured good-night to me. Upstairs, I lay down to Locke myself to sleep.

That was the skeptic's trick, I thought, the figured detachment which protected the author so he could write with the other hand that it is man's duty to oppose tyranny. Only our skepticism had been translated to Absalom whole, without the presumption which justified all the indecisive speculation. A tourist trick even, this Locke, the display of irony to emphasize one's own security; like the entrepreneur, the philosopher tells men they are free so that he may control them. I recalled how Absalom had recoiled on the balcony from that non-view to which he must have been subjected a thousand times—and add to that the inconceivable endless stairs, the nameless twisted streets, the soaring fragrant palace walls, and the absurd green mountains.

The production of power and initiation of motion are only perceived in ourselves . . . our only idea of power is unwarranted and confused . . .

Priscilla knocked on my door somewhat later, calling my name, but I did not answer, and she did not use her housekey.

Infinity is a negative idea . . . it expresses simply the inability of the mind.

Today I received word from Ray in San Francisco that the psychedelic anthropologist is dead from an overdose, and I am more than nauseous.

I suppose no contemporary journal would be complete without the mandatory word on drugs, especially since I've saved sex, this long year, for fiction; for in my experience, sex is always, sometimes detrimentally so, exemplary—while drug hallucinations are almost always one-dimensional, mere literacy, and psychedelia have only served to confirm this prejudice. Whatever else they are, drugs are lousy metaphors.

In any case, when I first came to Tangiers I was twenty. I holed up in a hotel much like *L'Incroyable* where, in short order, through the help of an enormous Lebanese who called himself Octavian, I collected an elaborate store of mind blowers, which I shall not list here for obvious cautionary reasons, and began to experiment, as they say. I'm afraid, however, that my conclusions will enrage aficionados and the police alike—for while I will testify that the euphoria of morphine is pretty hard to beat, it works best if you have something more than existential pain against which to test it; I preferred that administered so liberally by our armed forces to Octavian's purer stuff. But, in my defense, one must remember that drugs had not yet been assimilated into middle-class white culture; and the elaborate rules for group behavior had not yet been developed. I had, of course, learned how to act drunk before I ever drank, but I had no public manner for hash or coke or horse, and, moreover, I had no one to have a hallucination with, or even for. Worse, true to my practical Huguenot stock, I expected such experience to be usable beyond itself; in fact I assumed it would help my writing, or at the very least provide what book jackets call "an intense personal and illuminating vision." I thought an hallucination to be merely another art form. So every evening, I would dutifully scramble into bed with the requisite paraphernalia, administer the dosage, and with my spiral notebook propped on my knees, my PaperMate at the ready, would await my Kubla Khan. After several months of this, I became rather depressed—not from the physical debilitation, which wasn't as much as you would expect, but from the fact that my various euphorias, nightmares, faintings, vomitings, orgasms had not produced a scrap of verse, nor even an interesting clinical dossier. A few sentences on visual disorientation, the intensification of color and sound, some frankly indescribable long falls were not sufficient for my pains. So very little happened that I could not have *imagined!* So it was, unreinforced by my peers, unpunished by the authorities, and unconvinced of the substance's aesthetic merit, I at length regretfully informed Octavian that I would no longer be requiring his services. For this, he hit me in the neck with the heel of his hand and, as I was going down, kicked me expertly three times in the balls.

There's no moral, of course; I suppose this can be written off to the fact that when I was little I could never sleep since I thought losing consciousness was a sin, or that now I do not believe in any experience which is not translatable into some language beyond the self. . . .

But for my young friends who are now heaped up in the streets of this city like so much cordwood; for my dear friends who now stagger so insouciantly through the evenings on the lower East Side, unfinished

Sooooooooooooooooooooo:

If it's got a mind, stump it.
If it stands too high, slump it.
If it willn't budge, bump it.
If ya don't like it, lump it.
But if it's got a hole, hump it!

|Ronald Tavel, Gorilla Queen|

Time is dead—henceforth there shall be no years, no months, no hours— eternity is quite exhausted and had to end sometime.
Good Lord, I cried, suddenly conscious of a new idea. If time exists no more, when shall it ever be eleven?
|Charles Baudelaire, *The Poem of Hashish*|

poems like pistols on their hips; for my friend who sits in the foun-
tained foyer of a millionaire queer in Tangiers, his all-state halfback's
body now sheathed in diaphanous white Turkish pantaloons, an ame-
thyst in his navel, his veins the color of dung, who tells me in ten words
a minute that at least it's better than teaching gym in Carbondale, Illinois—what can I say? They tell me it's likely I have a high resistance.
I tell them they are vulnerable. They concur. They ask me if I will forgive them if they do not confuse their life with *my* aesthetics. I cannot
use Locke or Thoreau on them—I cannot convince them of anything, if
it's premised on the existence of individual *will,* on a self that's *made.*
If I say it's all subjective, they will only concur happily. And if I use
Marx, if I tell them they're victims of a conspiracy to anesthetize us all,
they say, "I told you so." They have achieved a kind of synthesis to answer all objections, by accepting the determinisms of *both* Marx and
Freud, without either their analysis or their solutions. And if I tell them
simply that I love them and don't want them to die, they say "Why
not?" to both. So if I were a father, I'd give my kid this sure fire-test:
Take whatever drug you want, then turn on the TV. If it doesn't improve the show, turn both off. If it does, you have only two alternatives
left. Then you'll know where you're at, who'sa boss, baby.

☐ 1
☐ 2   Check your alternative

It is out of season, and the beach is completely deserted in the morning.
The wind rasps in the boarded-up snack bars. On the way to lunch, a
child leading a blindman follows me for three blocks and secures a
franc. I would have given them all I had to be alone. They had waited
patiently on the edge of the sand near the defunct rails while I swam,
and had taken up my step almost nonchalantly as I passed. . . .
Restaurant Pergola was recommended by Priscilla—a charming place
managed by the Pergourdines: French family, four persons, three generations, two sexes, and all the same insufficient height of five feet two.
They have a white poodle named Couscous who rests his cold nose between your thighs during the meal, and two bored doves which sweep
back and forth from the bar to the front window. They also have an
Arab cook, working upstairs in a kitchen which overhangs the bar. It

has been decorated as a balcony with two gauzed windows, which occasionally feature the blurry profile of that Arab lady between two gilded garbage cans heavy with rubber dahlias. Getting the food downstairs is a difficult problem, however, so the door at the bottom of the stairwell is rigged with a sliding panel, and the plates, full and empty, are deposited on the stairs. If you look closely when the panel is opened, one may see two brown sinewy legs, dissected for a moment by the sweep of a hand with a plate—the same motion presenting or retrieving—and then the legs will turn heavily and ascend out of sight. I know this must mean something.

On the beach in the afternoon, the beggars come again demanding gifts, although my own sole property is a YMCA swim-suit, and at eight that evening Absalom is waiting beneath a street lamp. We walk again through the maze of winding streets. He remains silent—waiting patiently until my fancy will presumably be caught by something, and he can claim a commission. He is neither urgent nor relaxed, subservient nor indifferent: just proximate. But again I buy nothing, and apologize, saying that he should find someone else to guide.
"It is all right," he says with only mild disappointment, "I like my work," and he disappears softly into the dusk with my debt.
I eat at *Pergola* and stare at the Arab legs as they flex and pivot in their window.
Peter is not in, but Priscilla gives me "one on the 'ouse" and says that the boys from the American *base* always come in on weekends, and that I must be sure to meet some of my wonderful countrymen.
What base? I keep asking. I thought they were all phased out?
She pushes the gin across to me and smiles a smile which she must imagine to be transparent.

I lie on the beach, body-blacking for most of the weekend, trying to capture, more out of precious boredom than anything, what my impact on the city meant.

I lie on my belly rereading Locke and later turn on my back to ponder the city. The sun burns vaguely through my eyelids, and the only fact which proves my existence is the perspiration which runs into the gully of my neck and from there into the sand. Is this the sensation for my reflection? Because I can no longer see through my sweat, Locke thrusts his shooting dagger upwards from the sand, and beneath the purging sun I am the *tabula rasa:* born with nothing, yet born to much, to too much, like the label which reads, "Nothing removed, nothing added."

But I am interrupted by an elderly gentlemen whom I recognize as sharing the hospitality of *L'Incroyable,* a lawyer from Cologne who speaks little English, but enough.

"Français?"

No, American.

"Have you made the Turkish bath?"

Nope.

"Ach, it is something; I come now every year . . . ach, the little boys . . ."

I pick up my towels and start to go.

"But it is sad, is it not?"

What?

"That for the Mussulman it is *verboten* to drink alcohol."

Yeah, I guess so.

"Non français?"

Non, américain.

"Ho ha, the land of hambuggers!"

Yes.

"The land of the free and the home of . . ."

Yes.

"But *here* is the land of the free; do what you like, say what you like . . . here there is no . . . no . . . no civilization."

I must be getting back.

"You will come again, *bitte?"*

Sure.

The hotel is gained only twenty steps ahead of the blindman and his guide who have literally run up the hill after me. Why do I resist them? What's a franc? Priscilla has on a new frock, and has laid in a new supply of old magazines. Why do I resist her? What's a night? "Tonight," she announces peremptorily, "your *friends* are coming." Why do I resist . . . ?

To the *Pergola* for dinner, but there is the inevitable voice behind me, "Hey friend," and thinking it is Absalom I turn—but it is a new face, a face with a full set of gold teeth set in a blue mohair sweater.

"German?"

No, American.

"Hitler good man, right?"

No thanks.

"No like it here?"

Not yet.

"You want to change money?"

No.

"How 'bout ladies? Spanish, Moroccan ladies? Girls here mostly sick, though. Maybe boys?"

No.

"*Toujours rien?*"

C'est juste.

I escape into the restaurant to realize that I have been talking to an American, at least the *persona* of an American: the casual braggadoccio, the functional sincerity, the latent toughness which is both worthy and threatening, and then I eat with the cool nose of Couscous in my groin and the bright scrubbed legs behind my dinner.

The lazier beggars come out at twilight in clusters (gimme peseta tank-oo-ver-mush) and at *L'Incroyable* the American presence has arrived. Seven of our deterrents lounge about the bar in sport clothes, young faces toughened forever by boredom.

But I thought we haven't had any bases here since *1964*, I complain. No answer. Introductions by Priscilla and the talk inevitably turns to the Moslems—although that term is not used, for after so many years of refueling B-52s in the desert, Moslems have become "the Mos," or "ninety-day shitters," a euphemism referring, I presume, to Arab pantaloons.

"Some colored folks is my best friends," begins one, "an' back home we're no Little Rock! But I doan unnerstan these buggers, no ambition, no keepin up with the Joneses, no nuthin. I tried to be frens with one on the base an he stole me blind—and I doan think it was the money neither, I got the feeling when the MPs got 'im that he jest done it to make a *fool* outta me . . ."

"But these ain't *real* niggers, Joe, they doan know how to protec themselves. A nigger in the states got a whole repetoire to tell the white man who to get off; evertime he yassahs or yassams, he's laughing his fool head off inside—that's why whites think the nigger's so damn happy, he allus got a guffaw on his face."

"That's true," a sergeant chorused.

"But these A-rabs here—all they got is . . . silence . . . and when you break that, there's nuthin left."

How long you stationed here, I ask.

"Oh hell, they're not *really* niggers anyhow, I doan know *why* they're the way they are."

"I think it's the fuggin church that keeps 'em back."

"What kind of 'Indians' are they anyhow . . .?"

"Not like the first Americans," counseled Peter.

"Naw . . . you can say that again . . ."

Where are the planes, the nukes? I ask plaintively.

"One of the officers at the base told me that they were really Jews."

"Whaat! Kikes! Go on, get outta heah! They wanna kill the kikes!"

"Well, I doan care what they're called, I jes know in the back of my mine that I doan wanna mix with 'em—and doan tell me that everybody doan feel that!"

"We shouldn't, but we do, actually, don't we?" Priscilla interjected calmly.

Peter whips up more daiquiris. Priscilla is feeling me up again.

Whose peace are we keeping, my soldiers?

The next morning, sprawled around the bar waiting for the bus back to the "base," is our defense perimeter. Priscilla's magazines, their backs broken and pages warped, are scattered about the floor.

"Doan let the Mos get ya," a sergeant cried out as I left.

"They never wear their uniforms anymore," was all Priscilla said.

It is raining so I reach the *Pergola* unmolested. A man rides by on a donkey, his veiled wife and daughter walking behind. They are gazing at the squall line just beyond the mouth of the harbor, where the water is striped with shifting beds of plankton.

Inside, an American family is having breakfast, silently appreciative of the Pergourdines' frenetic service and their *Oeufs à la Grand Duke Meyerbeer.* The mother, a handsome woman, the tips of her bouffant hair graying, is teaching basic French vocabulary to two tow-headed boys. Her husband, horn-rims perched upon hard blunt features, grips an Arabic newspaper as though he hoped to order the opaque language by sheer tensile strength. He does not wait for the bill but walks to the bar to pay it, twice as tall as all the Pergourdines stacked one upon the another, including Couscous and the doves. The rest of the family exits except for the larger of the boys, who holds the door for his father.

As the tall man passes, his son slaps him on the back. "Let's hit the road, toad," he says, then *trips* his father, who breaks his long fall expertly with his hands. He hauls himself to his feet without a word, and with the kid still laughing, the four Pergourdines paralyzed with utter amazement, he puts an arm about his wife and saunters off, shaking his head, only a trace of disappointment in his eyes.

I have witnessed a scene which could have been enacted only by Americans of this age. Perhaps there is some hope for us after all.

This morning, the last of my year's "vacation," I went to the beach. It was deserted when I arrived, but no less than twenty-three people come to see me. This is what they offered: blanket, tea-mint, hashish, Berber doll, diamonds, Spanish ladies, taxi, Moroccan ladies, hassocks, ice cream, majoun, umbrella, honey, little boys, burro ride, kif, Turkish bath, genuine camel saddles. I refused all, growing angrier with each intrusion, until at last a small boy came and sat down beside me. He asked me to read what was in *das Buch* to him, and I began old Locke grudgingly:

The more compelled to choose, the freer we are. God almighty himself is under the necessity of being happy . . .

There he stopped me, saying that he knew I was an American, and that he would be pleased if I would tell him about that country. I replied that I just had. Between cultures, I think, we are all pimps.
The last thing I saw on that beach was a gigantic woman lying on her back surrounded by three beggar boys holding out their hands; she was groaning, *"Nada,"* roaring, *"Nada, nada!"*

I awake with no sun but Priscilla's underwear like a windsock outside my window. So *that's* Housey-Housey. The blindman and his boy are waiting for me across the street. The pattering commences as I head for the *Pergola*, pigeon-toed youth staccato between the splay-foot elder strides, and they catch me up just outside the eats. I give them another franc and they sit down in the gutter to wait until I finish brunch. The sliding panel displays the legs of our rusted Colossus again: she seems lighter on her feet today, perhaps this is her afternoon off! I resent the panel, the stumpy Pergourdines, the poodle and the doves more than usual.
I franc the boy for the last time in the twentieth century, and head off, but the jovial call is waiting around the corner. "Good-day, Mister." Absalom is exuberant. "Maybe you want something good to*day?*" He pulls an envelope out of his pocket. "Hash-hish, best quality, you try. Make happy, very happy. *Enfin!*"
The joint is as thick and long as a panatela, and I light her up.

December 7, 1968: The city is getting whiter. If anything is perceived strongly enough, it is true. And man sees only what concerns him. How to take offense? Why trade my vulnerability for consistency? My eye has been sullied, my curiosity worn out, my sympathies deadened. For this day, at the end of a crescent beach, at the edge of the world, among igneous lacerating rocks, I have come upon an Arab who, seeing that I was carrying a shooting-dagger of skepticism, sheathed in an apogee of individualism, presented me with a bouquet of yellow flowering lichen and beckoned me to follow—which I did, scrambling after him, ankles bleeding, flowerlets drooping absurdly in my hand, until we came to a grotto which held sea-spray as in the pockmarks of a Negress's neck, where mica blazed in the sun, and there he offered me a "life of Peace"—a life of primary qualities only—the city is white, the hills green, and the sky doesn't matter—different colors, maybe, but only one at a time, no seasons, no sea-change. no cycles, only the intensity of the wind telling the time of year.

But I've a problem, doctor; if my faults are universal, my virtues are my culture's. This is our true legacy, these funny self-absorbed men who, to assert their own freedom, and to insist upon it for others, end up talking about nothing but responsibility. On the wall above me, amongst the French and German graffiti, one of my young countrymen has written his version of their message—

The use of words then being to stand as outward marks of our internal ideas, and those ideas being taken from particular things, if every particular idea that we take in should have a distinct name, names must be endless. To prevent this, the mind makes the particular ideas received from particular objects to become general; which is done by considering them as they are in the mind such appearances,—separate from all other existences, and the circumstances of real existence, as time, place, or any other concomitant ideas. This is called ABSTRACTION. |*Mr. Locke*|

TO KNOW IS TO DO
TO DO IS TO LOVE
TO LOVE IS TO BE

imagining it, no doubt, to be a contradiction. Well maybe here, for us, this off-season. But such anti-geometry lacks both substance and symmetry. Locke knew: the absence of good does not necessitate volition. Thoreau knew: compassion is always untenable ground. I must leave for no better reason than I came, for I have several more lives to live. Our Arabs do not. And I no longer feel guilty, one way or the other, on this matter.
Simplify! Thoreau says it three times, as though he could not quite believe it. And Locke ends his work realizing that he has not increased

To one who habitually endeavors to contemplate the true state of things, the political state can hardly be said to have any existence whatever. [sic] |*H. D. Thoreau*|

|292|

his knowledge, but only created the necessity for another book to explain the one he has just finished. I leave them both to the library of *L'Incroyable*. They will need them.

"Happy now?" Absalom says.

In a way.

"No make happy?"

I nod dreamily.

Somewhat hurt, he takes out his wallet and produces three cards. The first is a Spanish health instructor's; the second, a British barrister's; the third a piece of folded stationery from a fraternity at a mid-western university. On it is scrawled:

OK Absalom, I say. What's up?

"Pardon?"

What's left to happen now? I'm ready for anything. So make me happy. I grasp at my last chance to give up, last chance for the victor to drive hence the spirit of victory.

Absalom looked straight at me then, almost longingly, certainly triumphantly, and then he is off at a trot, three strides to my one, and shortly we are in the depths of the Casbah, a long and narrow room in which a proprietor, dark, heavy as a bear, and his delighted family are falling over one another, enveloping me with garments. I do not resist. I would become a beggar; indistinguishable, indifferent.

But a word from Absalom and I am attired, not in shepherd's sack, but in yellow leather high-heeled shoes, crimson fez, a long hemless purple djalaba—one daughter slips bracelets on my wrists while another passes perfumed scarves about my shoulders—and then the son, not more than five, is there dancing about me, chanting in perfect mesmeric English: "Hello, Mohammed; hello, Mohammed!"

But if, from the impulse bodies are observed to make one upon another, any one thinks he has a clear idea of power, it serves as well to my purpose; sensation being one of those ways whereby the mind comes by its ideas: only I thought it worth while to consider here, by the way, whether the mind doth not receive its idea of active power clearer from reflection of its own operations, than it doth from any external sensation . . . |Locke|

I have done business with Mr. Absalom Araby-style and I find his wares to be without a doubt genuine and of A-1 quality.

Three abreast in the newest heavenly container, I on the aisle, knees to my chest, my limbs extend as my trunk shrinks, I am adapting amphibian-like. What was once powerful—for constricting, striking, foraging—is now for balancing; antenna, mandible, feathery and resilient. At the porthole through which she never looks, tough little face reflected in the clouds, there's a young girl the same age as I when I first came home from Europe; hair plaited straight, fingernails dark at the penumbra, insufferable because she is counting the years she has left to float as she will count her orgasms. When she turns her head, one can make out those two slight indentations in the skull, model of my very own difficult face-first presentation, and I scratch through my hair to find again the forceps marks. Yes, folks, we *were* all shot from the same gun.

She is not one to smile—the fact that she has experienced anything at all shows only in the taut corners of her mouth, but the eyes are still childish, and unable to fix, as if she had nothing *but* peripheral vision. I catch my own face in the window as I glance at her. My eyes are hard, a squint neither of age, nor myopia, nor lust precisely, but vaguely sinister nonetheless. But I have no lines about my mouth. I was told that I was the same as everybody else, and had to prove otherwise. She has been told she is different, new, and so must prove that she is the same. Perhaps all the degrading has not been for nothing. If everything has been reduced, become equivalent, then everything we do *is* new. The whole business has become more sad than startling.

Between us, his blunt fingers playing three-quarter arpeggios to the Muzak upon an attaché case smote from lava in his lap, sits a countryman in a certain shiny suit, his temples like the buttocks of a baby. His nails are laquered, manicured. Mine bitten. Hers filthy, whole. He is reading a book—*How to Make Money During Devaluation,* under which he has hidden a good porn book. When he goes forward to the toilet I open it where a page is dog-eared. She nearly smiles as I practice my gall. I'm afraid for him, this poor bastard. She's soon going to

|294|

ENVOI

I could not be certain whether I was really rich or really poor, really black or really white, really male or really female, really talented or a fraud, really strong or merely stubborn. In short, I had become an American . . . At that time it seemed only too clear that love had gone out of the world, and not, as I had thought once, because I was poor and ugly and obscure, but precisely because I was no longer any of these things. |James Baldwin|

GONE TO
P
LEAVE MY DRINK ALONE

The bed creaked when I rattlesnaked to strike, I hooked my right heel onto the bed spring. I raised myself on my right elbow. I drew my left arm back so that the back of my left fist touched

light into him and his dull-witted pleasantries. It's all on his clean hands, our American game, her seven rings, from an Oscar Mayer promo-souvenir to a Moroccan agate, glint against his IBM ring and college graduating class. I wonder why I've never worn a ring.
He has returned, sweating . . . I hope. His permapress which cannot breathe. He gives off a glow like mold. He threatens no one. In fact, it is quite clear that between us two, it is he who is threatened, and yet the three of us are equally responsible—in our various styles of staying alive—for the ooze to which we must now return. So instead of hating him, one must hate what he has to do; how he has had, in a word, the lack of an alternative. He is the true underprivileged man of our time, the captive majority, those whose only identity derives from increased production and maximal profit. What to do? She can only put him down or make love to him. I can only attack or ignore him. He fears her, fears me, because he thinks we're freer. We know better. It's the same movie up there on the bulkhead. The joyless bedroom farce in an airport motel—the mouths fluttering about some ghostly text with some bloody scuba diving and helicopter chases thrown in for continuity. Now he is watching me write this. He's not interested in what I'm writing; is simply afraid to look at her. For her little breasts are in disarray. Maybe I should write some good porn for him. If she attacks him, I would defend him—I sympathize with his accumulated burdens though I do not share them, more than her unwon aloofness and that programmatic scorn which I detest in myself as much as her. Uh oh. I believe he is going to speak. I scribble furiously. He thinks better of it.
But a shadow has crossed my page. Above us, her armpits so clean, so dry, sealed with some ingenious lacquer, airbrushed as it were, appears the leggy stewardess. No help for him. The pectorals of his non-breathing suit are already stained. Our blonde, however, smells like a girl in trouble. I'm tobacco and rags which have been used to wipe up and polish too many different things. We sweat the sweat of the comatose, staring at the wall which is not a wall, my knuckles white on the edge of my tray, where I have scribbled on the back of a brochure explaining how to get into a life raft and who's got the oxygen; above me this hard-easy mask, looking for a man. How to get out of the air! Pilot Meat!

|295|

my right cheek. I grunted for velocity and blackjacked my left elbow into her gut button. She groaned and wrapped and unwrapped her legs. She chattered her teeth like she was freezing to death. I could feel her groin and heavy black curtain inside my dome. Just before I went under, I thought, "I wonder if the runt can lug 150 pounds to that window." |Pimp, the Story of My Life, Iceberg Slim|

Whilst behind every door, the sounds of women talking, weeping, sighing.

She won't take silence for an answer, this last gasp of American eroticism; the mover, fair game, prepackaged, sauceless puddin, the pussy whip—Pythia squatting on her tripod over Hades, her endless, formless offspring devoured by wolves. She arches above us . . . he smiles, forcing back his leer, but she has her own toughness, and she has brought us our ravaged provisions; *mes compliments au chef!*

Glutinous salisbury steak, peas of the same luminescence as his suit. They glow like isotopes. The greenest goddamn peas you ever saw. Celery too. Another kind of green. And a hip salad bowl. I cannot open the packet in which there is a prewetted napkin to lube my lips. I fumble my notes. I can't start drinking this early. American eats. American pussy. Quintessential. Airbrushed.

Pythia has returned and leans ominously over us again. Her black nipples sheathed in acetate dangle above my nose. But she is not interested in me. Or him. We both need bulk, and our bowls are clean as the port engine's nacelles.

"What's wrong, honey? Not hungry?"

The girl is staring hard at her untouched tray. Our friend of the center looks at her in disbelief. Boy, is his plate clean. Attaboy. Her mouth is pursed, her molars grinding. How many dollars to straighten those teeth? She is informing on her food. Awaiting an answer, Pythia withdraws two trays, pointedly leaving hers—or can she only manage two at a time? We'll never know.

"What's the matter?" our friend asks the girl, his first lost word. "Airsick?"

"It's crap," she smiles.

He turns white. "Not at all bad for . . ."

"Carcinogenous."

"What d'ya mean?"

She means it's all preservatives, I interpret.

"I mean it's crap. That's all," she says.

He stutters. "Do you have any idea how much time and money went into that process. . . ."

Ah, brig, good-night
To crew and you;
The ocean's heart too smooth, too blue,
To break for you.
|Emily Dickinson|

He could have gone on: Look at this plane! Here you can afford to go to Europe, go to Europe in five hours, and all you do is complain about the food? Christ, this is the first time I've ever gone, look at all the damn kids on this plane. I haven't had a vacation in four years . . . The little bitch is not impressed. No sweetie she. To be equal, she will never conceive.

Pythia again arches her unreferenced melancholia across us.

He speaks: "Well, what the hell do you expect at 700 miles an hour? You should have flown in the old DC3s."

The girl picks up her food and sets it down on his tray. "Seconds?" she smiles thinly. Pythia doesn't know whether to take it away or not. The girl's eyes are now lasers.

"If you think we're going to live this way any more, you're crazy," she murmurs.

And oh, I think to myself, my monster is happy today.

Well, it's not *my* way. Which was to learn to eat anything that gets you through the night. And that's my advice to you. Our middleman would not misinterpret that notion as he did her bad consumership. And as long as we're going to have this feisty foolishness for some time, until something really gives, I'm just as glad I've got an outside seat and a foot in the aisle. But what we've got to remember is that it *stands for nothing*—that every time we try to make this quarrel into an analogy, a portent, a dialectic, we maim ourselves. It's a start, nothing more, but still, it's a beginning, and if not winning nor exemplary, it remains true to our condition and admirable for all that.

I'll have that drink now, Miss. I touch Pythia on the elbow and she is not unhappy for the work.

Now I'm blasted, going home, the body lifted slightly out of the seat courtesy of Mr. Heublein—the son-of-a-bitch is still gazing at my scribble. Is this my audience? Am I the antennae for *his* race? What's that make him; a carapace? I never much liked that metaphor, Ezra. We're not bugs here, after all.

Is she ascetic, or only a masochist? Does a decent man eat what's put in front of him? Well, peas *are* green, right? So what if they're *too* green? How do we get him off those too-green purblind peas, honey? How explain him to the peas which are too much with us? Begin with the *a priori*. Just exactly why are they *this* green? Who's responsible for such greenness anyway? Who's to say how green's *green?* How to prove the green's not the green we all desire? What's *natural* green anyway? Science, after all, has shown that green is the most accepted color. From what or with what are they too green? What would the *quintessential* green be? Greenness, greenity is what surrounds a question after all; a halo of sorts. What's the cost of peas? Not to mention greenness. What can peas do for you? Who are *your* peas? What have peas done for you lately? The pea beneath your mattress is not the perfect pea. Perhaps the perfect pea is not green at all. But we are not interested in the perfect pea, not even the nice pea. Possibly, the unadulterated pea is what we crave. Certainly not "peaness" itself, for the pea is an accompaniment. Are we equal to the pea? Can we put up with peas *as they are?* Or is it a matter, really, of transcending the pea? Or are we the pea? Are we at one with the sublimity and inblossoming of the pea? Does the pea know more than we? What actually happens to the pea? Some peas are my best friends. A short history of the pea would be too long. What rights do the pea have, and what right do we have to the pea? The pea should be what it is. Peas could save the world had we enough words for them. . . .

The pilot announces we're over the Statue of Liberty; she looks just like the lady in the hospital alongside of whom I spent the summer before I went to college, who lent me her Kafka, her Dostoyevski, her Dickens, her Shaden Freud. She explained the structure of personality formation by using one of her husband's monogramed golf balls. Its liquid unconscious core for distance, tensile ego winding to both transmit and absorb impact, and the infinitely pocked white superhide for endurance, but not for give ness.

As my diagnoses changed from leukemia to acute dysentery to ulcerative colitis, and my system reacted violently to the sulfa and other drugs, my weight dropped below 100, and I resolved to die cultured. If you couldn't play ball, maybe you could end smart. Though moved to a private room, I always kept myself covered, not wishing to be reminded of the loss of that Wonder Bread musculature, the corded muscles from a million pushups and squat thrusts, those relics of gristle which already hang upon young American men in their late twenties like the skins of other animals, gratuitous orders of merit. I was a new and minor mountain range—from my clavicle, into which I could insert my jaw, to my blade-like jaundiced feet. My sternum was a prong, my hip bones prosthetic handles—my parts had receded into a sudden declivity—then the kneecaps and the toes like the far Dolomites. It was then I discovered, despite that lady's insistent training, that Freud was wrong. I was not afraid of death. In the night I had heard the last screams of terminal cancer patients, the wrapping of the corpses, had seen the children half my age in more sophisticated states of colitis, colostomies already performed, and I knew I would perfunctorily throw myself from the window before I'd see my "system" in a bag above my bed. So it was not death, it was not even dying before I had done anything at all; it was dying *like anyone else* which was so disconcerting. Dying not only without consequences, but without being able to describe it, will it, without even being able to work at it; that I was denied the chance to be *better* at it than anyone was what most appalled me.

So it was that my best friend and I decided to make use of my circumstances rather than simply wallow in them. For a few nights every week, then, he would commandeer a date—a particularly naive young lady, who, in our judgment, needed to be disabused at that point in her gay life—a post-debutante, say, and bring her to the hospital on the pretext of visiting a sick friend—a unique preparation for her future charitable activities. He had given me a blue satin jock strap with Yale bull-dogs embroidered upon it, and clad only in this, my wasted body in the half-light, I would die for them during their visit. Sometimes in the midst of a pregnant whispered sentence, head suddenly twitching to the left, sometimes with gurgles and a final heart-rending scream, the eyes socked back in the head and gross pelvis arched in an effort for that last touchdown, and sometimes with epileptic throes and a Mephistophe-lean laugh worthy of the *commandatore.* It was the first time, for them. . . .

About this time I was startled by the visit of a local football hero, cur-rently the starting fullback at a Big Ten college, and it was his hands, the hands in which I would have placed the ball on the belly series, who now lifted my perforated buttocks, removed my bedpan, took my blood pressure. He was working as an orderly for the summer to discover if he wanted to be a doctor like his father. I turned my head away in silent shame. Later, we talked about the team.

"Look," he said one day, "why don't we talk about something else. Your books or something. You're never going to play anything again."

So we talked about the Freud, while his enormous forearms, now big-ger around than my thighs, rested on the steel railing of my crib. My literary lady friend was of the opinion that my illness was psycho-somatic. Otherwise, she said, I'd be dead.

You've seen the chart, I asked the fullback. What do you think?

"It isn't *only* physical," he concurred.

What do you mean?

"You shit your food before you can digest it. That's all I know."

"You've got to eat to live," the lady said.

You got to shit too, I said.

"The trick is," the fullback said, "holding on to it just long enough. And then letting go. It sounds easy, I know. But that's health."

He did not, I'm sorry to say, take up where his father left off. He be-came a professor of English.

At the end of the summer, they turned me upside down, put an illuminated telescope up my rectum; filled my bowels with barium sulphate; the doctor turned on a tiny light somewhere in my intestines; the ulcer had closed. Then they gave me enormous syringes of mega-vitamins, the worn needles breaking on my bony ass, removed the fistulas, scoring the anus as many times as there are spokes in a wagon wheel, and, insisting that I must heal "from the inside out," pronounced me fit enough. I closed out my life, died for a captive audience twice more before I was released. We had to hurry before the color returned to my face.

Then: "You can go back to school now," the doctor said one day. They hadn't cured me; but they had given me a profession.

Now we are welcomed to that mausoleum of the modern world where everything connects yet nothing happens—the airport. The illusion of the arcade, the synapse, the nerve center; don't never do anything in an airport, Mister, it will always disappoint you. The penultimate example of technological dehumanization, not to put too fine a point on it. After all, it is *our* Louvre. What's left of our vague remembrance of what on earth we ever wanted with this land, what we've managed to preserve from the barbarians who never came, testimony to our elaborate defenses and splendid isolation, those high points of our lootings, booty for posterity. . . . It is as if you took the Louvre, removed every painting, leaving the frames in place, swarming there on the wall, and then replaced each canvas with a clear pane of glass, a window—some giving access upon an alley, some on the blank sky, some upon the heating or electrical systems, and those between our corridors, framing the spectators staring through the walls, posing for one another. Fake artifacts. Phony mirrors. No view; though everywhere, transparency.

SOON TO BE A MAJOR MOTION PICTURE

It was then that he despaired of the country, or to put it exactly, that he perceived the Empire had eclipsed the country. |Stendhal at Orléans|

Access!

That is our cry. The final frontier of Western willfulness dissolves in its own mystique. ("Hey look, George, I'm a work of art!")

Access!

It doesn't matter that you don't ever go anywhere, and you don't much care how or why, but nobody can tell you that you *can't* go. I've got my rights, after all. (After all what?)

Access!

I want to go to . . . to . . . Istanbul! . . . yes . . . today. (Oh yes I can. And I want it in writing.)

Access!

Don't tell me about the past, don't warn me about the future. Give me *release* . . .

Waiting for my luggage, I wander the corridor of the glassed-in second level. In the middle of our terminus, upon a dais, a woman is playing Christmas carols on a demonstration organ. It's the end of the year again. Her body sways obliquely to "Good King Wenceslas." We are starting all over again.

Below me, through the glass, the immigrants are arriving and being searched. They look so neat in their clean conservative clothes. They look so happy. They are crying for joy. They can't wait to take their clothes off and look for work. The customs officials are gentler with them than with us. Customs; such a strange word. Occasionally there is an argument about food—a salami or strudel smuggled in the under-wear. Trichinosis, botulism invade us at every quarter; my God, they are still coming at us! Into this chaos, it is only they who are orderly. It is only the visitors who have nothing to lose. In the vacuum cell they look so swell, waiting to be inoculated with their Rights, waiting to be admitted where God's people have made their home. I tap on the glass. "No," I wave frantically, trying to warn them, "stay away for your own good. Keep out."

A woman in orange pants slipping below her hips of fifty-score, staggers up to me. Her hair is blue, her eyes are baked, her breasts hang about her. She is not crazy. She is no fool. She is merely totally disconcerted. She is *being free,* unhooked, if not unhinged. Her skin is incinerated. Her hands and feet are sausages. She living within her means.

"Where can I get a bus for Miami?"

Madam, this is an airport.

Beside me in the corridor, a teenage boy, one generation removed, watches his new relatives arrive with unveiled disgust. They are clearly not with it. Were the balcony not enclosed, he would probably spit. His aimlessness, his fecklessness, his pointless charm . . . his American character has relapsed from itself. We stagger like syphilitic savages to greet the newest refugees on the beach, the dying inflict themselves upon the dead. Our hair is a mess, our skin pustulate with the fury of spiritual miscegenation. . . .

When the element of the equivocal and personal character in history takes on, in New York, in addition to all the rest of the swarming ambiguity and fugacity of race and tongue, the result becomes for the picture seeker indescribably and luridly strong. The fascination was of course in the perfection of our baseness, and the puzzle in the fact that it could be subject, without fatally muzzling, without tearing and rending them, to those arts of life, those quantities of conformity, the numerous, involved accommodations and patiences, that are not in the repertory of the wolf and the snake. Extraordinary, we say to ourselves on such occasions, the amount of formal tribute to civilization is after all able to gouge out of apparently hopeless stuff; extraordinary that it can make a presentable sheath for such fangs and such claws. The mystery is in the how *of the process, in the wonderful little wavering borderland between nature and art, the place of the crooked seam where, if psychology had the adequate lens, the white stitches would show. |Henry James, "On the Baser Types" in* The American Scene|

The corridors are slippery with disinfectant. They shine, but not sufficiently to give a reflection, our fluorescence casts no shadow. Our bodies the only darkness here, and we walk upon tissue, on mucous membrane. Strange sourceless interior drafts scud and swirl, papers, photos, correspondence, documents, passports, genealogies . . . as if across a battlefield. Our indefatigable words have overtaken us. . . .

My baggage, as always, remains at several removes from me. But I shall pass the time. My stomach is acting up. I walk the long corridors of the lavatories, the urinals like so many propitious altars, their relics and offerings testimony to miracles and cures stolen away in the night. In my stall, there is a message for us.

THOSE WHO WRITE ON SHITHOUSE WALLS
ROLL THEIR SHITTING LITTLE BALLS
THOSE WHO READ THEIR WORDS
OF WHIT, EAT THOSE LITTLE BALLS OF SHIT

Peacefully emergent, credentials in order, I am returned to the museum of myself, where a battery of machines wait to entertain me while I wait. Their task, to test my potential against my enforced leisure. There are machines to take your picture, check your I.Q., analyze your handwriting, determine your weight, challenge your grip, and I use them all. The man who makes change for me will not reveal his face. His fingers slide the coins from beneath his folded newspaper, a headline of which promises new hope and a prosperity of sorts.

LEFTOVER HAM NO PROBLEM

|304|

The average weight for an American man, aged forty to forty-four years with shoes, coat and vest and a height of five feet eleven inches, is one hundred and seventy-five pounds (1,225,000 grains). |Actuarial Society of America|

According to the machines, I am a tanned and handsome enough, if somewhat hairy, young man in the prime of life, a genius rating in my chosen fields of "sports and general knowledge," though predictably weak in "entertainment" and "science." I weigh 168 hard pounds and have the grip of a thousand men.

I left to be a traveler in America; I returned to be a soldier in Europe. I did not fully carry out either of those careers; an evil genius snatched away the staff and sword, and thrust a pen into my hand. In Sparta, contemplating the sky during the night, I remembered lands that had already witnessed my peaceful or troubled sleep. . . . But of what use was it to complain to the stars, motionless witnesses of my vagabond destiny? One day their gaze will no longer tire in following me; it will stop on my grave. As for now, indifferent as I am to my own destiny, I shall not ask those unfriendly stars to shape that destiny with a milder hand, nor to give me back what the traveler leaves of his life in the places through which he passes. |*Chateaubriand*, Travels in America|

I am a double Gemini with Taurus rising, am slender, 7% water, and of two distinct natures. Ambitious, I tend to inflict my faults; if I marry, I will marry selfish. I am bad for women, too many irons on the fire, over-fond of examining my own thoughts. Nervous, flippant; ruled by Mercury, my stone is the aquamarine and I am subject to nasal catarrh and fainting fits. Secretly childlike, my own worst enemy, self-Karmic, I am in love with any invention which moves and/or eliminates distance, and though a talker, may leave my associates no wiser than they were at first. A spiritual birth or death may be indicated.

YOU HAVE LOST YOUR " "

WRITE YOUR NAME ACROSS MINE

CNewman

The electronic graphology machine balances the picture by making an appropriate distinction between my mind and brain, and as I sign my name, the IBM card is drilled with my aptitudes. I am, by the holes, by the numbers, discreet, forceful, dependable, sincere, aesthetic, friendly, imaginative, emotional, observant, realistic, reserved, patient, systematic, poised, perceptive, attentive, individualistic, analytical, sophisticated, unconventional, contemplative, dignified, original, funny, tender-hearted, mature, truthful, intuitive, tolerant, and very temperamental.

And what if the machines are wrong, if the testing has been fixed? Then of what use my mastery?

And if the machines lie, who is mine enemy?

I am also an American, a free man, and I have chosen to come home. No one will ever tell me what to do. But if this is all so, if the machines are correct, then what on earth am I doing *here?* Clearly, I deserve better.

|306|

A man has suddenly come up to me. Have I been recognized at last? He hands me his card without a word.

Let's Be Friends

I am a DEAF MUTE.

Forgive me for bothering you, WILL YOU?

I am selling this card to SEE my way through.

ANY PRICE you can pay will be appreciated.

C A L L   M E

THANK YOU.
(over)

Call me. Just call me. (over)

Charles Newman came to life in 1938. During the sixties, he traveled, studied at Yale and Oxford, traveled, was active in politics, traveled, edited *TriQuarterly* at Northwestern University, traveled, published two novels, *New Axis* and *The Promise-keeper.* He is now working on a series of interrelated novellas, *There Must Be More to Love than Death,* a novel, *Both Ways,* a play, *His and Hers,* and travels no more.

Lawrence Levy has won design awards from the New York Art Director's Club, the Chicago Three Show, the Warsaw Poster Biennale, and the American Institute of Graphic Arts. His films include *Ten Thousand Beads for Navajo Sam, Kfar Menachem: Crossroads,* and *Funeral,* which won awards at the Chicago International Film Festival and the San Francisco Film Festival. In addition to this book, he has collaborated with Charles Newman on *TriQuarterly* and on films.

The designer would like to note that this volume has been printed on RECYCLED PAPER; that the tiny wood fibers beneath these words perhaps once held poignant lines from Emily Dickinson, Theodore Roethke, or *New Axis;* and ecologists should note that Borges is therefore right.

THANKS